WILLIAM ARMSTRONG

MAGICIAN OF THE NORTH

Henrietta Heald

MᶜNIDDER | GRACE &

Published by McNidder & Grace
21 Bridge Street
Carmarthen SA31 3JS
www.mcnidderandgrace.com

First published in Great Britain in 2010 by Northumbria Press

Original paperback published 2012, reprinted 2015, 2016, 2021, 2022

A catalogue record for this work is available from the
British Library.

ISBN 9780857160423

Designed by Obsidian Design
Printed and bound in the United Kingdom by
Short Run Press Ltd, Exeter, UK

Contents

Illustrations

Illustrations are reproduced by permission of named organisations and individuals.

p.25 Pandon Dene (Newcastle Libraries); Jesmond Dene, Armstrong's house (National Trust Cragside)

p.70 Elswick in the 1840s (Newcastle Libraries); Elswick in 1887 (*Illustrated London News*)

p.109 Armstrong's first gun (Newcastle Libraries); gun trials at Shoeburyness (*Illustrated London News*)

p.183 The gunboat *Staunch* (*Illustrated London News*); HMS *Victoria* passes through the Swing Bridge (Newcastle Libraries)

p.188 The Japanese ships *Yoshino* and *Yashima* (both Newcastle Libraries)

p.250 Cragside lit by electricity (*Graphic*)

p.271 South-east Asia in the late 19th century (map by Bryan Kirkpatrick)

p.279 Admiral Togo with the Nobles; Japanese sailors in Newcastle (both Newcastle Libraries)

p.285 Cragside library and drawing room (both National Trust Cragside)

Between pages 118 and 119
William Armstrong at 21 (National Trust Cragside, *artist* James Ramsay)

Anne Armstrong senior (National Trust Cragside)

William Armstrong senior (National Trust Cragside)

Margaret Armstrong, née Ramshaw (Bamburgh Castle, *artist* J. C. Horsley)

Anne Armstrong junior (National Trust Picture Library, *photo* Derrick E. Witty)

Jesmond Dene map; Jesmond Dene banqueting hall (both Newcastle Libraries)

Armorer Donkin (National Trust Picture Library,
photo Derrick E. Witty)

Thomas Sopwith with the baloonist James Glaisher (Robert Sopwith)

James Meadows Rendel; George Rendel (both Vickers Archive)

General Grant visits Elswick (Newcastle Libraries)

Gun testing on Allenheads moor (Robert Sopwith)

Li Hung Chang at Cragside; the Chinese ship *Chih Yuan* (both
Newcastle Libraries)

Richard Norman Shaw's vision of Cragside (Laing Art Gallery)

Cragside today (author)

Between pages 224 and 225

Armstrong in the dining room at Cragside (National Trust Picture
Library, *photo* Derrick E. Witty, *artist* H. H. Emmerson)

Armstrong in baronial robes (Bamburgh Castle,
artist H. Schmirchen)

The royal family at Cragside (National Trust Picture Library,
top photo John Hammond, *bottom photo* Derrick E. Witty,
artist H. H. Emmerson)

Armstrong at Cragside; the launch of Pandora
(both Newcastle Libraries)

An architect's sketch of Bamburgh Castle; castle scaffolding
(both David Ash)

Bamburgh Castle today (author)

Launch card for Albany (Newcastle Libraries)

Launch cards for *Tokiwa* and *Asama* (Newcastle Libraries)

Image from *Electric Movement in Air and Water*
(Newcastle Literary and Philosophical Society)

Raising the bascules of Tower Bridge (Shutterstock.com)

Armstrong Mitchell crane in the Venice Arsenale
(Venice in Peril)

Front cover illustration

William Armstrong, 1946 (detail), James Ramsay
(Laing Art Gallery)

About the author

Henrietta Heald had a long and successful career in book publishing before taking up the pen herself. She was chief editor of the historical encyclopedia *Chronicle of Britain and Ireland*. A graduate of Durham University, Henrietta lives in Islington, north London, but spends much of her time in north-east England, visiting Armstrong's old haunts. *William Armstrong, Magician of the North* is her first book. It has been shortlisted for the Portico Prize and the H. W. Fisher Best First Biography Prize.

Foreword

I discovered William Armstrong in Jesmond Dene. I had visited Cragside a couple of times and, like millions before me (Cragside welcomed its four millionth visitor in the summer of 2009), had marvelled at Armstrong's amazing inventions, his taming of the landscape, and the quirky originality of the house he had built amid the bleak Northumberland moors. Later I learnt that he had made his money from industry on the Tyne, from the manufacture of cranes, ships and – sharp intake of breath – *guns*. But it was not until I had taken several solitary walks at dawn and dusk across the soaring Armstrong Bridge, a romance in wrought-iron and sandstone, and wandered along the banks of the Ouseburn that I really began to get the measure of the man.

Jesmond Dene is a unique urban gem. Little more than a mile from the centre of Newcastle, the vibrant heart of north-east England, the dene is a deep cleft in the landscape whose steep and wooded banks frame an enchanting burn that is sometimes gentle, sometimes tempestuous as it rushes past rocks and flows over rapids. Running north–south into the Tyne, the Ouseburn is the lure that induced Armstrong to make a home there in the 1830s with his new wife, Meggie Ramshaw.

As the years went by, the Armstrongs acquired, through purchase and inheritance, more and more land along the dene. Not content with the natural beauty of the place, they set out to improve what they found there, landscaping both the river and its banks, adding waterfalls, stepping stones, paths and bridges, and cultivating many exotic as well as native trees and plants. The aim – achieved more obviously and dramatically at Cragside – was to recreate the experience of being in the mountains, and to do it as unobtrusively as possible. 'I am a greater lover of nature than most people give me credit for,' wrote William Armstrong in 1855, 'and I like her best when untouched by the hand of man.'

The shaping of Jesmond Dene was much more than an act of self-indulgence, however. Like many of Armstrong's achievements, it had far-reaching significance. When he handed over almost 100 acres of his land in the dene to the city of Newcastle as a public park, he made it clear that his main motivation was to improve other people's quality of life. He had earlier built a banqueting hall in the dene – intended not for sumptuous feasting but as a place where he could hold tea parties for his employees at Elswick Works. The mighty industrialist, whose workforce would at times number more than 25,000, understood the importance to working people of leisure, reward and open-air recreation, and it was in this spirit that he made a gift of the dene to his fellow citizens.

By mid-2005 I was scouring shops and libraries for books about this enigmatic figure, but found nothing that could genuinely satisfy my hunger. At the same time, the more I talked to people, the more I realised that the name Armstrong had tremendous resonance in Newcastle. There was the Armstrong Building, the bedrock of Newcastle University, for example, and the elegant low Swing Bridge across the Tyne, which would swing open (as it still does after 140 years) to allow ships to pass either side of its central axis. Those in the know pointed out that the hydraulic mechanisms Armstrong had pioneered in the construction of the Swing Bridge were later adapted to open and close the giant bascules of London's Tower Bridge. There was even a statue of the great man and his dog outside the Hancock Museum, one of Newcastle's favourite institutions, now reincarnated as the Great North Museum. He had contributed £100,000 to the Royal Victoria Infirmary, opened in 1906. And didn't he have something to do with the Lit & Phil – that venerable institution near Central Station, founded at the time of the French Revolution, which played a leading role in Newcastle's intellectual flowering in the mid-19th century, and survives to this day?

Those with more recent memories mentioned Vickers-Armstrongs, the mighty defence contractor that continued as a major employer on Tyneside until well into the 1980s. Before that it had been Armstrong Whitworth with its formidable Walker Naval Yard and, even further back, Armstrong Mitchell, producer of gunboats and fast cruisers for all the world's leading navies. And how did the popular car-maker Armstrong Siddeley and the aviation firm Hawker Siddeley fit into the picture? Much later, I learnt that Bamburgh Castle on the Northumberland coast had been bought and restored by Lord Armstrong (as he was by then) in the last few years of his life – and that the castle was still owned and tended by members of the Armstrong family.

By the time I realised that 2010 was the bicentenary of William Armstrong's birth – he was born the year after Charles Darwin – I knew that I should be writing his biography. His 3,000-word obituary in *The Times* made it clear that he had been a national hero who was seen by many as Britain's saviour at a time of grave threat from hostile forces, and his fame stretched around the globe, from Chile to Italy to Japan. How could it happen that this remarkable figure had been almost forgotten in his native land – especially when dwindling energy supplies, industrial decline, and the threat of global warming meant that we were more than ever in need of his scientific genius, to say nothing of his inspirational business skills?

By reviving Armstrong's thoughts and ideas as expressed in his own writings, *Magician of the North* attempts to reach a deeper understanding of his achievements, and to penetrate the desires and motivations that spurred one great Englishman to pursue single-mindedly the path to true knowledge.

Henrietta Heald

Sources and Acknowledgements

Ken Wilson, a National Trust volunteer at Cragside for almost two decades, has an interest in William Armstrong that dates from the Second World War, when, as a young boy, he was evacuated from Tynemouth to Rothbury. Ken has amassed an extensive archive of written material, images, film clips, and sound recordings relating to Armstrong, Cragside, and the Armstrong family, to which he has allowed the author unlimited access. Without Ken's diligence and generosity this book could not have been written. Zena Chevassut, a friend and colleague of Ken, carried out useful research into Armstrong's father's family and uncovered some intriguing documents, including the younger Anne Armstrong's lakeland diary.

One of Ken Wilson's most important discoveries was an unpublished history of the Elswick Works, written in the late 1940s to mark the centenary of the founding of the works. A. R. Fairbairn, the author of this fascinating and detailed document, has been described as works architect at Elswick, but he died before the book could be published, and in the event a much shorter version of the firm's history was published by what was then Vickers-Armstrongs. Little more is known about Fairbairn except that he was an enthusiast for Esperanto. An anonymous preface to the Fairbairn typescript, a copy of which was deposited in the Vickers' archives at Cambridge University Library, describes his work as 'most accurate' and mentions that his research was 'used extensively' by J. D. Scott, the author of *Vickers: A History*, published in 1962. What is known about Elswick's history from other sources is corroborated by Fairbairn's account, and the author is indebted to him for many details not recorded elsewhere.

The largely unpublished journals of Thomas Sopwith, written over a period of 57 years, from 1822 until his death in 1879, are a treasure trove of information, not only about Sopwith's great friend

William Armstrong but also about the Victorian age and, in particular, its scientific luminaries. The diarist's descendant Robert Sopwith, the guardian of the original 168 leatherbound volumes, has kindly granted the author permission to quote freely from them and to reproduce the photograph of Sopwith and Armstrong taken in 1856. A microfilm version of the diaries forms part of the Special Collections at the Robinson Library, Newcastle University.

Peter McKenzie, a former employee of Vickers who wrote a short biography of Armstrong in 1983, also provided invaluable information, including helping to explain what happened to the various Armstrong companies after the merger with Vickers in 1927. Peter put the author in touch with Rosemary Rendel, the granddaughter of Armstrong's protégé George Rendel, who had herself carried out extensive research into the Rendel family and their engineering achievements, with a view to publishing her own book on the subject. Despite her advanced age, Rosemary was a fund of fascinating stories about the Rendels and gave permission for quotations from family correspondence. Thanks are also due to Jonathan and Jane Rendel and Christopher Rendel. Even before the author read Peter McKenzie's *W. G. Armstrong, the life and times of Sir William George Armstrong, Baron Armstrong of Cragside*, she had been inspired by Ken Smith's illuminating but all too brief account of Armstrong's life, *Emperor of Industry*.

Since virtually everything Armstrong said and wrote is either unpublished or out of print, the author has relied heavily on the assistance of librarians and archivists, in particular Liz Rees and her excellent team at Tyne & Wear Archives, which holds a vast collection of items relating to the Armstrong, Watson-Armstrong, and Rendel families and businesses, including hundreds of letters written by William Armstrong on both personal and professional matters; for the sake of space, these are not listed individually in the chapter notes. The author would also like to thank the staff at the British Library (especially those in the Rare Books reading room); Robinson Library, Newcastle; Durham University Library; Cambridge University Library; the Bodleian Library, Oxford; and the libraries of the London School of Economics (LSE) and University College London (UCL).

Particular thanks are due to Martin Dusinberre of Newcastle University for his insights into Armstrong's relations with Japan; Brendan Martin for his comments on industrial relations in late Victorian Britain; and John Clayson of Newcastle's Discovery Museum for his lucid explanation of scientific and engineering matters. John Clayson co-curated with Laura Brown a major exhibition at the Discovery Museum of Armstrong's life and works. Other individuals who helped with research and provided advice on improvements and amendments include Stephen White of Carlisle Library and Richard Sharp of the Literary and Philosophical Society of Newcastle upon Tyne (the Lit & Phil) (William Armstrong senior); Celia Lemmon (James Losh and the Losh family); Jo Hutchings and Frances Bellis of Lincoln's Inn Library (William Henry Watson); Michael Hush of the Open University (engineering); Adam Hart-Davis (hydraulics); Norman McCord (industrial relations); James Tree (Hollist family); and last, but by no means least, the redoubtable Ian Fells, emeritus professor of energy conversion at Newcastle University.

The custodians and staff at Cragside and Bamburgh have given generously of their time and wisdom. Among those currently or historically associated with Cragside, the author would like to thank, in particular, Alison Pringle, Andrew Sawyer, Robin Wright, John O'Brien, Pam Dryden, Dennis Wright, Pamela Wallhead, Justine James, Carole Evans, Caroline Rendell, Hugh Dixon, Helen Clarke, Sadie Parker and Kate Hunter. At Bamburgh, Lisa Waters and Chris Calvert have been unstinting in their help and support, and through them the author had the pleasure of meeting Francis Watson-Armstrong and Claire Thorburn; among others with a Bamburgh connection, the author would like to thank Carol Griffiths and Charles and Barbara Baker-Cresswell. Thanks are due also to Seamus Tollitt, Ouseburn Parks Manager, Robert Wooster and Sarah Capes, who enabled the author to consult the Jesmond Dene archives, and to Anna Newson, Tom Hope, John Penn, Carlton Reid, and other Friends of Jesmond Dene.

Special mention should be made of the architects and students of architecture who have directly and indirectly contributed to this book. Heading the list is Andrew Ayers, who, in the mid-1990s, was the first to whisper the name 'Cragside' to the author, then an ignorant Londoner. Next is Terry Farrell, whose autobiography opened the author's eyes to the wonders of Newcastle and introduced her to John Dobson, the man who, with Richard Grainger, rebuilt the town in the 1830s. Farrell quoted the traveller William Howitt, who, writing in 1842, captured the sense of surprise still felt today by newcomers to Newcastle: 'You walk into what has long been termed the coal hole of the north and find yourself at once in a city of palaces, a fairyland of newness, brightness and modern elegance.' The work of Richard Norman Shaw, the architect of Cragside, remains a continuing source of fascination, especially as elucidated by his biographer Andrew Saint. The list continues with the eminent architect David Ash, who, like Farrell, spent his undergraduate years at Newcastle University, where he wrote a thesis on the history and restoration of Bamburgh Castle, which remains unrivalled today in the depth and thoroughness of its research. Likewise, Jeremy Blake of Purcell Miller Tritton, a leading firm of 'green' architects, wrote a dissertation on Cragside during his student years. Both Ash and Blake have been generous in giving the author permission to quote from their works. Neil Cossons, Geoff Wallis and E. F. Clarke are among the engineers who have provided particular inspiration.

Other scholarly works that have proved invaluable to the author in writing this book include Marshall J. Bastable's *Arms and the State: Sir William Armstrong and the Remaking of British Naval Power 1854–1914*; Kenneth Warren's *Armstrongs of Elswick: Growth in Engineering and Armaments to the Merger with Vickers;* and a PhD thesis by Alice Short, *The Contribution of William Lord Armstrong to Science and Education* (Durham University, 1989).

Plans to mark the bicentenary in 2010 of William Armstrong's birth brought the author into contact with many people in Newcastle and elsewhere in Britain whom she would like to thank for their help and encouragement. In no particular order, they include: Penny Smith, Don MacRaild, Chris Dorsett, and Gill Drinkald of Northumbria University; Iain Watson and others at Tyne & Wear Museums; Graeme Rigby of Amber Films; Alex Elliot (actor); Matt Ridley (writer); Valerie Laws (poet); Sue Aldworth (artist);

Linda Conlon of the International Centre for Life; Caspar Hewett of the Great Debate; Kay Easson and Chris Sharp of the Lit & Phil; Paul Younger, Frances Spalding, Joan Allen, and Umbereen Rafiq of Newcastle University; Frances Clarke, Anna Somers Cocks and Nicky Baly of Venice in Peril; Neil Tonge, Ben Smith, Ian Ayris, Richard Faraday, Craig Brown, and other members of the Armstrong 200 Group; Phil Supple of Light Refreshment; Zoe Bottrell of Culture Creative; Andrew Ritchie of Goodenough College, London; Lawrance Hurst of the Institution of Structural Engineers; Steven Brindle of English Heritage; Mike Nicholson of the Soane Museum, London; Jennifer Speirs Grant of the Armstrong Studio Trust, Newcastle. Supporters at the BBC have included Julian Birkett (producer of Jeremy Paxman's *The Victorians*) and Martin Smith, who invited the author to take part in the BBC Free Thinking festival of ideas at the Sage, Gateshead, in October 2009. Thanks are also due to George Clarke and the production team at Tiger Aspect.

Broo Doherty of Wade & Doherty has proved to be the best literary agent any new writer could hope for. The author would also like to give particular thanks to Andrew Peden Smith of McNidder & Grace for believing in the project from the start and throwing his intellectual weight behind it; Laura Booth and Laura Hicks for astute copy-editing and indexing; Linda MacFadyen (friend and publicist) for her energy, loyalty, and original thinking; Mark Stafford for general assistance; and Andy Tough, the guiding hand behind the William Armstrong website (www.williamarmstrong.info).

Friends and relations who have contributed to *Magician of the North* are too numerous to thank individually, but I should like to single out a few for special mention: Max Eilenberg and Caz Royds for urging me to become a writer; Ariane Bankes for her support and encouragement at every turn; my loved and loving husband, Adam Curtis; and my wonderful children, Sophie and Jamie Curtis.

1

Xanadu

It was 19 August 1884 – a hot and dazzling Tuesday in Newcastle upon Tyne. At 5.25pm, two minutes early after its 5¾-hour run from London, the royal train steamed triumphantly across the High Level Bridge into John Dobson's magnificent Central Station, where a dense crowd surged forward, eager to catch a glimpse of the occupants. The portly middle-aged Prince of Wales was of secondary interest, but his popular Danish wife, Alexandra, and their five children, aged from 14 to 20, were greeted with exultant cheers and wild flag-waving. Never before had the young princesses, Louise, Victoria, and Maud, and their elder brothers, Albert Victor and George, accompanied their parents on such an expedition.

Although it was the first royal visit to Tyneside since 1854, there was no time at that moment for anyone to disembark. The train had halted for barely five minutes, taking on board a group of local dignitaries, before it swept north out of the curving station and disappeared into the distance in the same stately fashion as it had arrived.

For that evening, at least, a more rural destination beckoned. The royal party's chosen resting-place during its three-night stay in the English borderland was the village of Rothbury on the River Coquet. There the princes and princesses would enjoy the hospitality of Sir William and Lady Armstrong at Cragside – an astonishing modern house in the Old English style, carved out of bleak Northumberland moorland. As the Prince of Wales stepped out onto Rothbury's crimson-carpeted platform, one hour and a quarter after leaving Newcastle, a tall, elegant, top-hatted figure detached itself from the welcoming committee and stepped forward to shake hands with the heir to the throne.

William Armstrong had first met the Prince of Wales at the opening of Great Grimsby Docks by the Queen and Prince Consort 30 years earlier, when Albert Edward was a 13-year-old boy. On that occasion, the prince had been given a thrill by one of Armstrong's early inventions, when he, his father, brothers, and sisters were hoisted up the 300-foot-high water tower by a hydraulic lifting mechanism. Armstrong described in a letter to his wife how the Queen stood laughing at them below. 'Certainly the hydraulics were the great attraction,' he wrote, 'and I'll be bound for it will be talked about by the children as long as they live ... The Queen very nearly agreed to go up in the hoist but time was too pressing.'

At Cragside, furious preparations for the royal visitors had been under way for several weeks – ever since it had become clear that the Prince of Wales had spurned the Duke of Northumberland's offer of accommodation at Alnwick Castle in favour of an opportunity to stay at the home of the world-famous engineer. The size of the royal retinue had made it necessary for the Armstrongs to reserve the entire County Hotel at Rothbury, in addition to Cragside itself, for the use of the visitors. Twenty extra male waiters had been employed to serve the guests at meals – outnumbering the permanent staff in the house. Margaret, Lady Armstrong had engaged London caterers approved by the Prince of Wales and ensured he would be well supplied with his favourite champagne. The menu for the first dinner included oysters, clear turtle soup, pâté de foie gras, stuffed turbot, roast haunch of venison, grouse, and iced chocolate soufflé.

By good fortune, the architect Richard Norman Shaw had just completed his 15-year transformation of Cragside from an unremarkable sporting lodge into a residence fit for a 19th-century emperor. Shaw had not only wrought wonders on the outside of the building, perched on a rocky ledge above the Debdon Burn, but also commissioned interior work by the best craftsmen of the day. The Prince and Princess of Wales would occupy the Owl Suite, which had built-in plumbing, Venetian wallpaper by William Morris, and exquisitely carved American black walnut furniture, including owl finials on the bedposts. Elsewhere in the house were Turkish baths and every modern convenience for the royal visitors. In the evening, the guests would gather before dinner in the magnificent drawing room, hung with paintings by Constable, Turner, and Millais – and dominated at the far end by a spectacular inglenook chimneypiece made of Italian marbles in blue, salmon, orange, and pink, and weighing 10 tons.

Set into the south front of the house was the Gilnockie Tower, named after the stronghold of one of Armstrong's more notorious ancestors. Rather than the handsome high gable that Shaw had designed, the tower was topped off by a glass-domed observatory, where its owner would retreat to gaze at the stars.

But what entranced visitors to Cragside above all – and had won the house its reputation as 'the palace of a modern magician' – were the domestic gadgets created by Armstrong himself. Many were hydraulically driven, but others relied on electricity. In an astonishing development – following Armstrong's damming of the Debdon Burn and his installation of a water-powered Siemens dynamo – Cragside had four years earlier become the first house in the world to be lit by hydroelectricity.

The immediate impact of this advance in human civilisation was evoked a century later by the writer and broadcaster June Knox-Mawer: 'The wonders of science that Cragside could show were beyond any oriental palace-builder, even Kubla Khan himself. There were Sir William's hydraulic inventions, for instance, which automatically turned the spits in the kitchens, sent the trays up and down by lift, revolved the plants in the conservatories, and beat the gongs for family prayers and meals. Most marvellous of all were the incandescent lamps that blazed out from the windows at night with a brilliance quite different from candle or gas.'[1]

It was appropriate, therefore, that the arrival of the royal party at Cragside should be celebrated by a festival of light. Outside the house, Armstrong had fitted a network of lights that illuminated the whole valley. 'Ten thousand small glass lamps were hung amongst the rocky hillsides or upon the lines of railing which guard the walks, and an almost equal number of Chinese lanterns were swung across leafy glades, and continued pendant from tree to tree in sinuous lines,' according to a contemporary account.[2] 'Clouds of little lamps hung like fireflies in the hollow recesses of the distant hills, and symmetrical designs in coloured lamps were placed along the steep flights of rustic steps which lead from the depths of the valley to the upper grounds on either side.' The sight of the house itself was no less dramatic: 'From every window the bright rays of the electric lamps shone with purest radiance, and the main front was made brilliant by a general illumination.'

At 10pm a magnificent display of fireworks took place on Rothbury Hill under the direction of James Pain of London and New York: 'The woods and hills and dales were illuminated with every ray of the rainbow, rockets, monster balloons, shells, asteroids, and rayon d'or, batteries of Roman candles, electric shells, flights of tourbillons and "Mammoth Spreaders", said to be the largest shells in the world, climaxed by a superb "aerial bouquet".'[3]

Fears about setting fire to the heather having been overcome, a cone-shaped bonfire 20 feet high and consisting of huge logs of fir and pine and a large quantity of tar barrels was built on the highest summit of the nearby Simonside hills, with a similar one erected a few miles away at Elsdon. When the fires were set ablaze, they were visible not only from central Newcastle but also from Yorkshire, Cumberland, and the Scottish border, as well as from the most distant parts of Durham and Northumberland.[4]

Contrary to what the splendour of the event might suggest, the royal family's host that summer's night was no prominent local aristocrat. Although William Armstrong's father had worked his way up from counting-house clerk on the Newcastle quayside to prosperous corn merchant and town councillor, his father's father had made a meagre living in Cumberland as a shoemaker. Indeed, the Armstrongs were descended from a band of border reivers, or clannish outlaws, reputedly based in the ancient settlement of Bewcastle, north-east of Carlisle. In just two generations, the head of the Armstrong family had transmogrified from an unassuming artisan into a fabulously rich and sophisticated international businessman at home in the company of princes.

The festivities at Cragside – 'one of the greatest galas ever seen in rural England', according to *Newcastle Weekly Courant* – were a mere prelude to the substance of the official visit, which would not get under way until the following day. An original plan to invite the Prince of Wales to open a new dock at Coble Dene near the mouth of the Tyne at North Shields had expanded to include an extravaganza that would see the royal party progressing all over Newcastle, granted city status only two years earlier.

The outpouring of enthusiasm provoked by the occasion was reflected in the lavish decorations adorning the northern metropolis, with virtually every shop, public building, and monument festooned in flags, flowers, or evergreens, and triumphal arches spanning all the main roads on the route. Many otherwise unemployed local men had been paid to put up the decorations. The largest arch – 54 feet high and 42 feet wide – was built across Grey Street, with Grey's monument resembling a gigantic maypole. *The Times* was particularly struck by the mass of illuminations and decorations and noted that the streets were so crowded that 'locomotion was almost impossible'.

In a leader published the next day, *The Times* proclaimed that the arrival in Newcastle of the Prince and Princess of Wales was 'something more than an ordinary royal visit to a flourishing town'. Commenting on the excitement of the citizens and the unusually brilliant scenes in the streets, the newspaper elaborated on the significance of the occasion: 'As a guest of Sir William Armstrong, the Prince is regarded as identifying himself with Newcastle in an unmistakable way, for Sir William Armstrong's is a name which embodies all the great industries and interests of the city, and his fellow-citizens are proud of him.' This pride was well founded, for Armstrong's importance as a major employer who had attracted a great deal of trade to Newcastle was matched only by his acts of generosity to local people, apparently stemming from 'the pure goodness of his heart'.

The first task that the prince was due to perform – the opening of Armstrong Park – was an apparent reflection of this goodness of heart. Adding to an earlier gift of 20 acres, the industrialist was giving 62 acres of his land in Jesmond Dene, a renowned local beauty spot on the eastern edge of the city, to the people of Newcastle. The new public estate included a banqueting hall, built by Armstrong several years earlier as a place of entertainment for his employees at the Elswick Works – and since used to receive a multitude of eminent visitors.

Arriving at Central Station at noon, the royal family transferred to horse-drawn carriages and processed through the steamy city streets to the accompaniment of cheering crowds, followed by more carriages carrying Sir William and Lady Armstrong and other members of the party. 'Windows and roofs and every point from which a view could be obtained on the route was occupied,' observed *The Times*. 'On the roof of St Nicholas's Cathedral choirs of the town were gathered, and as the royal guests came into sight they sang "God Save the Queen" and "God Bless the Prince of Wales".' At the request of the prince, the procession also passed through some of the more industrial and poverty-stricken parts of the city, including Byker.

Crossing Benton Bridge, an elegant iron structure built by Armstrong himself high above the Ouseburn, the procession wound its way down into the deep cleft of Jesmond Dene shortly before 1pm and, watched by some 6,000 spectators, made its way to the banqueting hall, where the Prince of Wales was presented with a golden key and asked to perform the opening ceremony. He remarked how glad he was that the park bore the name of Armstrong, after Newcastle's great benefactor: 'His name is known in the British dominions – I may safely say all over the world – as that of a great man and a great inventor. Not less known are his great liberality and his great philanthrophy.' Then, a few yards from the banqueting hall, Princess Alexandra planted a young oak tree using a golden spade with a handle of black oak – a relic of Pons Aelius, the Roman bridge across the Tyne, which had survived for more than 1,100 years until its destruction by fire in 1248.

Ever since his parents had built a home there in the 1820s, William Armstrong had been under the spell of Jesmond Dene. Despite its proximity to Newcastle, the dene had a rugged, untamed appearance that reminded him of childhood visits to Coquetdale, the place that more than any other had captured his soul. In common with the contemporary Romantic poets, in particular Wordsworth and Coleridge, Armstrong was drawn to wild mountain landscapes, finding in them a thrill that amounted almost to a transcendental experience. 'I am a greater lover of nature than most people give me credit for,' he wrote later, 'and I like her best when untouched by the hand of man. The mountain air and the vigorous exercise suit my constitution, and produce an exhilarating effect which sometimes almost amounts to intoxication, while the total absence of all restraint inspires a glowing sense of liberty which I never elsewhere experienced.' At Jesmond Dene – and later, more dramatically, at Cragside – Armstrong sought to replicate the experience of being in the mountains. 'The solemnity also – and frequent awfulness of the scenes one meets with – excite feelings and reflections which may with all sobriety be described as tending to produce a moral and intellectual elevation, corresponding to the physical elevation of the body.' As the years went by, he acquired more and more land along the Ouseburn and moulded the landscape to resemble his ideal of nature. It was in this form that he now passed on the dene to his fellow citizens.

After the opening of Armstrong Park, the royal family and their retinue were entertained by members of the city corporation at nearby St George's Hall, where lunch was followed by speeches and toasts. It was the turn of Newcastle's radical Liberal MP, Joseph Cowen – editor and proprietor of the *Newcastle Chronicle*, and an old adversary of Armstrong – to take centre-stage.

Among his many provocative acts, Cowen had backed the strikers during the bitter engineers' dispute of 1871 – when Armstrong had led the employers to defeat over the issue of the nine-hour working day – but, despite their political differences, a mutual respect had since grown up between the two men. Cowen was a controversial choice as speaker. Not once did he mention the royal guests; instead, he proposed a toast to 'the industries of Tyneside' and went on to deliver a paean to Northumbria – her history, her achievements, and the enterprising character of her people. In a climax that must have astonished many of his listeners, the politician ended his speech with a breathtaking tribute to his former opponent.

'No name can be more appositely associated with northern industry and public spirit than that of the founder of Elswick, who has cast his thoughts into iron, invested them with all the romance of mechanical art, and achieved wealth almost beyond the dreams of avarice,' proclaimed Cowen. 'But he does not live for himself alone. He is happy when others can share in his bounty. Self-prompted, self-sustained, and, as regards his present profession, self-taught, he has worked his irresistible way through a thousand obstacles, and become one of the ornaments of his country when his country is one of the ornaments of the world.' The MP then reflected on the unique relationship between Armstrong and the people of Newcastle: 'He has interwoven the history of his life with the history of his native place, and has made one of the foundations of its fame the monument of his virtues. He has shown how the lofty aims of science and the eager demands of business can be assimilated, how the graces of social taste and embellishment need not be sullied by vulgar prodigality.'

Despite the audacity of its theme, Cowen's speech was received by loud and prolonged cheering, according to *The Times*. But Armstrong himself struck a discordant note in his response – with a veiled allusion to a backstage row with the organising officials – when he lamented that, since so many events had been included in the programme, there would be no time for the royal party to visit his factories at Elswick: 'An inspection of our places of industry which omits a view of the Elswick Works is rather like the play of *Hamlet* with the part of the prince left out.' He was determined that his guests should at least have a view of Elswick from the river.

That afternoon, the Prince and Princess of Wales inaugurated the Natural History Museum at Barras Bridge – a project spearheaded by the naturalist John Hancock and backed financially by many of Newcastle's leading citizens. The new building contained what was reckoned to be the most important collection of birds in the British Isles, including a specimen of an extinct great auk, as well as outstanding geological collections and a herbarium of British plants. It also provided a home for drawings of birds and animals by the engraver Thomas Bewick, and collections of fishes, mammals, reptiles, insects, fossils, and shells.[5] Moving on to the Free Library in New Bridge Street, the Prince of Wales formally opened its reference department.

As they returned to Central Station to board the train to Rothbury, members of the royal party might have spotted, a short distance to the left of the station portico, the restrained Neoclassical façade of the Lit & Phil building, where more than 40 years earlier Armstrong had demonstrated in front of rapt audiences some of his first inventions, including a hydroelectric machine and a hydraulic crane. As a member of the Literary and Philosophical Society since 1836, and its president since 1860, he had attended and conducted debates there on all manner of topical subjects, contributed to the society's vast and valuable collection of books, and put up the funds to build a 700-seat lecture theatre.

It was those early adventures in science and engineering that had captured the imagination of a knowledge-hungry public, invested the young Armstrong with a mysterious, otherworldly aura – and won him, at the age of 35, a fellowship of the Royal Society. John Wigham Richardson, who went on to found Swan Hunter shipbuilders, was growing up in Newcastle in the early 1840s and remembers being taken to see Armstrong deliver a lecture at the Lit & Phil: 'One dark night in the Christmas holidays, our father took us four elder children to see Lord Armstrong (then Mr William Armstrong, solicitor) exhibit his electrical machine ... It was a weird scene; the sparks or flashes of electricity from the machine were, I should say, from four to five feet long and the figure of Armstrong in a frock coat (since then so familiar) looked almost demoniacal.'[6]

During the final stage of the royal visit, Armstrong would have the chance to show off some of his greatest achievements to his future monarch – and he intended to seize it with both hands. But, before that, the royal family were looking forward to another sumptuous dinner at Cragside, from where they would observe the spectacular fireworks display, complete with bonfire, to be held at Cow Hill on Newcastle's Town Moor, 30 miles away.

Next day, at Fish Quay, the royal party joined the chairman and officials of the River Tyne Commission on board *Pará e Amazonas*, a palatial paddle-steamer built by Andrew Leslie of Hebburn to carry passengers on the Amazon, and lent specially for the occasion. In attendance were nearly 30 other gaily decorated steamers carrying Tyneside dignitaries and their hangers-on. Rather than heading east towards the sea, *Pará e Amazonas* first steamed upriver for a mile to offer its passengers a good view of Elswick Works, where, as the prince could see, a shipyard was under construction beside the long-established engine works and ordnance works. By the end of that autumn, the keel would be laid down of the first Elswick-built warship, the torpedo cruiser *Panther*, commissioned by the Austro-Hungarian navy.

Armstrong's gilded business career had recently entered a new phase with the formation of Sir W. G. Armstrong, Mitchell & Co., a public company that cemented the long collaboration between the Armstrong firm and that of Charles Mitchell at Low Walker in Newcastle's East End. Traditionally, Elswick Works had manufactured guns for warships built at Mitchell's yard – but a new era had begun in 1876 with Armstrong's building of the Swing Bridge between Newcastle and Gateshead, replacing an 18th-century stone bridge that had barred the passage of ships upriver. Driven by steam-powered hydraulic machinery that allowed it to swivel horizontally on a central pier, so that vessels could pass either side, the bridge had enabled the construction of ships at Elswick, 12 miles from the sea. The Tyne navigation had also been massively improved by dredging, and there were plans afoot to remove an entire island, known as King's Meadows, from the centre of the river opposite the works.

Described only three years later by the politician Lord Randolph Churchill as 'almost one of the wonders of the world', the Elswick Works was even then undergoing a huge expansion. In 1884 it employed fewer than 5,000 people; by 1900, the Armstrong workforce would have grown fivefold. During the last decade of the 19th century, Armstrong Mitchell would periodically occupy first place in the league of British shipbuilders.[7]

Having turned around at Elswick, *Pará e Amazonas* led the long line of steamers back downriver, passing under Robert Stephenson's High Level Bridge and through the Swing Bridge to be greeted by a crowd estimated to be around 80,000 on the Newcastle quayside. 'On the high roofs of the houses, on the perilous tops of the most lofty chimneys, too, adventurous persons had perched,' recorded *The Times*. 'Wharves, wherries, the roofs of sheds, and the masts of ships, all were occupied; and even the pinnacle of the massive 80-ton crane carried its human burden. Everywhere the enthusiasm was unbounded. There was a continuous roar of cheering from the banks as the royal craft sped on.' On the south bank of the river at Hebburn, more than 1,000 children were seen sitting on the side of a hill in a pattern based on the design of the Prince of Wales's feathers; as the line of steamers approached, the children shouted and cheered, each vigorously waving a single white handkerchief.

Soon after two o'clock, the royal procession arrived at the deep-water dock at Coble Dene, nearly nine miles from the Newcastle quayside, where it was surrounded by hundreds of small boats heavy with sightseers. Although it had cost £740,000 to build, the new dock was a triumph of the Tyne Improvement Commission, which had striven for more than 30 years to upgrade the river in order to maintain Tyneside's pre-eminence in the shipping world. Their success had been highlighted by Joseph Cowen the previous day: 'Three centuries ago the Tyne was the eighth port of the kingdom. Now it ranks second in number of ships that enter it, third in the bulk of its exports, and first in the universality of its trade.'

One of the commission's first great works had been the erection of two piers at the mouth of the river, which would eventually measure lengths of 3,000 feet (north pier) and 5,500 feet (south pier) respectively. Until 1860 there had been a sand bar at the entrance to the river, which gave a depth of only six feet at low water, and the entrance to the harbour was narrow and tortuous. Since then, 72 million tons of sand had been dredged, with the dredging carrying on at the rate of about 100,000 tons per week. The dock at Coble Dene had a depth of 30 feet at high water on a spring tide – a greater depth than any other dock on England's east coast. A large staith had been constructed, on each side of which were four spouts for loading coal, meaning that coal could be taken on board waiting ships at a rate of 800 to 1,000 tons per hour.

At the west side of the dock was a warehouse for storing up to 40,000 quarters (500 tons) of grain and fitted with the most modern hydraulic machinery available. The dock had a tidal entrance 80 feet wide and a lock entrance 60 feet wide, each fitted with gates made of 'greenheart' oak and operated hydraulically – again making use of one of Armstrong's earliest and most far-reaching inventions. Indeed, everywhere on the river, and in a myriad other places around the globe – from coal-mines to railway stations to great ports – were visual manifestations of Armstrong's marvellous achievements in the field of hydraulics. The phenomenon was captured in a memoir by Evan R. Jones, who had served as American consul in Newcastle from 1868 to 1883: 'For ten years of patient industry Armstrong thought and wrought to perfect and realize his idea. Now the freights of nations are swung by his crane. His hydraulic machinery is found on every mart of commerce in the civilized world.'[8]

The Prince of Wales named the new dock Albert Edward and declared it open, whereupon lunch was served in a pavilion on the west side of the dock entrance. Afterwards, remarking on the indelible impression made by the Swing Bridge, the Prince expressed the hope that a similar bridge might one day be built across the Thames near London Bridge to serve the Port of London.

Reboarding *Pará e Amazonas*, the royal party led the line of boats to the mouth of the river, where there was time for a close inspection of the massive piers. As the steamer approached the landing stage on the north pier, the Tynemouth Life Brigade impressed the audience with a hair-raising demonstration of its rescue work. Landing on the lower part, the visitors were taken up to the higher level in an improvised carriage and drawn by a small locomotive along the wagon way of the pier to a platform erected in the shadow of the old Tynemouth Priory and Castle. After another round of adulatory speeches, the princes and princesses were conveyed through the crowded and festooned streets of Tynemouth to the station, where a train was waiting to take them back to Rothbury.

The royal family's momentous visit to Cragside ended very much as it had begun, with a splendid formal dinner in advance of the departure by rail to Edinburgh the following morning. However, the visual record of those three days in August – a series of vivid watercolours by local artist Henry Hetherington Emmerson – portrays an atmosphere that is far from formal. Although he was the guest of a *nouveau riche* industrialist rather than someone of ancient lineage, the Prince of Wales showed no snobbery in his dealings with Armstrong. One of Emmerson's paintings shows the prince and his two sons sitting in relaxed fashion on the terrace at Cragside, dressed in easy country garb – one smoking, another holding a local newspaper – all listening intently to their host's words of wisdom. The Prince of Wales had inherited some of his father's passion for scientific enquiry and engineering innovation – and Armstrong was the very embodiment of all that was new and exciting in the world of technology. In another painting, Emmerson depicts Armstrong in his library in the congenial company of Princess Alexandra and her three daughters. In a fatherly guise – which throws into relief his own childlessness – Armstrong points out to the young princesses an item of interest in a book. Again, even in a royal milieu, it is he who is the centre of attention.

Despite the thrills they had experienced in Newcastle and along the Tyne, it was the magician's palace that had most entranced the royal visitors. Invited to taste the fruits of their host's personal Xanadu, they liked what they saw and succumbed to its delights. Not least among the attractions of Cragside, it was acknowledged, were the extensive rock gardens, in which Lady Armstrong's creative hand was everywhere revealed. Cloaking almost five acres, much of it consisting of precipitous slopes, they took their character from the crags above the River Coquet and the Debdon Burn. Almost all the rocks and stones which make up the three gardens had been manoeuvred into place by men using only levers and pulleys. Local fell sandstone had been collected from the surrounding moors and placed to show its weathered sides, and cascades were included in the designs to the north and west of house to introduce movement and the sound of water. Among the plantings were thousands of heaths and heathers, ferns, azaleas, and numerous alpine species. Between them, the Armstrongs were reckoned to have planted on the Cragside estate more than seven million trees and shrubs.

Three years after the royal visit to Newcastle, in Queen Victoria's golden jubilee honours of 1887, Sir William Armstrong was raised to the peerage as Baron Armstrong of Cragside. However, some people muttered, as some always would, that Armstrong's great wealth had been wrung from the blood and sweat of thousands of men less fortunate than himself, whose demands for improved working conditions he had cavalierly dismissed. His fiercest critics would later argue that Armstrong himself deserved nothing but contempt as a robber baron and a merchant of death – a man responsible for creating, manufacturing, and selling to all the leading nations on earth some of the most ferocious killing machines the world had ever seen.

2

The Kingfisher

It all began with water. Even as a young boy, William Armstrong was inexorably drawn to the streams and rivers near his home in the rugged, hilly countryside east of the booming coal town of Newcastle upon Tyne. From an early age his passion was fishing, and he spent many happy hours with rod and fly, thigh-deep in the fast-flowing burns of Northumberland in pursuit of the elusive trout. By his own account a 'weakly' child, prone to recurring chest ailments, William also put great faith in the curative powers of water – a faith that stayed with him throughout his long life. During a recuperative fishing trip to Rothbury in 1843, he wrote reassuringly to his wife, Meggie: 'I am now getting well as fast as can be. I have been almost continually in the water this glorious day and there's nothing does me so much good.'

William George Armstrong was born in the hamlet of Shieldfield on the edge of Pandon Dene on 26 November 1810, eight years after the birth of his sister, Anne. The family home was a three-storey terraced house in Pleasant Row with a back garden running down to the dene. Like many of the deeply cut valleys that fed their waters south into the mighty Tyne, by the mid-19th century Pandon Dene had fallen victim to the eastward expansion of Newcastle, and then been severed by a railway embankment. 'Year by year Newcastle goes on filling up the denes and valleys which intersect her,' lamented a contemporary chronicler.[1] 'One after another they disappear, and the picturesque undulation of the old town promises in time to give way to the level monotony of a flat surface.' But in the early part of the century, when Anne and William were growing up there, the dene was a beguiling place, with the burn winding through it and the hum of watermills mingling with the sound of varied birdsong. 'The mass of apple-blossom and the teaming luxuriance of the foliage which covered the banks, the little summer-houses in the trim gardens, and the winding pathway from the town to the Shieldfield, formed a picture of rare sylvan beauty.' The original 'Shield Field' was the place where English soldiers would traditionally muster in preparation for their many battles against the Scots. Part of the attraction for children was the ruins of a fort built there in 1644, during the Civil War, to defend the Royalist garrison in the town against the Scots Covenanters. King Charles I had been allowed to play golf on the Shield Field during his captivity in Newcastle in 1646.

A mile or so north-east of Shieldfield, at Jesmond, was another, equally enchanting dene that would prove more resistant to urban sprawl – and which, as the 19th century progressed, would lure more and more of the prosperous families of Newcastle to create homes and gardens along its ridges. With its steep and densely wooded banks giving way to wide grassy clearings, Jesmond Dene follows the course of the meandering Ouseburn for two miles between South Gosforth in the north and Jesmond Vale in the south. The river either flows purposefully through old woodland or gathers pace briefly in rapids and waterfalls, once used to power the corn and flint mills lining the valley. Featuring unusual rock formations, stepping stones, and a variety of bridges, the dene has a magical quality. Although in Armstrong's day it was flanked by mines and small industrial works, even then it offered a wonderful respite from the urban world. The combination of its proximity to the centre of Newcastle and its aesthetic appeal made it a desirable place of residence for the emerging middle classes, and an influential community within a community evolved there. It was in this physically and intellectually alluring environment that William Armstrong would set up his first home in the mid-1830s.

During the early years, however, it was the seductive charms of Coquetdale, 30 miles to the north, which exerted the strongest pull on young William. His father's friend Armorer Donkin, a rich bachelor, had a country home at Rothbury on the River Coquet, and the Armstrong family were frequent visitors. Donkin – an early member of Newcastle's Literary and Philosophical Society –

numbered among his vast circle of friends the radical journalist James Leigh Hunt. Destined to play a seminal role in Armstrong's brilliant career, Donkin was 'most generous in the manner as well as the amount of his sacrifices', wrote Leigh Hunt, describing him as 'one of the men we love best in the world'.[2]

Donkin and the Armstrongs, father and son, fished together on the Coquet and young William developed a talent for the sport. Among his mentors was Mark Aynsley, a young Rothbury shoemaker so skilled in the art of dressing flies that they would nearly always 'fetch' a Coquet fish. 'I was scarcely ever away from the waterside and fished from morning till night,' Armstrong admitted later. 'They used to call me the Kingfisher.'[3] He confessed to a fondness for poaching, which he always did alone, his favourite stretch of water being on the nearby Brinkburn estate, whose fish were, in theory, carefully protected: 'I have many a time crept under the bushes close to the house and filled my creel.' Even during the harsh northern winters, when the rivers froze over, he couldn't keep away from the water, and he proved also a competent skater, who with his tall, slim physique and arresting good looks was said to have 'carved some graceful figures on the ebony surface of the Tyne'.[4]

To Armstrong, these childhood experiences were full of joy. 'I believe that I first came to Rothbury as a babe in arms, and my earliest recollections consist of paddling in the Coquet, gathering pebbles from its gravel beds, and climbing amongst the rocks on the crag. For many years I annually visited Rothbury with my parents and under well-known local celebrities I learned to fish. The Coquet then became to me a river of pleasure. As I grew up, I extended my explorations of it from its mouth to its source, and acquired an admiration for its scenery which has been a source of enjoyment to me through all my life.'

William Armstrong's love affair with water – which only deepened as he grew older – and his desire in general to commune with the natural world, had an intensely practical side: a fascination with channelling elemental power to useful ends. This sprang from his wish to know how everything worked and, once he had found out, to improve on it – a pursuit that was given free rein during the long periods, sometimes months on end, when he was kept at home because of ill health. From as young as the age of five or six, William delighted in getting hold of old spinning wheels and other domestic items, and he would construct from them mechanical devices that could be set in motion by primitive pulleys, made from weights hung on strings from staircase railings. His interest in toys – which, whenever possible, he would take to pieces – depended on how far they satisfied his curiosity. His very early inventions included a new basket for fishing bait, designed to preserve minnows at the proper temperature.

One of William Armstrong's favourite excursions as a child was to the shop of old John Fordy, who did joinery work for his maternal grandfather, the Walbottle colliery owner William Potter. With Fordy's help, he would make fittings for his miniature engines or earnestly copy the joiner's work, acquiring a skill in the use of tools that proved invaluable in later life. Armstrong later told his friend Thomas Sopwith that his childhood had been 'a continual study of electricity, chemistry and mechanics' – none of which would have been taught at school.

More than fifty years before the introduction of compulsory elementary education, there was already a number of thriving schools in the Newcastle area for the lower and middle classes, including charity schools, Sunday schools, and private academies such as the highly regarded Bruce's Academy in Percy Street, attended by the future railway engineer Robert Stephenson, Armstrong's near-contemporary. Armstrong's early education at a private school in Whickham, west of Gateshead, was greatly supplemented by the intervention of his ambitious father, who had proved himself a skilled mathematician and had begun to amass a vast collection of books. And, like Robert Stephenson – who had been encouraged to assiduous study by his brilliant but illiterate father, George – he would have immersed himself in the library that formed a core part of Newcastle's learned society, the Lit & Phil.

By 1826, when Armstrong was sent to grammar school at Bishop Auckland in County Durham, his passion for mechanics was clear, and his enthusiasm for experimentation was growing. But the 15-year-old boy would have little opportunity to pursue those interests at school, where instruction was confined to 'reading

English, writing and accounts' – in addition to the classics, a subject particularly valued by his father. A contemporary report reveals that there were, on average, 55 boys in the school, about 10 of whom received instruction in the classics. Classicists were expected to pay fees of 10s 6d a quarter.

In Bishop Auckland, Armstrong lodged with Reverend Robert Thompson, master of the school since 1814, and in one notorious incident smashed a window of a neighbouring home while testing a home-made crossbow with missiles fashioned from the stems of old tobacco pipes. The renegade's school career survived the incident, but it is an example of how his academic studies were clearly not sufficient to satisfy his curiosity. Years later he wrote to his friend Stuart Rendel about tactics for making time pass more quickly: 'At school before the holidays I used to try a stick notched to correspond with the number of remaining days – one notch was obliterated every morning until the happy day of release arrived.' Armstrong's frustration may have had something to do with the master's lack of commitment to his pupils. The governors later found that, during a particular five-year period, Mr Thompson had 'rarely attended the school', criticising the poor standards that had resulted.

Despite this unsatisfactory state of affairs, Bishop Auckland – the chosen residence of the Prince Bishops of Durham since the 13th century – had its attractions, among which was the small engineering works of William Ramshaw, where the young Armstrong spent every spare moment. Impressed with the keen interest that the young man took in the machines, Ramshaw invited him to his home, where Armstrong met the engineer's 18-year-old daughter, Margaret, three years his senior. Captivated by her quiet but arresting good looks, self-confidence, and strength of character, he must also have been struck by her intelligent grasp of her father's craft – and perhaps even then had a foretaste of what a good match the two of them might make.

One very large obstacle stood in the way of William Armstrong's professional and amorous desires, however: his father's iron determination that his son should pursue a career in law. Armstrong senior had worked his way up from lowly merchant's clerk to leading member of Newcastle's social and cultural elite – and would go on to become an alderman and, later, mayor of the industrial and commercial powerhouse on the Tyne. His own experiences had taught him that a combination of educational opportunities, hard work, and shrewd use of connections was the key to self-advancement, and – however persistently William tried to convince him – he could not see mechanics as a worthy occupation for his only son. Consequently, as William's school days drew to a close, the idea arose that he should study law in London under the tutelage of his brother-in-law, William Henry Watson.

A glamorous and clever former soldier, Watson had married Anne Armstrong in August 1826. As a member of the 1st Royal Dragoons, he had served under Wellington in the Peninsular War at the age of only 16. He shared in the Waterloo prize money and was present at the entry of the allied armies into Paris. Shortly afterwards, having decided to enter the legal profession, he moved to London from his native Bamburgh, in Northumberland, and occupied chambers in the Inner Temple, one of the four Inns of Court. He became competent to practise as a 'special pleader', an expert in drafting complex documents, and was later called to the bar. At the time of his marriage, Watson seemed set for great things, and his career flourished. In 1856, he would be knighted and made a Baron of the Exchequer.

Whatever the youthful Armstrong's feelings about the prospect of living and studying with his rather awe-inspiring brother-in-law in an unfamiliar city far from home, all protests about his father's plans were silenced in the summer of 1828 by an event that shattered the entire family. On 1 June, William's beloved sister, Anne, died suddenly aged just 25. Barely a year earlier she had given birth to her only child, John William Watson.

Armstrong's father, William senior, was a sympathetic but forthright figure who exerted a strong influence over his small family. Born in 1778 at Stanwix in Cumberland border country, within sight of the Roman Wall, he had the good fortune to grow up at Wreay, a few miles south-east of Carlisle, where in early life his path crossed with that of the dynamic Losh family. The son of a village cobbler, and descended from generations of yeomen, Armstrong senior numbered among his ancestors the infamous 16th-century border reiver Kinmont Willie.

There had been a chapel at Wreay since the early 14th century, and around it had grown up a village that by 1811 consisted of 21 houses and 108 inhabitants. A schoolhouse was built there in 1760 to replace an earlier school established in the chapel. In Armstrong senior's youth, the crowning glory of Wreay was Woodside, the Palladian manor on the northern edge of the village belonging to the Loshes. Originally known as Inglewoodside, the house had evolved from a simple pele tower in the forest of Inglewood into a many-roomed mansion surrounded by rolling parkland.[5] It was presided over in the mid-18th century by John Losh, a descendant of the Arloshes who had inhabited the area for at least two centuries. Although no family members had been honoured with a title, they had prospered as landowners and county gentry. John Losh, known as 'the big black squire' of Woodside, had many children, six of whom survived. They included James (born in 1763), George and William, all of whom would play a vital role in the Armstrong story.

James Losh, a prolific correspondent who also kept a diary, had radical and reformist leanings that would see him caught up in the fringes of the French Revolution. He reached the pinnacle of his career in 1832, when he was appointed Recorder of Newcastle, the highest judicial position in the north of England. Among his close friends were the poets Wordsworth and Coleridge and the liberal politician Henry Brougham, Lord Chancellor from 1830 to 1834, a key player in the abolition of the slave trade and renowned for his progressive ideas on schooling and the law.

All the Losh children received a good education and all proved to have an aptitude for learning foreign languages. They started at the village school of Wreay, where William Armstrong, who had developed an early interest in mathematics, would follow them a few years later. John and James went on to school at Sedbergh to study under the renowned mathematician John Dawson. James Losh held his maths teacher in high esteem, regarding him as a friend: 'He was a man of exemplary purity and simplicity of manners, profound knowledge of mathematics, and had the best manner of conveying instruction which I ever witnessed.'[6]

An introduction to Dawson by the Loshes would have done much to stimulate the young William Armstrong's growing passion for mathematical study.

At Wreay village school, meanwhile, their tutor was William Gaskin, the local priest, a man who – fond of hunting and cock-fighting as well as ecclesiastical pursuits – combined eccentricity and learning in equal measure. 'Mr Gaskin is uncouth in his manners and abrupt and confused in his manner of speaking,' wrote James, 'but is certainly a man of considerable powers of mind and when a young man was a law student and by no means a bad Latin and Greek scholar.' Gaskin enjoyed a special relationship with the Loshes: 'He lived many years in my father's family and was my principal instructor until I was 16 years old. He kept also a school at Wreay which my brother and I attended, and although this might not be the best possible mode of education, yet it had some advantages and perhaps I have not upon the whole had any great reason to regret that I was not brought up at a great public school.'

Gaskin remained in close touch with the Losh family for the rest of his life. Once asked to define a good classical scholar, he replied, 'You should be able to construe the Greek testament, anywhere, at sight, and to parse any verb. You should, also, be able to read any easy prose Greek author, as Xenophon, Lucian, Herodotus and also Homer.' But even that was not enough: 'Then all the common Latin schoolbooks; you should be able to read at sight Virgil, Horace, Caesar's Commentaries, Tully's Orations. Lastly you should be able to write pretty correctly Latin prose – and a Greek play or two should be added!'

This, then, was the intellectual climate in which William Armstrong, the shoemaker's son, spent his formative years. In the mid-1790s, entering into his late teens, Armstrong left Wreay and, again following in the footsteps of the Loshes, he crossed the Pennines to seek his fortune in Newcastle upon Tyne, where – his mathematical abilities being well recognised – he was given work as a clerk in the counting house of a Losh family firm on the quayside.

The Loshes had inherited coal-mining interests in north-east England, which gave them the financial means to set up new industrial ventures on the Tyne. The most successful in this respect was the youngest brother, William, who had studied chemistry at Cambridge and in the early 1790s developed an interest in the French chemist Nicolas Leblanc, who had discovered a cheap and reliable way to produce alkali, or soda (sodium carbonate), in large quantities. Alkali was in huge demand at the time, not only from the textiles industries but also from the makers of glass, pottery, paper, and soap. Drawing on the discoveries of Leblanc, William Losh pioneered the manufacturer of alkali on Tyneside and set up a production works at Walker in 1796, stimulating a period of massive growth in the Tyneside chemical industry, which continued through much of the 19th century.

Along with his brother George, and John Diedrich Lubbren, a naturalised British citizen of German origin, William Losh was a partner in the firm that employed young William Armstrong as a clerk. Described as 'ironmongers, dealers and chapmen', Losh, Lubbren, & Co. traded in some of the many commodities that passed through Newcastle docks at the time, including corn. George Losh, a popular, easy-going figure – whose wayward habits made him a constant source of worry to his brother James – also had an interest in the Newcastle Fire Office and Water Company and in an ironworks at Balgonie in Fife.

To begin with, Losh, Lubbren, & Co. prospered, but in the summer of 1803 the company was mortally wounded by the abrupt collapse of the Newcastle banking house of Surtees and Burdon. On 1 July, George Losh told his brother James of the bank's troubles and a few days later James wrote in his diary: 'Everything looks hopeless.' The company went bankrupt, embroiling the partners in several years of debt repayments. The iron foundry at Balgonie also failed, and George Losh's fortunes went from bad to worse, eventually forcing him to emigrate to France with his large family. William Armstrong, the firm's clerk – by then married and the father of a baby girl – was suddenly thrown out of work and had to rely on his own resources and contacts, including his wife's family, to keep him afloat. Picking up the pieces from Losh Lubbren, and possibly with some financial assistance from William Losh, Armstrong set out to make his own way in the corn trade, establishing an office at Cowgate, near his home in Pandon Dene.

While his brothers were preoccupied by the trials of commerce, James Losh was making his way in the law and developing an interest in parliamentary and social reform. His progressive instincts and rhetorical skills had made him one of the leading lights of the Lit & Phil – even today, a life-size statue of him in the guise of a Roman senator dominates the magnificent double staircase of the society's building in Westgate Street. In 1799, Losh and his wife Cecilia settled permanently in Newcastle, later buying a house called The Grove in Jesmond Dene.

Little did the Loshes know at the time that they were pioneers in what would become twin traditions in the town, for both the Lit & Phil and Jesmond Dene were to act as magnets for most of the powerful individuals in Newcastle during the decades that followed. And – thanks, no doubt, to James Losh's influence – among the very early members of the Lit & Phil was William Armstrong, the studious young clerk from Wreay.

The brainchild of Reverend William Turner, an educational pioneer, the Lit & Phil was the stimulus for what was to become Newcastle's intellectual and industrial flowering in the first half of the 19th century. Turner's idea had been to establish a conversation club that would 'provide an easy method of spending the evening agreeably and usefully'.[7] He proposed that the members should meet once a month to exchange views on literary and scientific matters, and that those with special knowledge should present papers relating to the particular topic chosen for the evening. Subjects thought worthy of study and discussion included 'mathematics, natural philosophy and history, chemistry, polite literature, antiquities, civil history, biography, questions of general law and policy, commerce, and the arts'. All talk of religion and politics, however, was strictly prohibited. In November 1802, Turner himself launched what proved to be a highly popular series of lectures on 'natural and experimental philosophy' that would continue without a break for more than thirty years. According to Robert Spence Watson, the historian of the Lit & Phil and a lifelong member of the society, 'The meetings were not only times when scientific observations, and the results of research and experiments, were brought forward, explained and discussed, but they had also

Pandon Dene, an idyllic rural spot east of Newcastle, was Armstrong's childhood playground. By the late 19th century the dene had been levelled, built upon, and absorbed into the city.

William and Meggie Armstrong made a home in Jesmond Dene after their marriage in 1835. The few surviving images of the house, demolished a century later, include this view of the glasshouses.

an immediate and important influence upon the entire district, and upon the social and intellectual advancement of Newcastle.'

The Lit & Phil lays claim to being the first organisation of its kind to open its doors to women (although women did not become regular members on the same basis as men until the middle of the 19th century). On 13 March 1799, the committee resolved that a new class of members be admitted to the society; known as 'reading members', they were expected voluntarily to relinquish the privileges of attending the general meetings and voting in the choice of members – but gender was no bar.

It is probable that William Armstrong met his future wife, the reputedly gifted and amiable Anne Potter, at one of the society's monthly meetings. Anne was a member of the ambitious and well-connected Potter family of Walbottle Hall in the coal-mining district of Tynedale. She married William Armstrong on 25 November 1801 at St John's Church, Newcastle. Their daughter, also Anne, was born the following September.

In the summer of 1809, when the younger Anne Armstrong was almost seven, she travelled with her mother, her aunt, and her maternal grandfather, William Potter, to Cumberland and Westmorland to see the lakes and discover her father's roots. Since her father was unable to join them, Anne, with the help of her Aunt Jane, kept a journal so that he could later share in their adventures.[8]

The party left Newcastle by mail coach at midday on 17 July and, travelling via Hexham, Haltwhistle, and Penrith, arrived at Keswick at eight o'clock on the evening of the 19th. Over the following days, they explored Derwent Water, Rydal, Windermere, Ullswater and the villages in between, before returning to Newcastle via Carlisle, where they met various members of the Armstrong clan, including Anne's paternal grandparents. At Carlisle they visited the home of her father's brother, where they found, according to the diary-writer, 'a charming and numerous family'.

Anne's mischievous sense of humour and lively curiosity shine through the medium of her Aunt Jane's elegant prose. She comments, somewhat indignantly, that, after an early change of horses, her mother and grandfather swapped seats with two men who had been sitting outside the coach. Then it started to rain: 'One of the gentlemen, in his anxiety for my mama, putting his head out of the carriage in haste, to desire her to come in, hit his nose such a blow against the heel of one of the outside passengers' shoes as made him return with his nose in his hand with full more speed than he set out. This, you may be sure, made one laugh heartily.'[9]

The majestic scenery they observed could not fail to impress the whole party, but the young girl and her aunt found some aspects of it alien and threatening. On their way to Windermere, for example, the record shows that they were 'struck with amazement at the wild disorder which seemed to reign among these rugged tribes of uncouth mountains and chaotic dells, as if ruin had unmolesting fixed his dreary empire there'. A little further on they passed Grasmere, where the poet William Wordsworth was living at the time with his family at Dove Cottage (though the journal does not mention this fact). Wordsworth's reverence for the awe-inspiring power of nature is reflected to some extent in Anne Armstrong's lakeland diary, and this interest in the natural world – and human behaviour – would come to be shared with her brother, William, who made his appearance 18 months later.

The final piece of the jigsaw in the early life of the Kingfisher fell into place with the appearance on the scene of the man who would become his patron and benefactor, the genial and charismatic lawyer Armorer Donkin. Son of a timber merchant, Donkin had spent his early life in North Shields before working as a legal clerk in London's Hatton Garden for several years.[9] He returned to north-east England after the death of his mother in 1801 and, still in his early twenties, resolved to set up a law practice in Newcastle. He had few contacts in the town and found it a struggle at first, but all this changed when he joined the Lit & Phil.

At the society's monthly meetings, Donkin became acquainted with many of the leading families in Newcastle, and it was not long before he had built up a large and lucrative network of clients. One of his many friends was the aspirational corn merchant William Armstrong, described by an observer as 'a warm supporter of the institution and a man of scholarly acquirements'.[10] Almost exact contemporaries, the two men were immediately drawn to each other: 'Their tastes were similar; their political views harmonized; their aims were practically identical, and they became as brothers.' According to Alfred Cochrane, a historian of the Elswick Works, 'They used to meet and hold long discussions and arguments over a good many glasses of what, I have no doubt, was very excellent port.'[11]

Although less radical in their inclinations than James Losh, both men had a strong interest in economic and social reform. In August 1824, at a public meeting at Newcastle's Moot Hall, they were appointed to a committee to recommend whether a railway or a canal would be the better transport artery between Newcastle and Carlisle. The issue was urgent since, as Armstrong pointed out, 'We can bring corn from the Cape of Good Hope to Newcastle cheaper than we can convey it between Newcastle and Carlisle.'[12] In opposition to Losh, he argued strongly in favour of a canal, dismissing the railway proposition as 'spiritless' and revealing an instinctive caution in the face of the new, relatively untried, technology. When the committee reported, it came down firmly on the side of rail transport, and James Losh was appointed the first chairman of the Newcastle and Carlisle Railway. Armstrong later supported Losh in his bid to set up a free-trade association between Newcastle and the Far East, and in his campaign for religious emancipation; however, he opposed the repeal of the Corn Laws, believing that the abolition of tariffs on imported corn would severely damage the interests of British producers. The Corn Laws were eventually repealed in 1846.

By the mid-1820s, with the corn trade flourishing, William Armstrong had moved his family from their terraced house in Shieldfield to a much larger establishment in upper Ouseburn valley. The 12 acres of land on which he built a house, The Minories, also known as South Jesmond House, was a mere stone's throw from Jesmond Park, the property recently purchased by his old friend Armorer Donkin. The Armstrongs had arrived in Jesmond Dene.

Gregarious and generous by nature, Donkin transformed his Jesmond home into an elegant place of entertainment and instituted a weekly event that became legendary as 'Donkin's Ordinary'. Every Saturday the bachelor host would throw open his doors to any of his friends who felt disposed to attend, as explained by the diarist Thomas Sopwith: 'No invitation or notice is given or received and the number varies from six to sixteen. Nothing can exceed the comfort and hospitality that prevails.' Events would follow a pattern. After conversation in the library, the guests would be ushered into a dining room adorned with numerous portraits by James Ramsay and other fashionable painters of the day. 'The dinner is always substantial and abundant ... the wines good and followed by an excellent dessert.'

Donkin's growing public prominence in Newcastle and his membership of the Society of Hostmen – a guild set up in Elizabethan times to control the coal trade on Tyneside – meant that he often mixed business with pleasure. All kinds of eminent visitors to Newcastle were royally entertained, among them the political writer and farmer William Cobbett, who was pleased that Donkin had followed his advice on tree planting. Indeed, the grounds at Jesmond Park were tended with the same care that Donkin gave to his hospitality.

Donkin's interest in creating a gracious home and 'pleasure grounds' for the enjoyment of himself and his friends would be reflected by other new settlers in Jesmond Dene, especially in years to come by his protégé and heir, William George Armstrong, the son of his closest friends. In 1835, drawn to the dene by its landscape, its familiarity, and the proximity of friends and family, Armstrong would build a house there for himself and his new wife, surround it with a fabulous garden, and begin an extensive programme of tree-planting. But it wasn't simply the presence of the Ouseburn that made the dene so attractive: it was the untamed character of the watery environment and the possibilities it offered for enhancing nature. Some of the Kingfisher's excitement at the discovery of such a place, and his sense of being a 'willing captive', is conveyed in a fantasy he wrote in the 1850s:

'When I arrived, I was delighted with the cleanness of the water, the brightness of the grass which fringed it, the various colours of the mosses which clung to the rocks – and the general beauty of the whole scene. The merry stream as she capered past seemed to be laughing at the nimble leap she had just performed, and at having so cleverly jumped over those rude rocks which had stuck up their jagged edges to injure her had she alighted there ... I then began to search for the path by which I had descended, but, strange to say, I could not find it. I saw many places like it, but on trying them I found them to be all impracticable.'

Although Armstrong would later identify electricity as his first love, it was water in all its forms and applications that would represent an unbroken thread linking his many achievements – and it was water that would prove the catalyst for his first great scientific discovery. In the summer of 1835, he embarked on a sporting expedition to the Pennines near Sedbergh. While fishing on the River Dee at Dentdale, he experienced a revelation: 'I was lounging idly about, watching an old water-mill, when it occurred to me what a small part of the power of the water was used in driving the wheel, and then I thought how great would be the force of even a small quantity of water if its energy were only concentrated in one column. When I returned to Newcastle, I set to work at Watson's works, where I had been in the habit of making mechanical experiments, trying to practically realise the idea.' It was the germ of his myriad hydraulic inventions. From that moment on, according to family lore, William had 'water on the brain'.

Seven years earlier, following the death of Anne, any hope that he would have the chance to experiment with the 'motive power' of water would have been inconceivable. The loss of his sister marked the end of William's childhood. In the autumn of 1828, acquiescing in his parents' wishes – and those of Armorer Donkin, who had promised him work as an articled clerk – the 17-year-old boy embarked on the arduous 37-hour coach journey from Newcastle to London, where he would be introduced to the intricacies of the legal profession by his grieving brother-in-law. His destination was the Temple.

3

Brilliant Sparks

The Inner Temple and the Middle Temple – which, together with Gray's Inn and Lincoln's Inn, make up London's four Inns of Court – have an association with the legal profession that goes back more than 600 years, and a history of influential tenants that is even older. Named after the Knights Templar who lived there in the 12th century, the two neighbouring Inns occupy several acres of land between Fleet Street and the Thames embankment; with its narrow cobbled streets, garden squares, and harmonious jumble of architectural styles, the enclave offers a haven from the turmoil of the city all around. To the writer Charles Lamb, who was born there in 1775, the Temple was 'the most elegant spot in the metropolis'. In an essay published in the 1820s, Lamb wrote, 'What a transition for a countryman visiting London for the first time – the passing from the crowded Strand or Fleet Street, by unexpected avenues, into its magnificent ample squares, its classic green recesses!'[1]

In the early 19th century, as had been the custom for hundreds of years, lawyers, clerks, and law students lived and worked in rented 'chambers' in the Inns and were expected to dine regularly in the magnificent halls built for the purpose. Chambers had always been places of both residence and employment, especially since – until relatively recently – a legal education depended on the community experience of living, dining, and talking together. No formal legal training was established at the Inns of Court until the mid-19th century, so the usual custom for would-be lawyers was to enrol (at some cost) with an experienced legal specialist for at least a year in order to master the technicalities and procedures of the law courts.

The novelist Charles Dickens, who had a much more jaundiced view of the Temple than Lamb, revealed his disdain in the *Pickwick*

Papers, set in 1827 and 1828, the time of Armstrong's arrival in London: 'Scattered about, in various holes and corners of the Temple, are certain dark and dirty chambers, in and out of which there may be seen constantly hurrying with bundles of papers under their arms and protruding from their pockets, an almost uninterrupted succession of lawyers' clerks ... These sequestered nooks are the public offices of the legal profession, where writs are issued, judgments signed, declarations filed, and numerous other ingenious little machines put in motion for the torture and torment of His Majesty's liege subjects, and the comfort and emolument of the practitioners of the law. They are, for the most part, low-roofed, mouldy rooms, where innumerable rolls of parchment, which have been perspiring in secret for the last century, send forth an agreeable odour, which is mingled by day with the scent of the dry rot, and by night with the various exhalations which arise from damp cloaks, festering umbrellas, and the coarsest tallow candles.' [2]

Dickens provides a vivid impression, no doubt exaggerated, of the singular world into which young William Armstrong was plunged on his arrival in the Temple in the autumn of 1828. Already promised employment by Armorer Donkin in Newcastle, Armstrong threw himself into his legal studies under the watchful but benevolent eye of William Henry Watson. Fourteen years Armstrong's senior, Watson had been admitted as a member of Lincoln's Inn in June 1817, after the conclusion of his youthful military career. He had established himself in chambers at 5 Inner Temple Lane and in 1826, on his marriage to Anne Armstrong, moved to 2 Lamb's Building, where he would remain until 1832; the Watsons also kept a home in the borough of Fulham, south-west of London. For a few years after Anne's death, their baby son, John, would be brought up in Northumberland, either by the Armstrong parents in Jesmond or by William Watson's family at Shoreston, near Bamburgh.

Watson's work as a 'special pleader' involved drafting arcane documents for use in the common-law courts, while his brother-in-law was supposed to watch, absorb, and learn, as well as performing clerkly duties. This role did not inspire Armstrong – he himself never became a member of an Inn – but, even though his heart was not in it, he made the most of the opportunity, partly because he felt indebted to Donkin. 'The law was not, of course, of my choosing; my vocation was chosen for me,' he said later, 'and for a good many years I stuck to the law, while all my leisure was given to mechanics.' Donkin had always taken a great interest in the Armstrong children and had helped to finance young William's studies in London in the expectation that he would in due course return to Newcastle and join the Donkin firm, which was what eventually happened. 'When I entered his office I was practically adopted by him: I was to be his heir. Such an opening in life was, of course, most attractive: here, it seemed, was a career ready made for me.'

There were many advantages to residing at Lamb's Building, at the heart of the British establishment and within easy reach of Westminster. Although exclusively male (as far as the legal profession was concerned), the Inns were highly sociable places where it was easy to make contacts and difficult not to absorb information about the mechanisms of government and how they interacted with the law – information that would prove useful to Armstrong on the many future occasions when he would present a case to Parliament or give evidence to a royal commission. Among fellow Newcastle men he might have encountered in the Temple was his father's friend James Losh, who had been called to the bar at Lincoln's Inn 20 years earlier.

Losh was a key player in the agitation for reform and, although he practised on the northern circuit, his political interests brought him often to Westminster. As a Unitarian, or protestant dissenter, he was disqualified from holding certain high offices, so he had campaigned vigorously against the Test and Corporation Acts, which had enshrined this discrimination in law. The eventual repeal of these acts in 1828 opened the way for his appointment as Recorder of Newcastle. Losh used his influence in the northern counties to aid the passage of the Great Reform Act of 1832, which was steered through Parliament by Charles, Earl Grey, the Liberal prime minister and MP for Northumberland.

Likewise destined for a successful legal career, William Watson was busy establishing his professional and social reputation at the Inns of Court. Among the friends he made during this period was a young barrister from Sussex called Hasler Capron who worked as an 'equity draftsman', a specialist in the drafting of the technical proceedings in the Court of Chancery, and who, in 1830, took chambers at 1 Pump Court, Middle Temple. Descended from a Norman family who had been recorded in the neighbourhood of Lodsworth, near Midhurst, in the early 12th century, Capron was the heir to large estates. Soon after their meeting, Hasler had introduced William Watson to his younger sister, Mary, and it was not long before the young widower was spending a great deal of time in her company.

Despite the reformist ferment taking place on his doorstep, Armstrong showed little interest in politics – unlike his brother-in-law, who would serve as Liberal MP for the Irish seat of Kinsale and, later, for Hull. Nor was Armstrong particularly diverted by the multitude of taverns, coffee houses, and theatres which dotted the area around the Temple and nearby Covent Garden. What did give him pleasure, however, was to attend the Friday evening discourses at the Royal Institution in Albemarle Street, Piccadilly, where he first encountered the fascinating man of science Michael Faraday.

Michael Faraday was the guru of the age. Of humble origins – his father was a Surrey blacksmith and he began his own working life as a bookbinder's apprentice – Faraday rose to become chief assistant to the leading chemist Humphry Davy; he was made a Fellow of the Royal Society and in 1825 became the director of the Royal Institution laboratory, the most advanced scientific laboratory in the country. Four years earlier, Faraday had discovered what he called 'electromagnetic rotation', the principle behind the electric motor. In the autumn of 1831, by which time he was professor of chemistry at the Royal Military Academy in Woolwich, he invented the first transformer and the first dynamo, thereby laying the foundations for the practical use of electricity. The year 1831 saw another event with far-reaching consequences for the scientific community: inspired by David Brewster, an Edinburgh journalist and natural philosopher (the term 'scientist' was not coined until 1833), the British Association for the Advancement of Science held its inaugural meeting at York.

Faraday was a dashing, charismatic figure with a head of thick dark curls and a compelling style of communication whose lectures at the Royal Institution drew huge crowds from all walks of life. To some extent, his popularity could be attributed to the British public's contemporary hunger for scientific knowledge, which had got into its stride in the mid to late 18th century and which would reach its climax in 1859, with the publication of the first edition of Charles Darwin's *On the Origin of Species*. One of Faraday's many fans was the painter John Callcott Horsley, who attended a lecture in the early 1830s on the chemistry of colours and was struck by 'the brightness of presence, the charm of manner and language, and the marvellous manipulative skill of the lecturer'. Horsley went on: 'I can see him now, as if it were yesterday, entering the laboratory, advancing quickly to the table, and looking round his audience with a beaming glance from eyes, which for beauty and intense intellectual power of expression I never saw equalled – then plunging into his subject without a moment's hesitation, with rapid but perfectly distinct utterance of words of real and true eloquence, powerful, yet simple and clear even to such unscientific dullards as myself, and illustrating his subject with experiments of unerring certainty.'[3]

It did not take much for William Armstrong – during interludes in his legal studies at the Temple – to fall under the Faraday spell, and when, in 1840, Armstrong made his first important electrical discovery, he was quick to approach Faraday, whose first volume of *Experimental Researches in Electricity* had been published the previous year.

Regular journeys home to Tyneside to see his parents also helped to sustain Armstrong during his student days in London. While in Newcastle, he would take every opportunity to visit the engineering works of his friend Henry Watson, where he could indulge in all sorts of mechanical investigations with the help of the handful of skilled mechanics employed there.

Armstrong was in Jesmond in the autumn of 1831 and, to mark his 21st birthday, a portrait was commissioned from Armorer Donkin's friend James Ramsay. The painting – a romantic representation of a handsome young dreamer with echoes of a Byronic hero – was designed to hang as a companion piece to the portrait of his late sister Anne, also by Ramsay, which had been painted to celebrate her coming-of-age. By that time it was clear that Armstrong's legal training in London would be coming to a close, not least because his brother-in-law's domestic arrangements had changed. On 17 August 1831 – with Anne's death still a recent memory – William Watson had married Mary Capron and the couple had set up home together in Kensington. Their only child, a boy named William Henry, would be born the following year, and his half-brother John, then aged three, was destined to become part of the new family.

Meanwhile, another – much darker – development that would have an indirect but important impact on Armstrong's career was taking place on the North Sea coast just a few miles south-east of Newcastle. In October 1831, *Cholera morbus* arrived in Sunderland; it was the first time that the disease had been seen in Britain. Originating in the Indian subcontinent, and transmitted to Britain via the Baltic ports, cholera reached Sunderland as a direct consequence of the growing trade between India and Europe. Described by a contemporary observer as 'that grim Asiatic fiend',[4] the disease would spread first to Tyneside and then all over Britain in the year that followed, terrorizing the population and claiming more than 50,000 lives, including some 540 in Newcastle and Gateshead alone.

Although there were continuing arguments about whether or not cholera and similar diseases were contagious, waterborne, or contracted in other ways, there was a general acknowledgement that the domestic water supply was in need of drastic improvement. And no group of people was more keenly aware of that need than those living in the vicinity of the increasingly polluted River Tyne, which drained the Ouseburn and a host of other streams that had become no more than open sewers and receptacles for industrial waste. Although there was a reservoir on the Town Moor, from which water was delivered by lead pipes to fountains and standpipes, in times of drought the fast-growing population of Tyneside drew supplies from the river.

Thirteen years later, Armstrong would address this problem with the establishment of his first commercial operation, the Whittle

Dene Water Company. In the short term, he left London and returned to Jesmond, where he took up residence with his parents at the Minories and began to practise as a solicitor at the renamed firm of Donkin, Stable and Armstrong. At the same time, increasingly absorbed by the potential of water power – a preoccupation that reached a climax with the Dentdale revelation of 1835 – he started to make daily visits to Henry Watson's works, where he got to know the Hutchinson family of engineers and made many experiments with hydraulic machinery. Although also attempting throughout this period to apply himself diligently to his legal duties, he was gently derided as 'swinging like an erratic pendulum between the law office and the lathe'.[5]

The results of Armstrong's investigations into hydraulic power first came to public attention in December 1838 with the appearance in the *Mechanics' Magazine* of his article about an 'improved waterwheel'. Highlighting the inefficiency of existing contraptions at harnessing the power of water, and drawing on his detailed knowledge of the countryside around Newcastle, he wrote:

'Hilly and undulating districts abound with little rivulets, which flow down the sides of declivities from elevations of one to three hundred feet, and which, on account of their diminutive size, are at present entirely disregarded. Such streams as these, however, would become most efficient sources of mechanical power if they were made to operate by their gravity throughout the whole, or greater part, of their descent, instead of the very limited portion of which a waterwheel is capable of employing. Streams of this description are to be met with on the banks of many of our navigable rivers, and in a multitude of other situations well suited for mills and manufactories, where hydraulic power would prove of the utmost value.'

He explained that he was working on a method of concentrating the power generated by streams during their descent and using it to propel machinery. 'The first step towards accomplishing this object must be to get quit of the necessity of having a perpendicular fall, and the only conceivable way in which this can be done is by conducting the stream in a pipe from the commencement to the foot of the descent, and bringing the column of water contained in the pipe to bear upon machinery at the bottom.'

He revealed in precise detail, with the help of a diagram, his design for a completely new kind of waterwheel, one which would make it possible to apply the pressure in a water main directly and continuously to produce rotary motion.

By the following autumn, a model of Armstrong's 'hydraulic engine' had been constructed at Watson's works and demonstrated at Barras's brewery in Gateshead. Armstrong's friend Thomas Sopwith, who saw the machine in action at Gateshead, described it in his journal: 'Water brought by pipes from a considerable height (say 130 to 150 feet) is admitted into the piston and its exact pressure is ascertained by a valve loaded in the manner of a safety valve. The entire pressure of the water is brought to bear upon the flat disc or piston and hence the wheel revolves with a power proportional to the altitude of the column of water.' Sopwith went on to record all sorts of facts and figures illustrating the potential of the machine, which impressed him hugely. 'It possesses the great merit of extreme simplicity and in many situations is calculated to be of great utility by concentrating the power of a descending stream.' For the time being, however, few other people seemed interested in the hydraulic engine, so Armstrong turned his inventive energies elsewhere.

Among other things, he designed a crane, in which the operation of lifting was performed by the single stroke of a piston. He made a working model of the crane, and tested it with the town water pipes, but – as before – the device was generally disregarded. 'The curious part about the crane,' said Alfred Cochrane, 'was that, as still no interest was taken in it, and no progress was made towards any practical adoption of the system, Armstrong seems to have given up the subject altogether for a time. It was not until five years later that an event occurred which suggested to him new opportunities for exploiting his inventions.'[6] The catalyst for this development – which would launch Armstrong on his business career – was the arrival on the scene of the great West Country engineer James Meadows Rendel.

On 14 October 1840, William Armstrong wrote to Professor Michael Faraday at the Royal Institution in London describing 'a very extraordinary electrical phenomenon' involving a steam engine used for hauling waggons at Seghill colliery in Cramlington, a few miles north of Newcastle, where his mother's family, the Potters, had an interest. It involved the escape of steam through a fissure in one of the engine's boilers at the point where a safety-valve was attached to the boiler. The engine-man had recounted how, with one of his hands accidentally immersed in the escaping steam, he had put his other hand on the lever of the valve – at which point, according to Armstrong, 'he was greatly surprised by the appearance of a brilliant spark, which passed between the lever and his hand, and was accompanied by a violent wrench in his arms, wholly unlike what he had ever experienced before. He next found that, while he held one hand in the jet of steam, he communicated a shock to every person whom he touched with the other.'

Armstrong said that he himself had seen similar events at Seghill and was conducting experiments to find out more about their cause. He asked Faraday, 'Can the explosion of boilers, about which so much uncertainty exists, have any connection with the rapid production of electricity which thus appears to accompany the generation of steam?'

In later years, this phenomenon – which continues to pose a threat to the unwary – became known as 'the Armstrong Effect'. (During the Second World War, explosions in German tanks in the desert caused by frictional electricity – and the failure, through ignorance of their origin, to prevent such explosions – were said to have delayed Rommel's advance towards Libya in 1941.)

Armstrong's first communication with Faraday concluded with the remark, 'You are at liberty to make any use of this letter that you think fit.' In the event, after addressing a list of suggestions and queries to Armstrong, Faraday sent the letter and its successor to the monthly *London, Edinburgh and Dublin Philosophical Magazine and Journal of Science*, which published both letters in its next edition.

By experimenting with a special apparatus of his own, Armstrong had deduced that the steam was electrified as it entered the atmosphere but was not in an electrified state when inside the boiler – suggesting that it was the effect of friction on the emerging steam that had caused the sparks. Faraday's comments, also published in the *Philosophical Magazine*, show that he was in no doubt about the importance of Armstrong's findings: 'The evolution of electricity by vaporization, described by Mr Armstrong, is most likely the same as that already known to philosophers on a much smaller scale, and about which there are as yet doubts whether it is to be referred to mere evaporation ... or to chemical action. This point it neither settles nor illustrates – but it gives us the evolution of electricity during the conversion of water into vapour, upon an enormous scale, and therefore brings us much nearer to the electric phenomenon of volcanoes, water-spouts and thunderstorms.'

Thomas Sopwith had again been a witness to events. 'Mr W. G. Armstrong, Mr W. D. Anderson and I went to Seghill and had a number of experiments on the newly discovered Electricity in Steam which were very curious and satisfactory,' he wrote in his diary. Sopwith, a land surveyor, engineer, and polymath, had been drawn into the Jesmond circle by his acquaintance with James Losh and Armorer Donkin – with whom he regularly breakfasted and attended concerts in London – and had begun to develop an interest in Donkin's intriguing protégé. Born in Newcastle a few years before Armstrong, Sopwith had started keeping a diary in the early 1820s in which he recorded in witty and meticulous detail his many exploits, as well as his revealing opinions of his friends.

By the early 1840s, Sopwith was a highly regarded figure in the worlds of engineering and science. A member of the Institution of Civil Engineers, he had written on many aspects of surveying, including an account of the minerals of Alston Moor in the north Pennines and *A Treatise on Isometrical Drawing as Applicable to Geological and Mining Plans*, and undertaken commissions that ranged from street improvements in Newcastle to surveys of the iron and coal-mines in the Forest of Dean. In 1842 he was awarded the Telford Medal for constructing geological models. By then he had started to watch Armstrong's activities with a very keen eye.

Inspired by his experiences at Seghill, Armstrong was experimenting with a boiler of his own which he called his 'evaporating apparatus'. It was a wrought-iron horizontal cylinder 3 feet 6 inches long and 18 inches in diameter with a chimney; the 'fire box' below was insulated by means of four glass legs. It discharged steam under very high pressure through 14 jets, 7 on each side, creating sparks between 12 and 14 inches in length. According to Sopwith, 'The hair or fingers held in the jet of steam are brightly illumined by electrical light and the effects are not less beautiful than curious, new and important.'

Sopwith knew a crowd-puller when he saw one – and he acted swiftly. On 5 December 1842, he described in his diary a meeting with Mr Seavier, the managing director of the recently established London Polytechnic Institution, based at Somerset House in the Strand, and some of his acolytes: 'I explained to two of these gentlemen Mr Armstrong's apparatus for producing electricity from steam, which I have suggested should be called "Armstrong's Steam Electrical Engine". The subject received from them that attention which its novelty and importance could not fail to excite when offered in terms so kind and liberal as those which Mr Armstrong has proposed.'

Armstrong, it seems, had offered (presumably free of charge) to construct a much bigger version of the engine for display at the Polytechnic Institution, but it was not clear whether there was sufficient space to accommodate it. There was also concern about the chimney. Sopwith wrote in his diary: 'By what mode do you insulate the chimney, which must pass through a wall?' A week later, he wrote to Armstrong explaining that: 'There appears to be a difficulty first in respect of space and second on account of the heat' and told him that some of the directors were sceptical about 'the enormous power [that had been claimed for] the apparatus'. One proposal was to construct the machine in several parts, and a special committee was appointed to look into the plan. However, when Sopwith suggested to the institution managers that Armstrong might prefer to consider 'some other large exhibition [space], such as the Colosseum', the committee at once sent a representative to Newcastle to discuss the matter with Armstrong in person.

At the time, Sopwith was living with his wife Jane and their family at St Mary's Terrace in Newcastle, a few doors away from the brothers John and Albany Hancock, who were starting to make their mark on the world of natural history. In his diary for

24 December, he noted that he had dined with Armstrong that evening in order to meet Captain Boscawen Ibbetson, who had come from London to examine the electrical engine. Also present on this occasion, at Sopwith's invitation, was the engineer Robert Stephenson, who was 'much surprised and pleased by the extraordinary results of Mr Armstrong's experiments'. As a consequence of Ibbetson's visit, it was decided to construct the machine 'to the full power proposed by Mr Armstrong'. In the event, two such machines were built to Armstrong's specification at Watson's works, one for display in the gallery of the London Polytechnic Institution and another for export to America.

As soon as the news about the hydroelectric machine got out, there was enormous interest in this extraordinary new phenomenon. In October 1843, in the midst of a long stay in London to supervise the assembly of the two machines, Armstrong wrote to Armorer Donkin to apologise for his prolonged absence from Newcastle and his failure to fulfil his commitments as a partner in Donkin, Stable and Armstrong. Events were gathering pace – and, for the first time, Armstrong's genius was coming to the attention of the wider world. 'The machine has produced a far greater sensation in the scientific world than I ever supposed it would do,' he explained to Donkin. 'Descriptions of it are daily appearing in all sorts of publications both English and foreign and I am informed that some of my former letters in the *Philosophical Magazine* are being reprinted in more popular journals – so you see I have gained reputation enough to satisfy any man, and whatever its advantage may be in Newcastle, it has certainly this advantage in London, that it gives me a degree of consequence that I never thought of aspiring to.' He felt moved to say to his friend and benefactor, 'I trust you will excuse all this egotism, which I only indulge in under the belief that you will be interested in what I say respecting my self.'

Playing on general credulity about what the hydroelectric machine was capable of, London's new satirical magazine *Punch* joined in the fun, claiming in its issue of 11 November 1843 that members of the British Association had discovered an intimate link between science and gastronomy. Heralding an event at the Royal Polytechnic Dining Rooms, the magazine made the following announcement: 'Seats formed by Leyden jars attached to Armstrong's Hydroelectric Machine will be provided for those affected by Torpidity of general action; and a series of shocks will eventually excite the liver to its proper sense of duty. The immense powers of this machine will also be brought forward in the attempt to solidify nitrogen gas, gelatine and albumen into animal fibre or muscle. The Professors entertain the most sanguine hopes of being ultimately enabled, by this new process, to get beefsteaks from cheap glue and bird's eggs.'

The following year, Armstrong delivered two lectures on hydroelectricity at the Lit & Phil. 'The attendance was so numerous that many were unable to gain admission,' wrote Sopwith. 'I was even told by one of the parties connected with the institution that more went away, unable to gain an entrance, than those who entered the lecture room.' One evening the press of people prevented Armstrong himself from gaining access through the door and he had to resort to getting in through one of the windows, 'the height of which required the use of a ladder both outside and within the room'. A contemporary report in the local press showered praise on 'our talented young townsman, Mr W. G. Armstrong, of the firm of Donkin, Stable & Armstrong, solicitors of this town, who has risen rapidly into celebrity,' and who 'gave his very interesting lectures on "Hydro-Electricity" in a crowded room'.

Part of the attraction was Armstrong's ability to explain complex subjects with exceptional lucidity and avoid 'technicalities known only to the initiated few'.[7] This was an early example of his skill at captivating an audience. Although not an outstanding orator, he had a clear, precise, authoritative method of delivery, shot through with wit and humour, which meant that his speeches were always listened to with the closest attention. He would end his spectacular demonstration of the electric machine by firing a small cannon with a spark from his finger.

In 1846, William Armstrong's achievements in electrical research were recognised by his election, aged 35, as a Fellow of the Royal Society. His sponsors included Michael Faraday, the inventor of the electric motor that drives almost every car in the modern world – whose discoveries would also enable the use of electricity in industry and the home – and Charles Wheatstone, one of the inventors of the electric telegraph, which marked the start of global communications. 'What is the Royal Society for,' demanded Faraday at the time, 'if not for such men as Armstrong?'

Judging by the enthusiasm with which Armstrong was received at a Lit & Phil gathering on 6 October 1846, the ladies and gentlemen of that society would have found little cause to question Professor Faraday's opinion. As noted by a contemporary chronicler, John Latimer, it was an occasion that marked a greater openness towards the involvement of women in the society's proceedings: 'The ladies, feeling more at home, generally threw aside their bonnets, and gave an appearance of greater ease and freedom to the scene.'[8] A highlight of the evening was a talk by Armstrong on the workings of the electric telegraph. Providing further evidence of his charismatic power, the event proved so popular that no sooner was it over than he was asked to repeat it to another, equally large, audience.

'Everyone, [Armstrong] observed, was now familiar with the marvellous wires along which a communication was transmitted to a distance of hundreds of miles,' wrote Latimer. 'To show how this was done, Mr Armstrong explained the structure of the telegraph part by part that his audience might comprehend the whole. Connecting a wire with a voltaic battery, and exposing it to electric action, he made two needles or pointers, one at each end of a table, oscillate on their pivots at the same moment. The same effect would be produced, he observed, if the one needle were in Newcastle and the other in York, or in London, or in Calcutta; and as the operator had full control over the movements of the needles, it was easy to see how they might be made to express letters and words. This had been done – a sort of deaf and dumb alphabet had been formed; and, indeed, it was exactly an alphabet of that kind, for no two persons could be more deaf and dumb to each other than the parties who carried on a conversation by means of the electric telegraph.'

Before transmitting a message by telegraph, it was necessary to attract the attention of the operator at the other end of the line. This was done by ringing a bell. 'A handle was moved and a magnetic action was then exercised on a piece of steel connected with the apparatus,' wrote Latimer. 'The movement of this steel set an alarum a-going, and the ringing was kept up until the distant attendant on the telegraph gave an intimation on the dial that he was at his post. The question was then put, or the information communicated, as the case might be ... Truly, said Mr Armstrong, this modern means of intercommunication, which originated with a discovery made by Oersted (namely, that a needle, when placed across a magnetized wire, moved to one side), was the greatest marvel of this marvellous age: the realities of the electric telegraph exceeded the wildest extravagances of fiction.'

The thrill of the Lit & Phil audience at hearing Armstrong explain the marvel of the electric telegraph was a manifestation of the general excitement that had taken hold in the country about the scientific discoveries of the age. This excitement had been stirred up and fostered at the annual meetings of the British Association for the Advancement of Science, to the point where it resembled a religious fervour. Dismissed by some as a 'vanity fair', the British Association's meeting at Newcastle in 1838 had been the target of particularly heavy criticism for the showiness and theatricality of its speakers.[9] Leading churchmen and politicians inveighed against what they saw as a philosophical travelling circus, and the radical journalist Harriet Martineau deplored the way in which scientific celebrities received the adulation of women admirers who 'wandered in and out, with their half-hidden sketchbooks, seeking amusement as their grandmothers did at auctions'.

It was this public mood that would help to propel Armstrong from relative provincial obscurity on to the national stage; but, before he could reach those exalted heights, he had an affair of the heart to attend to.

4

Rivers of Pleasure

When Armstrong returned to Newcastle in 1833, he felt more than simple relief at having escaped from the fusty world of the Temple, where the situation had become less comfortable since the marriage of his brother-in-law, William Watson, to Mary Capron. His first move had been to establish himself as an articled clerk in Donkin's flourishing law firm, which looked after the interests of many influential families, estates, and companies in north-east England. But, despite his father's continuing disapproval, he was also looking forward to immersing himself in mechanical experiments and rediscovering Rothbury and other delights of the Northumbrian countryside. Best of all, he could indulge his growing affection for Margaret Ramshaw, whose father's engineering works at Bishop Auckland had proved such an attraction during his schooldays.

William and Margaret, or Meggie as he often called her, were both effectively single children, the apple of their parents' eye, and had much in common. Intelligent and perceptive, Meggie had been educated to a higher degree than her successful but relatively unsophisticated father, and – although humility was a distinguishing trait throughout her life – she must have seen her relationship with William as opening up exciting new opportunities. Amongst other shared interests, they were both passionate about the cultivation of trees and plants. He was 24 and she 27 when they married on 21 April 1835 at Bishop Auckland's church of St Andrew.

The Ramshaw parents bought 16 acres of land in Jesmond Dene, on the west side of the Ouseburn, a short distance north of the Armstrong family home, and gave it to William and Meggie as a wedding present. The land had previously formed part of the Jesmond Grove estate of James Losh, who had died two years earlier, and was a stone's throw from the ruined St Mary's Chapel, dating from the 12th century, a place of pilgrimage since the early Middle Ages. There the couple set about building a house for themselves, planting an oak tree to commemorate the beginning of their married life. Somewhat confusingly, the house was given the name Jesmond Dene to match its location. Maps of the time reveal that it was eventually a substantial residence, perhaps half as big again as the houses built by Armstrong senior and Armorer Donkin less than half a mile to the south, but no precise description of its layout and only a rough sketch and a couple of photographs of its exterior have survived. (The house was demolished in the 1930s.)

William and Meggie both thrived on entertaining, and there would have been plenty of room in the house for receiving guests. Outside they laid out a garden in the style of parkland, based on individual specimen trees interspersed with lawns, and, as the estate grew over the years, planted elm, beech, chestnut, and more oak, with yew and holly as evergreens. Following the fashion of the times, they also planted newly imported North American conifers and hybrid varieties of rhododendron. Large glass-houses were added to the main building for the cultivation of more exotic species. Part of their property in the dene was given over to farming.

Part of the allure of Jesmond Dene was its abundance of birdlife, which drew many naturalists to the banks of the Ouseburn, including the Hancocks, John and Albany, and the artist daughters of the engraver Thomas Bewick. A survey of the birds of Jesmond Dene made a century later recorded 72 species, including peregrine falcon, spotted flycatcher, and yellowhammer.[1] There were regular, if occasional, sightings of kingfisher. Bessie Adamson, one of the contributors to the survey, had once been thrilled to see a family of five kingfishers in the dene, three young with their mother and father. 'The young remained on a branch while the parents caught fish for them. We watched them for some time,' she wrote. 'The young were duller in colour than the parents.'

No ordinary love letters between William and Meggie survive, but Armstrong's ideal of womanhood is revealed in a semi-autobiographical dream-story he wrote some years later, in which water is personified as the mischievous, irresistible Lady Brook, who, both saviour and temptress, leads him to ever more daring exploits: 'Most of all I admired the pretty brook which danced so merrily past saying – as one might fancy – in all sorts of tones, *Won't you come with me? Won't you, won't you come?* So away I went and rapidly descended the mountain by the side of my captivating guide. My spirits never flagged, for I was delighted with my companion. She amused me with her prattle, enlivened me with her jumps and gambols, ran races with me, and splashed me when I came too near.' But Lady Brook would prove unpredictable and mysterious. 'We had reached the forest region and trees were closing in on either side as if to forbid our separation. I advanced a little further and then I stood upon a jutting shelf of rock from which the stream descended with a single leap into a deep and narrow forest glen. I saw her at the bottom sparkling amongst the trees and still gaily tripping forward – but as she proceeded on her course the banks contracted over her, the trees became more densely crowded, and at a little distance she retired into absolute darkness.'

Meggie's instinctive *joie de vivre* was captured by a contemporary resident of Jesmond Dene who watched the young couple on their regular strolls beside the Ouseburn. 'Often did Mr and Mrs Armstrong walk along the footpaths through the plantations,' wrote William Gascoigne. 'Unseen by them, I have frequently observed Mr Armstrong walking along, absorbed in thought, doubtless studying out his inventions; while Mrs Armstrong, gathering wild flowers not far behind, would seize him by the waist, and spinning him round in her arms playfully, dart away from him like a deer, laughing at him as she went, and leaving me the impression of her being one of the most amiable of English ladies that I had ever seen.'[2] Gascoigne commented on the close resemblance between Armstrong and his father: 'Seen from the rear, I do not think it could confidently be determined which was which.'

In reality, it was William who would prove the more elusive of the pair, and Margaret, despite her evident resourcefulness, must have been sorely tried by his frequent absences. The couple were destined to spend much time apart – William regularly visited London, amongst other cities, and devoted practically every waking hour to his business interests. Moreover, there was plenty of competition for his attentions. Reputedly devoid of pride, he was a compellingly attractive man whose growing fame only added to his appeal, as exemplified by his popularity at meetings of the Lit & Phil, which he had joined in 1836. At one of the society's gatherings called a conversazione, he was described as 'galvanizing the ladies – and also the gentlemen'.[3] Disregarding such distractions, the Armstrongs had a long and mutually satisfying relationship. William regarded Meggie as his equal in everything and had no qualms about asking her to help with his projects and experiments. In May 1843, while in the midst of building his hydroelectric machine for the Polytechnic Institution, he was taking a brief fishing holiday in Rothbury, from where he wrote to his wife in Jesmond:

'I have now to trouble you with a little commission. I always feared that the boiler would shake when discharging the steam and I think that in order to obviate the probability of accident it will be necessary to apply diagonal props and stays between the legs. The props must be made of wood which must undergo a certain process in order to render it an insulator or non-conductor of electricity similar to the glass. The first stage of this process is to have the wood cut into thin lathes which must be covered up for some days in quick lime in order to extract or dry up the juices of the wood. The wood must afterwards be baked in an oven or before the fire, and then the thin pieces or lathes in which it is cut will have to be cemented together with shel-lac to form the props of the requisite strength and thickness.

'I have written a note to Henry Watson by this post to request that he will procure a piece of fir wood of the proper kind for this purpose and set his joiner to saw it up into lathes of about 6 feet long. I have also written a line to Joseph to tell him to get my mother's pony on Saturday or Sunday at the latest and take out to our house as much quick lime as can be conveniently put into their cart, which will be amply sufficient for the purpose required. I have likewise told him to call at Watson and Lambert's to get the lathes to send out by the same conveyance.

'And now comes your slice of the business – when the lime is received it must be laid down under cover (say, in the coach house) and a little water must then be sprinkled upon each clod so as to reduce the greater part of the whole into a shelly state. A small watering pan will be the best thing you can use for this purpose and the lime should be allowed to lie for about a day to afford time for the water to produce the full effect before the wood is put amongst it. The lathes must then be covered up in the lime, placing them in the centre and not at the bottom of the heap so that they may be surrounded on all sides by the lime, and there they must remain until I get home. The less water put on the lime the better, the only object of using it being to break up the clods and so to bring the lime into more perfect contact with the wood. The drying power of the lime is of course injured by the water, but very little will do to break the clods if time be allowed for the water to act.

'P.S. The lathes will be of fir about 6 feet long and about $^3/_8$th of an inch thick and about 2 inches broad. They should be of red and not white fir and will be all the better of having a good deal of resin in them. From this description you will have some idea whether they are all right when you get them.'

A few days later, he wrote to Meggie again, presumably in reply to a letter from her recounting what had happened during the treatment of the lathes: 'Hoping the lime dust has come out of your nose and eyes. Believe. Ever yours W.G.A.' It should be noted that lime is unpleasant stuff to handle, and would undoubtedly have done some damage to Mrs Armstrong's skin.

Women shared with men the enthusiasm for scientific discovery that was sweeping Britain at the time and, although few were allowed to become members of the most august learned bodies – the Royal Society admitted its first two women to honorary membership in 1835 – many found ways to attend the lectures and debates.

When the British Association held its annual meeting in Newcastle in 1838, the large number of women present was a subject of comment. Margaret Armstrong would no doubt have been among them, and the female contingent probably included Thomas Sopwith's wife, Jane; Armstrong's mother, Anne; and several other members of the Potter family. One woman who insisted on being there was Pauline Trevelyan, the 22-year-old wife of the geologist Sir Walter Calverley Trevelyan, who was paying her first visit to the Trevelyan family seat at Wallington in Northumberland, 25 miles north-west of Newcastle. A vicar's daughter from Suffolk, Pauline had met Trevelyan, 20 years her senior, at Cambridge five years earlier, and had captivated him with her brilliant mind. After 1846, when Trevelyan inherited Wallington, Pauline would establish there a vibrant literary and artistic salon, where she cultivated close friendships with the art critic John Ruskin and several members of the Pre-Raphaelite Brotherhood, including John Everett Millais and William Bell Scott. It was the influence of members of the Wallington salon that prompted William Armstrong to collect the Pre-Raphaelites and their followers when he came to furnish Cragside in the 1870s.[4]

At the time of their marriage, the place where William and Margaret Armstrong had chosen to make their home was in the throes of a magnificent renaissance, thanks to the vision of an inspired builder called Richard Grainger, who had bought up large parts of the town on the steep north bank of the Tyne and transformed a higgledy-piggledy medieval settlement into what was hailed as 'a city of palaces'[5] (although Newcastle would not officially become a city until 1882). At its heart was Grey Street, laid out in imitation of London's Regent Street, but with a more dramatic sweeping curve, leading steeply down to the river. Writing more than 70 years later, Alfred Cochrane described the building of modern Newcastle:

'I do not know that there is any other instance of an English town being practically pulled down and rebuilt in the course of a few years by the enterprise and energy of a single citizen. Mr Grainger, who was originally a stone mason, and rose entirely by his own ability, entered, in 1832, upon an extensive speculation in town property. He bought, partly with his own, and partly with borrowed capital, the whole of the centre of Newcastle, where there were then small houses with gardens, a few narrow streets, and some waste ground ... The architect was Mr Dobson, 2,000 workmen were employed, and nine streets, many public buildings and private houses, and 320 shops were built.'[6] A 135-foot-high monument to 2nd Earl Grey, the prime minister who had overseen the passage of the Great Reform Act, was completed in August 1838 and erected at the top of Grey Street in time for the arrival of the savants of the British Association.

The British Association meeting of 1838 – the year of Queen Victoria's coronation – was indeed a sparkling affair. Liberally sprinkled with lavish dinners, balls, and other elegant social events, it epitomised the glamour that had come to be linked in the public mind with the scientific merry-go-round. 'Everything was numbered in thousands,' a history of the association records.[7] 'No fewer than 10,000 yards of red and white calico were used for decoration. The attendance of members was 2,430, and that of ladies about 1,100 ... No less than £3,099 was raised for the local hospitality fund, and at the end of the meeting £3,742 was allocated in the form of research grants.' All the great institutions of Newcastle, from the City Corporation to the Lit & Phil and the Natural History Society, threw open their doors to host lectures and debates, and a particularly spectacular ball was held in the recently completed Grainger Market, 'the biggest covered market in the country and a showpiece of the new Grainger and Dobson town centre'.[8] The meeting was presided over by the Duke of Northumberland, the association's president for that year, and, although Faraday stood aloof, most of the scientific giants of the age were in attendance. They included the geologists William Buckland, Adam Sedgwick, and Roderick Murchison, the mathematicians Charles Babbage and John Herschel, and the influential Cambridge professor and writer William Whewell. Thomas Sopwith – an expert in geology and mineralogy as in so much else – was very much at the heart of proceedings, arguing persuasively for the need to preserve mining records. As had become customary, on the conclusion of the formal business, many of the members dispersed to country house parties in Northumberland and Durham, where they mingled with the local aristocracy and gentry.

Sopwith was a frequent visitor to Jesmond Dene in the early days, as the friendship he had forged with William Armstrong senior broadened to include his son and daughter-in-law. He was impressed by 'the rich and varied stores of literary and scientific treasures which Armstrong [junior] has gathered around him'. There were paintings, books, and instruments of all kinds to admire.

One evening he noted 'a recently purchased edition of the works of Lavater in five volumes containing a great number of admirable engravings – a treasure store of suggestive illustrations of the human face'. He also saw a folio of Shakespeare's works, printed in 1623 but in perfect condition, and 'a number of admirably executed views for the stereoscope, some representing the glaciers and lofty waterfalls of Switzerland and others some engineering works'. Sopwith developed a strong rapport with Meggie and would keep her informed about London news and gossip. 'My wife desires me to thank you for your kind remembrances,' wrote Armstrong to his friend on one occasion, 'and particularly for the amusing portrait of Her Majesty in her monkey jacket.'

For the time being, there seemed little prospect of children to share in the Armstrongs' material riches, so Meggie's maternal feelings were directed in particular towards her nephew, Johnny Watson, who lived for the most part with his father and stepmother in London and Sussex, but who often visited his late mother's family in Northumberland. In January 1837, eight-year-old Johnny wrote poignantly to Meggie in Jesmond telling her about the fun he had been having in the snow. 'I am generally snow-balling all the day, and making very large snow-balls for show. I am very glad to hear of the tortoise which Mr Sewell gave you ... Will you give my love to all friends. I forgot my poor pony on whom I often think and I hope he is quite well.' Meggie also kept in close touch with Mary Watson and her son, William Henry, Johnny's half-brother. Meanwhile, William Watson, the father of the two boys, was continuing his steady rise through the legal profession, and in 1841 he entered Parliament as Liberal MP for Kinsale.

When Armstrong was away from home on legal or scientific business, Thomas Sopwith would keep Meggie company, attending church, going with her to concerts and other local events, and engaging in conversations regarding their shared interest in the practice and appreciation of art. On 4 July 1843, he drove her to Newcastle to witness 'the entry of Van Amburgh and his lions'. Isaac Van Amburgh was a famous American lion tamer who was much admired by Queen Victoria. The culmination of his act was to make a lamb lie down with a lion – the biblical image of peace in Eden.

Other new arrivals in Jesmond Dene at this time included a branch of the Potter family, headed by the redoubtable Addison Langhorn, the brother of Armstrong's mother, Anne. In 1840, Potter bought the long-established Heaton estate, east of the Ouseburn, and from the remains of Heaton Hall built himself an imposing new residence in a style since disparaged as 'pastrycook Gothic'. A close associate of Armorer Donkin, Addison Langhorn Potter would become a key partner in Armstrong's early business ventures, and some of his children, particularly Annie, remained lifelong friends of William and Margaret Armstrong.

At the time of his marriage in 1835 and for ten years afterwards, Armstrong was diligently pursuing his career as a lawyer in Newcastle, first as a clerk and then as a partner of Armorer Donkin and George Waugh Stable – but all the time he continued to burn with ambition and experiment with new ideas, often frustrated that his putative inventions did not provoke wider interest. In later life he acknowledged that his long stint as a lawyer had had its benefits: 'As it turned out, of course, it meant the waste of some ten or eleven of the best years of my life – and yet not entire waste, perhaps, for my legal training and knowledge have been of help to me in many ways in business. And all the time, although I had no idea of abandoning the law and regularly attended to my professional duties, I was an amateur scientist, constantly experimenting and studying in my leisure time.'[9] The Vickers' historian J. D. Scott later confirmed that Armstrong did not regret the years he had spent in the law: 'He was an astute businessman, skilled in negotiating contracts; he liked such work, and did it well, although always with a characteristic note of aloofness.'[10]

There are references in Sopwith's diary to routine legal duties carried out by Donkin and Armstrong, most relating to property management and mining rights. Such activities provided Armstrong with invaluable knowledge – both physical and social – of the lie of the land around Newcastle and in the vast north-eastern coalfield. In May 1845, when Sopwith was appointed chief agent at Beaumont's lead mines at Allenheads in the north Pennines, Armstrong would take care of the legalities.

Armstrong's easy reintegration into the society of Jesmond Dene also allowed him to acquire many useful contacts. James Losh, his father's original benefactor, had died in September 1833, but a new generation was making its mark. 'Donkin's Ordinary' continued to be a highlight of the week. 'These Saturday dinners for so long a period given by Mr Donkin were very enjoyable,' wrote Sopwith. 'There were no special invitations, no formality as to evening dress. The number varied from about eight to twelve. Good substantial viands were provided in abundance and an extra side dish or two were in readiness if many came. The wines and port were excellent, the conversation hearty and free, and every one was charmed by the intelligence and kindness of the host.'

Among Donkin's guests in the early 1840s was Isambard Kingdom Brunel, the engineer of the Great Western Railway, who – following the recent completion of the Thames tunnel that he had built with his father, Marc – was doing surveying work with Sopwith in Northumberland. Brunel was interested in building an 'atmospheric railway' linking Newcastle with Berwick on the Scottish border. Such a railway depended on the theory that trains could be propelled along the tracks by compressed air – an idea derided by the engineering Stephensons, father and son. Sopwith's account of a chance meeting between Brunel and the veteran George Stephenson betrays the rivalry between the two great railway engineers: 'Just before Mr Brunel departed at two in the afternoon, I went into the coffee room of the Queen's Head Inn with him and encountered Mr George Stephenson. He good-naturedly shook Mr Brunel by the collar, asking him what business he had "north of the Tyne".' Sopwith struck up a friendship with Brunel, and the two later saw each other frequently in London and Newcastle, sometimes in the company of Armorer Donkin.

Donkin was not universally popular, however. In 1844, he and Addison Langhorn Potter, both members of the coal-owners' committee, had become embroiled in a battle with the miners of the Durham and Northumberland coalfield, where child labour was commonplace and conditions included long hours, low pay – and the ever-present threat of catastrophe. Some miners were still haunted by the accident at Heaton Main colliery in 1815, when

41 men and 34 boys had been drowned by the collapse of a neighbouring disused mineshaft that had been allowed to fill with water, but there had been many similarly ghastly incidents since. The miners were seeking to gain what they saw as fairer and safer working conditions, abolition of the fines system, and a guaranteed four-day working week. Faced with an unsympathetic response from the owners' committee, on 31 March all 40,000 miners went on strike. Three months later, with no sign of a resolution, the coal-owners applied the ultimate sanction and turned the pitmen out of their tied cottages. The strike continued for another two months, but the miners were eventually forced to concede on the employers' terms, leaving a bitter legacy and tarnishing the names of Donkin and Potter.[11]

Later that year, Potter, who also ran a brewery and, like Donkin, had served as an alderman, took office as mayor of Newcastle. His appointment coincided with increasing public concern about municipal services – in particular, the need for a reliable supply of clean water. Potter himself, and entrepreneurs like him, had business reasons for wanting cleaner water. But, more importantly, waterborne diseases such as cholera, dysentery, and typhoid remained ever-present threats, especially among the fast-growing population of Tyneside, where overcrowding and insanitary conditions encouraged the spread of disease.

In collaboration with his friend Thomas Sopwith – by that time recognised as the leading mine surveyor in the country – and the builder Richard Grainger, William Armstrong boldly proposed a resolution to the problem. Between them, the three men had devised a plan for supplying Tyneside with good-quality water from the Whittle Burn, a tributary of the Tyne west of Newcastle. The aim was to build a series of reservoirs at Whittle Dene, near Ovingham, from where water would be conveyed to households in both Newcastle and Gateshead. While Armstrong and Donkin prepared a petition for presentation to Parliament (a legal necessity), Sopwith worked behind the scenes to persuade the sanitary inspectors of the advantages of bringing water from Whittle Dene – a source so elevated that there would be no need for pumps. Armstrong and Grainger set about serving notices on landowners who would be affected by the laying of the pipeline, in particular Hugh Percy, 3rd Duke of Northumberland, who threw his weight behind the scheme while insisting that the diameter of the pipe be increased from 18 to 24 inches.

Conveniently, proposals for the water company were submitted to Parliament not long after the publication of Edwin Chadwick's *Report on the Sanitary Condition of the Labouring Population of Great Britain* (1843), which 'with graphic illustrations of filth and degradation among the lower classes, [had] connected the prevalence of disease and high mortality to grossly inadequate sanitary provisions, drainage, and water supply'.[12] Chadwick also contributed to the Royal Commission on the Health of Towns, whose shocking report appeared in 1844–45. The prospectus for the new water company stressed that a copious supply of clean water was not only 'essential to the health, comfort and convenience of the inhabitants at large' but also 'conducive, in the highest degree, to habits of sobriety and cleanliness in the working classes'.

By mid-1845, despite some opposition, the bill to create the Whittle Dene Water Company had won parliamentary approval, and the new firm had begun a legal process to buy the existing Newcastle Subscription Water Co. James Simpson, the engineer of Chelsea Waterworks in London, was commissioned to design the new reservoirs. By 1848 three reservoirs had been completed and a cast-iron pipeline 12½ miles long and 24 inches in diameter – then the largest in the world – had been laid.[13] Two more reservoirs were built later; all five together were capable of holding 515 million gallons of water.

William Armstrong, acknowledged to be the mastermind behind the project, was joined in the enterprise by Armorer Donkin, his uncle Addison Langhorn Potter, George Cruddas, a shipowner and railway director, and Richard Lambert, a lawyer. Potter, who naturally wielded considerable political influence in tandem with his mining and brewing interests, became chairman. Cruddas had been appointed to look after the financial side of the operation, while Lambert was an old friend of Armstrong from his London days. Donkin, Stable and Armstrong were appointed solicitors to the company, and at the first general meeting of shareholders, on 28 July, William Armstrong, then aged 34, became company secretary at an annual salary of £150.

Apart from the benefits that Whittle Dene could bring to public health, there was no doubt that the availability of a continuous supply of mains water at good pressure would be valuable to Armstrong in his attempt to make the case for hydraulic power, which had obsessed him for the past decade. So, after he had received the go-ahead for the water venture, using all his powers of subtle persuasion – and revealing the psychological and business acumen that was the hallmark of his brilliance – on 24 November 1845, he wrote to Newcastle town council's finance committee:

'Gentlemen,

'I beg leave to draw your attention to a plan I have matured for applying the pressure of the water in the streets' pipes in the lower parts of Newcastle to the working of the cranes upon the Quay, with a view of increasing the rapidity and lessening the expense of the òperation of delivering [unloading] ships.

'It will readily be perceived that whatever has a tendency to accelerate the unloading of ships at the Quay must not only be highly advantageous to the shipowners and merchants of the port, but must also have the effect of increasing the accommodation to shipping which the Quay is now capable of affording.

'A working model has been constructed for the purpose of illustrating the operation of a crane upon the proposed plan and I am fully persuaded, after a careful investigation of the subject, that the advantages to which I have adverted would be realized by such a method of lifting goods.

'In order to relieve the Corporation from the speculative outlet of making the experiment on a large scale, a few of my friends are willing to join me in the risk and expense of adapting the plan to one of the existing cranes; provided that should the experiment prove successful a lease be granted to us of all the cranes upon the Quay belonging to the Corporation for the period of ten years, at the present rate and upon the following terms and conditions.

'1st. That we shall be at liberty to apply the hydraulic principle to all the existing cranes, and shall have the exclusive right of erecting others on the same principle upon the Quay in situations to be approved of by the Corporation or their authorized agent.

'2nd. That we shall be bound to reduce the present rates of cranage to the extent of at least 20 per cent.

'3rd. That the Corporation shall take the machinery at a valuation at the end of the term.

'We will also engage, in case the experiment should fail, to restore the crane to be operated upon to its present state, if required.

'Should you think it proper to accede to this proposition and the result of the trial be favourable, the public and the port will reap the immediate advantage of the improved system, and the Corporation will eventually come into the receipt of an increased revenue, without sustaining any loss in the meantime.'

A few days later, Armstrong demonstrated a model of his hydraulic crane at a packed meeting of the Lit & Phil, explaining how it worked and what its significance would be for shipping and industry at large. He also put his invention in a broader context, identifying it as part of the march of progress represented by the industrial revolution. The *Newcastle Daily Chronicle* published an account of the evening, explaining that the lecturer had used various props to illustrate the nature of the pressure exerted by a column of water, including a machine that could be made to rotate by the water power that was generated. What follows is an edited version of the speech that Armstrong delivered to the great and good of Newcastle on that cold December night.

He began with a eulogy to the railways. 'There is no circumstance which in future ages will reflect so much honour upon this country as its having been the cradle, if not the birthplace, of the steam engine. It is scarcely possible to appreciate the influence which that admirable invention is exercising in elevating the condition and promoting the happiness of mankind. It is carrying civilization to the remotest parts of the earth. It is bringing nations into friendly communications with each other. And it is dispensing all those articles of manufacture essential to refined and cultivated life to millions of the human race who would otherwise be without them.

'But the brilliant results which have been accomplished by

steam ought not to have diverted attention from other sources of motive power. While steam machinery has been advancing with rapid strides towards its present wonderful state of perfection, the valuable agency of descending water as a means of propelling machinery has been almost wholly neglected.

'You will readily perceive that, if the vast quantities of water which pour down the brooks and watercourses of hilly countries in time of rain were to be arrested in spacious ponds or reservoirs, formed in hollows, upon the elevated lands from which the water is discharged, and were subsequently to be let out by degrees, so as to increase the volume of the streams when the natural quantity of water should be deficient, the transient produce of useless floods would become available as a permanent source of mechanical power.

'A method is required of concentrating the power of a stream, and bringing it into action at the place most eligible for the establishment of mills and manufactories. Water, if thus supplied as a motive power, would possess advantages greatly superior to those of steam for every purpose excepting locomotion, and localities favourable for the application of the system would, in all probability, become the sites of manufacturing towns.

'Suppose, then, that instead of delivering water in a stream from a collecting reservoir, and passing it over a succession of waterwheels, a *pipe* were to be laid for the conveyance of water from the reservoir to the foot of the descent. Suppose, further, that the column of water contained in the pipe were caused to operate by its weight or pressure upon suitable machinery placed at its lower extremity, we should then obtain, in the lowest and most valuable situation, the concentrated effect of the entire fall. Then, in order to effect the distribution of that power, it would only be necessary to ramify the lower end of the pipe so as to bring the pressure into operation at any number of points at which it should be required.'

Armstrong drew breath and, using experiments and diagrams, explained the action of a column of water and the workings of a rotary water engine of the kind he had devised seven years earlier. He named the Ouseburn and the Whittle Burn as examples of waterways that might be used for the purpose he had in mind.

He went on to argue that even the water already being supplied to towns for domestic and manufacturing uses could be applied to various mechanical purposes – 'and there are few towns in England more favourably circumstanced for making the experiment than Newcastle, where the great altitude of the service reservoirs by which the town is already supplied, as well as of those which are about to be constructed, offer peculiar inducements for such an employment of the water'.

Armstrong then offered a vision of how his invention – if adopted and properly used – might transform the nature of human labour: 'Human labour is at once the most costly and the least effective of all motive powers that are applied to machinery. Yet, for want of a suitable substitute, men are daily employed, to a great extent, in all trading and manufacturing towns, in no higher a capacity than beasts of burden, for the mere purpose of producing motion, in cases where the exercise of skill and intelligence are wholly excluded.

'Among the many examples that might be given of this kind of labour, I may mention the lifting of heavy goods upon wharfs or in warehouses. The numerous ships, for instance, which frequent the quay of this town, are all loaded and unloaded by mere personal strength applied to cranes or other lifting machinery – the whole of which might be worked, at much less expense, with far greater expedition, and consequently with much less detention to ships, by means of the pressure which exists in the street water pipes, than by the present method.' He turned to the model of the crane on the table in front of him – an exact representation of one of the cranes in use on the Newcastle quayside – to show how it could be adapted to unload goods from ships by means of water power.

The *Newcastle Chronicle* report indicates how chilly it must have been in the lecture hall that night: 'The machine was put in action by a supply of water conveyed into the room, at a high pressure, by a lead pipe and, although the sudden frost which had set in unfortunately interfered in some degree with the temporary means of supply which had been provided, Mr Armstrong was enabled to show, in a most satisfactory manner, the perfect precision of the machine – its great power, and the important saving of time and expense which would result from its employment. The operations of lifting and lowering weights, and of turning the crane to either side, were all directed and controlled by the motion of a pointer upon an index plate.'

The situations in which hydraulic pressure could be put to good use were 'exceedingly numerous', said Armstrong. Its usefulness in operating all kinds of lifting machinery was clear and, in workshops where there was not enough activity to justify investing in a steam engine, hydraulic power would prove very valuable as a means of 'giving motion to lathes, printing presses, machines for performing operations of drilling, boring, punching, planning and clipping metals, revolving saws, forge-hammers, and so forth, especially where such machines are only required to be in action at uncertain periods, and with frequent intervals of rest'.

The introduction of increasingly sophisticated mechanical devices would have a human cost, Armstrong admitted. 'The substitution of inanimate power for human labour must unfortunately always be attended in the first instance with the evil of depriving individuals of employment – but the general welfare of the community is unquestionably promoted in every instance in which we succeed in coercing insensible agents into our service for the purpose of moving machinery. Man was designed to work by his head rather than by the mere strength of his arm, and as he continues to extend his dominion over the powers of nature, his occupations will gradually assume less of the physical, and more of the intellectual, character.'

On 14 January 1846, Armstrong's proposals were endorsed by Newcastle town council and soon afterwards – under the auspices of the newly formed Newcastle Cranage Company – operations started at Watson's works on the conversion of the first crane to hydraulic power. In July, Armstrong registered a patent for an apparatus called a jigger for 'lifting, lowering and hauling'; it consisted of a ram and multi-pulley device that 'converted linear motion to rotary motion and thereby increased the effective stroke of the pistons'.[14] By the end of the year, four more hydraulic cranes, each weighing 5 tons, had been ordered and were under construction at Watson's. The crane mechanism itself was relatively straightforward. 'Very rarely has such simple machinery been the foundation of so vast an enterprise as Elswick Works,' commented the Elswick historian A. R. Fairbairn, 'yet it was on the success of the cranes that Armstrong's reputation was built.' A bold scheme put forward by Armstrong for the entire transformation of the Newcastle Quayside – which he undertook to capitalise and carry out as a private venture – proved too much for the council, who turned it down.

On 1 January 1847, a deed of partnership for W. G. Armstrong & Company was drawn up and signed by the same men who had set up the water venture a year earlier: Armstrong, Donkin, Potter, Cruddas, and Lambert. The new firm's capital was £22,500, of which Armstrong's contribution was £2,000 in cash plus his patents for the hydraulic wheel and the crane, valued at £1,000 and £2,000 respectively.[15] Later that month, Armstrong gave up his position as secretary to the Whittle Dene Water Company, while retaining his financial interest in the firm, and finally – with the blessings of his father and Donkin – resigned from his legal practice. Even then, this was regarded by some as a risky course of action, as Armstrong reflected later: 'When at length I resolved to give up my profession and start in business as a mechanical engineer, most of my friends thought I was very foolish. And, on the face of it, it was a bold thing to do – abandoning for an entirely new enterprise the large and old-established legal business which, in course of time, would become my own.'[16]

The partners paid £5,552 for slightly more than 7 acres of land on the north bank of the Tyne a short distance upriver from Newcastle, and started to build workshops there.[17] Although narrow and steeply sloping at its western end, the land had apparently been chosen in preference to the wider and more level ground nearer the town because it offered an independent water supply with a good head of pressure. Bounded by the Newcastle and Carlisle railway to the north, a riverside cart track known as the Curds and Cream Road to the south, and the Benwell salmon fishery to the west, the site of the new works was known as Elswick Haughs.

Writing 40 years later about the nature of genius, Evan R. Jones, who was the American consul in Newcastle from 1868 to

1883, captured the irresistible attraction that scientific endeavour had exerted on Armstrong, despite concerted attempts to steer him towards the law: 'The generous offer of a friend, and the solicitous guidance of parents, made William George Armstrong a lawyer. He locked himself up amid parchment rolls and tomes of decisions and authorities, gave his undivided heart to the pursuit of science – and made a column of water lift a hundred tons!'[18]

5

Maister o' th' Drallickers

In 1843, the year of the hydroelectric machine, a leading light of the Institution of Civil Engineers and former pupil of Thomas Telford visited Newcastle to carry out a survey of the River Tyne. His name was James Meadows Rendel and his main expertise lay in coastal works and in 'harnessing the effects of tide and sea to provide safe haven for the country's rapidly expanding maritime trade'.[1] The harbours and docks at Holyhead, Portland, Birkenhead, and Leith would be among his most notable achievements. Rendel was introduced to Armstrong (probably by Thomas Sopwith, whom he had met in London) and the two men warmed to each other. Rendel, who himself became a Fellow of the Royal Society that year, did not take long to recognise the important advances that Armstrong was making in the use of water power – which, until that time, had been largely confined to the disregarded waterwheel. Three years later, Rendel and Armstrong would be commissioned to build new docks at Great Grimsby on the Yorkshire coast and, in time, Rendel would introduce Armstrong to many of the leading engineers of the day.

When the possibility arose that Armstrong might give up his practice of the law and – in the teeth of his father's opposition – set up his own business, it was Rendel's intervention that proved decisive. Stuart, one of James Rendel's sons, who himself had had an early career as a lawyer, recounted the episode in his memoirs. 'Armstrong's father disliked the idea of his son deserting an excellent and a perfectly secure career for what he deemed an inferior as well as more precarious career as a mechanical engineer, nor was there in Armstrong's character any turn for manufacturing enterprise.'[2] But James Rendel was convinced of the huge potential of water power. He told Armstrong senior that, if the young man were to embark on the manufacture of hydraulic machinery, he would place orders large enough to keep a medium-sized factory busy in the short term. 'As my father was the leading hydraulic engineer of the country,' wrote Stuart, 'this promise amounted to a guarantee on which Armstrong could collect the requisite means.'

As it turned out, much more than just a business partnership would develop between Armstrong and the Rendels – indeed, as time went on, Armstrong came to treat them as virtually his own family. 'Armstrong and his father were thoroughly reconciled over the business,' wrote Stuart. 'My father visited them. Indeed, the attachment between him and Armstrong became a close one, and Armstrong was a constant visitor at my father's house whenever called to London on business.' The Rendel family – James, his wife, Catherine, and their many children – lived in a substantial house in Westminster, 8 Great George Street, from where they could closely observe the construction of Charles Barry's new Houses of Parliament. In 1851, the Rendels bought a mansion in Kensington, 10 Palace Gardens, which they occupied until after James Rendel's death in 1856.

The first buildings to rise on the fields of Elswick were a machine shop, a boiler shop, and a smiths' shop, with a tall chimney between them. On the south side was an erecting shop where all the components were assembled, which included the joiners' and pattern shop. Further east, in a modest two-storey building, were the factory offices. Six houses, in what came to be known as Foreman's Row, were built at the western end of the site, and another row of cottages appeared on the new turnpike (later Scotswood Road) near the works' entrance. Overlooked by the works, and extending for nearly a mile down the middle of the river, was an island called King's Meadows.

At the same time, Armstrong opened an administrative office in the centre of Newcastle, at 10 Hood Street – from where the first letter sent was addressed to Messrs. Whitworth & Co. of Manchester, the renowned manufacturer of machine tools. From the start, orders came in at a steady flow, but money was flowing out even more quickly, so Donkin and Cruddas decided to bring in new funds, raising the company's capital to £43,000 before the end of its first year of operation. Armstrong's mood during this period was captured in a story told by the Elswick historian, Alfred Cochrane: 'In his old age Lord Armstrong used to recall an occasion when he paced up and down Grey Street, turning over in his mind how he could find more capital to keep his Engine Works afloat. He finally had to cease walking the pavement because the soles of his boots became so hot that it was painful to continue his promenade.'[3] The uncertainty that characterised the first two or three years at Elswick was compounded by Armstrong's lack of business experience, but his partners never seemed to have lost faith in him.

In the summer of 1847 two people joined Armstrong from Watson's works in Newcastle, which had won the contract to build Robert Stephenson's High Level Bridge across the Tyne. They were George Hutchinson, who became head of the drawing office and Armstrong's right-hand man at Elswick, and Henry Thompson, appointed works manager. Hutchinson moved into a house built for him at the extreme eastern end of the works site. One of the two men put in charge of the machine shop was John Windlow, who would play a vital role in the creation of the Elswick Mechanics' Institute. By September, six young apprentices had been indentured. One of these, Robert Mills, remembered making his way to the site to start work at 6am and seeing Armstrong ahead of him driving in a phaeton pulled by a white pony – the earliness of the hour reflecting the eager single-mindedness that remained a constant feature of Armstrong's stewardship of Elswick Works. By the end of the year, the weekly wages bill had reached £42, indicating that there were about 20 men on the books; around 100 more men were working to complete the buildings and to install machinery.[4]

The employment of George Hutchinson was an early example of Armstrong's brilliance at spotting exactly the right man for the job and then giving him the freedom to excel. Thomas Sopwith remembered meeting Hutchinson in 1823, more than 20 years earlier, when he was already employed at Watson's works. Even then, it had been obvious that 'he combined great mechanical skill and ingenuity with an extreme soberness of judgment and steadiness of conduct'. Hutchinson had since played a vital role in helping

Armstrong to develop his hydraulic inventions. The first hydraulic engine built under his management at Elswick was applied to drive the machinery of the *Newcastle Chronicle* printing press in Grey Street, using the piped water supply from Whittle Dene.

Sopwith himself had turned down Armstrong's invitation to get involved in the new firm because, as manager of the Beaumont lead mines at Allenheads, he feared a conflict of interest. Since he expected to place large orders for machinery from W. G. Armstrong & Company, he felt he could not put himself in the position of profiting from those orders. He later came to rue the lost opportunity.

Another of Armstrong's inspired managerial acts during this period was the appointment of the young Edinburgh-born engineer Percy Westmacott, who joined the company in 1851 as a draughtsman. By the end of the decade, when he was not yet 30, Westmacott had become technical manager of the engine works. From then on, through his long association with the Elswick firm – of which he became a partner in 1864 and managing director in 1882 – he would retain responsibility for the hydraulic machinery department.

Westmacott had a childhood connection with the Potter family, Armstrong's cousins, and used to delight in relating anecdotes he had heard regarding his employer in his youth. He also had vivid memories of his first meeting with Armstrong, to whom he was introduced by his old friend Aubone Potter shortly after arriving in Newcastle from London by steam packet.

'When I was asked in, Mr Armstrong was seated at his desk. He looked up for a moment and then gave me a kindly smile, which I can recall to this day – indeed, it was the same old smile he gave me when he said goodbye at Bamburgh Castle a few weeks before his death,' recalled Westmacott later. 'He then put me through a short, sharp examination, looked at my hands, which were then bony and strong, gave me distinctly to understand what lay before me and that my advancement depended entirely upon my own exertions and character, and recommended me to be zealous in my work. I was to have four shillings per day wages and go under Thompson, the foreman in the works, in the fitting and erecting shops.' Assuring him that he would try to do his best, Westmacott rose to go, but just as he reached the door Armstrong called him back and asked him if he could draw. 'Now this was what I just could do, mechanical drawing and freehand with either hand or both together. It came somehow naturally to me,' said Westmacott. 'Here then was my chance, sooner than I expected. Fortunately, there was at that time much pressure in the drawing office. Mr George Hutchinson, the manager, was sent for and it ended in my being engaged as a draughtsman at four shillings a day and to start at six the next morning.'

One of the first orders received by W. G. Armstrong & Company came from the Albert Dock in Liverpool – in spite of the initial scepticism shown by the dock's chief engineer, Jesse Hartley. Armstrong was fond of recounting what happened when Hartley, 'a somewhat eccentric gentleman, who was very averse to novelties', made an unannounced visit to Newcastle to have a discreet look at the crane. When Hartley arrived, he got involved in bantering with the crane operator, who had become so skilled at working the machine that he had been nicknamed Hydraulic Jack. 'Being put upon his mettle by Mr Hartley's incredulous observations,' said Armstrong, 'Jack proceeded to show its action by a daring treatment of a hogshead of sugar. He began by running it up with great velocity to the head of the jib, and then letting it as rapidly descend, but by gradually reducing its speed as it neared the ground he stopped it softly before it quite touched the pavement. He next swung it round to the opposite side of the circle, continuing to lift and lower with great rapidity, while the jib was in motion. In short, he exhibited the machine to such advantage that Mr Hartley's prejudices were vanquished.

'Mr Hartley ... at once called upon [me], whom he laconically addressed in the following words: "I am Jesse Hartley of Liverpool and I have seen your crane. It is the very thing I want, and I shall recommend its adoption at the Albert Dock." With scarcely another word he bade adieu and returned to Liverpool. This anecdote marks an epoch in the history of hydraulic cranes which then passed from the stage of experiment to that of assured adoption.'

Two warehouse lifts were ordered for the Albert Dock at a cost

The first buildings to rise on the fields of Elswick in the late 1840s were a machine shop, a boiler shop, and a smiths' shop, with a tall chimney between them. In front of the factory was the River Tyne; behind ran a railway line.

By 1887, the year of the Royal Mining, Engineering, and Industrial Exhibition in Newcastle – and Queen Victoria's golden jubilee – Elswick had expanded to include a shipyard and steel works.

of £1,000, and the payment for these, received on 15 May 1848, constituted the new company's first revenue from sales. The following year, Hartley ordered two cranes. Production had begun the previous October on four 12-ton cranes for the Edinburgh and Northern Railway, designed to lift loaded carriages from a ferry in the Firth of Forth on to the railway, but Armstrong suffered an early blow when the contract was cancelled at the last minute, after the cranes had already been built.[5]

It was not long, however, before orders were pouring in from all over the country – from coal-mines, canal companies, docks and railway companies. Among the enthusiasts for the cranes were some of Britain's leading engineers. 'Mr Isambard Brunel, the celebrated engineer of the Great Western Railway, sent us many orders,' recalled Armorer Donkin. These included hydraulic locomotive turntables for Paddington Station in London. Machinery of different kinds was also in demand. In 1849 an order arrived from the Birkenhead dock trustees for a hydraulic swing bridge – the first of a series that would bring fame to Elswick. Armstrong adapted his system to the working of dock gates and secured the contract, worth almost £13,500, for the building of the docks at Great Grimsby, for which the Prince Consort – that great champion of engineers and scientists – had laid the foundation stone in 1848. He and James Rendel designed the hydraulic machinery that would operate the locks, sluices, and cranes for the docks. The most spectacular element of the contract was the 300-foot-high water tower, built in the style of the Palazzo Pubblico in Siena, Italy.

Elswick also won the lucrative contract to supply hydraulic machinery to the lead mines at Allenheads, where Sopwith had become chief agent two years earlier (and where he would remain for over a quarter of a century). A preliminary visit by Armstrong to the mines in February 1848 to determine what machinery was needed included one of the many hair-raising incidents that peppered his career – when the two men narrowly escaped being crushed to death. 'We returned by the underground waterwheels (four in number) and the passing under the moving beam of one of the engines was a matter the *frightfulness* of which scarcely presented itself to our minds until we afterwards reflected upon it,'

Sopwith later recorded in his diary. 'Imagine a dark subterranean cave – just large enough to hold the machinery of the engine. One of the attachments was a ponderous beam, which worked by the regular action of a waterwheel which kept slowly moving up and down – both of these movements being completed in about ten seconds. The only mode of passing was to *creep as flatly as possible* from one side to the other in the interval of about four seconds when it admitted of such a passage. Any detention beyond an instantaneous rush-through with great activity and speed – the hesitation or turning back of only two seconds delay must have been fatal – for no living animal could have resisted the powerful pressure. I went through at one of these intervals and Armstrong followed, but many a time have we since wondered at our adventure, although then it appeared to us one of the ordinary incidents of underground work.' Armstrong seemed to relish such close encounters with extreme danger.

According to A. R. Fairbairn, who wrote a history of Elswick a century later, the hydraulic machinery installed at Allenheads did more than simply bring prosperity to the Beaumont mines. 'It was to a great extent responsible for the success of the Elswick Works,' he argued – not simply through profits from the sale of machinery but through 'the justification of Armstrong's inventions and the resulting confidence and increased skill gained by the successful solution of mechanical problems'.

Years later, when Sopwith and Armstrong were reminiscing about the work at Allenheads, they hit on the subject of 'tails', or letters of distinction after an individual's name. 'Armstrong jokingly said that he valued none more highly than "MD",' noted Sopwith, 'which he thought he might assume as an abbreviation of the title bestowed on him by an Allendale miner of *Maister o' th' Drallickers* – by which was implied his mastership of the men employed in putting up the hydraulic engines.' Armstrong had not earned this title lightly, Sopwith noted, for he personally had supervised the installation of the equipment. In making an assessment of what was needed, he had shown no fear in going down the mines and moving about amid working machinery while investigating the existing deep drainage systems.

The excitement that attended the launch of Armstrong's business career was tempered by the serious illness of his mother, Anne, who for some time had been suffering from an 'affection of the womb' – from which she died on 9 June 1848, aged 70. Her place of death is recorded as The Minories, Jesmond, the house that William Armstrong senior had built for his family in the 1820s. Armstrong is said to have held his mother in the highest regard and to have always spoken of her in the most affectionate terms. His earliest joys sprang from childhood visits to Rothbury with his parents and his sister, and fishing expeditions with Armorer Donkin, and the loss of his mother must have brought memories of those times flooding back. In later life he built a row of almshouses in Rothbury and dedicated them to his mother's memory.

The only surviving letter from Anne Armstrong to her son expresses her continuing worries about his health – a concern that seems to have begun in his early childhood, and which probably intensified after the premature death of his sister. It was written from Jesmond a few years after William's marriage, when he and Meggie had gone away, perhaps to Rothbury, so he could recuperate after an illness. 'I have employed myself since yesterday in making you a flannel waistcoat, which I hope you will wear immediately as there is no better protection against cold than new flannel,' wrote the young man's mother. 'You will perceive that I retain my old predeliction for la couleur de rose. I am only sorry that you cannot well wear it outside.'

Anne's sense of humour and forthright opinions are also evident in the letter, as is her affection for her son's 'dear wife': 'Tell her I have not forgotten her in her absence for I have bought her a little butter tub with a white, not a red, cow upon the top of it, and a pretty white knife to cut said butter, both of which will be very glad when she brings her pretty eyes here to look at them.'

Anne Armstrong senior was described in a memoir by her great-grandson, William Watson-Armstrong, as 'a lady of considerable literary culture and greatly beloved by all who knew her', but little direct evidence of her character survives. (Watson-Armstrong, who never knew Anne, must have received his information from her son.) Her family, the Potters, coal-owners and brewers, was a force to be reckoned with in Newcastle society. The patriarch was William Potter of Walbottle Hall, one of the proprietors of the prosperous Walbottle colliery in Tynedale, who married twice. The three children from his first marriage were Addison Langhorn, Donkin's close friend, Anne, and Jane, who died unmarried in 1866.

Anne was clearly an intellectual match for her husband, the ambitious and bookish young merchant's clerk from Cumberland, whom she married in November 1801 at St John's, Newcastle. The eight-year gap between the births of her two children suggests that Anne may have had problems in conceiving children or carrying pregnancies to term, and the death of her daughter at the age of 25 would have come as a heavy blow. Anne probably took an active role in the early upbringing of her only grandchild, Johnny Watson, but the impression remains that she grieved for her daughter until the end of her days – while the motherless Johnny was an unhappy child and prone throughout his life to periods of depression.

The best clues to Anne's personality can be found in Thomas Sopwith's reminiscences about her sister, Jane, who survived well into her eighties, and was distinctive above all for her independence of mind and penetrating intelligence. (It was Jane who, in 1809, had helped Armstrong's sister, aged six at the time, to write a journal during their trip to the English lakes.) Sopwith knew Jane Potter for more than 30 years and was struck by her 'peculiar aptitude for acquiring information' and her 'retentive and accurate memory'. Her knowledge was gained not only from reading but from the broad general interest she took in worldly affairs.

Whilst candid in expressing her thoughts to family and friends, Jane was always open-minded in response to views that differed from her own. 'With sentiments of steady devotion and consistent adherence to her own conscientious belief, she always combined a liberal and even indulgent toleration of the views and conduct of others,' wrote Sopwith after her death, relating how she would often read his journal and make useful criticisms. 'Her loss will be long felt, not only in the absence of the friendly and intelligent communications she so frequently made, but also because she possessed a powerful influence by the force and candour of a highly endowed and powerful mind.' Among Jane's many anecdotes were stories about her nephew William's childhood obsession with machinery. She remembered how young William would repeatedly amaze visitors to the family home with a proliferation of elaborate devices constructed from simple household items.

Anne Armstrong's death occurred at a time when her husband had risen almost to the pinnacle of Newcastle's social and mercantile elite – although his achievements had already been somewhat eclipsed by those of his more famous son. In 1836, Armstrong senior had been elected to represent Jesmond ward on Newcastle town council after campaigning to curtail mayoral privileges. He was defeated in the election of 1839 but returned unopposed in 1842. His most important contribution as a councillor was to spearhead improvements to the Tyne navigation, a highly contentious issue on which he wrote a pamphlet during his first term. A river committee was established, with Armstrong as chairman, but progress was hampered by arguments about funding and alleged corruption, which continued until the passage in 1850 of the River Tyne Improvement Act.

Still smarting from the repeal of the Corn Laws three years earlier, Armstrong senior was unanimously elected as a Newcastle alderman in 1849 and in the same year was nominated for mayor. His proposer, Alderman Joseph Lamb, described him as having been a 'zealous, active and industrious merchant' for the past half-century and pointed out that he had been 'ten times a deputy to London and other places for the benefit of the town'.[6]

Although unsuccessful at the first attempt, Armstrong became mayor the following year, aged 72. One of his first duties was to host a ball for prominent citizens at the Assembly Rooms. Having lost his own wife two years earlier, he asked his son's wife to assume the role of mayoress for the occasion. Meggie's reply, dated 11 November 1850, reveals something of her forthright and punctilious personality. 'I am induced, though most reluctantly, to undertake the duties of Mrs Mayoress,' she wrote, 'but you must allow me to stipulate one condition, & that is, that you will enable me to pay *ready money* for all expenses which I may have to incur in connection with the office, & that you will not cause me any unnecessary trouble by procrastinating such payments. I strongly object to running bills, even on my own account, & much more in the name of another person.'

Despite her apparently cool attitude, Meggie was a naturally gregarious woman who liked nothing better than hosting a good party. On this occasion, she warmed to the challenge and the event was a huge success: 'Refreshments were served out with great profusion and liberality ... The arrangements for the occasions were conducted in the usual style of magnificence and hospitality and the whole affair passed off to the unmixed enjoyment and satisfaction of the brilliant gathering.'[7]

During Armstrong senior's mayoralty, Newcastle was riding the crest of a wave – as reflected in Queen Victoria's visit on 29 August to open the Central Station, an architectural triumph by John Dobson. The Queen had visited the town just a year previously to celebrate the completion of Robert Stephenson's High Level Bridge across the Tyne, but the opening of the station set the seal on the establishment of the first unbroken rail link between London and Edinburgh.

The year 1850 was also marked by one of William Armstrong junior's greatest inventions – since hailed as 'the key to the general adoption of hydraulic systems'.[8]

Armstrong's original inspiration for the development of hydraulics had come from his desire to concentrate, and thereby greatly intensify, the power derived from the fall of water in streams and rivers. Where such natural heads of water were unavailable, one solution was to build tall towers into which steam engines pumped the necessary supply of water – which is what he and James Rendel had done at Great Grimsby – but this was not always practicable.

In 1850, the Manchester, Sheffield and Lincolnshire Railway Company ordered nine 2-ton cranes to be erected at New Holland on the River Humber to deal with the conveyance of luggage and merchandise between train and ferry-steamer. There was no source of natural water pressure at New Holland, and it would have been impossible to build a tower because the foundations were mostly of sand. After much thought and experimentation, Armstrong found the solution in what he called an 'accumulator'. It consisted of a large vertical cylinder in which a very heavy weight was raised by a column of water driven by a pumping engine. When raised, the weight acted on a ram, forcing the water in the cylinder down to produce the required pressure in the distributing pipes that gave rise to the 'motive power'. This enabled the pressure to be raised from 90 pounds per square inch to 600 pounds, and soon afterwards to 700 pounds, meaning that the distributing pipes could be of smaller dimensions than would otherwise be needed. The accumulator had a tapered plug that prevented damage to the inside of the cylinder by allowing the descending ram to be brought gently to rest. In later years, higher and higher pressures became possible, reaching 1,500 pounds by 1901.

'By this invention, hydraulic machinery was rendered available in almost every situation,' noted *The Times*. 'Being very convenient where power is required at intervals and for short periods, it has come into extensive use for working cranes and hoists, opening and shutting dock gates, turning capstans, raising lifts, &c., and in many cases has procured important economies, both as regards time and money, at harbours and railway stations where large amounts of traffic have to be dealt with. In the navy its applications are almost infinite in number.'[9]

When London's Tower Bridge opened in 1894, the mechanism that made possible the opening and closing of the bridge's giant bascules in little more than a minute was driven by six of Armstrong's accumulators. And accumulators are still in use today; in modern aircraft, for example, they are installed as a back-up in case of the failure of the main hydraulic system.[10] By the time of Armstrong's death in 1900, it was generally acknowledged that, without hydraulic machinery and accumulators, the warships that were constructed in the second half of the 19th century would have been an impossibility.

Growing interest in his cranes and accumulator did much to increase Armstrong's fame in Britain, and honours followed. In 1850 he was awarded a prize by the Glamorganshire Canal Company for the best machine to transfer coal from barges to ships. In the same year he received the Telford Medal from the Institution of Civil Engineers in recognition of his patent of 1848 for water-pressure engines. The frantic pace of his life at this time is reflected in a letter he wrote to Meggie on 17 October 1850: 'At York at 7pm, at New Holland at 11 next morning, at Grimsby at 3, and in London at 11 at night. Today at Rendel's but found he was at Birkinshaw. At Fowler's, who wants more machinery at New Holland. At Brunel's, who I expect will require hydraulic coal drops. At Pickford's, where I hope for cranes, and at the present time am preparing for a meeting at the Engineers. This is the *multum in parvo* [much in little] of my proceedings.'

When the Great Exhibition opened in London's Hyde Park the following May, among the most popular attractions were examples of the latest achievements in civil and mechanical engineering. As well as a giant model of the new docks at Liverpool, the Crystal Palace housed models of Stephenson's Britannia Bridge linking mainland Wales with Anglesey, Brunel's Chepstow railway bridge, and Vignoles's suspension bridge across the Dnieper at Kiev. There was a wonderful array of steam locomotives, hydraulic presses, marine engines by Henry Maudslay, machine tools by Joseph Whitworth, and James Nasmyth's steam hammer, whose hammer head was propelled vertically downwards by an overhead cylinder and piston.[11] 'Of the hydraulic machines exhibited,' noted the exhibition handbook, 'there is none more deserving attention than the hydraulic cranes and other hydraulic engines of Mr Armstrong of Newcastle.' Many of the machines included in the Great Exhibition were shown in motion; the steam for this purpose was supplied from a special boiler house, equipped by Armstrong's Elswick Works, which stood outside the building.

Among the foreign sensations at the Great Exhibition was a 'monster ingot' produced by the German steelmaker Alfred Krupp of Essen, which won him a gold medal. Krupp's pride and joy, however, was a gleaming new cannon capable of firing a 6 pound shot, which he had been working on for several years, and which attracted great interest from the Queen and the British press. This first experience of public acclaim fed Krupp's ambitions. 'He began to see genuine possibilities in munitions, and the Crystal Palace had taught him how to realize them,' wrote his biographer.[12]

Armstrong's invention of the accumulator greatly stimulated

Maister o' th' Drallickers

the demand for cranes and other hydraulic machinery, and by 1852 Elswick was producing 75 cranes a year. This increased to an average of 100 cranes a year, a figure that held steady until the end of the century, when production started to decline. Initially the railway companies were the company's most important customers, but in the last quarter of the 19th century the company sought new customers abroad, especially in the colonies, and by 1900 the export share of sales had risen to 60 per cent. In 1878, in awarding Armstrong its Gold Medal (now known as the Albert Medal), the Society of Arts would cite his successful development of 'the transmission of power hydraulically, whereby the manufactures of this country have been greatly aided, and mechanical power beneficially substituted for most laborious and injurious manual labour'. This followed similar recognition by Cambridge University, which made him an honorary Doctor of Laws in 1862, and Oxford, which made him a Doctor of Civil Law in 1870.

Armstrong's company paid out its first dividend on share capital in 1854. The partners had earlier agreed that, as soon as Elswick began to prosper, they would limit any dividend to 5 per cent and would reinvest the remaining profits in the business. Indeed, in the opinion of the Elswick historian Alfred Cochrane, the whole management of the finance was 'masterly to a degree', and the company's cash reserves grew in the first 15 years from under £20,000 to nearly £100,000.

Not all Armstrong's ventures proved successful, however. For example, several attempts at locomotive-building ended in failure.[14] The first was in the early days of Elswick, at the end of the 1840s, and was said to have lost the company £2,000 – wiping out all the profits made in the rest of the business over two years. The model Armstrong produced, called the 'Flying Dutchman', was designed to increase power by means of a condenser. His idea was ingenious, but it needed a constant supply of cold water in order for it to work properly, a requirement that could not be fulfilled.

One clear success, however, was the building of the docks at Great Grimsby, which were formally opened by the Queen and Prince Consort, with all their children in attendance, on 14 October 1854. But, as it turned out, the royal visit to Grimsby would prove a brief interlude in a time of increasing upheaval. While trade at Elswick was booming and Armstrong's industrial enterprise was going from strength to strength, events were taking place on the borders of Eastern Europe and Asia that would catapult the inventor to international fame and change his life for ever. Earlier that year, Britain and France had made an alliance with the Ottoman Turks designed to check Russian expansionism in the Balkans. At the beginning of September 1854, following a dispute about control of the Holy Places in Jerusalem, the allies set sail for the Crimea peninsula with the aim of besieging Sebastopol, the headquarters of Russia's Black Sea fleet. For the first time for almost 40 years, Britain was at war.

6

What News from Sebastopol?

In the first week of October 1854, Catherine Rendel and her daughter Fanny were staying with the Armstrongs at Jesmond Dene to escape the cholera epidemic that had taken hold in London. Fanny's 21-year-old brother George, an engineer at Elswick, was a long-term lodger with the Armstrongs. On Friday, 6 October, following a night of high drama, Catherine wrote to her husband, James, at their home in Kensington: 'About a quarter past three o'clock we were most of us awoke by a loud report which shook the windows of the house. My first idea was that a gun had been fired close to my window, but everything was quiet after and I was inclining to the idea that it was atmospheric – some unusual meteoric discharge.' Others suspected an earthquake, but it was heard in the morning that a fearful explosion had taken place in Newcastle, the consequence of a fire. 'Mr Armstrong has sent us an account [from Elswick] that the effects are dreadful. Of course, at present the extent is not known of the loss of life etc. and the fire I believe yet burns.'

The Rendels had heard the sound of what was later described as 'the most terrible and appalling catastrophe which ever occurred in the towns of Newcastle and Gateshead'. It had begun with a fire which had broken out soon after midnight in a Gateshead clothing factory, as reported in *Illustrated London News*: 'The heat became so intense that it melted the sulphur which had been stored in an adjoining bonded warehouse. It came out in torrents, like streams of lava; and, as it met the external air, began to blaze: its combustion illumining the river and its shipping, the Tyne, the High Level Bridge, and the church steeples of Newcastle – spreading over every object its lurid and purple light. The flames towered far above the masts of the ships moored at the neighbouring quays.'

Nearby was another warehouse, filled with highly combustible materials – 'naptha, nitrate of soda, and potash, immense quantities of tallow and sulphur' as well as gunpowder. 'No sooner had the flames reached this compound, which was in fact nothing but a huge fulminating mixture, than an explosion took place, which no pen can describe, and which made Newcastle and Gateshead shake to their foundations. The bridge shook as if it would fall to pieces, and the surface of the river was suddenly agitated as if by a storm.' Although only 53 people were recorded as having lost their lives, more than 500 people were injured, and damage to property was estimated to be in the region of £1 million.

The disaster that befell Newcastle and Gateshead that night could be seen as a metaphor for the much greater disaster occurring at the same time thousands of miles away in the Crimea – and, if the great fire and explosion horrified the people of north-east England, reports of the Crimean War published in *The Times* were having a similar effect on the country at large. But even before it became clear that the war was a military and political disaster for Britain – not least because of the army's hopelessly outdated and cumbersome artillery – William Armstrong had been working on the development of a new gun.

Troops from the Anglo-French-Turkish alliance had their first major encounter with the Russians on 20 September at the River Alma. The allies ultimately triumphed but the human cost was huge; more than 5,000 of their troops died in the battle and many hundreds more were injured. There were no proper facilities on the ground to treat the sick and wounded. In fact, the administration of the war as a whole was to prove scandalously inept, and supply systems were abysmal.

In a first example of its kind, *The Times* had a reporter on the spot who filed eyewitness reports of events on the battlefield. His name was William Henry Russell, and his impassioned and provocative accounts prompted Florence Nightingale to set sail from England with 38 nurses during the third week of October and set up a nursing department at Scutari. The group arrived in time to receive the wounded from the Battle of Inkerman on 5 November.

Everyone in Britain, including the Queen, was captivated by the reports in *The Times* and readers were avid for the next instalment. 'We are, and indeed the whole country is, entirely engrossed with one idea, one anxious thought – the Crimea,' wrote Victoria in a letter to King Leopold of the Belgians, her uncle.[1] 'Our loss [at the Alma] was a heavy one – many have fallen and many are wounded, but my noble troops behaved with a courage and desperation that was beautiful to behold.'

There was general annoyance in Britain that news from the Crimea took so long to reach home. The nearest telegraph points were at Constantinople and Vienna, which meant that, at the very least, it took four days for a message from the war zone to arrive in Britain. Sometimes it took weeks. *The Times* itself was forced to carry apologetic articles with headlines such as 'What news from Sebastopol?' which were devoted to explaining why the whole process took so long.

However, when the reports did appear, they were dynamite. Russell pulled no punches in expressing his own opinions. After dismissing an earlier hope that wars might be a thing of the past, he went on: 'War has reappeared – war between civilized, scientific, mechanical nations – between states that have immense war establishments, national debts, and all the rest of it. And war turns out to be just the same as ever – the same uncouth, disagreeable, savage, inhuman thing that it ever was since the beginning of history. It is still reckless, malicious, wanton, and absolutely envious of happiness and peace; it still produces the most miserable scenes, the wildest adventures, the most perilous situations.'

The editorial was published on Friday, 20 October, four weeks after Alma, which it describes: 'Take the expedition as it arrives off the coast of the Crimea. The soldiers and sailors are falling by scores under the stroke of an inscrutable pest [cholera]. The army lands and bivouacs in the mud, and in rain. For several days it suffers an actual plague of thirst. Then comes the march, on the very first day of which baggage is sacrificed, and the rear is left behind. At last comes the battle, tardy to those who had expected it, though only the beginning of the end. It is no paper fight. The carnage, confusion, feats of daring, the collision of thousands with thousands, the medley of the victors and the vanquished, are those of the old battles. Then, after a night of triumph and horrid suffering, the sun rises on thousands groaning, writhing, and in worst agonies of thirst, over the bloody field.'

Although Sebastopol still held firm against the besiegers, the soldiers were hailed elsewhere in *The Times* as heroes. But the veneer was thin, and it was not long before awkward questions were being asked of the military chiefs and, in particular, the Duke of Newcastle, the secretary of state for war. Things went from bad to worse in early November, when the inadequacies of the British artillery were laid bare at Inkerman. During a Russian attack, Lord Raglan, the commander of the British force, had ordered two conventional cannon to be brought up to defend their position. Since no draught horses were available, the job had to be done by the men; it took 150 soldiers and eight officers three hours to haul the 2-ton guns through the mud into position.[2] The Russians were finally forced to withdraw, but only after the arrival of allied reinforcements and fierce hand-to-hand fighting, some of it with bayonets, resulting in 2,500 British casualties. Inkerman came hard on the heels of Balaclava, best remembered in Britain for the disastrous Charge of the Light Brigade.

At the time when the truth about the debacle in the Crimea started to emerge, William Armstrong was staying at 10 Palace Gardens, Kensington, with his old friend James Rendel. Like everyone else, Rendel and Armstrong devoured Russell's reports. What angered Rendel, above all, was the ludicrous inefficiency of the artillery that the British had taken out to the Crimea. His reaction made a strong impression on his son Stuart. 'I remember my father's animated outburst at the absurd ponderousness of the cannon so critically employed,' wrote Stuart in his memoirs. 'My father had been the first engineer to construct a continuous iron bridge over an estuary of the sea, near Plymouth. That bridge was, of course, of cast iron. Thirty years had passed and the use of cast iron for such a purpose had become utterly antiquated. He was indignant that military engineering should have lagged so far behind civil engineering as to be still retaining cast iron for the purpose of making cannon.'[3] No advance had been made in the science of gunnery in the 40 years since the end of the Napoleonic Wars.

Another engineer equally concerned about the shortcomings of Britain's weaponry was Isambard Kingdom Brunel. Angry at the arrogance and incompetence of military officials, Brunel would argue that some of the disasters in the Crimea might have been avoided if only the government would make use of the latest innovations in engineering. To give substance to his claims, Brunel made a model of a 'floating siege gun', a type of craft resembling a modern submarine with only its conning tower above the surface. It included a cylindrical turret housing a single 12-inch-bore gun capable of firing three rounds a minute; ammunition was stored in the submerged hull and loaded mechanically. Although he won the support of General Sir John Burgoyne, the head of the Royal Engineers, Brunel ultimately failed to persuade the Admiralty to endorse his new gunboat.

James Rendel, meanwhile, was busy explaining to Armstrong how the lightness and strength of a small-arm barrel constructed of wrought iron made possible the use of rifling and cylindrical bullets. He couldn't understand why the extraordinary advance in civilian small arms, mainly for sporting purposes, had not been extended by the military authorities to field artillery and even heavy artillery, but he attributed the failure to the snobbish attitude of the cavalry and infantry officers. 'He used to speak of the contempt shown in all the higher military circles for the scientific corps and base mechanical arts,' wrote Stuart. 'The Royal Engineers and the Royal Artillery were non-purchase corps and were entered solely by competition ... At the siege of Sebastopol it was out of the question that either an engineer or an artillery officer should take command of infantry or cavalry.'

In characteristic fashion, Armstrong rose to the occasion. 'I can see my father and Armstrong now before me with a bit of blotting paper between them on the table,' recalled Stuart, 'on which Armstrong drew out a scheme for an enlargement to field-gun size of the small-arm wrought-iron rifle – and I can almost hear my father's challenge to Armstrong to take up the question and bring artillery up to the level of the civil engineering science of the day. "*You* are the man to do it," he said.'

By 18 October, more than a fortnight before the Battle of Inkerman – and perhaps a couple of weeks after he and Armstrong had put their heads together over a piece of blotting paper at his London home – James Rendel was writing to his son George in Jesmond about a new project, a bridge over the River Nene at Wisbech: 'You do not say whether the work is all rivetted together as it will be when fixed in place, or whether it is partly screw-bolted.' Having insisted that George come soon to London to clarify and collaborate on the venture, Rendel ended his letter with the following request: 'Give my kindest regards to Mr and Mrs Armstrong and say to the former that I expect wonders from his gun.'[4]

As the navy's chief civil engineer, James Rendel could pull strings with the first lord of the Admiralty, Sir James Graham, to arrange a meeting between Armstrong and the Duke of Newcastle, the war secretary. The purpose of the interview, which took place in December 1854, was for Armstrong to present his plans for a new battlefield gun, a project on which he had been working for several weeks – although he claimed to have embarked on it 'more as an amusement for [his] leisure than for any other reason'.[5] Armstrong was not alone in his suit. Between June 1854 and the autumn of 1855, the War Office received nearly a thousand submissions relating to increased firepower for Britain's armed forces.[6]

Armstrong told the war secretary that his aim was to enlarge the ordinary military rifle to the standard of a field gun and to use elongated lead projectiles instead of cast-iron balls. While lightness and easy manoeuvrability would be crucial features of the new gun, improved range and accuracy would be even more important. Impressed with what he had seen and heard, and preferring Armstrong's proposals to those of his rivals, Newcastle commissioned the entrepreneur to make six such guns for inspection and testing. Seeing the exercise as an experiment, Armstrong built only one gun, delivered in July 1855. It weighed 5 hundredweight and its shot consisted of cylinders of solid lead, each weighing 3 pounds.

The design Armstrong came up with had four distinguishing features.[7] First, unlike previous cannon, it was rifled, giving it a much longer range and making it much more accurate than its predecessors, as well as allowing elongated shells rather than round balls to be used as ammunition. (A rifled gun has spiral grooves cut inside the barrel, making the projectile spin as it passes through.) Second, it was to be loaded at the breech, which was quicker than the traditional practice of loading at the muzzle. Third, crucially, it was made by the 'built-up' or 'coil' method of construction, which was only possible with wrought iron. And fourth, of course, it was made of wrought iron.

Giving evidence later to a royal commission on ordnance, Armstrong himself explained the importance of projectile shape and rifling. 'The resistance a projectile encounters in passing through the air is mainly dependent on the area of its cross-section, and the advantage of lengthening a bullet consists in augmenting the weight without increasing the sectional area,' he said. To realise this advantage, it was essential that the bullet be 'guided endways' on its course: 'This can only be done by causing it to rotate rapidly upon its long axis by firing it from a rifled bore.' But using elongated lead projectiles meant that the gun must be made strong enough to withstand the greater intensity of force needed to produce the required speed. And for the gun to be to light enough to move around easily, it would have to be constructed of steel or wrought iron rather than cast iron or bronze.

Armstrong's fascination with materials was evident in his speech to the Society of Mechanical Engineers in Sheffield a few years later, when he identified 'the true age of civilization' as the age of iron. 'Without iron, all our skill and ingenuity would have resulted in comparative nothingness, and – had it not been endowed with that singular property of hardening by sudden immersion after previous conversion into steel – we should have been deprived of the means of cutting and shaping it to those accurate forms which our mechanical constructions require.'

Iron's property of welding was almost equally essential to its usefulness, he said, and 'the combination of these remarkable quality in one metal, coupled with the fact of its natural localities being generally identical with those of coal, affords the most striking instance of adaptation to the purposes of man that can be found in the mineral kingdom'. The fact that Britain had led the way in the march of progress, he said, was chiefly attributable to the nation's skill and energy in producing this metal and applying it to mechanical purposes.

In designing his first gun, Armstrong drew on his knowledge of sporting guns, whose barrels were formed by twisting long strips of iron into spiral tubes and welding them together to form a continuous tube. While favouring a steel lining for the bore, he adopted what later became known as the coil principle. 'I made my gun with a core of steel enveloped in coiled iron cylinders, which being shrunk one [over] another upon the steel tube gave that state of initial tension and compression necessary to give the greatest strength to a cylinder.' Thicker tubes were used near the breech, where the pressures from the detonation of the charge were greatest, giving the weapon its distinctive telescopic shape.

The steel bore for the first gun was machine-rifled by John Bradley, a young workman at Elswick who had been taken on as an apprentice seven years earlier. The skilful operation was carried out at the factory during the night, watched over by Armstrong and George Stuart, one of his foremen, who were both too agitated to sleep.

The next step was to 'prove' the gun by firing a projectile from it – in this case, a solid-lead cylindrical shot. In the first of many such exploits, the trials were carried out at Whitley Sands on the Northumberland coast. Armstrong would go to the beach early to ensure that no one else would be around, but these and later tests exposed him to extreme personal danger, especially when he started to experiment with breech-loading, as Alfred Cochrane recalled: 'He fired his gun across the dene at Jesmond against the opposite hillside and the numerous adventures which he met with during these firing trials, as well as the narrow escapes he had of blowing himself to pieces, were most exciting.'[8] He goes on to write: 'In those days, there was no science of artillery such as there is today – nor was there any knowledge of what pressure metals would stand, and [Armstrong] deserves credit for his physical courage.'

In July 1855, the first prototype was presented to the War Office's newly formed ordnance committee, which consisted of civilians as well as military personnel.[9] They were struck by the gun's accuracy, range, and power, but, believing it to be too small for use on the battlefield – with some even deriding it as 'a pop-gun', good only for childish games – they asked Armstrong to enlarge it. The weapon was re-bored to take 5-pound projectiles, and the lead shot was replaced by a cast-iron shell thinly coated with lead, which caused considerably less recoil when the gun was fired. After much experimentation, Armstrong also produced a concussion fuse which would explode the shell on impact.

By the middle of 1856, Armstrong was trying out various models of his gun on the moors above Allenheads in the Pennines, where his friend Thomas Sopwith was chief agent of W. B. Lead Mines. For days on end, Armstrong would occupy a solitary hut high on the moors, some 2,000 feet above sea level. Installing a target on the other side of a valley, he would fire his projectiles at it by night as well as by day, shooting after dark being made possible by the use of a nyctoscope, an ingenious night-vision instrument of the gunmaker's own invention.

On 20 June, Sopwith noted in his diary, 'Mr Armstrong having yesterday made preliminary arrangements for his gun experiments, the first shot was fired about ½ past 9 this morning ... The children in Allenheads school were singing a hymn when the sound was heard. I sent for a telescope through which they all distinctly saw the gun.' Testing was still going on months later. On 11 October, wrote Sopwith, 'I walked to the moor to observe some of Armstrong's gun experiments. They gave results of extraordinary force as well as precision, a 5-pound leaden bullet passing through 30-inch thickness of solid elm at a distance of 1,500 yards.'

This bullet was probably fired by the gun that was finally purchased by the War Office the following January, after the official trials were over. With the encouragement of the government, Armstrong immediately set about designing larger-scale versions, producing 12-pounder and 18-pounder models that proved equally successful in performance. (The size of this type of gun was identified by the weight of the projectile that could be fired from it.)

Armstrong was helped in the creation of his gun by two of Britain's most eminent engineers, Brunel and James Nasmyth, both of whom had previous experience in the development of artillery.[10] Indeed, Brunel had originally sought advice from Armstrong on how to construct a gun by enveloping an internal tube with wire. 'In theory the idea was perfectly sound,' said Armstrong later, 'but there were various practical difficulties and objections. Mr Brunel determined to have a gun made upon this plan at his own expense, and I undertook to carry out the experiment for him.'

Armstrong corresponded regularly with Brunel while carrying out tests on his own gun. 'The practice comes off each morning at Jesmond between the peaceful hours of three and five, when people are all in bed and out of harm's way,' he wrote on 1 July 1856. 'The gun is placed in the field where the dung-heap was and I fire across the valley against a vertical bank at a distance of 435 yards.' He said that he had made good progress on developing the projectile and was 'beginning to understand the principles on which accuracy is dependent'. He later wrote to Brunel asking him 'to pull a few strings' for him at the War Office to get written authority (he had already been given verbal permission) to construct some guns and carry out experiments on them.

In a letter dated 26 July 1857, Armstrong described the successful test of his new 18-pounder gun at Allenheads: 'I have got a nice little hut on the moors and if you could manage to escape from business and join me on Thursday and Friday I am sure you would be much interested.' However, by this time, Brunel was almost totally preoccupied by the construction of his giant steamship *Great Eastern*, leaving little time for guns – and the correspondence came to an end.

A trial at the government's artillery range at Shoeburyness in Essex in January 1858 made clear the virtues of the 18-pounder gun, whereupon Armstrong was given orders for two more 18-pounders, one 12-pounder, and 400 projectiles. He described the event in a letter to Sopwith: 'The grand shooting match of my gun against a heavy regulation gun came off last week at Shoeburyness ... The opposing gun was a 32-pounder weighing 56 hundredweight. Mine is an 18-pounder weighing 12 hundredweight. Each fired so many rounds at a number of targets at 2,000 yards and then at 3,000 yards. I fired my own peculiar shells. They fired solid shot, having nothing else that would reach so far. The 32-pounder *never hit the target at all, at either distance,* while my gun made 397 holes in 22 rounds at 2,000 yards and 180 holes in 10 rounds at 3,000 yards. Moreover, my gun, when fired with the same elevation as the 32-pounder, sent its projectile 900 yards further and did equal distance in 10 per cent less time, which of course indicates the greater velocity of its projectile. The 32-pounder was fired with charges of 10 pounds while mine used only 2¼ pounds. The mean deviation from a straight line was only 30 inches in 3,000 yards with my gun, while with the big 'un it was about as many yards.'

While trials of the competing guns were in progress – and no decision had been taken by the government about which one to recommend to the army – fears had been mounting in Britain about the possibility of a French invasion. Not long after the end of the Crimean War in February 1856, evidence of unusual activity had been noticed in French dockyards, where ironclad ships were under construction, and reports circulated of major improvements in France's rifled cannon. By contrast, Britain's attempts to upgrade its defences had been lacklustre. There was a growing awareness that ports, harbours, and arsenals around the country were poorly protected, and even where fortifications had been built there were not enough men to garrison them – nor was the army judged strong enough to resist an invading force. In 1857, the outbreak of a rebellion in British India against the rule of the East India Company increased the sense of insecurity, and the clamour for military reform intensified.

Following the appointment of a Conservative administration under the 14th Earl of Derby, a select committee on rifled cannon was set up in August 1858 at the instigation of the new secretary for war, General Jonathan Peel, a brother of the former prime minister Sir Robert Peel. Its secretary was Andrew Noble, a 26-year-old artillery captain who had studied ballistics. General Peel asked the committee to compare the various models of cannon that had been submitted to them and to decide which one should be generally adopted by the army for battlefield service.

Armstrong's most serious rival was the Manchester engineer Joseph Whitworth, who had prospered as an inventor and manufacturer of machine tools. Two years earlier, the government had started to supply Whitworth with large steel ingots to rifle into artillery pieces and he had received £17,000 in research grants. But, after three months of testing and evaluation, the committee decided that Armstrong's guns were more accurate and had a longer range than Whitworth's. In addition, one of Whitworth's guns had burst during testing, as Armstrong mentioned in a letter to Meggie: 'There cannot be a doubt of the committee being all with me – the more so as Whitworth's 60-pounder burst the other day at Portsmouth. In fact, I think I now have the field all to myself.' Armstrong later attributed his success in the development of the gun to 'always keeping a definite aim before me and devoting my whole energies towards its attainment'.[11]

Armstrong's explanation of how he triumphed over his rivals in 1858 shows the dogged thoroughness with which he addressed any task in hand. 'I was enabled, by the private experiments I had carried on after the completion of my first gun, to lay before the committee a complete system of field artillery, with a carriage, projectiles, fuses, and all the necessary accessories – while the other competitors, with one exception, merely proposed methods of rifling existing cast-iron or bronze guns, and certain forms of projectile to suit the rifling,' he said. The committee reported in favour of Armstrong's guns on every point – the construction, the breech-loading, the range, the accuracy, and the destructive effect of the projectile, which, in the words of the inventor, 'far exceeded that of any shell in the service'.

On 16 November 1858, the ordnance committee recommended 'the immediate introduction of guns rifled on Mr Armstrong's principle for special service in the field'. The government ordered 100 guns and guaranteed the £12,000 investment needed to build a gun factory at Elswick. Impressed by Andrew Noble's knowledge of ballistics, Armstrong asked him to join the new operation – but Noble, reluctant to relinquish a promising military career, refused the offer. Whitworth's gun was rejected and his research funding was withdrawn – but this was only the start of a long-running battle between the two titans of industry.

In the eight years since James Rendel had persuaded Armstrong's father to give free rein to his son's business career, much had changed in the relations between the two families. Several of Rendel's children would pursue an interest in engineering, but the personal links that Armstrong forged with the Rendels were just as strong as the professional ones. The catalyst for this development was most likely to have been the absence of any children in his own marriage. William and Meggie had a loving and happy relationship, and both repeatedly demonstrated their fondness for children, so the lack of any offspring must have been a source of profound sadness and disappointment.

The particular object of William Armstrong's affections at this time was the Rendels' third son, George Wightwick, who in 1849, at the age of 16, had run away from Harrow school after suffering a perceived injustice. He worked briefly with his father at Great Grimsby docks, and then went to work with his brother Lewis on an Admiralty pier at Holyhead, before being taken on at Elswick. During the three-year apprenticeship, George lived with the Armstrongs at Jesmond and grew very close to both William and Meggie, to the extent that Armstrong – known by the Rendel children as 'Uncle W.' – made an unsuccessful attempt to adopt the talented young engineer.

Armstrong had also had to endure the loss of the man who had done so much to help him to establish his career. Armorer Donkin had died on 14 October 1851 after 30 years as a leading light of the legal profession on Tyneside and 15 years as an alderman. Donkin had been no less than a second father to Armstrong, perhaps even more influential than his own father, and had bequeathed to him the greater part of his estate. Jesmond Park – which had won local fame as the scene of 'Donkin's Ordinary' – became an extension of Armstrong's own property in the dene.

Donkin's most outstanding trait had been 'the extreme cordiality and sincerity of his attachment to his friends', according to the *Newcastle Chronicle*. He had been a larger-than-life figure with an unmistakable physical presence: 'His head and face, though not handsome, were cast in a noble and massive mould; and a look of peculiar intelligence, mingled with good humour, and great self-possession, generally lighted up his countenance.' Acutely aware of how much Donkin had contributed to his early success, Armstrong seems to have felt the need to assume a similar role for himself in relation to George Rendel.

His exploits with the Rendel children inspired Armstrong to write a mystical adventure story for them in which the narrator finds himself confined in a breathtakingly beautiful mountain fastness. Composed in 1855, during long train journeys between Newcastle and London, *The Trap Rocks of the Himalayas* takes place in a region 'on the verge of perpetual snow'. The narrator, an engineer, describes how 'On either side of me, as well as all round the horizon, rose towering peaks of naked rock with snowy garments resting on their shoulders, and green fantastic glaciers filling the hollow by which they were divided. A bright sunshine lighted up the greater part of this wonderful prospect, while just sufficient cloud and mist hung about the mountains to show their grandeur to most advantage.'

A character called George Rendel appears in the story and explains to the narrator that, although abundant in natural resources and able to sustain human life at the peak of comfort, this 'glorious place' – reminiscent of the Garden of Eden – suffers from one major disadvantage: no woman has ever been 'trapped' there. Therefore, since they are free from deprivation and disease, the male inhabitants must live for hundreds of years in the absence of female company. Before long, the narrator and his interlocutor agree on the urgent need for escape – an end that is eventually achieved by means of their combined insights and inventive ingenuity.

George Rendel's engineering talents had been evident from an early age, and he had inherited his father's energy and drive, so Armstrong had no doubts about taking him on at Elswick. When, in the autumn of 1854, Armstrong was approached by the War Office and – on the strength of his achievements at Great Grimsby docks – asked to find a solution to a problem that had arisen in the Crimea, it looked as though George might be sent out to deal with it.

The Russians had scuttled half a dozen of their own battleships at the mouth of Sebastopol harbour in an attempt to create an obstacle for the enemy, and Armstrong was asked to design underwater mines to blow up the sunken ships. After carrying out some experiments with George's help, he invited several of his employees to watch a trial in his grounds at Jesmond. 'The mines, planted in different parts of the field, exploded in the most exhilarating manner, and after tea had been served out, the party separated, delighted with the afternoon's entertainment,' recorded an observer.[12]

To his family's indignation, George was not sent to Sebastopol after all. 'The reason is that he can have no proper position,' Catherine wrote to Stuart. 'Sir James [Graham, first lord of the Admiralty] wished it, but some military person has disputed the propriety of a civil engineer having any prominent part in it.' It was a foretaste of the prejudice on the part of the military authorities that would dog Armstrong's later career. In the event, the mines were used in 1856 in an attempt to blow up the docks at Sebastopol – a purpose for which they had not been designed. When complaints reached him that the mines had not worked as well as expected, Armstrong pointed out that the men operating them had not been properly trained for the task.

When his old friend and mentor James Rendel died suddenly from a fever in November 1856, aged 57, Armstrong took charge of affairs at 10 Palace Gardens and attended to all the arrangements for the funeral, confirming his place at the centre of the Rendel family. Although their father's death would bring the Rendels even closer to Uncle W., its immediate consequence was that George Rendel returned to London to help his eldest brother, Alexander Meadows, known as Med, to run the family engineering firm. Their sister Fanny revealed her affection for William and Meggie in a letter to Stuart, written from Jesmond Dene: 'You cannot think what quiet care Uncle W. takes of me. He is *so* good – and Mrs Armstrong is more than kind. If I had been their own child, they could not take more care of me than they do.'

In another letter to Stuart, this time from London, Fanny wrote about shell-collecting, a hobby that Armstrong had taken up with the Rendel children. 'Yesterday evening we had music and work and nearly finished packing the shells up, preparatory to Uncle W. going tomorrow. We shall miss him very much. Last evening a beautiful microscope came, which he had bought for George ... Mr A. is coming to us again at the end of next month at latest and has promised to take Mama and me to Oxford [where Stuart was an undergraduate].'

George, meanwhile, was writing to Stuart about engineering matters: 'We have let the large bridge for the Soane to contract. Uncle W. has got it. I am very glad of this as it will take a great deal of anxiety from my mind and I shall have many a pleasant trip to Newcastle for inspection.' The contract was to a build a railway bridge over the River Soane (now known as Son or Sone), a tributary of the Ganges in north-east India. The Rendel family firm had recently been appointed consulting engineers to the East India Railway, and would later perform the same role for the secretary of state for India. Indeed, in the period up to 1913, the firm would be responsible for building many thousands of miles of railway and for bridging most of the great rivers of India.[13]

In a contemporary correspondence with Stuart, Uncle W. revealed his fatherly concern for the Rendel children. 'Your proposition about taking Fanny abroad is, I own, a good one, though I do not like the idea of her being beyond my reach for an entire winter,' he wrote. 'I have just been up at the new house [9 Hyde Park Street] with your mother and George ... George is by no means well and I intend to carry him off with me when I next leave London, as I shall then proceed to Allenheads to try the new gun.' Armstrong's work on the gun had begun to impinge upon the Rendel family routine, as Fanny admitted to Nellie Hubbard, who had become engaged to Stuart: 'We are not going to Whitby for six weeks as the gun will not be finished before then.'

By December 1857, Armstrong had virtually assumed the paternal role. 'What important additions I have recently had to my family,' he wrote to Stuart, alluding to Stuart's forthcoming marriage and the birth of a baby to Med and his wife. 'My family [that is, the Rendel children] keep up a sharp fire of letters at me and think themselves aggrieved if I do not return shot for shot, quite forgetting how many they are to me.' However, keeping up 'a little daily conversation' with the Rendels during his separation from them was clearly a source of pleasure to Armstrong. 'Worse than any of them is that wee sister of yours [Fanny] that you make such a pet of and who has come over me also to a most unwarrantable extent.'

Gun trials scheduled to take place at Shoeburyness in late 1857 had to be postponed when Armstrong was called away to northern Italy, where – following in the footsteps of James Rendel – he was advising the Italians on the modernisation and enlargement of Genoa. Three years earlier, Rendel had proposed redeveloping the port by building new quays and a seven-storey warehouse, as well as recommending the installation of Armstrong's hydraulic machinery for operating the dock gates and the dockside cranes – a plan acted on by the president of the council of ministers, Count Cavour.[14] Rendel had also masterminded the construction of a large modern base at La Spezia, further along the coast towards Pisa.

'Uncle W. has business at Genoa – and George wishes to go also,' wrote Fanny to Stuart from London. 'Uncle thinks he can start about 1 November but his gun has been ordered to Shoeburyness, and therefore to a day he cannot be certain ... Uncle has just given us a most beautiful black horse – its paces perfect. I am now going to ride with him.' Armstrong's trip to Genoa was his first recorded journey abroad. He may have travelled there through Switzerland, whose landscapes held such a central place in his creative imagination.

As the production of ordnance got under way at Elswick, the extraordinary industriousness of the place was captured in an account by the librarian to the Royal Society, Walter White, who visited the works on his travels through Northumberland in 1858.[15] 'To describe this place as it deserves would require, not a page or two, but whole chapters, such are the magnitude and variety of the operations there carried on,' he wrote. 'I saw brawny smiths forging chains link by link, and small mountains of finished chains lying ready for transport not far from the ruthless machine by which their strength had been tested. I saw an iron bridge being built for India, and small iron steamers for the navigation of Indian rivers; and huge engines for sundry purposes, besides which the men looked dwarf-like; and gangs of rivetters wielding their hammers with deafening din.'

White was fascinated by the hydraulic engines that had made Elswick famous and, above all, by their inventor, who directed his tour of the works: 'He lays a cylinder underground at the foot of a crane, attaches one end of the lifting chain to the piston, and then by turning on a supply of water, the crane does any required amount of work.' Armstrong's systems were now in use all over the country, and in many parts of the empire. 'Twelve hundred tons of coal were lifted out of a ship in one day by a hydraulic crane in the Victoria Dock on the Thames,' noted White. He was particularly impressed by the smooth operation of the machinery. 'There is no fire, no heat, no smoke, no outrageous uproar with blowing off steam when the engine stops; but a tranquilly energetic movement, and in the pauses the water-engine settles into quiet as comfortably as a good man folding his hands in repose.' And the source of this power was remarkably cheap: 'Even in London a thousand gallons of water can be supplied for fourpence.'

Walter White's readers would no doubt have been anxious to hear his account of Armstrong's latest invention. 'I saw the gun – the nine-pounder – and a pretty thing it is for one so astoundingly fatal,' he wrote. 'It rests on a slide which, by receiving the first shock of the recoil, saves the carriage from strain and disturbance. The sights are arranged to secure unfailing aim; it is loaded at the breech; the shot is smooth and cylindrical, some seven or eight inches long, with the foremost end finished to a point; and the bore of the piece being rifled, the gunner may hit every time he fires. "Ah! that's the one that went eight feet into a solid butt of elm," said [Armstrong], seeing me take up a shot for examination that lay in the office.'

The acknowledged superiority of the Armstrong gun prompted White to speculate that the weapon, through its very power, would contribute to the ending of war. 'Since rifles were improved, artillery-men have not been able to keep out of range,' wrote White, 'but the Armstrong gun overshoots the new rifles as far as ordinary guns overshot the old musket, not to say farther – and therewith war will perhaps be satisfied, as least until new tactics are invented.' It was a view that the inventor himself would have shared.

7

National Hero

Among the memorable events that took place in Britain during 1859 were the deaths, in September and October of that year, of the engineers Isambard Kingdom Brunel and Robert Stephenson, both of whom had played influential roles in Armstrong's early career. Brunel's death occurred just as his spectacular railway bridge across the Tamar at Saltash was nearing completion and in the same month as the launch of his monster ship *Great Eastern* – five times larger than any other vessel afloat – which would make possible the laying in 1866 of the first transatlantic telegraph cable. The Newcastle-born civil engineer Robert Stephenson, whose death caused an outpouring of grief across the country, was buried in Westminster Abbey beside his illustrious predecessor, Thomas Telford. It was a high-water mark in what would come to be seen as Britain's heroic age of engineering.

Meanwhile – following the return to power in June of Henry John Temple, Viscount Palmerston, at the head of a Liberal administration – the government had launched a large-scale programme of rearmament. As fears continued to grow about Napoleon III's belligerent intentions, Palmerston, who had cultivated good relations with the French emperor, was seen as offering the best chance of peace. The intellectual spirit of the times was captured in two literary sensations: John Murray risked huge controversy with his publication of *On the Origin of Species* by the 50-year-old Charles Darwin, while the journalist and biographer Samuel Smiles produced *Self-Help*, his groundbreaking guide to worldly self-enhancement, whose sales would exceed a quarter of a million copies during the author's lifetime alone.

The year 1859 would also see William George Armstrong elevated from the role of relatively obscure businessman in the north-east of England to the status of national hero – but, for him, the year began very much as the previous one had ended, with gun tests on the Essex coast at Shoeburyness.

One of these trials was attended by Thomas Sopwith, who – following his wedding the previous September to Annie Potter, daughter of Addison Langhorn Potter of Heaton Hall – was now related to Armstrong by marriage. As Sopwith related in his diary for 4 January 1859, the group at the artillery range that day included Prince Albert – that year's president of the British Association for the Advancement of Science – and the Duke of Cambridge, the commander-in-chief of the British Army and first cousin to the Queen.

'I went with Mrs W. G. Armstrong in a handsome carriage to Shoeburyness, distant about 4 miles from Southend, to witness experiments in artillery practice which are now being carried out there,' wrote Sopwith. 'These experiments are under the immediate direction of Mr W. G. Armstrong and are confined to repeated trials of guns invented by him.'

The trials were carried out in methodical fashion: 'The guns, five in number, were placed on a small battery commanding an ample range over the vast area of flat ground which stretches north-east from the mouth of the Thames. On this area, which is covered for a few hours at high water, targets are placed at the respective distances of 625, 1,500, 2,000 and 3,000 yards. All these were fired at from three of the guns, mostly from the 18-pounder (formerly at Allenheads) and with almost invariable success, the shots in a few instances falling short of the target. Some shots were fired into an oak butt, or block, at 625 yards distance, the first one being directed against it when only one foot above water and therefore presenting an exterior surface much less than that of a very small boat. It was a capital hit and the splinters flew a great height into the air.' (As noted earlier, the size of a gun was denoted by the maximum weight of the projectile it could fire.)

'Mr Armstrong tells me that, in former practice, the oak butt has been shot through its entire thickness of 6 feet, the shot passing another 600 yards, or in all 1,225 yards. The butt is 9 feet long, 9 feet high and 6 feet thick, weighing 10 tons. This power of penetration exceeds that of any gun hitherto known of any weight, size or description whatever. The range attained by this gun at an angle of 35 degrees was 9,175 yards (being 375 yards over 5 miles), which is quite unparalleled in gun practice.' The experienced army officers who witnessed the experiments had clearly been astonished by what the gun could do, and its qualities had particularly impressed the committee on rifled cannon presided over by William Wiseman.

The next evening, Sopwith and the Armstrongs attended a party given by the Rendels, where press stories were causing a stir: 'The *Globe* of 3 January mentions in a leader the influence of Armstrong's gun on naval warfare. The first number of a new series of the *Mechanics' Magazine* published 31 December 1858 calls it "the most effective cannon that the military man has yet had given him" and mentions its inventor Mr W. G. Armstrong as "an hydraulic engineer of Newcastle".'

Later that year, in explaining to the House of Commons the decision to adopt the Armstrong gun, the war secretary, General Peel, said that 'at equal distances, the Armstrong gun was 57 times as accurate as our common artillery'.[1] The Duke of Cambridge was even more astounded, claiming that 'The Armstrong gun could do everything but speak.'

By the end of January, Sopwith was back in Newcastle, where, during tea with the Armstrongs at Jesmond Dene, he learnt that Armstrong was to be made Engineer of Rifled Ordnance to the War Department – an appointment that would be accompanied by a substantial salary, together with a large order for guns. Many of the guns would be made at a new factory already under construction at Elswick, and Armstrong had been promised personal honours 'which will mark the favour of the Sovereign as well as the approval of her government'.

Armstrong was worried that the government might change its mind and decide to build all or most of the guns at the Royal Arsenal in Woolwich or contract out their manufacture to others – in which case, he and his partners would see no return on the new capital they were investing in Elswick. So he offered to hand over his gun patents free of charge, and agreed not to sell his guns to a foreign country, as long as the government would underwrite the security of the investment. In mid-January, a ten-year contract was signed, under which, in response to the granting of the patents, the government guaranteed £50,000 in capital; this was soon raised to £85,000.[2] The Elswick partners were banned from revealing any information about Armstrong's guns, even to their own employees, beyond what was strictly necessary to manufacture them.

Three weeks later, a letter arrived at Jesmond Dene from the War Office notifying the recipient that 'General Peel has sent your name for knighthood to the Queen. The other honour will shortly follow.' Armstrong was requested to wear 'ordinary court dress' for the investiture and warned to expect to be 'preferred for especial notice by the Queen and Prince Albert'.

The situation was later scrutinised by the magazine *London Review*: 'The government decided to manufacture, with great speed and secrecy, a large number of the new weapons, and at once prepared to treat with the successful inventor. General Peel, the gun's most energetic friend, has repeatedly said that they would have given him any compensation that he liked to name, but Armstrong quietly executed a deed transferring all his patents to the government and refused any remuneration. In return for his success and patriotic liberality, he was knighted and made a Commander of the Bath, and – as it was necessary to have his assistance in manufacturing the guns and maturing his inventions – he was appointed to the new office of Engineer of Rifled Ordnance, to which some dignity was attached by a salary of £2,000.' In return for this salary (backdated at Armstrong's request to 1856), the government became entitled not only to his services but also to 'all future inventions and improvements he might make in relation to gunnery'. In the event, the guns would be produced at both Woolwich and Elswick, and Armstrong's appointment would allow him to supervise the manufacture of the guns at Woolwich while continuing his research into larger and more powerful models.[3]

Elswick Ordnance Company had been created on 1 January 1859, and by the summer the initial stage of the new works was almost finished.[4] Of its five 'shops', two were devoted to producing the mechanical parts of the gun, one to making shot and shell, one to fitting out, and there was also a giant smithy, equipped with a hearth and hammers for welding the gun coils. Care was taken to preserve 'a mystery of secrecy', as it was described in *The Times*. 'Great strictness [must] be exercised as regards the men employed at the works,' the newspaper remarked. 'Each is to have assigned to him his own position and beyond it he is not to be allowed to advance.'

George Rendel, not yet 26, took on the management of the ordnance works, while Percy Westmacott remained in charge of the engine works. Commenting on his brother's promotion at such a young age, Stuart Rendel pointed out that '[George] had been Armstrong's constant companion during the experiments with the first gun. He had shared to the full the enthusiasm for the prospective development of artillery manufacture.'[5] The promotion was later seen as a prime example of Armstrong's genius at spotting men of exceptional ability and employing them as his lieutenants.

The following year, Rendel would be joined by the equally youthful Captain Andrew Noble, the former secretary to the ordnance committee, who was finally persuaded to leave the army and take control of the Elswick ammunition department. The other partners in the ordnance works were George Cruddas, who continued to look after the financial side of the Elswick businesses, and the lawyer Richard Lambert.

Seeking to avoid a conflict of interest, Armstrong was not a legal partner in the ordnance company – although he provided it with capital – but reserved the right to join the firm at any time following his departure from government service.[6]

Armstrong's skill at recognising aptitude in others was combined with a tolerance for those who had moral qualms about the direction in which his business was developing. In the mid-1850s, his chief draughtsman at Elswick was a Cornish Quaker, Richard Hoskins, who refused to become involved in the manufacturing of guns, as he told his employer during a meeting in the drawing office. 'Thou knowest, Mr Armstrong, that I cannot go against my conscience,' said Hoskins. 'Well, I cannot blame you, Richard,' his master replied.

There is no evidence, however, that Armstrong himself agonised over the decision to go into arms manufacture. 'If I thought that war would be fomented, or the interests of humanity suffer, by what I have done, I would greatly regret it,' he said. 'I have no such apprehensions.'[7] Indeed, he believed that his work in pushing forward the frontiers of science was likely to lead to a decrease in bloodshed: 'The power which science gives us, whether as applied to peace or war, is always on the side of civilization and the spread of civilization must tend necessarily to diminish war and to make it less barbarous.'

By the time General Peel had dispatched his letter confirming Armstrong's appointment as Engineer of Rifled Ordnance, Armstrong and Sopwith were already in London for the investiture, which took place on 23 February. 'At one o'clock I called on Mr William George Armstrong at the British Hotel in Jermyn Street and found him arrayed in his court dress ready to proceed to the levée at St James's Palace,' wrote Sopwith. 'I bade adieu to him in his name of Mr W. G. A., and at four o'clock I was the first out of the palace to shake hands and congratulate him on his elevation to knighthood as Sir William Armstrong.'

That evening, Armstrong described the day's events in a letter to Meggie, who had not made the journey south, perhaps because of illness: 'Your husband has cast his old skin and entered his new one and you have partaken of the change which I trust will be a happy one ... The Queen's face shone forth most radiantly when my name was announced and she said she had great pleasure in conferring the honour. The Prince then stepped forward and shook hands with me.'

A prominent report in the following day's *Times* was unrestrained in its enthusiasm for the gunmaker's achievements: 'The effect that will be produced upon our armaments by the introduction of the rifled ordnance invented by Sir William Armstrong is the most important branch of any question respecting the National Defences. If these new inventions turn out to be as formidable in practice as they are startling in description, it would seem as though all the old military and naval arrangements of the world must soon pass away like the airy *dramatis personae* of a morning's dream.' Armstrong himself was somewhat taken aback by the eulogy, as revealed in his letter to Meggie later that day: 'I suppose you would see *The Times* of this morning. It is extraordinary what a burst of notoriety the guns have at length brought upon me. I suppose I shall hear something about the CB [Companion of the Order of the Bath] tomorrow.'

Another family member whose absence had been keenly felt at the palace ceremony was Armstrong's father, William senior, who had died in June 1857, only a few weeks after relinquishing his various public offices.

Respecting his father's wish that, after his death, the Newcastle Lit & Phil should receive any scientific books and local tracts from his personal collection that might prove useful, Armstrong junior had donated 1,284 works to the society, giving it a collection of mathematical publications unmatched by that of any other provincial institution.[8] Armstrong senior had also been one of the founders of the local Natural History Society and helped to set up a chamber of commerce in Newcastle. But above all, as chairman since 1843 of the river committee, and a commissioner after the River Tyne Improvement Act of 1850, he had successfully campaigned to improve the navigation of the River Tyne.

William Armstrong senior was buried in what is now Jesmond Old Cemetery in the same place as his wife, Anne, who had predeceased him by nine years, and next to the grave of his old friend Armorer Donkin. Presumably commissioned by the younger Armstrong, the monuments to the two men – long, low, triangular caskets of granite, simply ornamented – are, apart from their inscriptions, identical.

His years of widowhood and the death of friends had led Armstrong senior to foster closer ties with his own family, in particular his only grandchild, Johnny, the son of his late daughter and son-in-law, Anne and William Watson. Having followed his father into the legal profession, Johnny Watson took an active interest in his father's career, as revealed in a letter to 'My dear Grandpapa', written from London on 28 May 1856, when Johnny was 27, referring to a possible new recruit to the 'exchequer bench'.

(William Watson was elevated to the judiciary five months later and rewarded with a knighthood.) Johnny then expressed a wish to visit his grandfather in Jesmond. 'I can well believe the Minories is looking beautiful – I sigh for a little fresh air, for my health for the last two months has been, I am sorry to say, very bad.'

Johnny's health, especially his mental stability, seems to have been a constant cause of worry to his family. His stepmother, Mary Watson, revealed her concern in letters to Meggie Armstrong, who herself took a great interest in the Watson family and had become something of a confidante. 'I am very anxious indeed to know your opinion of Johnny's health,' wrote Mary in one letter from her country home near Midhurst in Sussex. 'He makes me very uneasy at times. When he feels depressed, he writes me a detailed account of his ailments and then the next letter is all bright and cheerful. At the same time, he always owns that he is more comfortable after he thinks I know exactly how poorly he is.'

Johnny did not let his emotional state affect his relationship with his maternal grandfather, however. Indeed, the two of them enjoyed a close rapport. Up until the last weeks of Armstrong senior's life, Johnny had taken responsibility for supplying him with snuff. 'My dear Grandpapa,' he wrote in April 1857. 'I was quite ashamed about the snuff. I ought to have sent it before the circuit, on the which, while I was enjoying myself, your nose was perhaps going without its ordinary excitement. However, I hope that by this time you are enjoying the real genuine mixture as procured by me at the shop and carried to Newcastle by my uncle. I only sent one pound, thinking it was better fresh.'

It seems to have been a source of relief, as well as joy, to his relations when, on 5 May 1859, Johnny married Margaret Godman Fitzpatrick, the daughter of Patrick Persse Fitzpatrick of Bognor Regis, Sussex. Mary Watson described the wedding in a letter to 'My dear Lady Armstrong' (as Meggie had become a few weeks earlier). 'I must write a line to tell you that all went off well yesterday. The bride of course looked beautiful and I really think you would have admired her bouquet,' wrote Mary. 'Johnny was very nervous but recovered himself when it was all over. They went only to Windsor and today we had a letter from them saying they had taken a walk on the terrace "like any other people". They are going to Wales for a little time as at present it is not thought wise to carry out their original intention of going to the continent.' (There was growing tension at this time between Britain and France.)

As Thomas Sopwith recorded in his diary, William and Mary Watson had joined in the celebrations to mark Armstrong's knighthood. 'On my return to the hotel in Jermyn Street, I found Baron Watson congratulating the new-made knight, his brother-in-law,' he wrote. 'It is a very remarkable coincidence that the only son and only daughter of the late Mr William Armstrong should have fallen into a line of promotion – the former commencing life as a lawyer and now knighted on his appointment as Engineer to the War Office for Rifled Ordnance, and the latter, had she lived, would have shared the honours of her husband Baron Watson, who began life as a soldier and ended in the profession of the law.'

Two days later, Sopwith and Armstrong dined with the Watsons at their home in Eaton Square, Belgravia. 'The judge is a first-rate conversationalist,' noted Sopwith. 'Some of his Northumbrian recollections and imitations are inimitable – such as, for instance, the difficulty of London officials of the court in understanding the name "Turnbull" when pronounced by its owner as "Trummell".'

Sopwith recorded Armstrong's nonchalance in the face of sudden fame. 'The leading article in *The Times* on 24 February spread to the four corners of the earth an exact estimate of the merits of my highly gifted friend and of the favour of his Queen bestowed in so public and unmistakable a manner,' he wrote. But Armstrong remained resolutely indifferent. 'Indeed, his only apprehensions seemed directed to avoid as much as possible the influences of that tide of fashion which ever follows the smiles of royalty.'

Further evidence that Armstrong was now regarded as part of the British establishment appeared the following month with his admittance to London's exclusive Athenaeum Club in Pall Mall. Sopwith (already a member) was informed of the event in a note from Sir Roderick Murchison, the president of the Royal Geographical Society: 'Dear Sopwith, Sir William Armstrong was brought in as one of the eminently distinguished this afternoon, and is now an Athenaen.'

When the new knight returned to Newcastle in early March, he received a hero's welcome from his fellow townspeople. Shops and offices were decorated with flags and streamers, and cheering crowds lined the streets. The appearance of Sir William and Lady Armstrong was greeted by a fusillade from a row of cannon. In a speech on behalf of the Elswick workers, George Hutchinson pointed out that the powers of the Armstrong gun had 'excited the surprise and wonder [not only] of the British people and the British army and navy, but of the governments of all the powers of Europe and all other civilized nations on the globe – wherever the knowledge of its astonishing powers has been spread'.

The celebrations were followed by a meeting of Whittle Dene Water Company, of which Armstrong remained chairman. As reported in *The Times*, Armstrong told his audience that the chief grounds for congratulations were to be found, 'not so much in the fact of any personal aggrandisement of himself as in the additional employment which would be given to the skilled artisans of the district'. From these comments, said the newspaper, 'it may be inferred that the manufacture of the rifle-cannon will be extensively carried out at the Elswick Works'.

A few days earlier, *The Times* had noted that Armstrong's reputation had been established as the inventor of the hydraulic crane now in use in all the main dockyards of Europe, and that – apart from the guns – there were many other works involving great mechanical skill being turned out by the Elswick factory, including 'a large bridge of peculiar construction for India'. Recognising that the enterprise at Elswick was something out of the ordinary, *The Times* noted that the workers 'maintain their own library and newsrooms, and both they and their employers take a lively interest in educational questions'. Armstrong, it was recorded, had recently donated a handsome sum of money to the Newcastle Lit & Phil, with a view to making it more useful to 'a superior order of mechanics'.

Some elements of the press were less enthusiastic about Armstrong's latest invention, however. *Punch* was exercised about the popular thirst for deadly weaponry. On 12 March 1859, a fortnight or so after Armstrong's visit to the palace, the magazine

Armstrong's first gun was a light breech-loading field gun developed after the Crimean War. It fired elongated 5-pound shells rather than round balls, and its barrel was rifled rather than smooth.

Armstrong went on to design heavy naval guns, some weighing more than 100 tons. His guns were tried out against rival models at the government's Shoeburyness testing range on the Essex coast.

quoted the view of 'an insane Shakspearian student' who claimed that 'the Swan of Avon clearly foreshadowed Sir W. Armstrong's dubbing with ceremonial sword of knighthood in the lines "It is the sport to see the engineer/Hoist with his own petard."' Elsewhere in the same edition was a piece about the practice among 'old heraldic writers' of describing men who had received honours as 'sons of their works'. On this principle, asked the magazine, 'Will Sir W. Armstrong take it as an offence to be styled "son of a gun"?'

On 10 May, a sumptuous banquet was held at the Assembly Rooms in Newcastle in recognition of Armstrong's services to his country. The guests included Earl Grey, the lord lieutenant of Northumberland and son of the former prime minister Charles Grey, the Earl of Durham and Lord Ravensworth, the mayors of Newcastle and Tynemouth, and 200 people described by Sopwith as 'the most respectable inhabitants of the vicinity'. The Whig politician Sir George Grey, MP for Morpeth, presided. Armstrong gave an account of his latest discoveries relating to the design and manufacture of rifled artillery and shells. 'The dinner went off admirably well,' wrote Sopwith, noting that, in paying his tribute, Robert Stephenson had alluded to 'the great change effected in the character and capability of the skilled workmen in engineering factories'. In this, Armstrong had led the way, remarked Sopwith, 'in the excellent regulations at his works and by the admirable expositions of practical science which I have heard him address to his assembled workmen'.

Despite all the public acclamation, Armstrong was still happiest when solving mechanical problems, and he was soon busy with everyday matters such as advising Sopwith on the installation of hydraulic equipment. He had also embarked on a large-scale landscaping project at his estate in Jesmond Dene, including the installation of 'fine masses of ornamental rockwork', which had taken place under the direction of the naturalist John Hancock.

On a visit to the dene, Sopwith took a stroll with Armstrong and George Rendel during which he and Armstrong reminisced about their frequent walks together in former days, 'when, as I reminded him, he was apt to come out – as I thought, wonderfully strange for an attorney – on electricity, lights, magnetism, space and materialism, subjects on which he had well considered and readily grasped the prominent points of each. How often since then have I been surprised by his extreme aptitude in talking up, as it is called, the general features of any great problem or the study of science.'

As much as he might enjoy his occupations in the north, Armstrong was obliged by his new position to spend a large amount of time in London, among other activities mingling with the great and good – something he regarded as more a duty than a pleasure. 'Last night Sir William dined with Sir John Pakington [First Lord of the Admiralty] at eight and found the Marchioness of Salisbury at home at eleven,' wrote Sopwith. 'These invitations arise from the government's recognition of the new and important appointment made under their auspices, and in that point of view cannot but be gratifying – the more so as Lady Armstrong was included in the invitation to the "At Home" of the noble marchioness. So far, however, as the mere elements of rank or greatness – or fashion, pomp and display – are concerned, none cares less than Armstrong, whose views and feelings are rather too much in the opposite scale of absolute indifference and neglect.'

On 28 June, Armstrong gave the Queen a model of his gun that, at her express request, he had made especially for her. He told Sopwith about the encounter the following evening, when both men were attending a party hosted by the Rendels at their new home in Hyde Park Street. 'The beautiful model of the gun was yesterday presented by Sir William to HRH the Prince Consort or through him virtually to the Queen. Her Majesty and the Prince gave a private audience to Sir William at eleven o'clock, which lasted an hour and a half and the particulars of construction and contrivance were given in much detail – the Queen making many enquiries and evincing much care and judgment. The Prince of Wales was also present.'

By early August, operations were in full swing at the new Elswick Ordnance Works. A 70-pounder gun, the first of its kind, was nearing completion and work had started on building an even bigger gun – a 110-pounder. Meanwhile, Armstrong had been asked by Sidney Herbert, Palmerston's war secretary, to experiment with applying a new principle of rifling to the existing cast-iron ordnance. Fears of war with France had prompted Herbert to launch a campaign of military expansion, including a programme of fortifications along the south coast of England and elsewhere. When Armstrong's new gun design was inspected by Herbert and the Board of Admiralty it gave great satisfaction, but the pressure on Armstrong was starting to show; during a visit to Jesmond Dene, Sopwith noted his care-worn countenance.

On 21 October, the two men were in London for Stephenson's funeral, which came hard on the heels of Brunel's at Kensal Green cemetery a month earlier. Soon after ten o'clock, they walked past Stephenson's former home. 'As we were passing, the hearse was moving from the door,' wrote Sopwith. 'A large crowd was assembled and about a dozen mourning coaches and forty carriages were in attendance.'

By special permission of the Queen, Stephenson's funeral cortège was allowed to pass through Hyde Park on its way to Westminster Abbey; the entire route was lined by silent crowds. 'I drove with Sir William to Great George Street, where he went to join the Members of Council,' wrote Sopwith, 'and I reached the abbey at a few minutes after eleven. A large number of persons were already assembled. I took a place beside Mr Decimus Burton close to the entrance to the choir. From this time until 12, the numbers were greatly augmented. Men of every profession – many of them of the most distinguished rank in their respective walks – were to be seen. Every art and science was thus represented. On every face sincere grief and marked respect, nay reverence, seemed to be imprinted and at length – a few minutes after twelve o'clock – the solemn pealing of the organ, the chanting of the choristers and the deep-toned funeral bell indicated the arrival of the funeral procession.' On the day of Stephenson's funeral, all shipping lay silent on the Tyne, Wear and Tees; all work ceased in Newcastle and nearby towns to make way for services of remembrance; and flags were flown at half-mast.

On 4 November, Armstrong took up a further appointment, as superintendent of the Royal Gun Factory at Woolwich, where 3,000 men were employed. By the middle of the month, at a lunch with Sopwith at the Athenaeum, Armstrong admitted that all his time was taken up by business at Woolwich, 'where the entire management is now committed to his care as regards rifled artillery'. They met again at the club on Christmas Eve, when Armstrong explained that he was 'very actively engaged at Woolwich often to a late hour at night and a commodious house has been placed at his disposal'. Armstrong's assistant John Anderson (later the arsenal's general manager) would live at the house, but Armstrong would keep rooms for his own use.

Usually, when in London, Armstrong stayed with the Rendels, continuing a tradition established long before the death of James Rendel. 'I saw more than ever of Armstrong [at this time],' wrote Stuart later. 'Since he had to spend the greater part of his time in London, he lived in my mother's house and made her family his.'[9] Despite the necessity of being away from Newcastle for long periods, Armstrong accepted the presidency of the Lit & Phil, succeeding Robert Stephenson, who had occupied the post for the previous five years.

Meanwhile, he was contemplating the likelihood that, for the first time, his guns would be used in anger against a foreign foe. On 5 October, he had written to Meggie, 'Amongst other things, two batteries of my guns are to be got ready for China in six weeks from this date, and carriages, ammunition and equipments are all to be arranged for them.'

Britain and China had been engaged in hostilities for 20 years, since the outbreak in 1839 of the Opium Wars. Britain was seeking to increase its commercial penetration of China and was insisting on the ratification of the 1858 Treaty of Tientsin (Tianjin), which opened several ports in north-eastern China to foreign trade, and established a Chinese maritime customs service under British supervision. The failure to ratify prompted a British attack on the Taku forts guarding the Peiho River. When a British gunboat foray up the river came to grief, a larger, Anglo-French force was got ready to set sail for China early in 1860. This expedition would carry Armstrong breech-loaders.[10]

Another groundbreaking development under way in the defence field was the gradual replacement of wood by iron, and later steel, in the construction of ships. The building of Britain's first iron battleship, *Warrior*, had begun in the summer of 1859, after the award of the contract to the Thames Iron Shipbuilding Company. *Warrior* was intended to outclass her French equivalent, *La Gloire*, also under construction, which had an iron skin 4½ inches thick, attached to a wooden hull. *Warrior*'s hull was made entirely of iron and the ship was longer and narrower than *La Gloire* – all of which made it possible for her to travel through the water at speeds of up to 14 knots, 2 knots faster than her rival.

Naval artillery experts had at first been confused about how to respond to the advent of iron ships, since no conventional weapon would have been powerful enough to penetrate the new armour. However, the trials carried out under the auspices of the committee on rifled cannon had alerted them to the efficiency of Armstrong's guns, and they took particular interest in the 40-pounders and 70-pounders, as well as the relatively untried 110-pounders, which had a range of about 2½ miles.

In the event, *Warrior* was the first ship to be armed with Armstrong guns, carrying four 70-pounders and ten 110-pounders, a pattern that would be replicated in other ships of the Warrior class.[11] With half the weapons being built at Elswick and the other half at Woolwich, this was a very profitable turn of events as far as Armstrong was concerned. However, there was more than simply money at stake. As the naval historian Marshall Bastable has pointed out, the orders from the Admirality not only gave his business a good start but established his international reputation as 'the man whose guns were aboard the historic ship *Warrior*, the most powerful ship in the greatest navy in the world'.

8

A Bigger Bang

No sooner had Armstrong taken charge of the Royal Arsenal at Woolwich than the vultures started to circle. Every army officer who could dream up a reason for opposing this non-military upstart from Newcastle made his voice heard. As before, Armstrong's chief business adversary was Joseph Whitworth, who advocated the use of cast-steel and hexagonal rifling in gun construction. Whitworth insisted that he had been unfairly treated by the committee that had preferred Armstrong's gun to his. He pursued his cause with such vigour that, eventually, seven different official committees would be obliged to examine his claims.[1] Another man with a grudge was Colonel Eardley Wilmot, the former superintendent of the Woolwich factory, who had been forced to make way for Armstrong after showing scant enthusiasm for his gun.[2] Wilmot would prove a useful ally to Whitworth in the battle ahead. There was some opposition in the upper echelons of government and the armed forces, and there were other inventors who felt aggrieved that their creations had been passed over. Among the latter were Henry Bessemer and Theophilus Blakely, a retired captain of the Royal Artillery.

Bessemer, who had invented a revolutionary process for manufacturing 'mild steel' and who had set up his own steel works in Sheffield, had been making plans – before Armstrong's appointment – to produce guns from Bessemer steel at Woolwich. To his indignation, the war secretary, Sidney Herbert, consulted Armstrong, who declared that the new metal was quite unsuitable for the purpose. 'Why go to my rival?' complained Bessemer. 'Why go to the gentleman who has a scheme of his own to carry out instead of mine?'[3] Blakely, meanwhile, had designed a 'built-up' gun and presented it to the government for inspection in July 1854, several months before Armstrong came up with a similar design. At the time, Blakely's model evinced little interest but he took out a patent on it in 1855. When Armstrong's gun won official support in 1858, Blakely claimed that it was based on his invention. He began a determined, bitter – and ultimately unsuccessful – campaign to have it publicly acknowledged that he had been first with the design.

Armstrong's wrangle with Blakely, coupled with his attempt to collaborate with Brunel on gun design during the Crimean War, had crystallised his opposition to the patent laws, which, being derived from medieval laws on monopolies, were in urgent need of reform. In this, Armstrong and Brunel were agreed. Believing that patents stifled invention rather than encouraging it, Brunel had refused to protect any of his own ideas – with the result that Armstrong's work on Brunel's gun design had to be halted when it was discovered that a patent had recently been taken out for the same idea. Armstrong used this event to illustrate his opposition to the patent laws, insisting that 'it was unjust to give the monopoly to another without proof of priority of idea'. He argued that cases of this kind would continue to occur because 'similarity of circumstances will constantly suggest similar ideas to different minds, and the man who first applies to the patent office puts a stop upon all others who are directing attention to the same subject'. This complemented Brunel's view that 'most good things are being thought of by many persons at the same time'.[4]

In July 1861, Armstrong explained his views to the Society of Mechanical Engineers in Sheffield. 'We are obstructed in every direction by patented inventions which will never be reduced to practice by those who hold them, but which embrace ideas capable of useful application if freed from monopoly,' he complained. In an impassioned argument that drew heavily on his own experience, he insisted that the merit of invention was found not merely in an original idea but in 'the subsequent elaboration, and in the successful struggle with difficulties, unknown to the mere theorist, and often requiring years of labour, blended with disappointment, for their removal'. He claimed that scientific advancement was being obstructed by the very laws intended to encourage its progress.

'Nothing can be more irrational than to give equal privileges to the mere schemer and to the man who gives actual effect to an invention. Primary ideas ought to be the common property of all inventors, and protection, if we are to have it at all, should be sparingly awarded to those persons alone who, by their labour and intellect, give available reality to ideas.'

Later that month, in a speech to the Patent Law Reform Association in Manchester, Armstrong reminded his audience that he had become an inventor before he had had much money or been engaged in a business where he could exploit his discoveries. 'In some instances I have availed myself of the patent laws and in others not,' he said, 'and I am satisfied that if those laws had not existed I should have been substantially in the same position as at present.' He reserved his most devastating fire, however, for the injustice of the system. 'Philosophers who furnish the light of science to guide to useful discovery go altogether unrewarded and unrecognized,' he argued. 'Practical men, who, like James Watt and George Stephenson, devote the best part of their lives to perfecting inventions of immense importance to the world seldom derive from patents any greater emolument than would flow to them without the aid of a restrictive system, while they are frequently involved in tormenting litigation about the priority of idea.' On the other hand, there were many people who had become very rich even though their only merit had been 'promptitude in seizing upon and monopolizing some expedient that lay on the very surface of things, and required no forcing atmosphere of protection for its discovery'.

The iniquity of the patent laws was a subject that continued to exercise Armstrong, as the *Economist* magazine noted in June 1869: 'Sir William Armstrong complains of "the necessity which I am under of taking out patents, not for the purpose of obtaining for myself a monopoly, but simply for the purpose of preventing other persons from excluding me from my own inventions".' He came up against all sorts of opposition to his stance, epitomised by an article in *Scientific American* that proclaimed, 'Not content with appropriating the ideas of others right and left, he would have larceny legalized by the world.' Much of the heat was taken out of the issue by a series of legislative measures, culminating with the Patents, Designs, and Trade Marks Act of 1883, which included a large reduction in the initial cost of a patent, making the system accessible to many more people.[5]

The most effective opposition to the Armstrong gun was directed at its performance rather than its evolution, however. In 1860, the gun was used in the field in China 'with remarkable effect', according to *The Times*, proving 'a weapon of great power and wonderful precision'[6] and helping to secure an Anglo-French victory against the Chinese. The Duke of Cambridge, the army commander-in-chief, insisted that the expedition had established beyond doubt the weapon's excellence. But the previous year, during a debate in the House of Commons, Sidney Herbert, the war secretary – while acknowledging that the gun was 'a discovery of the utmost importance' – had pointed out that there was 'some doubt as to its efficiency in naval warfare'.[7] So far, only the smaller models, which had been tested at Shoeburyness in 1858, had proved themselves in battle. The larger 110-pounders, which weighed 4 tons, had been manufactured in haste without proper trials. A later government report noted that the political necessities of the day did not 'allow time for maturing the design previous to its manufacture', so 'the first 100 of these were constructed before any experiments on them had been concluded'.[8]

As Armstrong was well aware, the problem with the larger breech-loading guns stemmed from a part of the breech mechanism called the 'vent-piece'.[9] There were claims that, when the 110-pounder gun was fired, the vent-piece could be damaged or blown out altogether – causing a terrible hazard for gunners. In the smaller guns, the vent-pieces were of sufficient strength to be able to withstand the explosion of their charge, but the more powerful explosion in the 110-pounder led to much more unpredictable results. Also, tests had shown that projectiles from the gun were not able to penetrate iron, convincing Armstrong that, for the time being anyway, breech-loading had reached the limits of its strength with the 110-pounder.[10] Future development of breech-loaders – which did not start until the late 1870s – would depend on the

William Armstrong at the age of 21, in the guise of a Byronic hero, painted by James Ramsay, a friend of his patron, Armorer Donkin. Armstrong was studying law at the time, at London's Inns of Court.

Armstrong's mother, Anne, a member of the ambitious Potter family, was 'a lady of considerable literary culture, greatly beloved by all who knew her'.

William Armstrong senior worked his way up from lowly merchant's clerk to leading member of Newcastle's social elite.

Margaret Ramshaw, who married Armstrong in 1835, played a crucial role in every aspect of her husband's life. The couple had no children.

Armstrong's only sibling, Anne, died at the age of 25, barely two years after her marriage to William Watson, a glamorous former soldier.

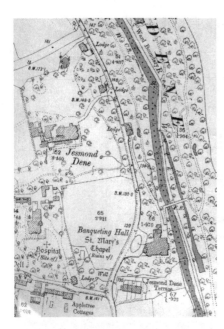

An 1898 map of Jesmond Dene shows Armstrong's house of the same name and its proximity to the banqueting hall.

The Jesmond Dene banqueting hall occupied a prominent position on the west bank of the Ouseburn. Built in 1862 by John Dobson, it was later extended by Richard Norman Shaw.

Patron: Armorer Donkin, a rich bachelor, invested in Armstrong's commercial ventures and left most of his estate to him.

Diarist: Thomas Sopwith (left) kept a journal for 57 years, recording the exploits of his many friends. He is shown here with the balloonist James Glaisher.

Mentor: James Meadows Rendel prepared the way for Armstrong's business career and encouraged him to develop his first gun.

Surrogate son: George Rendel, who inherited his father's engineering talent, was virtually adopted by the childless Armstrongs.

Ulysses S. Grant (with right hand visible), a pugnacious Union general who served as US president from 1869 to 1877, visited Elswick in the late 1870s to inspect monster guns.

Testing an early Armstrong gun on the moors above Allenheads in the Pennines – as captured in a watercolour sketch in the diary of Thomas Sopwith.

Visiting Britain in 1896, the Chinese statesman Li Hung Chang was entertained at Cragside by Armstrong and Andrew Noble (centre).

Built at the Elswick shipyard and launched in 1886, the Chinese cruiser *Chih Yuan* was sunk eight years later in a battle with the Japanese on the Yalu river.

Cragside as envisaged by Richard Norman Shaw in the early 1870s, with the rock garden in the foreground. Shaw is reputed to have sketched his initial scheme for the house in a single day.

The west or glen front of Cragside as it appears in the early 21st century.

availability of improved steel and new propellants. In the meantime, he turned his attention to rifled muzzle-loaders.

Meanwhile, Joseph Whitworth had been pursuing his campaign against Armstrong with determination and building up support in official circles. 'If the disciples of the Whitworth school were to be believed,' reported *The Times* later, 'the Royal Navy had been supplied at a fabulous cost with guns that are worse than useless. Bows and arrows, according to these authorities, were more serviceable than the Armstrong pieces of large calibre, for the former annoyed the enemy without danger to the archer, while the latter were said to be constantly bursting or blowing out their vent-pieces, and scattering havoc among the gunners.' Although the argument about breech-loaders rumbled on for several years, it soon became largely irrelevant as far as naval defence was concerned. Originally conceived as field weapons, the breech-loaders could also do considerable damage to wooden vessels, but one development had changed everything: the advent of the ironclad warship. The 110-pounder had clearly not been designed to sink an ironclad.

As part of a strategic defence review, the Palmerston government had come up with a plan to construct coastal and offshore forts to protect government dockyards and arsenals from attack by enemy (particularly French) ironclads. Work started in July 1860 on building two forts to flank the approach to Portsmouth, which, along with Plymouth, was one of the two most important naval bases in southern England. Located off Spithead in the Solent, the forts would be separated by 2,400 yards of water – so their protection would depend on being armed with guns powerful enough to send a projectile through an ironclad hull at a distance of up to 1,200 yards.

Realising that his existing breech-loaders were inadequate for the purpose – since generating the required speed of shot over such a distance would destroy the breech mechanism – Armstrong began to develop much larger built-up guns that could be loaded through the muzzle. The eventual result was a new class of 'monster' guns: rifled muzzle-loaders weighing 6, 12, and 22 tons.[11] Based on the size of shells they could fire, these were called 150-pounders, 300-pounders, and 600-pounders; they were also known as 'shunt guns' from a modification to their rifling mechanism. The two larger models were nicknamed 'Little Will' and 'Big Will' after their creator.

Popular criticism of Britain's fort-building programme, always vigorous, had been fuelled in March 1862 by a key incident in the American Civil War that took place at Hampton Roads, near the mouth of the James River in Virginia: the first encounter in history between two ironclads, the *Monitor* (for the Union) and the *Virginia*, formerly known as the *Merrimack* (for the Confederacy).[12] Although *Virginia* caused plenty of damage to the Union's wooden ships blockading the harbour, neither of the two ironclads could get the better of the other, despite a closely fought battle lasting several hours. The inconclusive outcome confirmed to sceptics that ironclads were impervious to even the most powerful guns, even when fired at close range – and led directly to the suspension of work on the Spithead forts.

Meanwhile, however, Armstrong's new muzzle-loaders were being put to the test at the Shoeburyness artillery range. The first trials of the 300-pounder took place on 9 April 1862, witnessed by the Duke of Cambridge and, representing the Admirality, the Duke of Somerset and Lord Clarence Paget.

The gun was tried at a distance of 200 yards against a target replicating the strength of *Warrior*, Britain's first ironclad, whose all-iron hull was 4½ inches thick. Although the results were supposed to be kept secret, the next day's *Times* published an exuberant account of one of the tests: 'With an indescribable crash that mingled fearfully with the report of the gun, the shot struck upon a comparatively uninjured place [on the target], shattering the iron mass before it into little crumbs of metal, splintering the teak into fibres literally as small as pins.' Another shot went completely through the target, reported the newspaper, and 'even the fondest believers in the invulnerability of our present ironclads were obliged to confess that against such artillery, at such ranges, their plates and sides were almost as penetrable as wooden ships'.

Although it was soon obvious that the *The Times*'s report was exaggerated – the shot had not actually passed right through the target – it suited the government to let it be believed and, following a fiery debate in the House of Commons in early June, it helped Palmerston to win a vote of confidence on the issue of forts and guns. The Duke of Cambridge continued to back Armstrong, reiterating the inventor's insistence that he would soon be able to make a rifled gun that would achieve at 2,200 yards what was now possible only at 200. Armstrong himself believed that, however sophisticated the armour of ships might become, it would be always be possible to produce a weapon powerful enough to penetrate it. After his first success against the Warrior target on 9 April, he wrote to *The Times*: 'We must be prepared for vessels stronger than these – stronger even than the *Warrior*, and should, therefore, go on increasing the size of our guns until we reach some practical limit. The weight of such guns, however objectionable, must be accepted as a necessity, and ships must be adapted for their reception.'

When Queen Victoria asked her prime minister to explain why work on the Spithead forts had come to a halt,[13] Palmerston pointed to the inconclusive result of the battle between the ironclads at Hampton Roads. In a letter of 22 June, he described why the defence of the forts posed such a problem, but he reassured the Queen that Armstrong was near to finding a solution. 'The proposed forts at the east end of the Isle of Wight will be 2,400 yards apart, so that a ship steaming through the middle of the space between them would be 1,200 yards from either fort,' wrote Palmerston, 'and it yet remains to be seen whether any gun can send a shot which will make an impression on the iron plating of a ship at so great a distance. Sir William Armstrong says he can and will make a gun that will send a shot which even at that distance will pierce armour plating.'

At this point, Joseph Whitworth re-entered the fray with renewed vigour. Determined, as he saw it, to right past wrongs, Whitworth set about enlisting the support of all sorts of powerful personalities, taking up residence near Westminster and lobbying persistently until he had built up a 'Whitworth party' in the country. He, too, had been working on the development of giant muzzle-loaders, with the aim of penetrating the Warrior target before Armstrong could – and this he succeeded in doing. On 25 September, a projectile fired by a Whitworth gun from 600 yards went right through the iron plate, and Whitworth demanded that he be given proper recognition for the achievement. The gun fired on this occasion was described by *The Times* as 'an ordnance muzzle-loader manufactured at Woolwich on Sir William Armstrong's wrought-iron principle, but with the beautiful hexagonal bore of Mr Whitworth's mode of rifling'. The Whitworth system of rifling small arms had earlier drawn high praise from the military authorities – especially his 1857 design for a gun to replace the unreliable Enfield rifle. Even the Queen was an enthusiast; on 2 July 1860, she had opened the first meeting of the National Rifle Association at Wimbledon by firing a Whitworth rifle and hitting the bullseye at a range of 400 yards.[14] After an exchange of fusillades between Whitworth and Armstrong – mostly conducted through an interminable and highly detailed correspondence in the columns of *The Times* – a new select committee on ordnance was asked to look into Whitworth's claims.

The theory had emerged that, as signalled by *The Times*, the Whitworth gun that had proved so successful against the Warrior target had in fact been based on Armstrong's design. The crucial witness on this point was John Anderson, the civilian engineer appointed as Armstrong's assistant at Woolwich in 1859, who had supervised the production of breech-loaders. The committee learnt that Anderson had looked at the design of Whitworth's cast-iron gun and, with Whitworth's agreement, changed it into an Armstrong built-up gun made of wrought iron.

To get across his case to the committee, Armstrong relied heavily on the forensic skill of Stuart Rendel, the 28-year-old son of his old friend James, and younger brother of George, then in charge of Elswick Ordnance Works. Stuart had graduated in Classics from Oxford and aimed to become a barrister, but he had not begun to practise law before getting embroiled in what became known as 'the battle of the guns'. Stuart's first motivation appears to have been loyalty towards his father's old friend. 'Armstrong found that he was being exposed to publicity in a form peculiarly obnoxious to his reserved and reticent character,' Stuart wrote in his memoirs. 'He suffered acutely under the sting of heated and personal controversy.'[15] The young man had already been useful to Armstrong in a secretarial capacity, providing administrative and legal advice, and dealing with official correspondence, 'and I became almost necessary to him when he was confronted with serious controversy in the press and in Parliament'.

Although Stuart Rendel described himself as 'half man of culture, half man of the workshop', he never showed the same inclination towards engineering as his three brothers, Alexander Meadows (who had taken over management of the Rendel family firm), George, and Hamilton. In fact, Stuart suffered from a disability caused by too much rowing while at school: 'My spine became curved, my false ribs stuck together, all prospect of making anything of my youth and education vanished,' he wrote later.[16] As a result he developed a 'scholar's stoop', which became pronounced in later life.

By closely briefing Armstrong's supporters on the committee, and by ensuring that John Anderson made it quite clear that Whitworth had used an Armstrong weapon to penetrate the Warrior target, Stuart Rendel was vital in helping Armstrong defend his reputation as the man who made the first built-up gun. He was spurred on by the strength of feeling reflected in Armstrong's complaint that Whitworth and others had had 'guns made for them in the Royal Gun Factory upon my principles, by my methods and according to drawings supplied by persons who have derived all their information and experience under me'. Armstrong was particularly upset that 'these guns should be used in competition with my own guns and should go forth to the world as the inventions of my opponents'.

It could not be denied, however, that a Whitworth shell had been the first to pass right through the Warrior target. Since both Armstrong and Whitworth said that they had now developed weapons capable of penetrating the target from a range of at least 1,000 yards, the government instigated a competition to decide which gun would be most likely to sink ironclads more effectively. In January 1863, the Special Committee on the Armstrong and Whitworth Guns was established by the Admiralty and the War Office to put the rival claims to the test. Although both of the guns under examination were modelled on the Armstrong built-up principle, each used different projectiles and each had a distinct form of rifling. As Armstrong would repeatedly insist, 'The projectile should rule the gun, not the gun the projectile.' In this instance, he used conical shells with between three and six studs attached to them to produce the required spin as they passed through the gun barrel, while Whitworth preferred flat-headed shells and hexagonal rifling.

The Armstrong Whitworth Committee was largely composed of naval and military officers, but each of the principal players was allowed to choose a civilian representative. Stuart Rendel was appointed to represent Armstrong in succession to William Pole, professor of civil engineering at University College London, who had found the strain of attending the relentless series of weapons tests unendurable. Whitworth was represented first by the marine-engine builder John Penn and then by John Macdonald, the manager of *The Times*, but, according to Rendel, his greatest champion on the committee was General Sir Lintorn Simmonds of the Royal Engineers. Rendel found the debating sessions much more challenging than the work in the field. 'The attendance at all the experiments on land and sea, during which some fifty thousand rounds were fired and the result of each round examined, was of great interest to me and was unaccompanied by any anxiety,' he wrote. 'We burst some guns with some risk to ourselves and, of course, the excitement over the competitions was sometimes extreme ... I led the case for Armstrong, while General Simmonds led the case for Whitworth, and how we came to produce a report generally favourable to Armstrong I can scarcely understand.'

Rendel did not doubt the importance of his own contribution, but what amounted to almost three years of observing numerous tests and analysing endless streams of statistics eventually took its toll: 'I over-strained either nerves or mind or both, and have suffered from over-sensitiveness of the brain from that day to this.'[17]

The question of whether projectiles could penetrate armour at the required distance would be resolved on 16 March 1864 when Armstrong's 600-pounder – 'Big Will' – fired a 344-pound round steel shell which smashed through an iron plate 11 inches thick, and a separate plate, 6 inches thick, behind it. The shell struck the front target at a speed of 1,560 feet per second. 'Never, probably, has a more tremendous blow been struck by human agency,' reported *The Times*. 'The mass of steel driven by the tremendous charge of powder must have struck the target with a power almost inconceivable, for everything went down before it. The solid oak beams behind the plate were crushed into splinters, and the plate itself hurled bodily back against the 6-inch target and split into two pieces. The 11-inch plate was torn apart.' It was a personal triumph for Armstrong, but it did not end the competition with Whitworth – and it would be two more years before the Armstrong Whitworth Committee was ready to deliver its report.

As the arguments about his guns hotted up, Armstrong had found it necessary to cultivate his allies in government and the defence establishment by involving himself in London high society. He often stood back from the crowd at the more glittering occasions, however – not through feelings of intimidation but because he saw himself as an outsider, as suggested in a letter to Meggie written in October 1860: 'On Friday I dined with the Peels and [there were] the Duchess of Cambridge and the Princess Mary with a small party of diplomatic people from some of the Embassies... Thackeray and Garibaldi were at a tremendous discourse with the whole party – the former for his lectures on the four Georges and the latter for his revolutionizing tendencies. How can you account, said the Duchess to me, for this Garibaldi fever. I cannot account for it, I replied, but I must confess to being somewhat smitten with it. Uh! said she, turning good-humouredly to General Peel, I see your friend is a "radical". I was reminded of poor Mrs Ibbetson who often called me by that name and in much the same manner.'

Meeting his social obligations could seem closer to an endurance test than a pleasure. 'I went to the levee yesterday and got through all smoothly,' Armstrong wrote to Meggie in March 1861. 'The Queen seemed in good humour ... I must say my taste for court does not increase.' It was a time of tension, when the controversy about his breech-loaders was coming to a head: 'Today the Army Estimates came on the House of Commons and I am rather looking out for squalls. However, it is not my fault if Baring [the under-secretary at the War Office] is not well prepared for any attack. There have been lots of lies in some of the papers of late and I dare say that some of my opponents will found charges against the government and myself upon them. I rather wish they may ... I consider that I am at the most critical stage just now and if I get well through with all I have in hand the course will then be easy.'

A few months later, in his Sheffield speech, Armstrong argued persuasively in favour of maintaining strong defences. Although usually wary of making any moral or political pronouncements on a public platform, he had been prompted by vociferous critics into taking a stand on the perennially controversial subject of war.

'We shall all agree in condemning war and deploring the suffering it entails, but we must not regard it as destitute of all admixture of good,' he said. 'The conquests of ancient Rome scattered the germs of civilization over the whole of the then known world, and similar effects have attended many of the conquests of more modern times ... Courage, patriotism, self-devotion and honour have found their brightest examples among those who have followed the profession of arms.' He went on to advocate pragmatism in international disputes: 'We know that nations, like individuals, are liable to quarrel, and when they do so, having no common jurisdiction to control them, they resort to arms. So long, therefore, as any one nation maintains its armaments, it is an absolute necessity that others should do the same, unless they choose, by their inability to resist, to tempt a rupture, and are content to succumb to the event of its occurrence.'

Armstrong was under intense scrutiny from the press at this period, not only in mainstream newspapers but also in popular periodicals such as *Punch*, which had been keeping an eye on him ever since he burst on to the national stage in early 1859. *Punch* took delight in painting him as a warmonger and in making fun of the absurd arms race under way in Britain between the navy (synonymous with the Admiralty) and the artillery branch of the army. The navy was claiming it could build ships that were so strongly reinforced that they would resist any missile. The artillery, represented on this occasion by Armstrong, was out to prove that, regardless of the strength of any ship, a weapon could be made that was powerful enough to penetrate it. Meanwhile, as an apocalyptic mood took hold, influential religious figures were 'proclaiming the millennium' – which amounted to predicting the second coming of Christ – and ordinary people were complaining that taxation was spiralling out of control. *Punch* ridiculed this state of affairs in an article of 19 April 1862 called 'Pull Armstrong, Pull Admiralty' and subtitled 'a probable chronology':

1860. MR ARMSTRONG of Newcastle-upon-Tyne invents Rifled Ordnance that will knock any ship to pieces. He is knighted and the Admiralty is benighted.

1861. The Admiralty recovers, and invents iron ships that resist any known cannon-balls.

1862. SIR WILLIAM ARMSTRONG invents a gun that smashes the Iron Ships into blacksmithereens. The Admiralty collapses.

1863. The Admiralty re-expands and invents Platina Ships fastened with diamond cement, and Sir William Armstrong's balls fly to pieces like bons-bons.
MR GLADSTONE doubles the Income-Tax.

1864. SIR WILLIAM ARMSTRONG invents Brazen Thunderbolts (supposed to be the original Jupiters) and in a pleasing experiment sends the greater part of the British Fleet to the bottom of the sea.

1865. The Admiralty invents Torpedo vessels which sail under water, and below any range of guns.
SIR WILLIAM ARMSTRONG tears his hair and swears in the Newcastle dialect.

1866. SIR WILLIAM ARMSTRONG invents a Vertical gun that discharges Greek fire straight down, and a second time he destroys the greater part of the British fleet. The Lords of the

Admiralty are about to hang themselves, when a thought
strikes them, and they don't.
MR GLADSTONE again doubles the Income-Tax.

1867. DR. CUMMING, who has for some weeks been having
in his coals by the sack only, suddenly proclaims the
millennium. As there is now to be peace everywhere, the
Admiralty does not invent anything, but waits to see.

To test DR. CUMMING's veracity, and to find out whether
lions will lie down with kids [lambs], the Zoologicial Society
(against the advice of their excellent Secretary, MR. SCLATER)
lets loose their biggest lion while a charity school is in the
Gardens. As the lion, instead of lying down with a kid, only
lies down to digest him, the Admiralty thinks there is some
mistake somewhere, and determines to invent a new fleet.
MR. GLADSTONE once more doubles the Income-Tax.
1868. The Admiralty invents a Stone Fleet, with cork keels,
and defies SIR WILLIAM ARMSTRONG.

1869. SIR WILLIAM ARMSTRONG invents the Hannibal, or
Alp-shell, which contains the strongest vinegar, and melts the
Stone ships. Having for the third time destroyed the British
Fleet, he is raised to the peerage as LORD BOMB.

1870. The Admiralty invents an Aërial Fleet, which sails in the
clouds, out of shot range, and the First Lord takes a double
sight at SIR WILLIAM ARMSTRONG.
MR GLADSTONE a fourth time doubles the Income-Tax.

1871. LORD BOMB invents a Balloon battering-train, and in
an experimental discharge brings down all the British fleet
into the German ocean.

1872. The Admirality, in desperation, invents a Subterranean
Fleet, which is to be conveyed by tunnels to all the Colonies,
but MR GLADSTONE blandly suggests that, as everybody

now pays twice his income in taxes, the people may object to further imposts unless some proof of economy is given.

Government therefore stop the pensions of a hundred superannuated clerks, discharge some extra night-porters at the Treasury, and bring in Estimates for the Subterranean Fleet.

1873. LORD BOMB invents his Typhaeons, or Earthquake Shells, and suffocates the British Fleet in the Tasmania Tunnel. MR GLADSTONE a fifth time doubles the Income-Tax.

1874. THE EMPEROR OF THE FRENCH proclaims the Millennium, which of course immediately occurs, no more warships are wanted, and the collectors remit the quarter's Income-Tax not yet due.
LORD BOMB invents his Volcano Fireworks in honour of the occasion, and by some accident burns up the Public.

The controversy about the doings of Lord Bomb spread its tentacles far and wide, even provoking interest in the colonies. In Australia, for example, *Melbourne Punch*, which had begun publication a few years earlier, carried an article on 10 July 1862 relaying the 'latest news from England': 'Sir William Armstrong has designed a revolving breech-loader to carry a ball as big as a hogshead, a single discharge from which would send a shot through the great wall of China and leave a clean orifice.'

A contemporary group portrait by Thomes Jones Barker, *The Intellect and Valour of Britain*, reflects Armstrong's national standing in the early 1860s. The 36 men depicted in the painting include Palmerston (Prime Minister), Gladstone (Chancellor of the Exchequer) and Russell (Foreign Secretary), shown discussing the terms of the recent free trade treaty with France with its main architect, Richard Cobden MP. Another group is focused on Professor David Brewster demonstrating his lenticular telescope to a group that includes the writers Dickens and Tennyson as well as other leading scientists such as Faraday and Murchison. But the largest group, on the right of the portrait, centres on Sir William Armstrong 'explaining the peculiar structure of his famous cannon' to a clutch of generals and field marshals with the architect Charles Barry, the explorer David Livingstone, and the writer William Thackeray in attendance. On one side of Armstrong sits Robert Stephenson, engineer and MP for Whitby, whose death in 1859 had caused an outpouring of national grief.

In August 1863, following an Anglo-Japanese diplomatic incident, Armstrong 110-pounders were used in a British bombardment of Kagoshima at the south-western tip of Japan. Some of the vent-pieces were reported to have blown out, prompting a renewed attack by the gunmaker's critics. Despite Armstrong's insistence that the 110-pounder, while not perfect, had been falsely maligned, its fate was sealed when, during another expedition to Japan, the vent-piece again appeared unreliable.[18]

In a later correspondence with Lord Clarence Paget of the Admiralty, Armstrong hinted at the possibility that there may have been a deliberate attempt to damage his standing through false reports about the 110-pounder. 'It is perhaps scarcely fair to connect my name so emphatically with the 110-pounder breech-loader – the least successful of my guns,' he wrote, 'and to disconnect it from my larger muzzle-loaders, such as the 6- and 12-ton guns – acknowledged by your lordship to have given highly satisfactory results.'[19]

In the event, the Admiralty concluded that the 110-pounder gun was not suitable as a naval weapon, and by the end of 1865 all breech-loaders had been withdrawn from service; this type of gun would not be adopted again by the British armed forces for another 20 years.

The intense conservatism of leading military officers hastened Armstrong's eventual rift with the government. Some apparently opposed the breech-loader in principle, arguing that it was much harder to maintain than the familiar muzzle-loader. There was also a controversy about the cost of the Elswick operation, and an official enquiry concluded that half of the £500,000 spent at Elswick during the period in question might have been saved if the government had asked Woolwich to fulfil all its defence requirements. The financial basis of the report was fiercely contested by the Elswick managers, some of whom believed that the government was using the dispute as an excuse for capitulating to service diehards.

In September 1862, the contract that had been signed three and a half years earlier between Armstrong and the government was suspended, and production of artillery at Elswick ground to a halt. Over the next few months, all government orders were transferred to Woolwich. According to Marshall Bastable, during the period of the agreement, about 3,000 Armstrong guns of all sizes had been manufactured, of which about half were made at Elswick, and the total revenue for the Elswick Ordnance Company in the years from 1858 to the end of 1862 was more than £1 million. Now, the absence of government orders combined with a ban on overseas sales imposed by the 1859 deal brought the Elswick firm to the brink of bankruptcy and the directors sought compensation.[20] (They eventually settled for £85,000, more than £19,000 of which was in payment for machinery and stores.)

The crisis that had arisen between Armstrong and the defence establishment was kept under wraps during W. E. Gladstone's visit to Newcastle in October 1862 – an episode that soon became internationally notorious for Gladstone's disclosure of sympathy for the Confederate states in the American Civil War (in spite of official British neutrality). Armstrong was among the assembled worthies in the town hall to whom the chancellor's revelatory speech was addressed.

Following a ceremonial procession along the Tyne from Gateshead to Tynemouth, Gladstone spoke to a large crowd at South Shields, describing the tremendous impression made on him by the endeavour and industriousness he had witnessed on Tyneside: 'I know not where to seek – even in this busy country – a spot or district in which we perceive so extraordinary and multifarious a combination of the great branches of mining, manufacturing, trading and shipbuilding industry, and I greatly doubt whether the like can be shown, not only within the limits of this land, but upon the whole surface of the globe.'

The spirit of optimism prevailing in Newcastle at the time was reflected at Elswick, where the workers and directors refused to be defeated by the withdrawal of government patronage. While Armstrong himself remained Engineer of Rifled Ordnance and might have continued his work at Woolwich on the development of his successful muzzle-loaders, he was put under pressure from the Elswick directors, especially Stuart Rendel, to return to Newcastle and help to secure the future of the ordnance works. In his talks with the chief, Rendel highlighted foreign interest in Armstrong guns, in particular a recent enquiry from the Brazilian government. Having applied in vain to Elswick, which was then under War Office monopoly, the Brazilians had instead placed orders with Joseph Whitworth in Manchester. 'Nothing could be more unfortunate for the reputation of the Armstrong gun,' wrote Rendel, 'than that it should be known by the British public that foreign governments were preferring an English gun of a rival system.' He warned Armstrong that he was in danger of being ousted from his pre-eminent position in the armaments field.

Armstrong insisted that, given his past commitments to the British government and people, he could not honourably start selling guns to foreign powers so soon after leaving office, but he was influenced by Rendel's argument that 'the manufacture of arms for foreign powers was far from an unpatriotic act'. Rendel's reasoning was that, if Britain sold arms to foreign countries, those countries would then be 'dependent on us for their munitions of war', which would increase British influence in the world. Armstrong still looked on the matter with 'much indifference', but he made a concession. 'If these are your opinions,' he told Rendel, 'you are perfectly at liberty to try to give them effect, and if you can obtain any orders for Elswick by all means do so, and to make it worth your while we will give you five per cent commission upon the orders you bring us.'

It was not only his concern about the future of Elswick but also his sense of obligation to his friends and business partners that finally prompted Armstrong to act. On 5 February 1863, he wrote to Sir George Cornewall Lewis at the War Office, pointing out that the termination of the agreement between the government and Elswick Ordnance would leave the company 'burdened with a much larger plant than is covered by their guarantee'. Friends who had invested large amounts of money in Elswick felt that they had a claim on him to join their firm and 'lend my aid in rendering their unrecovered expenditure productive', he explained. 'As I cannot join the Elswick company in capacity to be useful without interference with my official duties, I am induced to tender my resignation, relinquishing, of course, all claim to further payment.' He said, however, that he would be willing to give the War Office any advice it needed on the development of ordnance. Armstrong later noted that, from the time that the Elswick contracts were cancelled by the government, the firm had 'no alternative but to commence a new career, based on foreign support'.

As surprised as everyone else by the turn of events, *The Times* reassured its readers that government weaponry would continue to be produced at Elswick, 'This resignation was, we believe, as unexpected as it was unwelcome at the War Office,' the newspaper reported. 'The causes are wholly unconnected with the forthcoming experimental trials between the Armstrong and Whitworth guns, and Sir William only retires that he may attend more closely than his official duties permitted to the extensive works of the Elswick Ordnance company, in the success of which he has so large an interest. That company will, as hitherto, continue to manufacture rifled ordnance both for the army and navy.'

When, a week later, the War Office replied to Armstrong's letter, the tone of regret was clear. 'The offer of your resignation being perfectly spontaneous, and the result of arrangements of a private and personal nature, altogether unconnected with your official position as Engineer for Rifled Ordnance and Superintendent of the Royal Gun Factories,' wrote Lewis's subordinate, 'Sir George Lewis has only to express his acquiescence in the course which you desire to adopt; but he cannot permit your official connection with this department to cease without conveying to you, as I am now directed to do, his high sense of the zealous and efficient manner in which you have invariably discharged your public duties, and of the advantage which Her Majesty's Government have derived from your services while holding the appointments which you have now resigned.'

But it was too late. They had allowed him to slip through their fingers. Armstrong was already back in Newcastle and about to embark on a period of expansion in both his professional and personal life which would see him fêted all around the world, from Valparaiso to Tokyo – and which would eventually make him one of the richest and most influential men in Europe.

9

Restless Spirits

On 1 May 1862, the International Exhibition opened in London's south Kensington, on the site where the Natural History Museum and the Science Museum now stand. It would last for five months and attract more than six million visitors. According to the popular magazine *The World*, 'instead of the Crystal Fountain [which had captivated visitors to the Great Exhibition of 1851], the cynosure of neighbouring eyes was the Armstrong gun ... none overlooked the queerly shaped gun with massive breech-piece. During the preceding years this weapon made no little noise in the world [but], as Sir William quietly remarks, the battle of the guns is not over yet.' The *London Review* commented on 'the beautiful specimens of Armstrong guns, showing by the veining of their surface the twisted structure of the iron. The separate coils are also exhibited of all sizes and in all stages of their manufacture.' Another set of guns that made an unforgettable impact at the Kensington exhibition were those of Alfred Krupp. The *Spectator* described 'ladies standing in mute delight' at the sight of Krupp's weapons and men dreaming of 'the battle music of the future'.

On 5 July, Johnny Watson wrote to Lady Armstrong in Jesmond to commiserate on the death of her mother, Mrs Ramshaw. Johnny mentioned that he had met his uncle by chance at the exhibition and had related a conversation overheard in the crowd: 'I was fortunate enough to come in for a description which he gave of *the* gun and its belongings. Of course, a fairish crowd soon collected, to whom the lecturer was unknown even by sight. Of whom one said to his friend, "Ah! There's a fellow thinks he knows all about it." "Yes," said the other. "Armstrong would be rather surprised if he heard his gun described *that* way." Such, you see, is the effect of invisible fame.'

In the same letter, Johnny recalled 'the many acts of kindness which, in my boyhood, I received both from [Mrs Ramshaw] and from your father. I dare say you well remember the rides he used to give me on the old grey.' Since the loss of his own mother in his infancy, Johnny Watson had been peculiarly close to the Armstrong family, even when he was of such a young age to know little about it. And in the past two years he had come to rely more on his relationship with William and Meggie following the sudden death of his father, William Watson, Armstrong's early mentor.

A glittering legal career had been rudely cut short when Watson senior had suffered a heart attack in court, while addressing a jury at Welshpool in Montgomeryshire on 12 March 1860, and died the next day. After his youthful military exploits, Watson had made his mark in public life, serving as Liberal MP for Kinsale in the south-west of Ireland and, later, for Hull. Having excelled as a barrister and author of law books, in 1856 he became a baron of the Exchequer (a judicial position that no longer exists) and was honoured with a knighthood. Baron Watson would be remembered not only for his 'hearty and forcible style of address' but also for his 'friendly disposition and cordial bonhomie'.[1] His death meant that the only surviving familial link between Armstrong and his sister, Anne, was her depressive son, Johnny, then aged 32.

Baron Watson's second wife, Mary, was herself in frail health, as indicated in a letter sent by her sister to Jesmond on the evening of the baron's death. 'Dear Lady Armstrong, I feel how anxiously you will look for some account of my dear sister under her sudden bereavement ... I would first tell that she had been suffering from a *very severe* attack of bronchitis since their return to Bognor, attended by most violent pain in her ears and *extreme* deafness.' There was concern about how to inform Johnny Watson, who was travelling in France. 'We scarcely venture to expect that he will not have heard of it before any private tidings can reach him. From the last account, he had evidently very much improved in health.' In the event, Mary Watson herself wrote to Johnny expressing her intense grief and sympathy for his loss.

Already emotionally fragile, Johnny Watson would continue to be touched by tragedy. After the birth of their son, William Henry, in 1863, he and his wife lost two very young children before the arrival a decade later of Susan Dorothea, nicknamed Tottie. The babies were buried in the Sussex churchyard of West Lavington, not far from Johnny's stepmother's home in Midhurst.

While the subject of Armstrong's guns continued to attract intense interest in London and, increasingly, around the empire – sowing the seeds for a revolution in his business career – a transformation of a quite different kind was under way on the eastern fringe of Newcastle. 'Sir William has purchased an extensive range of the Ouseburn banks,' wrote Thomas Sopwith in his diary, 'and is now engaged in improving them by laying out roads, planting trees and ornamental shrubs, with bridges, lodges and all suitable means for convenient access to what bids fair to be a very handsome though immature Bois de Boulogne in the vicinity of Newcastle.'

As the Armstrongs acquired more and more land in Jesmond Dene, they threw their combined energies into expanding their home there and enhancing its beauty and usefulness; in addition to building large glass-houses and initiating a vast planting programme, they turned over some of the estate to pasture and agriculture. Although always nurturing a grand vision, William never disregarded the minutiae of daily life, and his letters to Meggie from London at this time are peppered with homely references. 'The two cows will be sent off on Monday night and must be expected on Tuesday,' he wrote on one occasion.

During an early evening walk to Jesmond, Sopwith – unobserved – noted an example of Armstrong's customary dedication to the task before him. 'When I approached the dene, I saw for the first time the vast quantity of cutting and quarrying and alteration which is made evident by the broken and uncovered rocks and soil, studded with workmen and with trains of carts ascending and descending newly made roads,' he wrote. 'In the midst I saw Sir William giving directions apparently, and by his action it was evident even at a distance to understand how earnestly he was intent on the work in hand.'

On another visit to Jesmond Dene, in early 1861, Sopwith found the master of the house at home and anxious to talk about the controversy caused by *Essays and Reviews*, a polemic published by a group of Oxford academics challenging the conventional interpretation of the Holy Scriptures. Headed by Benjamin Jowett, the group had argued that biblical writings should be read in the sense in which they had been originally intended, stripped of the, sometimes forced, meanings they had acquired.[2] But what most irked Jowett's opponents was his insistence on the progressive nature of divine revelation – which carried with it the idea that each generation should interpret the scriptures in its own way. 'Great is the sensation caused by the breadth and independence of thought of these *Essays and Reviews*, of which a fourth edition has appeared,' wrote Sopwith. Armstrong, it seems, was strongly attracted by Jowett's arguments, later making a point of visiting him personally to discuss them.

The *Essays and Reviews* controversy was particularly topical in that it came hot on the heels of the row about Charles Darwin's theory of natural selection that had dominated that year's meeting at Oxford of the British Association.[3] Two of the leading protagonists in the drama were Professor Richard Owen and the biologist Thomas Henry Huxley. A former president of the British Association, Owen was one of the most highly regarded scientists of his day, especially in the fields of physiology and palaeontology. He was also a staunch opponent of Darwin's theory. Huxley was an ardent supporter, who had written laudatory reviews of the recently published *On the Origin of Species*, and who cast himself as 'Darwin's bulldog'. (Darwin himself was absent from the Oxford meeting because of illness.) After opening skirmishes between Owen and Huxley, the tension rose with the intervention of Samuel Wilberforce, bishop of Oxford, who famously defended the divine creation of mankind and ridiculed many of Darwin's claims, taunting Huxley about whether he was descended from an ape on his grandfather's side or on his grandmother's. Huxley replied in like manner, demolishing the anatomical arguments used by his adversaries and gaining the enthusiastic support of his audience.

Although its immediate outcome was unclear, the confrontation sparked off a momentous battle between the church and science, between faith and rational thought, whose reverberations are still felt today. Many people believed that the two opposing positions were irreconcilable. Instinctively and intellectually, Armstrong was drawn to the Darwin camp, but when he himself assumed the presidency of the British Association in 1863 he was careful not to antagonise the traditionalists. T. H. Huxley became a firm friend of the Armstrongs, and he and his family would make many visits to Cragside in later years.

Meanwhile, a fundamental change in the national consciousness was under way. The outpouring of grief that had marked the funeral of Robert Stephenson in October 1859 had proved an apex in public perception of engineers and scientists in Britain. Soon afterwards, a sense of disillusionment with scientific progress gradually took hold, fuelled by the publication of *On the Origin of Species*, which challenged many deeply held religious beliefs, and the rows in Oxford. The engineers who had been revered since James Watt's invention of the steam engine a century earlier would come to be seen by some as part of the conspiracy of scientists who were seeking to undermine the whole structure of faith and morals on which the country was built. As Brunel's biographer L. T. C. Rolt observed, 'The very earth, which had seemed so firm set, now shook beneath men's feet. Suddenly all became unsure and bewildering. Was this really the right way, the path that man was predestined to follow or had he taken a wrong turning? The older generation looked back wistfully to the England before railways as to some lost garden of Eden.' A crucial destabilising event occurred in December 1861, when typhoid took the life of the Prince Consort. With the death of Albert, the once buoyant fraternity of scientists and engineers lost their most influential and vigorous champion.

A new recruit to Jesmond society around this time was Andrew Noble, the brilliant young ballistics expert who had served on the ordnance committee in 1858, and who had eventually agreed to come to Newcastle on what his wife described as 'a sort of trial, to see how Elswick suited him'.[5] A native of Greenock, Noble had joined the Royal Artillery at the age of 18 and spent most of his military career abroad. While in Canada, he met his future wife, Margery Campbell, whom he married in 1854. Six years later, the Nobles migrated to Newcastle and lived in temporary accommodation, where their son Saxton William Armstrong was born, before moving into what Mrs Noble described as 'a picturesque house in Jesmond Dene, built for us by Lady Armstrong'. This was Deep Dene House (now Fisherman's Lodge), just across the Ouseburn from the Armstrong domain.

Andrew Noble would make a vital contribution to Elswick's industrial and commercial success, but he was a far from easy character to deal with. 'Noble was a fanatical worker; except for a day at a time he never took a holiday, and it was often midnight before he left the works,' wrote the Vickers' historian J. D. Scott.[6] 'He was as ambitious as he was able, coercive, tenacious and choleric; in course of time there was to be trouble, but meanwhile his heroic capacity for work was invaluable.'

Noble's arrival marked the beginning of a new chapter at Elswick, in which he and George Rendel would be in joint charge of the ordnance works. 'It speaks very highly of both Rendel and Noble,' remarked the Elswick historian A. R. Fairbairn, 'that these two forceful personalities were able not merely to carry on the joint managership of the ordnance company without explosion, but were able to run in double-harness for more than 20 years.' The Nobles, like the Rendels, became much more than business associates of the Armstrongs; they too would gradually be absorbed into the wider Armstrong 'family' – a development that prepared the ground for a bitter rivalry at Elswick between the Rendel and the Noble factions after Armstrong's death.

Like Sopwith, the Nobles were fascinated by the Hancock brothers, Albany and John, who lived in St Mary's Terrace, a short walk from the dene, with their two sisters. The brothers were close friends of William Armstrong and stimulated his love of the natural world, John in particular playing a major role in the landscaping of Jesmond Dene. Apart from his charm and charisma, John had a prodigious knowledge of birds, gained in a way that seems exceedingly odd to modern sensibilities.[7] An excellent shot, he was known to rise regularly at 3am and walk to the coast with his gun, which was often put to effective use – his house soon became a museum of specimens he himself had collected. He set new standards in taxidermy and came to be regarded as the best exponent of the art in Britain. 'In his wanderings after birds, and his hawking, he had seen many things,' wrote Margery Noble. 'He could remember and tell us his experiences so vividly, his countenance and expression changing with the incidents he told ... He set up a series of stuffed falcon to illustrate falconry.' John's major literary contribution to the ornithology of the area was his *A Catalogue of the Birds of Northumberland and Durham*, published in 1874.

The elder Hancock brother, Albany, won international renown for his expertise on shells and invertebrates, encouraging Armstrong to buy a collection of shells from the leading conchologist Hugh Cuming, and conducting a long correspondence with Charles Darwin about barnacles. Apart from his scientific talents, Albany had literary leanings and was a great lover of books. 'It was like reading a particularly good criticism from the *Saturday Review* to hear him give his opinion on books,' remarked Margery Noble. 'I cannot understand why he didn't write. He was very fond of my eldest daughter, Lilias, and would invent fairy tales as they walked in the dene, or on the sea shore, where we sometimes went together.'

Albany and John Hancock and their sisters remained at the heart of Jesmond Dene society, as they had been since Thomas Sopwith first came across them in the 1840s. They introduced the Nobles to other inhabitants of the dene, including the two elderly daughters of Northumberland's nationally acclaimed engraver Thomas Bewick – 'delightful old ladies, full of love and fun and kindness', according to Mrs Noble. Like their father, they were great lovers and observers of nature. The Nobles rejoiced in the friendship of these 'bright spirits', as well as appreciating 'the intercourse with Sir William Armstrong and the frequent visits of learned and scientific men, such as Professor Owen, and Professor Huxley and his family'.

In the early 1860s Armstrong had conceived of the idea of building a banqueting hall in Jesmond Dene. The original plan was to have a place where he and Meggie could entertain large numbers of Elswick workers and their families. John Dobson – the architect who had worked with Richard Grainger to transform Newcastle into 'a city of palaces' – was given the commission to design the original hall; an imposing gatehouse was added later. Dobson's new creation, measuring 40 feet by 80 feet, was set on the west bank of the Ouseburn, down the hill from the Armstrongs' house. Sopwith saw it in its finished state for the first time in August 1863. 'The walls are of white brick with quoins of red brick and other facings of the same,' he remarked. 'The roof timbers are stained dark-oak colour and the plaster between is coloured a pale blue. Several niches are filled with statues, and pedestals are surmounted also with larger statues which appear to great advantage in front of crimson flags which descend like drapery.' Sopwith's visit took place a few days after one of the Elswick workers' parties. 'Three rows of tables were in the hall and 210 chairs,' he wrote. 'Last Monday, from one to two thousand persons had tea here, and probably more than ten (some of the papers say sixteen) thousand people enjoyed themselves by Sir William and Lady Armstrong's invitation.'

Simultaneously with his creation of the banqueting hall, Dobson was working on improvements to the Armstrongs' house and on Jesmond parish church. These were the great architect's last recorded works, rounding off an association with the dene that had begun some 45 years previously, when he had designed Jesmond Grove for James Losh and improved Jesmond Park for Armorer Donkin. In the 1820s Dobson built Black Dene House for Dr Thomas Headlam and made additions to the nearby West Jesmond House for Thomas Burdon Sanderson; later known respectively as Jesmond Dene House and Jesmond Towers, these imposing residences would in time be occupied by two of Armstrong's closest business associates, Andrew Noble and Charles Mitchell.

Thomas Sopwith's favourable opinion of Armstrong's works in the dene was cemented during a walk he took there with his friend in the days leading up to the 1863 meeting in Newcastle of the British Association, whose members would be shown around the estate. '[The grounds] extend a mile and a quarter in length and the new roads and walks are about three miles in extent. The prospects are as various as they are pleasing,' noted Sopwith. 'Here a vista of trees, there a broad expanse of fields fringed with woods. Now the eye is confined to a narrow and romantic valley, then a few minutes after it is ranging over distant hills. The breadth of landscape which is usually present to view is something quite remarkable in a place so near a populous town.' As the landscaping work had been finished only recently, large parts of the estate were bare or only thinly clad with young plants. 'But in two or three years these broad areas will be vast masses of beautiful flowers, and the whole then will be a landscape garden of the most exquisite beauty,' wrote Sopwith. 'Certainly the hall and gardens and grounds are works of creative genius such as few could plan and still fewer accomplish.'

Armstrong would later extend the banqueting hall to accommodate a 12-foot-high painting showing 'Prince Hal' (later King Henry V) taking the crown from his father's bedside by his friend John Callcott Horsley, originally commissioned to hang in the new Houses of Parliament. Acting on the recommendation of Horsley, Armstrong invited an up-and-coming young architect by the name of Richard Norman Shaw to design the extensions to the hall. During Shaw's visit to the dene in 1869, to inspect progress, Armstrong took him to see the small hunting lodge which he had recently built in the hills outside Rothbury.

When Armstrong had resigned his position as Superintendent of the Royal Gun Factory in Woolwich and returned to Newcastle in early 1863, it had been with a renewed sense of purpose. Despite his mauling by the British military and political establishment, at whose hands he had suffered, in Sopwith's words, 'all manner of insidious attacks and ungenerous imputations', he was on the brink of a dramatic, and highly profitable, new era in his business career.

As a first step, the two Elswick concerns were merged under the banner of Sir W. G. Armstrong & Company; extra land was acquired to the east of the existing site, more than doubling the area occupied by the works; and new engineering 'shops' were built to deal with the anticipated rise in production. Blast furnaces added a dramatic aspect to the site, with 'their tall structures by day and the glaring lights at night', wrote A. R. Fairbairn, but even more startling was the hammer shop, where 'the 30-ton steam hammer undertook the heavy forging work, and shook the houses around, day and night'. At this time, the Ridsdale iron mines, 25 miles to the north-west, were worked by the firm for a supply of iron ore.

No less important than its gun-making counterpart, the Elswick Engine Works had continued to grow at a breath-taking rate. 'Up and down the country, railways were lengthening, docks expanding, while the constantly increasing shipping brought prosperity to the numerous wharves on the Thames and elsewhere,' wrote Fairbairn. 'Never before or elsewhere had there been such commercial and industrial expansion, and from the Forth to Plymouth they clamoured for hydraulic installations, till the order books of that period read like a gazetteer of industrial England. Docks at London, Liverpool, Birkenhead, Swansea, Newport and Bristol placed large orders, but the smaller ports like Maryport and Goole (requiring a complete dock and cranage installation) were also in the market ... Every principal railway was a customer and the installations for which they called were so extensive that 30 identical cranes would be only one item of their order.' During this period, the Elswick firm also became renowned for its hydraulically operated swing bridges, which steadily increased in size and sophistication. An outstanding example was the bridge over the River Ouse near Goole in Yorkshire, built to carry the railway from Doncaster to Hull, and still operational in the early 21st century.

The astute negotiator Stuart Rendel remained in London and, while still fighting Armstrong's corner on the Armstrong Whitworth Committee, masterminded Elswick's arms sales to foreign buyers. Originally given what he called 'no more than a roving commission', for which he received 5 per cent of the proceeds from sales, Rendel finally joined the firm when Armstrong sold him a ¹⁄₂₅th share for £19,600.[8] He saw to it that Elswick's first foreign clients were the two sides in the American Civil War. Orders followed from Egypt, Turkey, and Italy, but it was clear from the start that nothing would be simple, especially when it came to dealing with money-grubbing middle-men.

The British government had banned the export of arms to the belligerents in the American war, and Rendel knew that, if any breach of this rule were revealed, there would be public outcry, particularly from Armstrong's opponents in Parliament and the War Office. So, when agents for the Union sought to buy Armstrong muzzle-loaders for the defence of Boston harbour, talks had to be conducted in total secrecy – and a go-between was hired. He was John Scott Russell, a naval architect and shipbuilder whose business was on the verge of bankruptcy. Scott Russell received a first instalment of several thousand pounds from the American envoy in London, out of which he was expected to pay Elswick for guns as they were completed. Elswick would therefore be able to claim that it was selling guns to Scott Russell rather than to a participant in the war.

'Scott Russell communicated with Armstrong and an order was arranged,' wrote Stuart Rendel in his memoirs.[9] 'I think this was the first foreign order accepted by the Elswick company. It was, however, run very close by orders from the Southern States, whose London banker, Mr Gilliat, afterwards Governor of the Bank of England, was an intimate friend of mine ... I went to Paris to see the military agents of the Southern States there.' Many of the early deals arranged by Rendel seemed to have depended on personal contacts. 'I really cannot say which orders were first obtained,' he went on. 'However, I soon became mixed up in the Northern order. For Benjamin Morane, the secretary of the American legation, was also a friend of mine.'

Rendel apparently had no scruples about sidestepping his government's policy or about selling arms to both sides. It eventually emerged that Scott Russell, after making some payments, had been diverting the money for his own purposes and using all sorts of subterfuge to cover his tracks. He had also led Andrew Noble to believe that further orders of £100,000 were in prospect when, in fact, 'as time passed and the threat to Boston faded, the Americans were considering ways to cancel the existing orders'.[10]

By early 1865, Armstrong had a set of guns in his yard ready and waiting to ship to America but was still awaiting payment by Scott Russell. When his scheme was exposed, Scott Russell was disgraced and expelled from the Institution of Civil Engineers, and the Elswick company, which he had cheated out of £5,000, had to put the episode down to bitter experience. 'The American difficulty having blown over I am a little relieved from that pressure which was getting stronger every day,' wrote Armstrong to Meggie in Jesmond. 'I hope the Yankees will now let us alone till we get our artillery quite perfect and then if they will have a brush let them come on.' But, with the end of the civil war later that year, the demand for British guns in America disappeared.

Thanks again to Stuart Rendel's connections, the Khedive of Egypt was another of Elswick's early customers. 'Through my college friend Mr (now Lord) Goschen, who had just negotiated the first Egyptian loan,' wrote Rendel, 'I learned that the Khedive had a design for securing armaments to promote his independence of the Porte.'[11] Shortly afterwards, Goschen introduced Rendel to Colonel Efflatoun, a personal friend of the Khedive, who was visiting Europe on an arms-buying mission. 'The result was that Efflatoun Pasha placed himself entirely in the hands of the Elswick firm,' wrote Rendel, 'and for some time I was the intermediary through which his very important orders for guns were placed. Later on, he visited Elswick itself and became greatly attached to Sir Andrew Noble.'

An even earlier client was Turkey, whose links with the British government had strengthened on the back of Turkey's decision to commission the building of a new ironclad fleet in British shipyards. The Turks later resolved to arm their new ships with guns made at Elswick. 'It was left to me,' recalled Rendel, 'to negotiate the contracts as the London representative of the firm direct with Musurus Pasha, the Turkish ambassador.'

Yet another of Stuart Rendel's friends, George Gibbs, was a partner in the South American firm of Antony Gibbs & Sons and lived in Valparaiso, Chile. 'Through him we obtained introductions which led to Chilean orders in which we dealt directly with the government,' wrote Rendel.

In 1857, Stuart Rendel had married Ellen (Nellie) Hubbard, the daughter of William Egerton Hubbard, an influential English merchant based in Russia. Shortly after starting his 'roving commission', he had spent six weeks at the Hubbard house in St Petersburg and was allowed 'to sit upon [the Russians'] artillery committees and witness their artillery experiments'. He later secured a similar introduction in Vienna. However, he came up against a problem: 'In both cases, I found the Krupp interest too powerfully installed, politically and otherwise, for successful opposition.'

With military conflicts breaking out in many parts of the globe, there was no shortage of demand for armaments in the 1860s and 1870s. Indeed, it could hardly have been a more promising moment for Elswick to enter the international arms trade. The following list, compiled by Marshall Bastable, identifies the wars in which Armstrong guns were used: 'the American Civil War from 1861 to 1865; the Schleswig-Holstein War of 1864; the Austro-Prussian (Seven Weeks) War of 1866, which included naval battles between Italy and Austria; the continual civil war in Spain between 1868 and 1876 and her wars against Peru in 1864–65 and Chile in 1865–66; the war of Paraguay against Argentina, Uruguay and Brazil between 1864 and 1870; the War of the Pacific, 1879–84, which pitted Chile against Peru and Bolivia; and the continual wars between Turkey and the Balkan peoples which culminated in the Russo-Turkish War of 1877–78'. China, also, was keen to build up its defences following the Japanese invasion of Formosa (Taiwan) in 1874. According to Bastable, 'World demand for weapons, especially for warships, increased during the 1880s and accelerated in the 1890s, when the great powers launched the armaments races and naval power entered a period of rapid growth and technological development.'[12]

Elswick did not, however, stand unchallenged on the world stage. Across the North Sea in north-western Prussia was a rival establishment equally awe-inspiring in its industrial might – the Krupp works at Essen on the River Ruhr. Fifty years earlier, Alfred Krupp's father had set up a steel foundry in the town, and it was as a producer of steel that Krupp had so far made his mark. Armstrong had acknowledged this fact in 1861 in his Sheffield speech: 'It is seldom that the enterprise of English manufacturers is exceeded by that of foreigners, but in this production of steel forgings of large dimensions Krupp of Essen has taken the lead of all steelmakers in this country. He has met the difficulty of toughening large masses of cast steel by using hammers of extraordinary weight, and I believe that equal success will never be attained in England without adopting similar measures.' There were still many improvements to be made in the manufacture of steel. 'It will be a great era in metallurgy when a material possessing the toughness and ductility of wrought iron, combined with the homogenous character of a cast metal, can be economically supplied in large blocks,' commented Armstrong. It was the development of a new type of steel that would later rekindle his interest in breech-loading guns.

By the early 1860s, Krupp's other main preoccupation had become the production and sale of armaments – and his exhibits at the International Exhibition had confirmed his dominant position in the field. As Krupp's biographer William Manchester explained, the private arms manufacturer of the time was allowed to sell his wares to any country. Only during a war could he rely on local trade; in peacetime, he had to keep his factories going by selling abroad. 'Thus, Krupp sold guns to Russia, Belgium, Holland, Spain, Switzerland, Austria and England. Berlin knew this. The government not only encouraged him to maintain a large establishment; it was prepared to act as his accomplice.'[13] However, Krupp did not like the taste of his own medicine. Soon after securing an agreement to sell some of his arms to the British, he discovered that some Prussian admirals were seeking to buy guns from Armstrong – and he solicited the support of the Prussian Prime Minister, Otto von Bismarck, to scupper the plan. A huge arms deal with Russia at the end of 1863 won Krupp international notoriety as 'the Cannon King'.

Armstrong made clear his competitive feelings towards Krupp in a letter of December 1863 to Stuart Rendel. 'As to Krupp's guns, I presume you know that the report that one of them had burst was not strictly true,' he wrote, adding that another gun of the same design had since indeed burst in dramatic fashion: 'and that too with a vengeance, flaying into a thousand pieces'. Armstrong attributed this to 'the intrinsic unfitness of the material' and said that he had had 'this nice piece of news' conveyed to the under-secretary for war.[14]

The rivalry between the two men came to a head again a few years later when Krupp heard that the navy of the new North German Federation was about to submit a large order for Armstrong's 9-inch muzzle-loaders. (From March 1864, by order of the War Department, all heavy Armstrong guns were designated by their calibre or diameter of bore rather than the weight of their projectiles. After that date, the terms '110-pounder', '70-pounder', and so on, were no longer recognised by the service.) The guns had made a favourable impression on King Wilhelm and Prime Minister Bismarck when fired in their presence. Krupp acted quickly. He went to St Petersburg and, using his influence with Tsar Alexander II, persuaded the Russian admirals to testify on oath that his 8-inch and 9-inch guns were superior to all others, and to urge the Prussian king – who was later presented with the testimonials by an intermediary – not to buy the British weapons. To the astonishment of many, the strategy worked. Wilhelm capitulated and Krupp's pre-eminence in Prussia was preserved. As a result, according to William Manchester, Armstrong's men 'gave up on the Germans ... and never came back'.[15]

There would be only one further near-encounter between the two great arms barons, which came hot on the heels of Krupp's acquisition of a vast new firing range at Meppen near Osnabrück. 'Now that he had his own incomparable trial ground he was eager to try it out,' wrote Manchester. 'His first thought was to challenge Armstrong to a duel. Let the British and German goliaths stand hubcap to hubcap and blaze away, he gleefully told [his lieutenant]; customers would be invited to watch and then to write their checks – in millions of marks.' In spite of the temptation – there was a strong possibility that Armstrong would have won such a competition – the invitation was politely declined. Armstrong and Krupp and the French arms manufacturer Schneider came to be known collectively as 'Europe's deadly triumvirate'. In Manchester's words, 'Over the next eighty years they were to be celebrated first as shields of national honor and later, after their slaughtering machines were hopelessly out of control, as merchants of death.'

Armstrong himself, however, was stung by accusations that the invention of ever more sophisticated weaponry encouraged international hostilities. In fact he believed the opposite, and would have staunchly supported the modern theory of deterrence. 'The tendency of mechanical invention, as applied to war, is to discourage aggression and thus to maintain peace,' he insisted in a speech to the Institution of Mechanical Engineers in Newcastle in 1869. 'We may consequently hope that it will hasten the arrival of a period when civilized nations will abandon the arbitrament of arms and settle their differences by rational and peaceable methods.' He also believed that by improving the quality of weapons, and making hand-to-hand combat less likely, he was helping to reduce the brutality of war. He argued that the scientist and the engineer supplied the means for war but it was society that had to decide on its justification and purpose: 'It is our province, as engineers, to make the forces of matter obedient to the will of man; and those who use the means we supply must be responsible for their legitimate application.'[16] All in all, in the second half of the 19th century, he was seen as a great national benefactor – a man who had played a crucial role in increasing the security of Britain and the defence of the empire.

10

'However High We Climb'

August 1863 was an exceptionally wet month in the British Isles, with rain falling heavily almost every day, but the weather did little to dampen the spirits of the members of the British Association as they assembled for the annual spectacle of the scientific merry-go-round. They were meeting in Newcastle upon Tyne for the first time in 25 years – and their host and *primus inter pares* on this occasion was Sir William Armstrong.

'I esteem it the greatest honour of my life that I am called upon to assume the office of your president,' he told them in a speech on 26 August. Since the 1838 conference, extraordinary progress had been made in scientific knowledge; in mechanical science, the advances had no parallel in history. 'The railway system was then in its infancy, and the great problem of transatlantic steam navigation had only received its complete solution in the preceding year. Since then, railways have extended to every continent and steamships have covered the ocean.' Armstrong reminded 'the parliament of science', as *The Times* had dubbed the gathering, that the site of its meeting was the birthplace of the railways, and that the coal-mines of the district had done more than any other 'to supply the motive power by which steam communication by land and water has been established on so gigantic a scale'.

The presidential oration would later be described by Charles Darwin as 'Armstrong's admirable speech' and hailed by the veteran scientific luminary Sir Roderick Murchison as 'the best address that has ever been delivered at the British Association'. He held his audience rapt with his absorbing analysis of the march of human knowledge, using the history of the railways to show 'what grand results may have their origin in small beginnings':

'When coal was first conveyed in this neighbourhood from the pit to the shipping place on the Tyne, the pack-horse, carrying a burden of 3 hundredweight, was the only mode of transport involved. As soon as roads suitable for wheeled carriages were formed, carts were introduced, and this first step in mechanical appliance to facilitate transport had the effect of increasing the load which the horse was enabled to convey from 3 to 17 hundredweight. The next improvement consisted in laying wooden bars or rails for the wheels of the carts to run upon, and this was followed by the substitution of the four-wheeled wagon for the two-wheeled cart. By this further application of mechanical principles, the original horse-load of 3 hundredweight was augmented to 42 hundredweight ... The next step in the progress of the railways was the attachment of slips of iron to the wooden rails. Then came the iron tramway, consisting of cast-iron bars of an angular section: in this arrangement the upright flange of the bar acted as a guide to keep the wheel on the track. The next advance was an important one, and consisted in transferring the guiding flange from the rail to the wheel: this improvement enabled cast-iron edge rails to be used. Finally, in 1820, after the lapse of about 200 years from the first employment of wooden bars, wrought-iron rails, rolled in long lengths, and of suitable section, were made in this neighbourhood, and eventually superseded all other forms of railway.

'Thus, the railway system, like all large inventions, has risen to its present importance by a series of steps; and so gradual has been its progress that Europe finds itself committed to a gauge fortuitously determined by the distance between the wheels of the carts for which wooden rails were originally laid down. Last of all came the locomotive engine, that crowning achievement of mechanical science, which enables us to convey a load of 200 tons at a cost of fuel scarcely exceeding that of the corn and the hay which the original pack-horse consumed in conveying its load of 3 hundredweight an equal distance.'

Armstrong's purpose in tracing this evolutionary process was to demonstrate the extraordinary scope of the inventive faculties of human beings. 'No sooner is a road formed fit for wheeled carriage to pass along than the cart takes the place of the pack-saddle – no sooner is the wooden railway provided than the wagon is substituted for the cart – and no sooner is an iron railway formed, capable of carrying heavy loads, than the locomotive engine is found ready to commence its career. As in the vegetable kingdom fit conditions of soil and climate quickly cause the appearance of suitable plants, so in the intellectual world fitness of time and circumstance promptly calls forth appropriate devices. The seeds of invention exist, as it were, in the air, ready to germinate whenever suitable conditions arise, and no legislative interference is needed to ensure their growth in proper season.' He was eloquently elaborating the view he had expressed earlier in the year to the Royal Commission on Patents: 'The great majority of inventions are the result of mere accident – if you let them alone, they will turn up of themselves.'

In his most penetrating and prophetic passage, Armstrong then turned to the generation and consumption of power in order to highlight mankind's dependence on fossil fuels and to speculate about how the human race would meet its future energy needs. He began with a reference to one of Tyneside's most famous sons: 'The philosophical mind of George Stephenson, unaided by theoretical knowledge, rightly saw that coal was the embodiment of power originally derived from the sun. That small pencil of solar radiation which is arrested by our planet, and which constitutes less than the 2,000-millionth part of the total energy sent forth from the sun, must be regarded as the power which enabled the plants of the carboniferous period to wrest the carbon they required from the oxygen with which it was combined, and eventually to deposit it as the solid material of coal. In our day, the reunion of that carbon with oxygen restores the energy expended in the former process, and thus we are enabled to utilize the power originally derived from the luminous centre of our planetary system.'

The part played by the sun in the creation of coal does not stop there, however. 'In every period of geological history the waters of the ocean have been lifted by the action of the sun and precipitated in rain upon the earth. This has given rise to all those sedimentary actions by which mineral substances have been collected at particular localities, and there deposited in a stratified form with a protecting cover to preserve them for future use. The phase of the earth's existence suitable for the extensive formation of coal appears to have passed away for ever; but the quantity of that invaluable material which has been stored up throughout the globe for our benefit is sufficient (if used discreetly) to serve the purposes of the human race for many thousands of years. In fact, the entire quantity of coal may be considered as practically inexhaustible.' But a worrying situation was developing in Britain: 'The greatness of this country much depends upon the superiority of her coal in cheapness and quality over that of other nations; but we have already drawn from our choicest mines a far larger quantity of coal than has been raised in all other parts of the world put together, and the time is not remote when we shall have to encounter the disadvantages of increased cost of working and diminished value of produce.'

Armstrong then attempted to calculate how long it would be before all of the accessible coal in the British Isles were exhausted. 'The quantity of coal yearly worked from British mines has been almost trebled during the last 20 years, and has probably increased tenfold since the commencement of the present century; but as this increase has taken place pending the introduction of steam navigation and railway transit, and under exceptional conditions of manufacturing development, it would be too much to assume that it will continue to advance with equal rapidity. The statistics collected by Mr Hunt of the Mining Record Office show that at the end of 1861 the quantity of coal raised in the United Kingdom had reached the enormous total of 86 million tons, and that the average annual increase of the preceding years amounted to 2¾ million tons. Let us inquire, then, what will be the duration of our coalfields if this more moderate rate of increase be maintained.

'By combining the known thickness of the various workable seams of coal, and computing the area of the surface under which they lie, it is easy to arrive at an estimate of the total quantity comprised in our coal-bearing strata. Assuming 4,000 feet as the greatest depth at which it will ever be possible to carry on mining operations, and rejecting all seams of less than 2 feet in thickness, the entire quantity of available coal existing in these islands has been calculated to amount to about 80,000 million tons, which, at the present rate of consumption, would be exhausted in 930 years, but with a continued yearly increase of 2¾ million tons would only last 212 years. It is clear that long before complete exhaustion takes place, England will have ceased to be a coal-producing country on an extensive scale. Other nations, and especially the United States of America, which possess coal-fields 37 times more extensive than ours, will then be working more accessible beds at a smaller cost, and will be able to displace the English coal from every market. The question is, not how long our coal will endure before absolute exhaustion is effected, but how long will those particular coal-seams last which yield coal of a quality and at a price to enable this country to maintain her present supremacy in manufacturing industry.

'So far as this particular district is concerned, it is generally admitted that 200 years will be sufficient to exhaust the principal seams even at the present rate of working. If the production should continue to increase as it is now doing, the duration of those seams will not reach half that period. How the case may stand in other coal-mining districts I have not the means of ascertaining; but as the best and most accessible coal will always be worked in preference to any other, I fear the same rapid exhaustion of our most valuable seams is everywhere taking place.'

Armstrong's warnings about the future of coal must have had a similar impact on his audience that predictions about human-induced climate change have today. Then, as now, the profligate use of limited resources was at the centre of the debate. 'Were we reaping the full advantage of all the coal we burn,' he said, 'no objection could be made to the largeness of the quantity, but we are using it wastefully and extravagantly in all its applications.' He went on to provide examples of how this wastefulness was evident in industry and to lay down a challenge to engineers to devise 'improved practical methods of converting the heat of combustion into available power'.

It was widely believed that, before coal was exhausted, some other motive power – such as electricity – would be found to take its place. 'Electricity, like heat, may be converted into motion,' said Armstrong, 'and both theory and practice have demonstrated that its mechanical application does not involve so much waste of power as takes place in a steam-engine; but whether we use heat or electricity as a motive power, we must equally depend upon chemical affinity as the source of supply. The act of uniting to form a chemical product liberates an energy which assumes the form of heat or electricity, from either of which states it is convertible into mechanical effect. In contemplating, therefore, the application of electricity as a motive power, we must bear in mind that we shall still require to effect chemical combinations, and in so doing to consume materials. But where are we to find materials so economical for this purpose as the coal we derive from the earth and the oxygen we obtain from the air? The latter costs absolutely nothing; and every pound of coal, which in the act of combustion enters into chemical combination, renders more than two and a half pounds of oxygen available for power. We cannot look to water as a practicable source of oxygen, for there it exists in the combined state, requiring expenditure of chemical energy for its separation from hydrogen. It is in the atmosphere alone that it can be found in that free state in which we require it, and there does not appear to me to be the remotest chance, in an economic point of view, of being able to dispense with the oxygen of the air as a source either of thermodynamic or electrodynamic effect. But to use this oxygen we must consume some oxidizable substance, and coal is the cheapest we can procure.'

There was another source of energy, however, that – although he did not say so – went to the heart of Armstrong's very being. 'I allude,' he said, 'to the power of water descending from heights to which it has been lifted by the evaporative action of the sun.' He referred to the efficiency of the waterworks at Greenock 'where the collecting-reservoirs are situated at an elevation of 512 feet above the River Clyde', making them useful in the generation of hydraulic power. 'But the hydraulic capabilities of the Greenock reservoirs sink into insignificance when compared with those of other localities, where the naturally collected waters of large areas of surface descend, from great elevations in rapid rivers or vertical falls. Alpine regions abound in falls which, with the aid of artificial works to impound the surplus water and equalize the supply, would yield thousands of horsepower; and there is at least one great river in the world which, in a single plunge, develops sufficient power to carry on all the manufacturing operations of mankind if concentrated in its neighbourhood. Industrial populations have scarcely yet extended to those regions which afford this profusion of motive power, but we may anticipate the time when these natural falls will be brought into useful operation. In that day, the heat of the sun, by raising the water to heights from which to flow in these great rapids and cascades, will become the means of economizing the precious stores of motive power, which the solar energy differently directed has accumulated at a remote period of geological history, and which, when once expended, may probably never be replaced.'

Lamenting other examples of waste in the burning of coal, Armstrong complained that 'combustion in common furnaces' was so imperfect that 'clouds of powdered carbon, in the form of smoke, envelop our manufacturing towns, and gases, which ought to be completely oxygenized in the fire, pass into the air with two-thirds of their heating power undeveloped'.

The use of coal for domestic purposes also involved waste and extravagance. 'It is computed that the consumption of coal in dwelling-houses amounts in this country to a ton per head per annum for the entire population; so that upwards of 29 million tons are annually expended in Great Britain alone for domestic use. If anyone will consider that one pound of coal applied to a well-constructed steam-engine boiler evaporates 10 pounds or one gallon or water, and if he will compare this effect with the insignificant quantity of water which can be boiled off in steam by a pound of coal consumed in an ordinary kitchen fire, he will be able to appreciate the enormous waste which takes place by the common method of burning coal for culinary purposes. The simplest arrangements to confine the heat and concentrate it upon the operation to be performed would suffice to obviate this reprehensible waste. So also in warming houses we consume in our open fires about five times as much coal as will produce the same heating effect when burnt in a close and properly constructed stove. Without sacrificing the luxury of a visible fire, it would be easy, by attending to the principles of radiation and convection, to render available the greater part of the heat which is now so improvidently discharged into the chimney.'

Touching on many other subjects, ranging from the invention of the Davy lamp to the nature of matter, Armstrong identified 'the dynamical theory of heat' (thermodynamics) as probably the most important discovery of the century. 'We now know,' he said, 'that each Fahrenheit degree of temperature in a pound of water is equivalent to a weight of 772 pounds lifted one foot high, and that these amounts of heat and power are reciprocally convertible into one another. This theory of heat is chiefly due to the labours of Mayer and Joule, though many other names, including those of Thomson and Rankine, are associated with the development.' Earlier thinkers, including Lord Bacon, had been fascinated by the relationship between heat and motion: 'Even Aristotle seems to have entertained the idea that motion was to be considered as the foundation not only of heat but of all manifestations of matter.'

Armstrong explained how he and Andrew Noble had used the dynamical theory of heat to advance their knowledge of the science of gunnery. He devoted special attention to recent discoveries by the physicist John Tyndall, the author of *The Glaciers of the Alps*, 'respecting the absorption and radiation of heat by vapours and permanent gases'. Tyndall's experiments had shown that 'the minute quantity of water suspended as invisible vapour in the atmosphere acts as a warm clothing to the earth. The efficacy of this vapour in arresting heat is, in comparison with that of air, perfectly astounding. Although the atmosphere contains on an average but one particle of aqueous vapour to 200 of air, yet that single particle absorbs as much heat as the collective 200 particles of air. Remove, says Professor Tyndall, for a single summer night, the aqueous vapour from the air which overspreads this country, and you would assuredly destroy every plant incapable of bearing extreme cold. The warmth of our fields and gardens would pour itself unrequited into space, and the sun would rise upon an island held fast in the grip of frost.' The science of meteorology, still in its infancy, was starting to yield some interesting clues about how to forecast the weather, with the help of information derived from a series of hair-raising balloon ascents by the intrepid James Glaisher – one of which would take place above Newcastle later that very week.

Amid all these marvels, 'the facility now given to the transmission of intelligence and the interchange of thought' was one of the most remarkable features of the age, argued Armstrong. 'Cheap and rapid postage to all parts of the world – paper and printing reduced to the lowest possible cost – electric telegraphs between nation and nation, town and town, and now even (thanks to the beautiful inventions of Professor Wheatstone) between house and house – all contribute to aid that commerce of ideas by which wealth and knowledge are augmented.'

However, he complained, 'the fundamental art of expressing thought by written symbols remains as imperfect now as it has been for centuries.' He advocated introducing a form of shorthand, and went on to recommend the adoption in Britain of the decimal system of weights and measures that was being used in continental Europe (in place of pounds and feet), arguing that both science and international commerce suffered by the 'want of uniformity' in this area: 'Valuable observations made in one country are in a great measure lost to another from the labour required to convert a series of quantities into new dominations.'

Hailing the recent discovery of the source of the Nile by Captains Speke and Grant, Armstrong acknowledged the vital contribution of Sir Roderick Murchison and the Royal Geographical Society. But he reserved his final accolade for the great and rapid strides made in 'the science of organic life', highlighting the profound sensation caused by the work of Charles Darwin in promulgating the doctrine of natural selection. 'The novelty of this ingenious theory, the eminence of its author, and his masterly treatment of the subject, have, perhaps, combined to excite more enthusiasm in its favour than is consistent with that dispassionate spirit which it is so necessary to preserve in the pursuit of truth.' He summarised the intense controversy provoked by Darwin's claims before setting out his own views on the subject.

While broadly welcomed Darwin's theory – which did not, at this stage, include explicit reference to humans – Armstrong found parts of it difficult to accept. 'The Darwinian theory, when fully enunciated, founds the pedigree of living nature upon the most elementary form of vitalized matter,' he said. 'One step further would carry us back ... to inorganic rudiments; and then we should be called upon to recognize in ourselves, and in the exquisite elaborations of the animal and vegetable kingdoms, the ultimate results of mere material forces left free to follow their own unguided tendencies.' Like most of his listeners, he realised the shocking implications of these ideas – and partially refuted them in his comments on Darwin's mentor, the geologist Sir Charles Lyell, whose book *Antiquity of Man* had been published earlier that year. Lyell had shown, said Armstrong, that is was no longer possible to doubt that 'the human race has existed on the earth, in a barbarian state, for a period far exceeding the limit of historical record; but, notwithstanding this great antiquity, the proofs still remain unaltered that man is the latest as well as the noblest work of God'.

Having touched on all of the important scientific issues of the day, Armstrong wound up his address by expressing the hope that, when the British Association next met in Newcastle, its members would have found the intervening period to have been as fruitful as the period on which they now looked back – a hope that, as was clear from his closing remarks, he expected to be fulfilled:

'The tendency of progress is to quicken progress, because every acquisition in science is so much vantage ground for fresh attainment. We may expect, therefore, to increase our speed as we struggle forward; but however high we climb in the pursuit of knowledge we shall still see heights above us, and the more we extend our view, the more conscious we shall be of the immensity that lies beyond.'

The rapturous response that Armstrong received in Newcastle's packed New Town Hall was replicated in the days that followed in a sustained demand for transcripts of his speech. Reproduced word for word in national and local newspapers, it was also printed separately in pamphlet form and widely circulated. Meanwhile the scientific savants, as they were known, dispersed to their respective 'sections' in different parts of the town and the routine work of the conference got under way.

Armstrong's comments on the coal supply would lead directly to the setting up three years later of a royal commission to enquire into the duration of British coalfields, to which he contributed as both a member and witness. And he would return to the subject of coal conservation in his presidential address to the North of England Institute of Mining and Mechanical Engineers in 1873.

Each day of the British Association's meeting was rounded off by feasting and celebration, and it was for this purpose that John Dobson's banqueting hall in Jesmond Dene really came into its own. The diarist Thomas Sopwith was entranced by the sparkling hospitality he experienced there: 'As night advanced, the glass arches over the doorways assumed a deep indigo colour which formed a striking contrast to the crimson drapery below. The temperature is agreeable – there are no currents of air – and all these advantages conduce much to the enjoyment of the guests. As to the sumptuous repast I can only say that it gave unmixed satisfaction, including as it did every delicacy of the season with such variety and abundance as left nothing to be desired. Soft and gentle airs were played on the organ during dinner. There followed "Non Nobis Domine" by a select choir from Durham, who sung several fine compositions during the rest of the evening. One toast and only one was given – viz. the Queen – by Sir William Armstrong, and the company could then enjoy the pleasant and instructive conversation of so intelligent an assemblage.'

Apart from attending the daily meetings of the scientific sections, visitors to the British Association were entertained by outings to local places of interest, including Durham Cathedral and the iron works at Middlesbrough. Early one morning, Armstrong organised a session of 'shell practice' using wooden targets on Whitley Sands. (Although this sort of activity had become common, there were increasing objections from local people to such a dangerous use of public space.) Among the most popular excursions – despite the wet weather – was a visit to the lead mines at Allenheads, in a particularly bleak part of the Pennines, where Thomas Sopwith was manager, and where Armstrong had installed various hydraulic engines.

'I rose before six and went to the Central Station where a party of about 200 were gathering to depart in a special train to Allenheads mine,' wrote Sopwith in his diary for 3 September. 'A dull-looking morning, an overcast sky and even a few drops of rain did not appear to have discouraged the active-minded ladies and gentlemen who were intent on this adventurous inroad into Allendale. Sir William Armstrong arrived with his wonted punctuality and he, Mr Stuart Rendel and myself were accommodated in a separate carriage. At five minutes past seven we started and went express, in about an hour, to Haydon Bridge. Here, a most extraordinary assemblage of omnibuses, cars, coaches and other conveyances were ready to receive the party. Some gleams of sunshine appeared on the hills, and blue skies overhead presented a promising aspect. Sir William, Mr Rendel and I got into my own carriage and led the way, reaching the northern boundary of Allendale parish half an hour before the first of the excursion vans.

'Rain began to fall, the cold grey-looking clouds seemed too much in harmony with the leaden attractions of Allenheads, and the "hydraulic" features of the weather seemed to be unmistakably developed. I proposed to divide the party, some going on, as Sir William and Mr Rendel had done, to breakfast and to the Blackett Level at Allen Town, others to join me in a walk to Allen Smelt Mill ... As only a few can look into the oven-like opening at once, I advised them to walk slowly past, to look in as they passed, then to go out at one door and come in at another, forming a continuous circle and every one seeing the silver every four or five minutes.'

In its report on the excursion, *The Times* divulged that, in certain years, enough ore had been raised here by the London Lead Company, which owned the mine, to provide 10,000 tons of metal. 'Mr Sopwith, the director of all the mining operations here, explained with great clearness the various processes through which the ore passes before it reaches the market,' according to the newspaper, 'but the greatest attraction was the extraction of a large cake of silver by Mr Hugh Lee Pattinson's well-known desilvering process. In this process, the chief feature is that – the lead crystallizing first – the silver is left behind, squeezed out as it were from the less valuable metal during congelation. The crystals, still containing some silver, are melted again a second and a third time.' Pattinson had calculated that by his process at least 50,000 ounces of silver were added annually to Britain's national supply.

As the viewing of the mine continued, Armstrong led the visitors through the various engine rooms and – in what was, according to Sopwith, 'one of the crowning events of this week of wonders' – gave an account of his own inventions. 'When at length all had seen the large waterwheel, the forcing pumps, the accumulator, the winding and pumping engines, the ventilators and the ascent and descent of the cages in the shaft, when all had heard Sir William's lectures on the details of each separate construction (accompanied as his voice was by the sound of his own machinery), the party once more entered or climbed upon their respective vehicles. Sir William and Mr Rendel entered my conveyance and, soaked in rain which fell in pitiless torrents, we at length reached Allenheads.'

Sopwith explained that many of the party had travelled direct to Allenheads. 'Some went in carriages down the Gin-hill shaft, others went in an adventurous pedestrian excursion down the horse track, a subterraneous pathway which descends by a succession of rugged inclined roads into Allenheads mine. The "dripping savants", as *The Times* calls them, who had now arrived with me, were shown to warm fires in the miners' room and many offices prepared for their reception. Mr Beaumont, who was there to receive and welcome them, took the ladies up to the Hall, where they remained until the hour of dinner. Here again Sir William Armstrong and Mr Bewick greatly exerted themselves in giving the most clear and ample explanations of the engines and machinery – the washing and dressing of ores, the crushing mill, bouse teams – in short the whole of the appliances by which the lead ore is converted into a form suitable for being sent to be smelted.'

Their hosts – Wentworth Blackett Beaumont, the proprietor of the London Lead Company, and his wife, Lady Margaret – then laid on a banquet followed by dancing. 'After dinner, Mr and Lady Margaret Beaumont went down to see the festive throng accompanied by Lord Canning [Lady Margaret's brother], Mr Percy Westmacott and myself,' wrote Sopwith. 'Dancing was kept up until near eleven o'clock, her ladyship joining most cheerfully in several of the dances. Indeed all seemed bent on amusement and, selecting such partners as came to hand, Lord Canning and others took an active part in country dances and Scotch reels, in which I also participated.'

In summing up the 1863 conference, *The Times* concluded that, despite the shortcomings of the weather, it had been 'one of the most successful meetings as to numbers, pecuniary profits, and the ability and varied interest of the papers read, ever held by the British Association'. As the visitors prepared to make their way home, the paper predicted that they would 'never forget the kindness and the warm-hearted hospitality with which they have been received by the people of Newcastle'.

In need of rest and recuperation following the departure of the savants – he had not taken a proper holiday for 15 years – William Armstrong looked north to Rothbury, where he had spent so many happy times as a child fishing and paddling about in the River Coquet. 'I thought I should like to see the old place once more,' he explained later to a visiting journalist. He travelled there in mid-September and stayed over a weekend. According to Andrew Noble's wife, Margery, her husband was in Rothbury at the time recovering from a bronchial infection. Armstrong had recommended Rothbury on account of its health-giving qualities. 'It cured me as youth when I was almost given up,' he told Mrs Noble. 'I went there, drank goats' milk, and fished, and I was almost able to walk all the way back to Newcastle when I left.'

The morning after his arrival, Armstrong took a stroll along the banks of the Coquet with Noble and George Rendel, who was also staying in Rothbury with his family. 'We walked down by the side of the river beyond the Thrum Mill,' said Armstrong. 'And I scrambled along what is now called the Cragside hill, sat upon a boulder and had a look at the surroundings. I observed then it was a pretty site for a house.' He spoke to a man leaning over a nearby gate and asked him if there were any fields for sale. 'This is for sale,' replied the man, indicating part of the gorge behind him, which included an old mill. 'Well, I thought nothing more about it at the time,' Armstrong recalled later, 'but on my return to Newcastle, the house at Rothbury haunted me so much that I made enquiries about the site – and after a little negotiation I bought it.

'The original intention was that I should build a house of eight or ten rooms and a stable for a pair of horses. And I spent the whole of my spare time planning the transformation of that bleak Northumbrian moor into an earthly paradise. You'll admit that I've made it almost as famous as my guns. I can't begin to give you the faintest idea of the pleasure that it's given me. I feel certain that, had there been no Cragside, I shouldn't have been talking to you today – for it has been my very life.'

11

Paradise on Earth

Building began at once on the site near Rothbury, in the glen of the lonely Debdon Burn – and so eager was Armstrong that the work should proceed rapidly that he and Meggie took lodgings in an old mill cottage at Debdon Burnfoot, from where they could direct operations at close quarters. A group of workers arrived, many drafted in from Elswick, and William Bertram and his wife joined them from Jesmond Dene; Bertram would remain Armstrong's 'faithful and confidential manager' until his master's death.[1] There were just four rooms in the mill house; the Armstrongs occupied the upper floor and the Bertrams the lower one.

The 20 acres of rocky, heath-covered, treeless moorland that Armstrong had acquired was described much later by the architectural historian Mark Girouard as 'a lunatic site for a house'.[2] Indeed the spot chosen was on such a steep slope that, once the building was finished, people entering through the front door and walking up to the second floor would look out at the back and find they were only at ground level – since the ground had come up behind them. 'But that's part of the drama of the place,' remarked Girouard. 'They had to dynamite to make a platform to put the building on in the first place, and when they extended the house with a billiard room at the back, they had to dynamite holes to fit that in.' The original space for the house had been carved from solid rock and, as it grew, more rock had to be clawed and blasted away under Armstrong's direction.

'Some of his friends thought him mad to build on such a spot,' wrote Winifreda Watson-Armstrong, who became mistress of Cragside in 1901, 'but his quick eye saw what could be made of the place and, nothing daunted, he began to work. Roads were made, the house was built, and the planting began. A staff of about eighty men was employed on the roads alone, the hours of work from 6am to 6pm, the highest wage being 16s. 6d. a week.' The Armstrongs gradually acquired more and more land, eventually laying out 36 miles of drives and 9 miles of footpaths.

More attention was devoted at this stage to clothing the bare hillsides with vegetation than to creating a luxurious residence. Exposed ridges and summits were planted with a countless number of pines, while at lower levels, approaching the water's edge, rhododendrons were the favoured species. Naked boulders were covered by beds of flowering mosses and heathers, and hardy trees and creepers were introduced in abundance.

In the early days, Armstrong was still obliged to spend much of his time in London or Newcastle, leaving Meggie in charge of the construction work at Rothbury. By the time he wrote to her on 17 March 1865, operations were progressing well: 'I will bring down the clock I have got for the upper sitting room at Rothbury. It can stand in the sitting room of the old house until the new one is ready. I hope you find your quarters comfortable and that you like the appearance of the new building and the grounds.'

Three months later, the new house was almost ready for occupation: 'I was glad to have your letter this morning giving so cheering an account of the prospects of more rapid progress. It will be an immense comfort to go into the house next time I am there, though at present I do not see much chance of being able to leave London early enough to get to Rothbury for the Race Week [an annual public holiday]. I met Dodds the plasterer at the railway station as I was coming away and he urged that the floors should be laid down in order that he might get on with the ceilings, which would otherwise be much shaken by nailing down the boards. If this were done he might be prepared to send more plasterers.'

As he mentioned later in the same letter, Armstrong was continuing, with considerable reluctance, to fraternise with the rich and powerful in London society: 'We had a tremendous swell party at the Count de Paris's, including the Prince of Wales, the Duke of Marlborough, the Prince Mustapha Pasha of Egypt, the Duke and Duchess d'Aumal and a dozen others of the same sort.

The count made himself very agreeable to everyone, but I get tired of these things.'

In the event, the Armstrongs moved into Cragside that summer – but by March 1866 they were still sharing the place with decorators, as Armstrong complained in a letter to Stuart Rendel: 'We are in a horrid state at present with painters and paperers who make dust and smells enough to drive one out of the house.' That year, Armstrong started to write letters on paper headed 'Cragside, Rothbury' and embellished with a raised-hammer motif – the emblem of an engineer.

Conceived as a simple weekend retreat, the original two-storey building at Cragside resembled a boxy sporting lodge of little architectural distinction, but – presumably as a result of Meggie's influence – only the very best and most fashionable materials were used for decorating the interior. For example, two of the earliest wallpapers designed by William Morris and produced by Morris and Company – 'Fruit' and 'Trellis', both dating from 1864 – were used to cover the walls in two of the bedrooms. Meggie could also now indulge to the full her talent for gardening and her passion for plants, both of which had evolved with the development of Jesmond Dene. Over the years, she used her skill and vision to transform the bare hillsides and narrow valleys into what would become one of the finest examples of Victorian horticulture, incorporating almost 5 acres of spectacular rock gardens.

The Armstrongs clearly worked well as a team, as observed later by Winifreda Watson-Armstrong. Although Meggie must have taken on much of the burden of overseeing the transformation of the estate, Armstrong himself 'took the keenest interest in the work, every detail being submitted to him ... Lady Armstrong was often up and round the estate at six in the morning, in order to see his wishes carried out, and the whole work was ably superintended by the steward, Mr William Bertram.' Many wild stories were apparently told about what Armstrong was doing, and the great feats he was achieving. 'A lady visitor from the south solemnly assured me that [Sir William] had had every rock brought to Cragside and placed in the position they are now occupying,' wrote Winifreda, 'and nothing would make her believe to the contrary.'

As time went by, the Armstrongs added to their estate at Cragside by buying land from neighbouring landowners until they owned most of the land from Rothbury to Warton along the Coquet and as far to the north-west as Netherton, extending to almost 15,000 acres.[3] Their acquisitions included Debdon Moor from the Duke of Northumberland, the Cartington estate from the Beck family, the Trewitt estate from the Smart family, and the Warton estate from the Pawson family. They planted several million trees and shrubs, as well as constructing five lakes and several miles of private drives. 'Practically not a tree or shrub has perished, testifying to [Armstrong's] care in his first choice of plants, which he knew would be congenial to the soil, and, secondly, to the manner of planting trees. He was well rewarded for his care and patience,' wrote Winifreda.

The earliest visitors to Cragside, in August 1865, were I. K. Brunel's widow, Mary (née Horsley), and Sophia, Lady Hawes, her friend and sister-in-law. The friendship between the Armstrongs and the Brunels had been cemented after I. K.'s death by the employment of his son Henry as an apprentice at Elswick. Henry would be invited regularly to Jesmond, and his affection for his hosts was evident in his letters home. 'Lady Armstrong eats very little herself but I think she is fond of organising her friends,' he wrote to his mother. 'Lady Armstrong has given me a cheese toaster in which I luxuriate.'

It wasn't until the summer of 1866 that the Sopwiths visited Cragside for the first time. 'I went with Annie by express train to Morpeth, whence we took a barouche to Rothbury,' wrote Sopwith in his diary. 'We arrived at Cragside at about 3pm and had a most enjoyable walk, first by the sides of a picturesque burn with precipitous and rocky scenery, fringed with natural wood and at every step presenting new and remarkable combinations of rock and wood and water ... We passed along roads and an iron bridge in course of construction, and then proceeded to a lake of about 16 acres which Sir William has formed over what was a nearly flat and meaningless morass.' Armstrong then retrieved a small boat from a rustic boathouse and rowed the Sopwiths across the lake.

The vessel had recently been acquired in London by Stuart

Rendel, who had been commissioned by Armstrong to find a rowing boat 'of the Richmond wherry class – safe, commodious and sufficiently good-looking'. Armstrong had been keen to avoid anything too ostentatious. 'In painting and general fitting it should be very quiet and suited to the character of this place. Probably varnished wood without paint would be best.' He had also considered the problem of transport. 'As to getting it here, it could be rowed down to the wharf where the Newcastle steam boats go and there put on board for Newcastle. Thence I would send it to Cragside on a wagon.'

A few days later, the Sopwiths awoke to a scintillatingly clear morning, 'every object on the distant hills as well as in the adjacent landscape being sharp and crisp and as distinctly visible as in a pure mountain atmosphere'. After breakfast at Cragside, William and Meggie took them in an open carriage to nearby Cartington, where Armstrong went out to shoot for a couple of hours and the others walked to the ruins of Cartington Castle. 'As we walked,' noted Sopwith, 'we heard from time to time the sharp clear click of the "Armstrong Gun".' At the foot of Cartington Hill was a small, square house in a walled garden that Armstrong would later lend to Andrew Noble and his family, and where they spent many happy summers.

It would be the first of several visits to Cragside by Thomas and Annie Sopwith, who were enthralled by the wonders of the place, although they found the 'awful punctuality' with which Armstrong conducted his affairs something of a trial. More to their liking was his love of trees: 'The varieties of pines and other trees formed a subject of much interesting explanation from Sir William, who enters most thoroughly into every detail connected with their natural history and progress.'

Armstrong was equally punctilious when it came to modern conveniences. 'I am very much in want of a telegraph to this place,' he wrote in March 1867 to Stuart Rendel, who was expected to deal with practical as well as commercial problems. 'I must have one of my own from Alnwick, which is the nearest station.' A major concern was that the post arrived in Rothbury late in the morning and left early in the afternoon, 'so that the inhabitants and visitors must either remain in the house during the best part of the day or run the risk of not being able to answer important letters by return of post'. Although Armstrong believed that it would be a worthwhile investment for one of the established telegraph companies to install the necessary wiring, especially since Rothbury was becoming a popular holiday resort, he offered to make a personal contribution to the costs and help set up the service: 'I could arrange for a respectable and intelligent hotelkeeper to take charge of the instrument and receiver to deliver the messages,' he wrote. 'Would you be good enough to call upon the secretary of the International Telegraph Co. and ask what can be done.'

Another early visitor to Cragside was John Callcott Horsley, the artist brother of Mary Brunel, who believed he had an ancestral connection with the nearby village of Longhorsley. 'I was invited to stay at Cragside, [Sir William's] beautiful home in the moors, near Rothbury, in Northumberland, which was but a few miles from the village of Long Horsley,' wrote the painter in his memoirs. 'I need not say that I quickly told my host of my interest in this place and the castle, and we thereupon went to see it. The castle was then inhabited by a Roman Catholic priest, who most kindly showed us the place.'

It was John Horsley who introduced Armstrong to the man who did more than any other to transform an unremarkable country cottage into what became known as 'the palace of a modern magician':[4] a relatively unknown, Edinburgh-born architect by the name of Richard Norman Shaw. Shaw had made some elegant additions to Willesley, John Horsley's old farmhouse at Cranbrook in Kent, and gone on to build two new houses at Groombridge in Sussex – Glen Andred for the marine artist E. W. Cooke and Leys Wood for his own cousin James Temple. In May 1868, Meggie Armstrong visited the Horsleys at Cranbrook to inspect Shaw's work on Willesley[5] and reputedly took 'glowing reports' back to Newcastle.[6]

Although heavily influenced by Augustus Pugin, champion of the Gothic Revival, Shaw and his partner William Eden Nesfield had moved beyond the prevalent architectural fashions in order to establish a new, more fluid style of architecture, one which came to be called Old English. Old English was a romantic reaction against everything considered 'modern' at the time. Many of its features – half-timbered, tile-hung façades, steeply pitched roofs, Tudor chimneys, and gables, leaded windows, galleried towers – harked back to the Middle Ages, but were arranged and combined in an innovative way, presenting a vision of an idealised past that was highly attractive to the aspiring middle classes. Shaw's drawings for Leys Wood caused a sensation when they were exhibited at the Royal Academy in 1870; apart from its nostalgic appeal, here was a house that, rather than sitting sedately in the middle of a formal garden, seemed to soar out of the rocky eminence on which it stood.

Shaw's first task for the Armstrongs was to design an extension to the Jesmond banqueting hall to accommodate John Horsley's *Prince Hal*. In September 1869, while staying with the Armstrongs at Jesmond Dene, he wrote to his wife, 'I had a tremendous talk with Sir William about his gallery this morning, and think I am to have my own way. I dearly like my own way and not other people's.'[7] On his return from Elswick that evening, Armstrong had taken Shaw on a long walk when 'he talked of guns and engines no end'.

That weekend, Shaw was summoned to Cragside and asked to draw up plans for adding a library and dining room to the north end of the house, with a plunge bath and hot-air heating system in the basement, and two storeys of bedrooms above. The architect apparently sketched out the whole of his initial scheme for the additions in just a single day, while his host and other guests were out on a shooting expedition. This feat was elucidated a century later by the poet John Betjeman, a keen admirer of Cragside: 'In those days, architects had long cuffs, and it was always said that they would just sketch out something during dinner "on the cuff". Well, you could add on here and draw a plan – and that would be how the house would be created. Shaw was a very funny man – a man of the greatest possible charm – and he could sketch out rapidly for you what your house was going to look like, rather like Lutyens could.'[8]

Armstrong approved Shaw's designs on the spot and told him to put the plan into action without delay. 'It will be very satisfactory working for Sir William,' wrote Shaw to his wife, 'as he knows right well what he is about.' He went on to mention 'wonderful hydraulic machines that do all sorts of things you can imagine'.[9] Although the two men had their own, sometimes conflicting, views about the development of Cragside – according to Shaw's biographer Andrew Saint, Shaw was never given the free rein he wanted at Cragside – they would remain on good terms throughout the 15 years that Shaw worked on the house. During this period, Shaw commissioned some of the finest craftsmen of the age to enhance the medieval qualities of his building. They included William Morris, James Forsyth, Philip Webb, and William Richard Lethaby, who later became the first professor of design at London's Royal College of Art.

Armstrong had been attracted to the site of Cragside not only by its natural beauty but also by the potential it offered for the use of water power. Consequently, he lost no time in damming the nearby Debdon Burn and Black Burn to create reservoirs, eventually five in all, from which water could be piped all over the estate.[10] Crucially, the artificial lakes also provided heads of water that could be harnessed to drive hydraulic machinery. The water from Debdon Lake powered a turbine which operated the estate sawmill, and it was here that Armstrong carried out his first experiments in the production of hydroelectricity.

Tumbleton Lake was formed by damming the Debdon Burn lower down, creating a head of water to serve the pump house of 1866, where pumps driven by a hydraulic engine provided water to Cragside house. Meanwhile, the main course of Black Burn was dammed to form the largest of the five lakes, which was used for boating and fishing as well as the provision of hydraulic power to Cragend Farm. Most impressive of all, two more lakes were created by diverting water from Black Burn high up on the moors and channelling it through a canal, a pipe, an open wooden flume, and a stream to feed two new lakes in the area known as Nelly's Moss. The lower lake provided a head of water to drive all the hydraulic machinery in the house as well as the cascades in the rock garden.

By the time the Sopwiths visited Cragside in November of 1870, radical changes to the property were already under way.

For the first time, Thomas and Annie were able to travel all the way from Newcastle by rail, a journey of two and a half hours, part of which took them along the newly opened line from Scots Gap to Rothbury. They were met at the station by Johnny Watson, Armstrong's nephew, who drove them to their destination in a wagonette.

'A single glance at the house suffices to show the extensive additions now being made to it, viz. an entirely new dining room, drawing room, lobby, Turkish and other baths, etc.,' wrote Sopwith in his diary. 'These are now from 10 to 15 feet from the ground and were, during our stay, fully explained to us by Sir William. The arrangements for warming and ventilating appear to be most complete, and when finished the house will certainly be replete with comfort as well as elegance, for nothing can exceed the scientific skill brought to bear upon all the building, or it may rather be said upon all the engineering appliances by Sir William and the good taste for economic and suitable matters in which Lady Armstrong eminently excels.'

Based on the idea of ancient Roman baths and introduced to Britain in the 1850s, Turkish baths were all the rage at the time. (In 1872 Armstrong's cousin Addison Potter, who was mayor at the time, set up a Turkish bath company in Pilgrim Street, Newcastle, whose directors included the prosperous local coal-owner John Joicey.) The complex that Shaw built at Cragside included a steam bath, a cold plunge, a hot bath, and a shower, as well as water closets and a changing room. Ingeniously, it also helped to heat the rest of the house, since the space occupied by the baths was situated between chambers containing huge coiled waterpipes, which, heated by nearby boilers, were the source of hot air that was ducted up to the rooms above.

Another groundbreaking phenomenon was the kitchen, built to twice the height of the other rooms in order to promote cool temperatures and to let in an abundance of light.[11] It included a huge Eagle range by H. Walker and Son and roasting fire and ovens by Dinning and Cooke of Newcastle. In front of the fire was a wooden plate-warmer, and above the sink was a rudimentary dishwasher, intended mainly for rinsing plates. Hydraulic mechanisms were installed to rotate the spits in front of the range and to operate the dumbwaiter (lift) used to transport food and pots and pans between the kitchen and the sculleries below. Electric gongs were used to summon guests to meals, and there was even an internal telephone system. The greatest boon to servants was the hydraulic lift which could be used to carry coal to the upstairs rooms and transport laundry, warming pans, and bedroom china between the various floors. Indeed, most of the technical wonders were designed to limit routine tasks, lighten loads, and improve efficiency. As Hugh Dixon of the National Trust points out, Armstrong was the first to unite elements that would come to be taken for granted in ordinary homes during the 20th century: hot and cold running water, central heating, mechanical aids, and electricity. 'It was here that modern living began,' wrote Dixon.

The Turkish baths were used for the first time on 4 November, the day of the Sopwiths' arrival – only one of the interesting elements of their visit, as the diarist recorded: 'After a conversation, we had lunch at about (perhaps exactly) one; at two we were in the grounds, or rather among the rocks and crags which form the immediate foreground or basis of the house. Here, tree after tree was visited, all of them remarkable for their rapid growth and many of them for botanical excellence or pecularities. It seems strange to look at trees between 15 and 20 feet height which have all been planted, as Sir William told us, within the last five years.

'Of the extraordinary character of the scenery near the house, there can be only one description: it is unique – wild yet beautiful, rugged yet in every part easily accessible, rough yet grand with beautiful foliages. It is a romantic, bold and gigantic piece of landscape gardening. It is now some time since a lake of 17 acres gave a great charm to the general effect and now Sir William is making a river – literally – a stream of considerable width which will be a great addition to the view from the house.'

Still imbued, even today, with Armstrong's personality, Cragside is a welcoming house despite its size and large quantity of rooms – 'one for every day of the year, and for every mood', in the opinion of John Betjeman. Many of the rooms are characterised by relatively modest proportions and subtle but confidently conceived interior schemes.

The library, originally the drawing room, is panelled in light oak, elaborately carved by Shaw's favourite craftsman, James Forsyth, and lined on two sides with bookcases to a height of five feet; it includes an intricate beamed and coffered ceiling, also by Forsyth, and a fireplace of Egyptian onyx, red marble and blue majolica tiles.[12] Wallpaper in two shades of green was supplied by Cowtan of London. The deep bay window incorporates stained glass supplied by Morris & Co. and designed by Edward Burne-Jones, Dante Gabriel Rossetti, and Ford Madox Brown. In the dining room, the inglenook fireplace made of grey stone is large enough to accommodate two heavy oak settles. Behind these, on either side of the fire, are stained-glass windows of the Four Seasons by William Morris. The lintel is supported by massive capitals, carved with cocks and wolves.

This was only the beginning, however. As time went by, the house grew and grew. Betjeman, who admitted that he would have liked to have lived at Cragside, had a theory to explain its genesis.[13] 'First, I think, [Armstrong] was going to create a castle. And then he decided, or somebody decided, later to add a ballroom, so the castle as you came in was immense, its stone arches ... and passages never quite ending, leading you on to another corner. And then they suddenly decided to go for pleasure and not be such a fortress, so there is a bit of it, which is the ballroom part, which is in the Renaissance style – most beautifully done, and a fireplace as big as a house in the ballroom with alabaster carving all over it. I've never seen anything like it, never seen anything so big before.'

Even when Shaw had finished his work, the house remained dramatically exposed in its setting. In Mark Girouard's opinion, it must have looked more like a castle than a house: 'It was floating on the top of a craggy hillside, as you can see in the old photographs. Now the trees have grown up all round it, which give it a curious, rather spooky character. It's a kind of magic place.'[14]

Writing in 1881, the architect and painter Thomas Raffles Davison described the indelible impression that Cragside had made on him:

'Imagine a great hill covered from bottom to crest with huge grey boulder stones, and halfway up, cut out of a steppe on the hillside, the site and placing of a building of the most picturesque kind imaginable. Then, having chosen the site and placed the house, call forth your gardeners by the hundreds, and bid them make amongst and around those crags and boulders cunningly winding walks, every one formed of steps of the natural grey stone. Then bring your evergreens and rare heathers by the tens of thousands, plant them over and about the place till there is hardly a spot of bare soil left; then with the rarest and commonest ferns plant every crevice among the boulders. Form two artificial lakes in the valley near the house, so that you can defy suspicion of the manufacture. Make a carriage approach from opposite ends of the valley, so easy and pleasant that it might have been transplanted from Hyde Park; and, beside these, let there be rolling along the hill, at two heights above, carriage drives that for views and healthful breezes shall be immaculate. Along the valley let there by a brooklet teeming with fish, and covered and bordered with trees and rocks forming a veritable glen: span the stream by rustic and iron bridges, which form the centres of a score of perfect pictures.

'As for the hall itself, you will not sum it up in words – for beyond its charming rooms, which give an added pleasure and refinement to life, there are in it such stores of art, pictures, sculptures, pottery and books as only a princely and discriminating wealth can bring together.'[15]

The Armstrongs' residence at Cragside attracted many friends and visitors to the area. In particular, the Nobles and the Rendels took out a joint tenancy on nearby Lorbottle Hall, which each family occupied alternately for two months at a time. 'We had the happiest time of our lives there,' remarked Margery Noble.[16] Among their many eminent guests were the biologist T. H. Huxley, his wife, Henrietta, and their family.

Some of the magic of that time is captured by Mrs Noble in her memoirs. 'One evening when the Huxley girls were staying with us, and some young men, we decided to cook our own dinner in the woods called Maiden Chambers on the hill above the house,' she wrote. 'We carried up our cooking utensils and food, but it was nearly dark before the food was ready and quite dark when we had finished. As we sat round the blazing fire, Miss Rachel Huxley and Mr Harding played chess – like Ferdinand and Miranda in Shakespeare's *Tempest*. We heard the sound of music out of darkness. It sounded fairy-like and mysterious. It was our gamekeeper, John Dickinson, and his sons; he played the violin very well, and his sons were musical. The young people danced reels in the firelight among the trees while they played.'

12

High Tide on the Tyne

In early August 1867, Thomas Sopwith paid a visit to Elswick Ordnance Works, where he found Armstrong 'in the midst of red hot iron, blazing furnaces, enveloped in the gloom of thick darkness and dust'. The scene bore 'no slight resemblance of what one may conceive the "infernal regions" to be – and this was Sir William's own expression for it'.

In these same 'infernal regions' an entirely new chapter was beginning in the history of industrial Tyneside, for Armstrong had recently signed an agreement with the shipbuilder Charles Mitchell to collaborate on the construction of gunboats. The vessels were to be built at Mitchell's yard at Low Walker, about six miles downriver from the Elswick Works, while the weapons would be manufactured and fitted at Elswick. Mitchell's had been preferred to the much larger firm of Palmer Brothers at Jarrow, on the south bank of the Tyne, which had built one of the earliest ironclad warships, as well as the world's first screw collier (a motor-powered ship for transporting coal). Mitchell was a skilled linguist with useful foreign connections – since 1862, he had been building ships for the Russian navy at St Petersburg.

Armstrong's original association with Mitchell came from the need to test guns at sea. Armstrong had habitually sought remote areas for weapons testing, such as the Northumberland moorland and beaches, but although these areas were sparsely inhabited there was still a regular stream of complaints – as well as the occasional invasion scare – and testing far offshore would seem to avoid these problems. George Rendel realised that a squat barge-like boat would make an excellent vehicle for mounting guns and, as the

Elswick historian Kenneth Warren points out, it would prove to be 'a short step from a gun experimentally mounted in a barge to a floating gun usable as a coastal battery'.[1] The man charged with building the required vessels was Charles Mitchell.

Born into a Methodist family in Aberdeen, Mitchell had travelled south in 1842 to take a job at the Tyne yard of his fellow Aberdonian John Coutts. The two men had met at an Aberdeen iron foundry and engineering works, where Mitchell was an apprentice draughtsman, while also finding time to attend evening classes in science at the local Marischal College. He was a diligent student with a passion for carving model ships from pieces of wood. By the time Mitchell arrived in Newcastle at the age of 22, shipbuilding was well established on the Tyne, serving an ever-growing coal trade with London and south-east England, but most colliers were wooden and dependent on sail for their propulsion. John Coutts was a pioneer in the building of iron ships.

Mitchell had left home with very little money, and most of what he did possess was borrowed from his father and repaid at the first opportunity. Always punctilious in the settling of debts, he displayed a 'rugged independence' when it came to financial matters, according to his biographer; this was sometimes interpreted as meanness but was rather 'an indication of a man of very firm character, determined to stand on his own feet'.[2]

After two years, Mitchell migrated to London to work for a firm of marine engineers, from where he journeyed around France, Germany, and Italy and discovered a talent for languages. During his travels, he was captivated by the Renaissance churches of Italy with their frescoes, stained glass, and campaniles, taking a particular interest in the fabulous Byzantine mosaics at Ravenna. In 1852, however – acknowledging that his first love was the sea and ships – he returned to the Tyne to set up his own shipyard at Low Walker, where many other expatriate Scots had settled.[3] His marriage in 1854 to Anne Swan, from a large local family, brought him useful social and business connections. Two of Anne's brothers, Charles Sheriton and Henry Frederick, joined Mitchell's firm as apprentices; Charles would later be instrumental in the founding of Swan Hunter shipbuilders.

The Russian connection had begun in 1857, when Mitchell was commissioned to supply canal and river steamers to transport grain from the interior of Russia to the Black Sea. A few years later, after the Russians had decided to convert their yards at St Petersburg for the construction of iron ships, he was asked to train the workers in the new techniques. Five warships were built at the yards under the English firm's auspices; the Russians were so impressed by Mitchell's work that they presented him with a gold snuffbox, inlaid with diamonds, and also conferred on him the Imperial Order of St Stanislaus. When Mitchell was obliged to return to Tyneside, he left his 20-year-old brother-in-law, Henry Swan, in charge at St Petersburg, where he stayed until the Russian contract ended in 1865. Swan then entered into formal partnership with Mitchell and became manager of Low Walker.

The Russians kept up contact with Mitchell, placing orders for turret ships (with guns mounted in a revolving turret) as well as canal and river vessels. When the Russian High Admiral, the Grand Duke Constantine, visited Newcastle with his retinue in 1871, Mitchell and Swan led the reception party at Central Station.[4] The visitors were taken to Jesmond Towers, Mitchell's home, where they were joined for dinner by local dignitaries.

Meanwhile, Mitchell and Swan's business prospered and orders flooded in from all over the world, for merchant ships, passenger ships, barges, and other vessels. The firm provided specialist craft for the laying of undersea cable along the coast of South America and elsewhere. Between 1853 and 1883, some 450 ships would be launched from the Low Walker yard.

The first product of the collaboration between Armstrong and Mitchell was *Staunch* – a 79-foot-long 'floating gun carriage' ordered by the Admiralty, designed by George Rendel, built by Charles Mitchell, and completed in 1868. Carrying a single 'disappearing' 9-inch muzzle-loading gun – which was raised from the shallow hold to its firing position by hydraulic action, and lowered for reloading – *Staunch* had no protective iron skin, making it much lighter, faster, and cheaper than a lumbering ironclad, and its low draught made it ideal for patrolling shallow coastal waters. *Staunch*'s key features reflected Armstrong's abiding belief that it would always be possible to produce a gun that was superior to armour – and that battleships should therefore be designed with the prime aim of exploiting the latest developments in gunnery. Writing to *The Times* in May 1869, he emphasised 'the value of small vessels for defending our numerous sea ports against the sudden inroads of hostile ironclads in time of war'.

In the event, *Staunch* was a resounding success for Low Walker.[5] During the 1870s and early 1880s, the yard completed 21 of these vessels, including 3 more for Britain, 2 for the Netherlands, 4 for Australia, and 11 for China, and the same basic design was used for orders from Brazil, Chile, and Italy.[6] By 1877, Elswick was shipping dismantled *Staunch* gunboats in crates to various parts of the world and having them reassembled at their destination under the supervision of experienced engineers from Elswick.[7] The Rendel brothers never felt entirely happy about the link with Charles Mitchell, however. 'In dealing with Mitchell and Co. we are preparing a rival who may turn against us,' wrote George to Stuart on one occasion.

The biggest impediment to Armstrong's commercial ambitions at this time was the state of the River Tyne itself. As the size of vessels using the river increased and shipyards had to expand to accommodate them, the relative shallowness of the water presented an ever more serious challenge. However, extensive dredging operations had been under way since 1860 under the auspices of the Tyne Commission. Millions of tons of sand and other obstacles had been removed, eventually providing a 26-foot depth of water at Elswick. By 1878 Elswick had been equipped with a wharf from which guns and machinery could be shipped.

Another crucial event was the removal of the 18th-century river bridge, with its low, obstructive arches, and its replacement with a steel swing bridge – an innovation which, for the first time, made it possible for big ships to pass upriver beyond Newcastle. The foundation work was carried out by the Tyne Commissioners, and the bridge's wrought-iron superstructure and hydraulic operating machinery were both supplied by Armstrong. It gave him a gateway to the sea – the prelude to opening a shipyard at Elswick.[8]

Armstrong collaborated with Charles Mitchell to create the gunboat *Staunch*. Designed by George Rendel and launched in 1868, she became the foundation of a shipbuilding empire.

The first battleship built at Elswick was *HMS Victoria*, named in celebration of Queen Victoria's golden jubilee year. She passed through the Tyne's Swing Bridge on 6 April 1888.

Occupying virtually the same site as the bridge built in AD120 by the Roman emperor Hadrian, the 560-foot-long Swing Bridge has three piers of solid masonry set into cast-iron cylinders sunk to a depth of 45 feet below low-water mark and filled with concrete.[9] Its two central openings are spanned by the twin parts of the superstructure that swing around the central pier. Each of these openings provides a clear passage of 104 feet – wide enough to allow the largest ships in the navy at the time to pass through. Opened and closed with apparent ease by means of hydraulic power, its movable section is 281 feet long and weighs more than 1,450 tons. The Swing Bridge was the latest in a series of such groundbreaking bridges built by the Elswick firm.

Reflecting a decade later on the marvellous ingenuity of the Swing Bridge, the antiquarian expert John Collingwood Bruce pointed out that the first ship that passed through the bridge, on 17 July 1876, was the Italian ship *Europa*, which continued upriver to the Elswick Ordnance Works to take on board a huge gun for the Italian government. 'In the second century, Rome exhibited on the banks of the Tyne the triumphs of her engineering skill,' he wrote. 'In the 19th century the chieftains of Tyneside showed Rome how largely Britain had profited by her instruction.'[10] Still operational today, though opened only rarely, the Swing Bridge had its busiest ever year in 1924, when it opened more than 6,000 times. By the early 21st century, it had been swung open well over a quarter of a million times. The Swing Bridge also proved a fitting companion to Stephenson's High Level Bridge of 1850, slightly to the west, which was high enough above the waterline to allow large ships to pass underneath it.

By this time, Elswick was producing truly monster guns and, by necessity, the plant for making them was steadily increasing in capacity; massive lifting machinery was also needed wherever the guns were to be moved or offloaded from ships. Eventually, as Marshall Bastable wrote, 'It was hydraulic machinery to manipulate the enormous guns that became the main point of the innovator's imagination.'[11] In 1876 the Elswick Works notched up an extraordinary series of world records. That year saw the opening of the Tyne's Swing Bridge, an Elswick creation – the largest swing bridge in the world. The first ship to pass under the bridge was *Europa*, which had come to Elswick to collect a 104-ton gun – the largest gun ever constructed. It was lifted on board the vessel by the new hydraulic 'sheer-legs' hoisting device, the largest of its type in the world and capable of lifting 120 tons. At La Spezia, in Italy, the gun was lifted out of the ship by an Elswick-made hydraulic crane weighing 180 tons – again, the largest in the world.

The Italian connection with 'the chieftains of Tyneside', already a decade old, would become more important as the years went by. It dated from a meeting in London in 1866 between Stuart Rendel and Captain Augusto Albini of the Italian navy. 'I cannot remember how I met Albini, now admiral and senator,' wrote Rendel in his memoirs. 'He had invented a rifle which he was pressing on Belgium, and he was acting as the Italian naval attaché.'[12] In fact, Albini had come to London at the height of the Austro-Prussian War, intent on buying Armstrong guns for the Italians, who were fighting at sea on the Prussian side. Rendel used his acquaintance with Albini for 'the furtherance of the first order for guns from the Italian government'. For several years afterwards, Stuart Rendel was the sole channel of communication between Albini and Elswick: 'This was the origin of our great Italian connection, and Admiral Albini is now, some 35 years later, head of the Rome office of the Armstrong firm.'[13]

In the summer of 1866, Albini bought a large quantity of Armstrong 150-pounders, each weighing 6 tons, and urged the firm to let him have more. After some hesitation – and following the Italian defeat by the Austrians at Lissa (Vis) in the eastern Adriatic – Armstrong won favour with Albini by agreeing to divert to Italy a consignment of guns ordered by the Turks but not paid for.

Over the next 18 years, thanks largely to Albini's agency, Italy would remain Elswick's most important client for large naval guns, and the close commercial relationship would eventually lead to the setting up of a branch of Armstrong's company at Pozzuoli in the Bay of Naples.[14]

Stuart Rendel's business dealings with Albini took him often to Rome, Naples and La Spezia, but his brother George soon became an even more familiar sight in Italian naval circles. Since George was, in his brother's words, 'the most original and successful engineer in the mounting and working of heavy guns at sea', the Italians held his opinion in high regard and would regularly invite him to Italy to solve any problems in person.

Stuart Rendel was the prime mover in securing foreign sales for Elswick over 12 years, from 1864 to 1876.[15] He believed that his strength as a negotiator sprang from his 'intimate and personally acquired knowledge and experience of facts deeply concerning the countries that I visited'. In the early years, he sometimes felt at a disadvantage because he was an outsider. 'I was not an inventor or even an engineer, and I was invading a citadel jealously garrisoned by military officers and officials,' he wrote.[16] Stuart was relieved when Armstrong eventually agreed that he should join the firm.

In Marshall Bastable's view, 'Armstrong and Rendel constituted one of the great partnerships in business history. Like Boulton and Watt, or their contemporaries and rivals, Albert and Tom Vickers, their different talents, personalities and backgrounds complemented one another.' While Armstrong looked after technological development and the overall direction of the firm, Rendel promoted Elswick's reputation abroad and developed a worldwide network of agents and clients. 'Armstrong was the great engineer and businessman, Rendel the salesman and negotiator, the man who had the right friends and contacts to help get the company off to a strong start.'[17]

During the late 1870s, another remarkable Elswick pair were making world-changing discoveries – this time, in the field of gunpowder. They were Frederick Abel and Andrew Noble, and together they determined the nature of the chemical changes produced by firing explosives. To find out exactly what happened inside a gun when fired, Noble invented a chronoscope, a device that recorded – to one millionth of a second – the speed of the shot when passing any point in the gun's bore; he also devised an electrical mechanism to record the pressures inside a gun. Abel was a former professor of chemistry at the Royal Military Academy in Woolwich whose friendship with Armstrong dated from Crimean War days. He and Noble carried out many hazardous experiments at the Elswick laboratories until they eventually created gunpowder with such slow-burning properties it resulted in a dramatic increase in the speed at which projectiles could be fired. 'At one bound,' reported Noble, 'muzzle velocities were increased from 1,600 feet per second to 2,100 feet per second.' He convinced the defence establishment that, to obtain the most advantage from the slow-burning powder, gun barrels needed to be lengthened.

Noble's advances were all based on mathematical deduction, and he conducted his scientific research in the intervals between his management obligations at Elswick. 'It was largely because Andrew Noble spent not merely strenuous days in the Works, but also laborious nights in the laboratory, that employment in the Works steadily expanded,' wrote A. R. Fairbairn.

A longer barrel made it much more difficult to load a gun from the muzzle, so a major consequence of the adoption of the Abel–Noble system was a return to breech-loading. Revolutionary improvements in steelmaking also helped to rekindle interest in large breech-loaders, which had been generally disregarded by the British establishment since Armstrong's departure from Woolwich in 1863. The new 'open-hearth process' of steelmaking, developed by William Siemens and Pierre Emile Martin, was a great advance on the earlier Bessemer method, resulting in a product virtually free from phosphorus, and therefore much more suitable than any other form of steel for the manufacture of guns.

Other new weapons appearing on the market at this time included the Gatling gun, a forerunner of the modern machine-gun, designed by the American inventor Richard Gatling during the American Civil War.[18] Even though it had to be cranked by hand, the original Gatling caused great excitement in military and naval circles. In 1870 Armstrong became the British licensee for the Gatling Gun Company, and by the end of the following year he had 36 Gatling guns, considerably modified from the American model, ready for delivery to the British government.[19] The Gatling provided good business for Armstrong over a long period, and a whole department at Elswick was later devoted to its manufacture. It was used both as a field gun and for arming ships until it was superseded in the 1890s by the Maxim gun, the first truly automatic weapon.

By the end of 1879, Armstrong had constructed two breech-

The Japanese cruiser *Yoshino*, designed by Philip Watts, and launched at Elswick in 1892, was hailed as the fastest cruiser in the world after exceeding 23 knots in trials.

Yashima was the first battleship constructed in Newcastle for the Japanese imperial navy. In 1896, shortly after launch, she was moored at the Newcastle quayside for public viewing.

loaders using Andrew Noble's slow-burning powder and had them tested at Shoeburyness; the Admiralty men were so impressed when they saw what the guns could do that they swiftly placed a large order. A few years later, he was asked to make two 12-inch guns of 43-ton weight to government specifications, but he objected to using mild steel for the outer sleeve that would enclose the steel barrels. In the event, he was allowed to construct wire-wound barrels – something he had been unable to do until an unexploited patent on the method expired in 1877 – and eventually convinced the ordnance committee that the steel-and-wire gun was superior to the all-steel gun.[20]

As demand for gunboats from Low Walker increased, and the possibility arose that Armstrong and Mitchell might collaborate on more sophisticated warships, pressure grew for a more formal relationship between the two firms. George Rendel, who saw Mitchell as a wily operator looking for a chance to take advantage of Elswick, was worried. 'I dread commencing shipbuilding,' he wrote to Stuart in April 1881. 'We shall lose money at first, besides getting entirely overweighed with work. At the same time I am not satisfied to create a fine business for Mitchell for nothing, and I doubt if the present plan of contracting for ships to be sub-let can long be maintained, especially for important vessels like ironclads or large cruisers.'

When it came to it, Armstrong offered to buy the Low Walker shipyard from Charles Mitchell and Henry Swan and invited the two men to become directors with him in a limited liability company to be known as Sir W. G. Armstrong, Mitchell and Company Ltd. The company was launched in November 1882 with a capital of £1,575,000; the board members included William Siemens and Josiah Vavasseur, an expert in gun mountings who brought with him his valuable patents and designs, as well as Andrew Noble, William Cruddas, Stuart and Hamilton Rendel, and Percy Westmacott. (William Cruddas had succeeded his father, George, as Elswick's financial director in 1861.) The future prosperity of the firm would depend on guns adapted for greatly increased charges of powder. Combined with the Siemens–Martin method of steelmaking, the improved powder would enable the construction of guns of unprecedented firepower, ushering in a new era in artillery.[21]

As far as the Elswick managers were concerned, the merger with Mitchell had absorbed a potential rival, and the public sale of shares had raised £665,000 towards the financing of new ventures, but Stuart Rendel regretted the 'mischievous separation between capital and management' inherent in a limited liability company.[22] In July 1884, in a letter to the governor of Madras, he wrote, 'The Elswick company flourishes and gives us no anxiety as yet, but all the charm of the works has gone out of it for me now that we are no longer a family firm.' Rendel maintained his opposition for a long time afterwards. 'We put a needless million into the Mitchell and Swan pockets over the purchase of Low Walker,' he would say in later life.

Hot on the heels of *Staunch*, and coinciding with the formation of Armstrong Mitchell, came a new Elswick warship inspired by the gunboat but much larger and faster. Introduced in 1882, *Esmeralda* carried two 10-inch breech-loading guns and six 6-inch guns, and could reach speeds of more than 18 knots – making her, in Armstrong's words, 'the swiftest and most powerfully armed cruiser in the world'. *Esmeralda* had no armour, but the vessel's engines, boilers, and other vital parts were contained inside steel decks below the waterline, so that she would be 'almost absolutely secure against the worst effects of projectiles'. This was the first of a group of deadly, well-protected warships that would gain universal fame as 'Elswick cruisers'.[23]

Although *Esmeralda* was another triumph for George Rendel, he and Stuart both fell out of favour with Armstrong during this period for having pursued their own independent interests, supposedly at the expense of Elswick. George's contribution to two government committees on ship design had attracted the attention of leading members of the Admiralty, and two first lords in succession had invited him to leave Elswick and join the navy's board of control. A third offer coincided with pressure from his second wife for a move away from Newcastle – and this time George accepted. There was also a suggestion that he had had a serious disagreement with Andrew Noble over the management of Elswick. In 1882 he left the firm for which he had worked for some 30 years to become a civil lord of the Admiralty, a new post created to allow the admittance of 'practical men of science'.[24] By this time, George was married to Licinia Pinelli, whom he had met on a trip to Rome. His first wife, Harriet Simpson, had died in 1878 after bearing him five sons.

Stuart Rendel, meanwhile, had fulfilled a long-held political ambition by entering Parliament in 1880 as Liberal MP for Montgomeryshire. 'Though I never suspected it, and I think Armstrong himself scarcely knew it, the effect upon his mind of my brother's going to the Admiralty and of my going into Parliament was as though we had both rather deserted Elswick and himself,' wrote Stuart.[25] 'He was not in the least a jealous man, yet I can now see that his regard for Elswick was the one overwhelming passion of his life. He did not feel flattered by the striking recognition of my brother George's high qualities, nor consider that his situation was a tribute to Elswick.' Also, although Armstrong had always instinctively sympathised with the Liberal viewpoint, within a few years he would split with the Gladstonian Liberals over Irish home rule. According to Stuart, 'My politics he detested and his dislike of them was needlessly stirred by others. Thus, my entering Parliament, though with his assent, estranged him and, in conjunction with my brother's joining the Admiralty, threw him more exclusively into reliance on others.'

In fact, the establishment of Armstrong Mitchell coincided with a shift in the balance of power at Elswick in favour of Andrew Noble and his family. Noble's work on gun construction had won him recognition as one of the world's leading experts on the subject. He also had a conspicuous passion for Elswick, apparently equal to that of Armstrong's, and served it with single-minded loyalty. On the formation of the limited company, he became its vice-chairman, and although Armstrong remained its titular head, the reins of management were taken up by Noble. Noble was an intensely driven character whose favourite form of recreation was the physically demanding game of real tennis (the original indoor racquet sport from which the modern game of lawn tennis is descended), which he played in a specially built court near his home in Jesmond. Yet, according to A. R. Fairbairn, it remained true that 'part of the wages of every skilled man and labourer received in the works, week by week, had been earned for him by the incessant activity and Herculean toil of Andrew Noble, for he, more than anyone else, created the steady and increasing employment which the works enjoyed'.

Meanwhile, Armstrong, who was 72 years old when Armstrong Mitchell was formed, was happy to delegate more of the day-to-day running of the company to his able lieutenants so that he could give more time to his favourite pursuits, including experiments with electricity.

Another aspect of the merger with Mitchell was the plan to set up a steel works at Elswick. The ideal man to run such an operation was identified as Henry Dyer, a retired Royal Artillery colonel who had worked at Shoeburyness testing range before joining Whitworth's in Manchester. Armstrong and Noble persuaded him to jump ship. Dyer would 'supply excellently the kind of experience we want for our steel works', wrote Armstrong to Stuart Rendel in October 1882. The Elswick Steel Works, incorporating two Siemens–Martin open-hearth furnaces, opened in 1884, having cost £15,000 to build.[26] Output increased rapidly, reaching more than 2,500 tons a week by the end of the century. The plant was designed to supply the firm with castings and forgings for the production of giant guns; steel for shipbuilding continued to be purchased from other sources.

With the opening of the new shipyard at Elswick in October 1884, the firm embarked on its period of greatest expansion. From that time onwards, warships – including gunboats for the Royal Navy – would be built at Elswick and all other types of ship at Low Walker. The first vessel launched at the yard, on 13 June 1885, was *Panther*, a torpedo cruiser for the Austro-Hungarian navy. Spectators who had gathered to witness the momentous event were also invited to watch Armstrong strike the first rivet into the structure of a new battleship called *Renown*, destined to be the heaviest and costliest vessel constructed on the Tyne thus far, with a displacement of almost 11,000 tons. The events of that June day marked the start of a 33-year period in which Elswick would be at the forefront of the world's major naval yards.[27]

Shortly before her launch in April 1887, *Renown* was renamed *Victoria* in honour of the Queen's golden jubilee year. The first war vessel to be entirely built, armed, and fitted out by one establishment, she cost £724,855 – more than £41 million in today's money.[28] Her building at Elswick had been made possible by the installation of the Swing Bridge, and her size was such that she would only just pass between the bridge's piers. However, the fate of *Victoria* herself was less than triumphant. In 1890, the vessel was adopted as the flagship of Britain's Mediterranean fleet, under the command of Vice-Admiral Sir George Tryon. A terrible fate awaited her in the summer of 1893, during training manoeuvres off Tripoli in Lebanon. A bungled order by Tryon led to a collision with the battleship *Camperdown*, which struck *Victoria* on the starboard bow, causing her to capsize and sink within 10 minutes, taking with her 358 men, including the admiral.

In the years after the opening of the Elswick shipyard, the demand for Esmeralda-class cruisers was almost overwhelming, with orders arriving from Austria-Hungary, Italy, China, Spain, Romania, Argentina, Norway, Portugal, Turkey, Brazil, and the USA. New technological developments meant that the ships' speed of travel was increased dramatically – and they were less than half the price of a battleship.

Armstrong, meanwhile, was campaigning for a change in Britain's naval defence policy. In a presidential address to the Institution of Civil Engineers in 1882, he spoke in forthright fashion about the pursuit of peace, insisting that enlightened engineering skills could, and should, be used to promote the best interests of the human race. There was no country in the world less inclined to aggression than Great Britain, he insisted – but, equally, there was none so likely to incite the greed of an assailant. Britain had more than one half of the ocean-carrying trade of the whole world in its hands, and its ships, swarming over every sea and conveying merchandise of huge value, would, in the event of war, inevitably attract the interest of hostile cruisers.

Since the advent of steam navigation, naval power had come gradually to depend on engineering supremacy rather than seamanship. The most recent stage of this revolution was the introduction of torpedoes, against which 'our ponderous ironclads are no more secure than ships of thinnest iron'. Britain's early ironclads, such as *Warrior*, had been protected all over by thick armour. To resist the most powerful guns now afloat, armour of a thickness of at least 2 feet was required, and clearly this could not be applied to the whole vessel because of the weight and speed implications, so the armoured surface had been restricted to ever-smaller areas, leaving a large part of the ship unprotected.

Armstrong argued that, for the cost of one ironclad, the British navy could have three unarmoured ships of far higher speed; steel plates should be used for the hulls, and the guns and engines should be as light as was consistent with their efficiency. He drew attention to the light unarmoured warships designed by George Rendel and built at Elswick for foreign powers, which had attained speeds of up to 18 knots an hour. It was hard to know what defence could be put up if several of these vessels were to attack a British merchant convoy, he warned. At present there was not a single ship in the Royal Navy carrying a complement of arms sufficiently powerful to engage them, or which was fast enough to overtake them in pursuit or evade their attack in retreat.

Armstrong's intervention did much to stimulate the debate then raging about Britain's place in the world. Ever since the early 1860s, when Palmerston had decided to concentrate the nation's defence resources on army-run coastal forts, the navy had been relatively neglected – until 1879, when a war scare led to demands for a change of policy. In 1884, William Thomas Stead, editor of the *Pall Mall Gazette*, caused a sensation by publishing a series of articles arguing that the Royal Navy was falling behind its rivals and required vast public investment. Stead found an ally in the influential naval strategist John Fisher, an early champion of torpedoes, who understood the British people's fear that their country was in danger of losing its dominant position. Eventually, Prime Minister Gladstone, who had always opposed an increase in defence spending, was forced to add £5 million to the naval estimates.

British arms manufacturers then embarked on a period of rapid expansion, which received a huge boost when the Naval Defence Act of 1889 stimulated innovations in the design of warships and weapons. 'There was also a tightening of the relationship between the British state and the private manufacturers of arms,' wrote Marshall Bastable, 'as the government became overwhelmingly the single most important customer.' Bastable argues that, between 1884 and 1914, an 'intimacy' developed between Armstrong's firm and the British state – 'a complex relationship of mutual dependency, acrimony and cooperation' – which would eventually deprive Elswick of much of its entrepreneurial independence. As a consequence of the 1889 act, naval engineering was reinvigorated and 'national power and status were given their highest expression in the mighty ships and guns which poured out of the dockyards and factories of the world's armaments companies'.[29]

Since the cold-shouldering of Armstrong two decades earlier, the Royal Ordnance Factory at Woolwich had gradually fallen far behind Elswick in all important respects, and in 1885, when Armstrong was asked to join a committee to advise on design and production of the new breech-loading naval guns, the balance of power shifted decisively in favour of Elswick. The following year, John Fisher, the new director of naval ordnance, was given permission to acquire guns directly from private manufacturers as long as it was economical to do so – and he promptly placed orders for Elswick's quick-firing gun developed by Josiah Vavasseur for use against torpedo boats. The War Office monopoly had finally been broken.[30]

As the arms race of the mid-1880s took hold, Armstrong's old adversary Alfred Krupp re-entered the fray, challenging Elswick's domination of the foreign market for naval guns. Count Albini encouraged the Elswick chieftains to spoil their rival's plan of setting up an ordnance works in Italy by getting there first, and enlisted the support of the Italian government. It was eventually agreed that Elswick would establish a factory at Pozzuoli in the Bay of Naples.

As chance would have it, George Rendel had recently been advised by his doctor to retire from the Admiralty and move to a warmer climate. Italy was an obvious possibility, especially since his wife was Italian, so – although reluctant to leave the Admiralty – George jumped at Armstrong's offer that he should rejoin the company as a director and run the Pozzuoli Works jointly with Count Albini.[31] He took a villa on the coast at Posillipo, not far from the works, and established himself there with his family, gaining a reputation as a generous host. The ships launched at Pozzuoli from 1888 onwards were built on the Armstrong principle of combining the biggest guns with the greatest speed. Although the works were initially profitable – and would prove an essential part of Italy's industrial growth in the late 19th century – the arms business in Italy remained intensely political and competitive.[32]

In what deserves rather more than a footnote in history, during the early 1880s Henry Frederick Swan, the manager of the Low Walker shipyard, came up with the idea of using a ship's hull as a container for oil. Henry Swan, who had met the oil-exporters Robert and Ludwig Nobel during his time in St Petersburg, had already won a reputation for promoting new ideas in the Armstrong Mitchell firm. He went on to design *Gluckauf*, launched in 1886, the first vessel specially constructed to cross the Atlantic with a cargo of oil.[33] From that date, the success of the oil tanker was assured, and during the next two decades the Armstrong Mitchell firm was at the forefront of tanker developments. In that period, shipyards in north-east England were responsible for 200 tankers; 21 were built on the Wear and 32 on the Tees, but the Tyne built 147, with the Armstrong company taking the lion's share of 96.

Henry Swan also took a prominent part in building ice-breakers for the Russians, and when the Russian Admiral Makharoff was commissioned to build a powerful ice-breaking vessel capable of keeping the Baltic open all winter, he approached Swan with a scheme for what became the world-renowned *Ermack*, launched in 1898.

Another mighty creation of the Low Walker shipyard was a train ferry to carry passengers, carriages, and trucks across Lake

Baikal in Siberia, the world's deepest and oldest lake, linking two sections of the Trans-Siberian railway.[34] In the 1890s, before a line was built around its southern shore, the lake, whose average width is 30 miles, was a formidable obstacle to the completion of the railway, especially since its waters froze for around five months of the year. The immense ferry, named *Baikal*, was built in Newcastle and then dismantled; the different sections and pieces were marked and shipped to St Petersburg, from where the parts, weighing more than 3,000 tons in total, were transported in about 6,900 packages by rail and river to Irkutsk, the largest town on the western side of the lake. The items were then carried by pony-drawn sledges to a village on the lake shore, where the ship was reassembled and launched in June 1899. The amazing impact created by *Baikal* – emblematic of the triumph of the Low Walker yard – was captured by the British journalist John Foster Fraser, who in 1901 travelled from Moscow to Vladivostok and recounted his exploits in *The Real Siberia*:

'Presently there came steaming down the lake a huge four-funnelled vessel, white painted, by no means pretty, and rather like a barn that had slipped afloat. That was *Baikal*, one of the most wonderful vessels in the world, coming back from Misovaya, and carrying two goods trains fully laden. If necessary she could carry three trains and 800 passengers. *Baikal* passed sufficiently near for me to appreciate her great size, and as the fore gates were open I caught a glimpse of red-painted goods waggons. The ship is of over 4,000 tons, close on 300 feet long, and has nearly 60 feet beam. She has three triple-expansion engines of 1,250 horsepower, two amidships and one in the bow.' This tremendous power was required for ice-breaking. *Baikal* was capable of breaking through ice 36 inches thick. Her bow was curved, so that, when confronted by even thicker ice, she could be reversed and then proceed at full steam towards the ice, partly climbing on it and crushing with her weight. This meant that *Baikal* sometimes took an entire week to cross the lake.

13

Enlightenment

The year 1863 was Armstrong's *annus mirabilis*. He dramatically severed relations with the British government, launching himself on a new career as the world's first international arms dealer; he hosted the stellar meeting of the British Association in Newcastle and gave the speech of his life as its president; and he bought land near Rothbury and begun to build Cragside. On a more personal note, a son – a possible Armstrong heir – had been born to his nephew, Johnny Watson.

A less momentous but no less far-reaching event took place on a site next to the Elswick Works on 22 September, the date of the annual Elswick employees' soirée and distribution of prizes, hosted by William and Meggie Armstrong. It was the formal opening of the new building of the Elswick Mechanics' Institute, designed by the eminent architect John Dobson, and including specially equipped classrooms and a 500-seat lecture theatre. Of the 37 people then employed as draughtsmen in the Elswick drawing office, 33 had been promoted from the workshops after gaining qualifications from the Institute, set up shortly after the founding of the works itself.

Even though he himself had received little formal teaching, Armstrong believed passionately that education was the key to self-fulfilment and success in life. 'It is by means of books that working men can bring themselves into communion with highly gifted cultivated minds, and they will derive instruction, refinement and amusement from doing so,' he said to the assembled company. 'It is in an institution like this, where a working man, surrounded by books of the best authors and in communication with the most respectable and most intellectual men of their own class, can best acquire those qualifications which will increase his happiness and exalt his nature.'

This step forward in education was only part of a wider social revolution in the district that had been spearheaded by the expansion of the Elswick Works. The first and most conspicuous effect had been a transformation of the landscape. While rows of small houses sprang up around the works in an explosion of speculative building, Newcastle itself expanded westwards towards the growing industrial heartland. 'Steadily the tide of bricks and mortar crept out from the town ... streets of houses, tiny back-yards and dingy back lanes swallowing up the green fields, till the works was joined to the town by a continuous housing area on both sides of Scotswood Road,' wrote A. R. Fairbairn. As the demand for living space grew, many workers' homes took the form of the typical 'Tyneside flat' – a three- or four-roomed apartment built as part of a pair, one occupying the ground floor and the other the upper floor of the ubiquitous two-storey terraced buildings. There were many complaints about the standard of accommodation, especially the lack of adequate space between the terraces, but in some cases it was a great improvement on the insanitary slums that had gone before. Another distinctive feature of this new urban area was the exceptionally large number of public houses – eventually totalling more than 40 along the mile and a half of Scotswood Road.

Shortly after the works opened in the late 1840s, a more salubrious establishment could be found right next to its entrance: the house of John Windlow, a machine-shop foreman, who had begun to arrange meetings with about 20 of his fellow workers for the purpose of 'mutual improvement'. At first, the men assembled regularly at Windlow's humble home, to be taught arithmetic and the art of measuring by their more experienced colleagues, but they were soon provided with the space and means to set up a reading room and library. This organisation would take on a more formal guise as the Elswick Engine Works' Literary and Mechanics' Institute. Driven as much by his need for a skilled workforce as by his concern for the social good, Armstrong had not hesitated to throw his weight behind the venture, which achieved greater momentum with the opening of the new building in September 1863.

Workers who attended classes at the institute were expected to study not only the 'three Rs' but also geography, history, elocution and phonography (Pitman shorthand), along with technical subjects such as hydraulics, pneumatics and hydrostatics.[1] As the educational historian Alice Short has observed, the curriculum reflected Armstrong's personal philosophy, combining the ideology of self-help with 'the promise of upward social mobility which was the reward for hard work and temperate living'. He realised the need for a scientific understanding of the underlying principles of engineering and the importance of relating theory to practice. 'When the Elswick Works complex was complete,' wrote Short, 'the factory, the Mechanics' Institute and the elementary schools were integral parts of the same unit, both in place and in purpose. Armstrong appeared to encourage the development of the institute so that it would become the training ground for his future foremen and managers.'

Prominent among the current managers at Elswick was George Hutchinson, formerly of Henry Watson's High Bridge Works, who had joined Elswick in 1848 as Armstrong's assistant, becoming head of the drawing office and, later, works manager.[2] At the opening of the Mechanics' Institute building, Hutchinson – who would be president of the institute for 20 years – highlighted the personal interest taken by Armstrong in working men, especially those employed at Elswick. 'There are young men who came to these works with no other prospect before them but that of earning their bread by the sweat of their brow,' he said, 'but who, having availed themselves of the instruction given in this institution, now hold respectable and responsible positions.'[3]

Hot on the heels of the opening of the new building came proposals to set up elementary schools for Elswick workers' children, to be overseen by a committee representing both workers and managers.[4] It was agreed that the institute and the schools could both be financed by a tax of twopence a week on the higher paid workmen and a penny a week on those earning less than 15 shillings. Anticipating by four years the 1870 Elementary Education Act, the

Elswick Elementary Schools opened in 1866 and grew to become the second largest educational establishment in Newcastle; it remained independent until the Education Act of 1902, after which it was transferred to local authority control.

Other developments included the construction of a chemistry lab behind the existing institute building; offering places for up to 75 students from all over the district, it was long respected as the largest and most efficient laboratory of its kind in the north of England.[5] A 'day science class' begun in 1891 swiftly grew into a Day Technical School admitting both boys and girls. Along with the establishment of the Mechanics' Institute and the Elementary Schools, the Technical School was the third of the pioneering educational initiatives championed by the Elswick firm – all well in advance of any comparable moves by the British government.

The Elswick Mechanics' Institute continued to thrive and expand until, in the early years of the 20th century, its student numbers were between 600 and 700 in each session. Apprentices took exams under the auspices of the Society of Arts and other national bodies, obtaining a high standard of results and winning numerous awards and scholarships. Some moved on to Newcastle's College of Science, then part of the University of Durham. After that, with their qualifications validated by Durham, they could assume senior management roles not only in Britain but in other industrialising nations around the world.

As illustrated in *London Review* magazine for May 1862, an apprenticeship at Elswick was regarded as an extremely desirable goal, allowing those with 'superior ability and conduct' to be promoted from the workshops. Everyone with 'the disposition to improve himself' could attend evening classes in drawing, mathematics, and natural science, and have access to an extensive library of useful books. 'Prizes are given for proficiency in each branch of education, and once a year masters and men meet at an immense tea party to bestow the prizes on the successful competitors,' noted the *London Review*. 'All this produces reciprocal good feeling and a clan-like sympathy in the common work.'

Armstrong would always encourage aspiring young workers and, whenever he could, allow them an opportunity to prove themselves. A. R. Fairbairn cites the example of John Bradley, taken on as an apprentice in 1848, who by 1855 was skilled and trusted enough to be given the task of rifling Armstrong's first gun. From the early days of the works, 'an aristocracy of skill' was recognised by both management and men. 'In a works where production depended more and more on carrying out exact and delicate mechanical operations, the operators became depositories of acquired skill and accumulated experience. Paradoxically, the more production ventured into new and ever more complicated mechanisms, the more the old, skilled men were called upon.' The result was that Elswick Works gained a reputation among the men as 'a job for life'.

Among the institute's most distinguished graduates was Charles Parsons, who was attracted to Elswick after excelling in maths at St John's College, Cambridge, and went on in later life to invent the steam turbine. Henry Brunel, second son of I. K. Brunel, the famed engineer of the same name, also served an apprenticeship at Elswick, and later helped to construct the hydraulic mechanism to operate the bascules of London's Tower Bridge. The building that had been opened with such fanfare in 1863 would remain the home of the Elswick Mechanics' Institute until its demolition in the 1970s.

Armstrong believed that mechanics' institutes could do much to rectify the deficiencies of an imperfect early education. 'There is no difference in intellectual power between the working man and those who are placed in a higher sphere,' he argued. 'The only difference is in the amount of knowledge and mental cultivation possessed by each.' In supplying the pathways to knowledge, such establishments gave those from less advantaged backgrounds a great opportunity to improve their condition in life. 'Armstrong's initiative in combining industrial and technical education on the same site was revolutionary,' wrote Alice Short. 'His vision of Elswick as a centre of excellence for the training of engineers became a reality, through the twin agencies of the workshops and the Mechanics' Institute.'[6]

During the early years of Elswick, a separate but parallel movement was under way to establish a college of science in Newcastle – a movement that sprang from developments in coal-mining, which remained the region's principal source of wealth. The North of England Institute of Mining Engineers, the first organisation of its kind in Britain, was established in the town in 1852, just a year after a School of Mines had opened in London – and a few months after an explosion at the newly opened Seaham colliery in County Durham had claimed six lives. The disaster at Seaham was by no means the worst of recent mining accidents, but it proved the spur that would unite mine managers and workers in a common mission to improve mine safety. The Mining Institute's first president, Nicholas Wood, identified the organisation's top priorities as accident prevention and the improvement of technical knowledge.[7] It was intended, he said, 'to raise the art and science of mining to its highest practicable scale of perfection, in safety, economy and efficiency'.[8] Membership was extended to coal-owners as well as miners, and to people in 'other institutions, professions or occupations whose labours, talents or professional experience can aid our efforts'.

Three years later, at the time of the Crimean War, a committee was formed to investigate the setting up in Newcastle of a 'British College of Practical Mining and Manufacturing Science'.[9] Its members included Nicholas Wood, the industrialist Isaac Lowthian Bell, the surveyor and lead-mine manager Thomas Sopwith, and the proprietor of Elswick Works, William Armstrong. Although the Duke of Northumberland agreed to become patron of the college and promised a generous contribution to its endowment, coal-industry leaders were unable to raise enough money to fund the enterprise, and – after long and convoluted wrangling about what form such a college might take, and where it might be based – the idea was shelved. Wood, who became chairman of the Mining Association of Great Britain, continued to campaign tirelessly for a college of mines, but his death in 1865 made the establishment of such an institution seem even more remote.

A power struggle persisted between those who believed that a mining college should be part of Durham University and those who argued for a completely separate entity in Newcastle. Created in 1832 principally as an ecclesiastical institution, the University of Durham was under the control of the Dean and Chapter of Durham

Cathedral; and a serious obstacle to the founding of a new college at Durham was the firm application of the Test Acts, whereby no one could be admitted to the university who did not adhere to the tenets of the Church of England – a situation that persisted until 1871. While the arguments raged, men and boys continued to suffer death and injury in the mines through a series of horrifying incidents, culminating on 16 January 1862 with the disaster at Hartley Colliery near Seaton in Northumberland, which claimed 204 lives – a record toll for a mining accident in Britain.

When the Mining Institute decided in 1866 to admit mechanical as well as mining engineers, Armstrong joined the organisation, becoming vice-president two years later and president in 1873. At the time of his joining, the clamour for technical education was growing ever louder, especially after the Paris International Exhibition of 1867 revealed that Britain was falling behind in the technological race among nations. More than a quarter of a century earlier, the Senate of Durham University and the South Shields Committee, set up to improve mine safety, had jointly agreed on the urgent need for 'a course of practical engineering in some fitting institution in the heart of a mining district'[10] – since when the initiative had stalled and restarted several times. But everything changed in 1869 with the arrival of William Charles Lake as Dean of Durham, an appointment that carried with it the wardenship of Durham University – for Lake was an ardent supporter of the idea to establish a college of science in Newcastle.

That summer, in the centenary year of the first running of James Watt's steam engine, Armstrong spoke to mechanical engineers in Newcastle about the achievement of technological progress. As a result of Watt and those like him, he said, the human race had entered a 'golden age of mechanics'. Watt had devoted the full powers of his intellect and battled against the odds to make available for practical use 'a force derived from the action of the sun through countless ages, stored up in wood, or packed still more closely in coal'. Since it had been brought under control, this force had 'subdued the wind and waves, removed mountains, and enabled mankind not only to increase and multiply and people the far-off regions of the earth, but even to annihilate time and space as far as concerns mutual communication'.

Similar leaps in human progress should be possible in the future – but there was always a danger, warned Armstrong, that workers might forget that their skilled 'hand labour' had been made possible by the 'head labour' that preceded it. 'Industry alone is no match for combined industry and education,' he insisted.

He emphasised the need to find a source of energy to replace coal as the remaining stocks of the fuel in Britain became increasingly inaccessible. However, there was no cause for despair because – as had so often proved to be the case – necessity was the mother of invention. 'When an agent more powerful than the hand of man was wanted to supply man's necessities, the agent was found and brought under subjection by Watt,' and there was every reason to suppose that this pattern would be repeated. 'The rays that shone upon the plants whence, in the form of wood or crushed into coal, men now draw their supply of heat have shone also on the whole surface of the globe, and if it should indeed come to pass that our supplies of one mineral should fail, we have little doubt that another will be found to take its place.' As a last resort, the human race would have to 'call upon the science which found us electricity' to find us some other available source of power. 'There is time enough and to spare for the intelligence of men to seek and find means hitherto uncontemplated for the subjugation of nature,' he said.

Armstrong saw the expansion of education as a vital step in the quest for solutions to humanity's most pressing problems. He rejoiced in the fact that the nation was now 'alive to the duty of educating the people', but stressed that this development had come none too soon, since the greatest obstacle to Britain's social and industrial progress was its low standard of education, especially among the working classes.

This awakening to the importance of a formal education had come relatively recently to Armstrong. Only a few years earlier, Thomas Sopwith had recorded a conversation between himself and Armstrong in which Sopwith had argued in favour of setting up a practical school of science in Newcastle. Armstrong apparently retorted that 'the mechanics' institutes such as that established at

Elswick meet all the requirements and the supply of scientific education is equal to the demand'. He thought, noted Sopwith, that 'there was no difficulty in young men obtaining classical or scientific instruction at nights, concurrently with their daily avocations'. Given his own patchy experience of formal education and later enlightenment through personal experience and experimentation, Armstrong may have found it hard to separate in his own mind the twin pursuits of labour and study. He believed that Britain's success in the technological race would depend on both elements coming together in a human drive for self-advancement. In a speech to the National Association for the Promotion of Social Science, he argued against all forms of protectionism, including restrictive practices by trade unions, while extolling the role of labour. 'Labour, physical and mental, is the creative element of our nature. Nothing possesses value until labour has been expended upon it; not even raw material is exempted from this rule,' he said. 'Analyse as we will, we always come to labour as the foundation of value.'

He opposed the manipulation and regulation of labour in the quest for a more equal society, believing that individual ambition should be given a free rein within the law. 'Struggle for superiority is the mainspring of progress. It is an instinct deeply rooted in our nature. It shows itself in the keen interest which contest of every kind excites in our minds, and in the homage which we render to success, even in matters of little moment. To what a dead level of mediocrity would our country sink if struggle for superiority were stamped out amongst us, and how completely would we fall back in the race of nations!'

The meeting of social scientists, held in Newcastle in September 1870, was presided over by Algernon Percy, 6th Duke of Northumberland, a keen advocate of expanding formal education to all social classes. Among other prominent speakers was Dean Lake, the new warden of Durham, who expressed concern that most of the men responsible for mine safety were still being inadequately educated. On his appointment as warden, Lake – a high-church Liberal and man of wide interests – had been urged by Gladstone to infuse life into the moribund university, whose student numbers had fallen below 50.[11] Rejecting the idea of making

Durham a miniature Oxford, Lake decided instead to concentrate on its development as a leading school of theology, and to promote the establishment of a scientific college in Newcastle.

In March 1871, setting aside previous rows, the Institute of Mining Engineers organised a meeting at the Lit & Phil, with Armstrong in the chair, to consider whether 'by the united action of the University of Durham with the scientific societies, manufacturers and gentlemen of the district, some provision could be made for the establishment of classes for the teaching of physical science'.[12] Isaac Lowthian Bell, the prominent iron and steel manufacturer, was the first to take the floor.

Industrial enterprises in the area had traditionally relied heavily on 'rule of thumb', argued Bell. In many cases, much had been learned in this way. But the time had come for the 'rule' to be elevated to an exact science. This would be the purpose of the new school, and Newcastle was the obvious place for it. Newcastle was the centre of the great manufacturing district of the north, with excellent transport links. As well as an outstanding lecture theatre, provided by Armstrong himself, the students would also have access to a fine museum, which, especially for geological studies, was unsurpassed in the kingdom. Bell reckoned that about £3,000 would be needed to pay for the initial equipment to get the scheme off the ground.

Among other things, Dean Lake had proposed that, were a college to be created in Newcastle – a college that would be part of Durham University – the professors might divide their time between Newcastle and Durham. This was a potential stumbling block. Armstrong was strongly opposed to the idea, presumably believing that it would seriously weaken the new institution. He advised that Durham should transfer all its scientific education to Newcastle, so that the duties of the professors could be exercised there exclusively.

A fortnight later, the *Newcastle Chronicle* published a leader identifying the previous Saturday, 25 March 1871, as 'a new red-letter day in the calendar of the social and scientific progress for the North of England'. On that day, said the *Chronicle*, 'the hopes and wishes of 40 years found expression in an effort to establish classes in the town of Newcastle for the diffusion of knowledge in those branches of science which bear a direct relation to the staple industries of the district'. The appointment of Dr Lake as Dean of Durham had been crucial to this outcome, reviving 'the failing confidence of those who had long alternated between expectation and despair of help in that quarter'. Lake's revised scheme – which excluded the idea of divided services – stamped him emphatically as a man for the times, 'a man of broad conceptions, liberal sympathies and high administrative talents'.

Virtually every prominent individual in the region was present at the Lit & Phil to hear Dean Lake announce his plan. Again in the chair, Armstrong pointed out that, even though Lake's plan was distinguished by 'still greater liberality [than the previous scheme] in a money point of view', it would involve 'a corresponding display of munificence' on the part of the assembled company. If they rose to the spirit of the occasion, he said, they would succeed in establishing in Newcastle a school of science which would be in every way worthy of 'the great wealth, intelligence and importance of the district'.

Dean Lake said it was not intended to offer a general education at the new college, covering literature as well as science, although that might happen in the future. The aim rather was to provide a two-year scientific training consisting of four broad subjects: pure and applied mathematics; chemistry; experimental physics, embracing pneumatics, hydrostatics and hydrodynamics; and mineralogy and geology. Success in final examinations would give students a distinction such as 'associate in physical science'. At least four professorships would be needed for the successful operation of such a course. The cost of employing the professors, along with several skilled assistants and a secretary, was projected to be about £2,000 a year. It was a crucial task of the meeting to decide how these costs would be met. The dean questioned whether they were prepared to raise such a sum themselves.

In outlining the plan for the new college, Lake felt the need to explain Durham's role in its genesis. Glossing over previous tensions, he said that, since his arrival in Durham the previous year, he had found that the university was 'animated by the most friendly spirit towards Newcastle and the north of England generally'. Durham

University had been founded 40 years earlier, right at the start of the railway age, when it was believed that it would become something similar in character to the old universities of Oxford and Cambridge. But many changes had since taken place, and the university had suffered in consequence, particularly in the past decade, as reflected in its dwindling student numbers. The university was now anxious to play its part in 'assisting the education of the population amongst whom its lot was cast'. There was a growing awareness of the need for 'a more scientific training in those trades and professions which were followed by those around them'. Although many arguments had been made in favour of Durham as the seat of such studies, the thinking on this matter had now moved on.

Among other financial contributions, Durham University proposed to found ten scholarships for students at the Newcastle school of physical science, each valued at £20 a year. It would also give £300 towards the laboratories, which it was felt best to establish immediately. The school would be officially part of Durham University, in parallel with the Newcastle College of Medicine, formed as an independent body in 1834 and incorporated into the university in 1852.

Amid the animated discussion that followed Dean Lake's speech, it was an intervention by the journalist Joseph Cowen that finally set the seal on his proposals. He and his fellow townsmen, said Cowen, all thought the dean's proposal so liberal and handsome that they could not have expected anything better. If they did not carry it out efficiently, therefore, it would be to the 'lasting disgrace' of the town. But, since it could only be carried out by 'the sinews of war' being supplied, he proposed that they should subscribe £1,000 before they left the room. All it needed was for 20 of them to guarantee £50 each. Cowen pointed out that Sir William Armstrong had already given £100 a year; he would himself give £50 a year, and, if others only did likewise, he was sure the dean and his colleagues might go home congratulating themselves on the success of the movement. The University of Durham would, he trusted, be improved by its contact with the people of Newcastle – and he was satisfied that the people of Newcastle would improved by their contact with it.

Cowen went on to give his frank views on the likely outcome of the new association. In a speech frequently interrupted by outbursts of laughter and applause, he characterised the inhabitants of Tyneside as 'a rough population' obsessed with making money – 'as if the making of money were the be-all and end-all of existence'. In the struggle for wealth, he said, they often conducted themselves like eels stuck in a jar, all struggling with each other to reach the top. But if they could be brought into contact with the soothing influence of that soporific institution, the university, they might improve each other, wear off the corners of each other's prejudices, and in that way gain mutual benefit. Cowen ended by saying that the best way of acknowledging the actions of the dean and his colleagues would be by practically carrying out their project – and guaranteeing £1,000 a year for the six years over which the 'experiment' would last.

The *Newcastle Chronicle* later published the subscription list that was compiled before the men left the meeting: 'Sir William Armstrong, £100 a year for six years; Mr I. L. Bell, £50 a year; Mr J. W. Pease MP, £50 a year; Mr J. Straker, £50 a year; Capt. Hunt, £50 a year; and Mr J. Cowen, jun., £50 a year. The following gentlemen promised the amounts stated, to be spread over six years: Mr H. L. Pattinson, £100; Mr E. F. Boyd, £50; Mr R. S. Newall, £180; Mr L. W. Adamson, £100; Mr Thos. Hodgkin and friends, £200; Mr J. B. Alexander, £30; Messrs. Walker, Parker and Co, £100; the Mayor of Newcastle, £100; Mr J. M. Redmayne, £100; Mr R. R. Redmayne, £60; Dr Charlton, £60; the Rev. Mr Tait, £35; and Mr T. W. Bunning, £30.' The amount pledged in this way came to more than £3,000, or more than half of the sum required to fund the college for the initial six years of its existence.

The College of Physical Science was finally inaugurated six months later, at a grand ceremony on 25 October 1871 involving people from all walks of life. 'The peerage was represented by the Duke of Northumberland ... and Earl Grey,' noted the *Chronicle*. 'The House of Commons was present in considerable force to learn how much could be done, by a strictly undenominational effort, to educate the rising generation of Englishmen. The Corporation of Newcastle ... the clergy ... The merchants, manufacturers and shopkeepers of the district came forth to signalize their sympathy with the new-born plan for consolidating England's commercial supremacy.'

In seconding a vote of thanks to Armstrong for his seminal role in the creation of the college, T. E. Headlam, the local MP, emphasised that the founder's whole life had been 'a proof of the value of a study of physical science', and during a lunch at the Central Exchange News Room the 3rd Earl Grey proposed a toast to the 'success to the College of Physical Science, coupled with the name of Sir William Armstrong'. Grey went on to highlight Armstrong's contribution to technological progress. 'The name of Sir William has a European, or rather a worldwide, celebrity for the success with which he has applied physical science to useful productions,' he said. 'Not only in regard to those fearful instruments of destruction with which his name is so closely associated, but also, and of far more importance, to a variety of machinery and contrivances of the utmost value for supplying the wants of mankind.' Armstrong's success, asserted Grey, was the strongest encouragement that could be given to students of the new college.

Armstrong responded by saying he hoped the example shown in Newcastle would be rapidly followed elsewhere – and proceeded to deliver a rousing wake-up call to Britain's industry: 'It is only by scattering local colleges over the whole land that we can bring about that widespread diffusion of scientific knowledge that is so essential to the advancement of the nation from a moral as well as an intellectual point of view.' That aim would not be achieved by great national scientific colleges, but by bringing scientific instruction to the doors of the people. 'We must enable people to have instruction at home and not allow them to be any longer deterred from seeking it by the great expense and inconvenience of travelling to distant places.' He was surprised how little had yet been done to spread scientific knowledge among the British people. 'Had scientific instruction not been confined, as it has been, to a few persons, we should have a vastly greater amount of practical and beneficial results arising from the application of science than we have.'

The value of scientific education had been fully recognised by Britain's industrial rivals on the European continent. 'We were far more ahead of our rivals 20 years ago than we are today,' he insisted, 'and unless we wake up to the necessity of improving our condition by the promulgation of science, we can expect to be rapidly overtaken.' Although Armstrong may have been slow to embrace the idea of a school of science, he had come to see that it was a vital weapon in the fight to maintain Britain's industrial supremacy. As Alice Short has pointed out, the Elswick Mechanics' Institute and the company's apprentice scheme would continue to serve a very useful purpose, but it could at last be said with confidence that 'the day of the professional engineer – equal in every respect to other professions – had arrived'.[13]

Despite the mood of celebration and self-congratulation that attended the opening of the College of Physical Science, and the substantial funds raised by the inaugural appeal, the first students and teachers had plenty of practical problems to contend with – a situation that, in the event, would persist for more than 15 years. In the absence of any proper classrooms, 'accommodation was provided in the "cellars and attics" of the Mining Institute, while the facilities of the Literary and Philosophical Society, of the College of Medicine and of the Natural History Society were placed at the disposal of the burgeoning College'.[14] The Natural History Society of Northumberland, Durham and Newcastle upon Tyne, itself an offshoot of the Lit & Phil, had been closely involved in the discussions that led to the setting up of the College of Physical Science, and its collections were made freely available to the college for teaching purposes.

When, in 1887 – not before time – a new site was chosen at Lax's Gardens near Barras Bridge to accommodate what by then was known as the Durham College of Science, William Armstrong laid the foundation stone of the edifice which would later bear his name and which, in today's Newcastle University, is still known as the Armstrong Building. It was officially opened on 5 November the following year by Princess Louise, Marchioness of Lorne, the fourth daughter of Queen Victoria.

Some 16 years later, after Armstrong's death, building began on a front extension to the College of Science, paid for by 'a fund of £50,000, raised to commemorate the life of the first Lord Armstrong, whose name the college will henceforth bear'. As well as housing several academic departments, the new building was designed to include administrative offices, a library, a museum, common rooms, and a large public lecture theatre.

In 1906, when King Edward VII and Queen Alexandra visited Newcastle, the college had more than 1,760 students on its academic roll. As well as maths, science and engineering, its courses now included art, literature, music, law, languages, history, and political economy. The monarch's duties on this occasion included opening both the new Tyne Bridge and the Royal Victoria Infirmary – to which Armstrong, through his great-nephew, had contributed £100,000, one third of the total cost needed to build the new hospital and nurses' home. Then, on 11 July, he inaugurated the Armstrong College of the University of Durham. 'The name of Armstrong,' proclaimed the King with calm confidence, 'will always be identified with scientific discovery and industrial success.'

14

Stormy Undercurrents

By the beginning of the 1870s, reflecting the huge expansion in Armstrong's business enterprise, the Elswick Works stretched for three-quarters of a mile along the north bank of the Tyne, and the population of the Elswick district was approaching 28,000, an eightfold increase on 20 years earlier. The promise of work in the booming engineering and armaments industries had attracted men from all over Britain to seek work in the northern metropolis. 'Houses and streets were thrown up in a constant attempt to keep up with the flow of immigrants,' wrote David Dougan.[1] 'What had been a large spread of bare land was quickly covered by row upon row of houses and streets, all climbing precariously up the steep slope that led from the river.' Scotswood Road, once a simple country lane, had become the centre of one of the most concentrated industrial and residential areas in Britain.

But, while Elswick rode the crest of a wave in terms of productivity and international fame, a confrontation loomed that would thrust Sir William Armstrong into the very eye of a storm and severely harm his public image. It would later be characterised as one of the most significant industrial battles of 19th-century Britain. The paternalist Elswick masters had little experience of being challenged by their men – a protest in 1862 about reduced pay for night-workers had fizzled out – so, when the engineers' dispute erupted in the spring of 1871, they were not well prepared to deal with the sea change that was under way in both local and national industrial relations.

A resurgence in miners' militancy had occurred in the 1860s, when – at a time of increasing prosperity – it was mirrored by demands from workers in engineering and shipbuilding for a share of the spoils. Before the end of the decade, widespread pressure was growing for a reduction in the basic working week from 59 hours to 54. In addition to the established ten hours of work on weekdays and nine on Saturdays, there were two hours of meal breaks, which meant that workers in many industries spent up to 12 hours a day, six days a week, at their place of employment.

Wages at Elswick were fixed according to the agreements in the engineering trade of the district. By 1900, they amounted to some 36 shillings a week for a skilled worker, and about half that for an unskilled labourer. 'It was an age of cheapness,' wrote the historian A. R. Fairbairn, 'and the Elswick workman could find entertainment on a Saturday afternoon and evening, or satisfaction for his thirst, all for something between sixpence and a shilling. Amusements were few, hard drinking was common.' But in the last three decades of the 19th century, encouraged by the progress of national and international labour movements, an increasingly disgruntled workforce embarked on a campaign for better conditions.

The Nine Hours' Movement took hold on Wearside in March 1871, when local engineering workers met at a Sunderland hotel under the able leadership of Andrew Gourley and drew up a petition to present to their employers calling for a reduced working week.[2] Playing on popular enthusiasm for 'self-help', the workers argued that, as well as benefiting their health, the extra five hours of time not in employment would give them the chance to improve the education of themselves and their families. These advantages apart, the existing economic conditions made it likely that a shorter basic working week would also be a subtle way of ensuring that the men could earn more from longer periods of overtime.

When the Wearside employers dismissed the petition, a meeting of about 1,000 workers voted by a large majority in favour of industrial action, and in early April most of the Wearside engineering works were at a standstill. The strike did not last long. Despite a pledge of support from other local employers, including those on the Tyne, after less than a month the Wearside firms capitulated to their employees' demands and conceded the nine-hour day, resulting in a swift return to work.

Meanwhile, in the wake of the victory on Wearside, a Nine Hours' League was formed in Newcastle, with John Burnett as its president. The league's committee sent a letter to all engineering employers in Newcastle and Gateshead, asking them 'kindly' to consent to 'the reduction of the hours of labour from ten to nine hours per day – or, more properly speaking, from 59 to 54 hours per week'.[3] This was, said the letter, 'a concession, we believe, that might be made with little or no injury to your own interests, and with great advantage to ours'.

The employers' response – communicated through the solicitors Stanton and Atkinson of Pilgrim Street – was abrupt: 'At a meeting of the Manufacturing Engineers of the Newcastle upon Tyne and Gateshead District held at the Station Hotel, on Saturday, 6 May 1871, Sir William George Armstrong in the chair, a circular having been read from the Acting Committee of the Nine Hours' League, requesting a reduction of the hours of labour, from 59 to 54 hours per week. It was unanimously resolved that the above application be declined.'

The league members were taken aback by the cold impersonality of this letter. Past industrial disputes on Tyneside had been marked by openness and directness between masters and men, and there was genuine indignation that the employers had adopted such a high-handed approach. In particular, the mutual respect that had traditionally characterised relations between Armstrong and his employees at Elswick was put in serious jeopardy.

Most of the engineering employers on Tyneside had come together under the banner of the Associated Employers to resist the demands of the league and, although Armstrong had agreed to lead the group, the work of organising the employers' resistance was largely undertaken by the management team at Elswick, in particular Andrew Noble and George Rendel. All the Elswick managers were entering uncharted territory, and their inexperience in industrial relations was evident in the clumsiness of their early moves. Andrew Noble – who clearly did much in the background to stiffen his fellow directors' resolve – was particularly ill suited for his role in the crisis. Described by Fairbairn as 'imperious, autocratic, emphatic in his expressions, [and] sudden, almost volcanic, in his decisions',

Noble treated everyone at Elswick Works alike, 'so that managers of departments and the latest junior office boy all hurried to carry out his orders'.

By contrast, John Burnett, the president of the Nine Hours' League, was an intelligent and wily operator, a leading light of the Newcastle Mechanics' Institute with strong socialist instincts. His active involvement in the campaign for parliamentary reform in the 1860s had won him some useful local contacts, including Joseph Cowen, the radical editor of the *Newcastle Chronicle*. Burnett believed that it was possible to progress towards a more just and equal society by a policy of cooperation with the more enlightened members of the ruling class.[4] In John Burnett, Armstrong would encounter a new kind of opponent – an opponent for whom his disputes with rival inventors and died-in-the-wool military chiefs had offered little preparation.

Burnett's next move was to propose a meeting between the two sides to discuss how strike action might be avoided, but, before the employers could respond, workers at Clark, Gurney and Watson, a small engineering firm, jumped the gun by going out on strike. This angered the rest of the league because it gave the masters the excuse to reject the offer of a meeting – which they promptly did. A second letter arrived from the solicitors, saying that the employers would have suggested a written communication from the league, in preference to a meeting, 'but for the fact that a strike had already taken place'. Under the circumstances, the letter went on, all the employers could do was 'to refer the Nine Hours' League to their former communication, dated the 6th inst., and to request them to consider it final'.

The employers had laid down the gauntlet. At a meeting of the league on 20 May, a resolution for strike action was overwhelmingly carried. Two days later, the men handed in their notices, to expire the following Saturday, 27 May. Two of the leading Tyneside firms, Palmer's and Stephenson's, had stayed aloof from the dispute. Charles Mark Palmer was not willing to concede the nine hours, but he told his workers that he would accept the nine-hour day if and when it was generally accepted by other local engineering firms. Stephenson's, less explicitly, followed a similar course.

At a meeting at Newcastle's Station Hotel on 23 May, the employers pledged their united opposition to the strike, as reported by George Rendel in a letter to his younger brother Stuart: 'The masters agreed unanimously to hold out and to make no concessions without the consent of our association.' The elder Rendel – a leading manager at Elswick since his appointment as head of the ordnance works in 1859 – argued that the men's demands should be resisted in the interests of the whole district. 'A weak opposition and a quick concession would lead to further demands that would ruin the district,' he wrote, 'not to speak of the immediate loss it would inflict on employers on their existing contracts. We are in for a severe contest but it cannot be helped.'

Two days later, the league representatives met the mayor of Newcastle, Richard Burdon Sanderson, who had offered to mediate between the parties, and presented him with a manifesto explaining that a shorter working week would allow them to improve their education while giving them less excuse for excessive drinking. 'There is a vast amount of ignorance amongst us, and a vast amount of drunkenness in our midst,' they admitted, 'but we contend that one of the most powerful preservatives of ignorance and one of the most seductive agencies of drunkenness has been the long duration of the hours of labour, and its consequent effect in the almost total exhaustion which it has produced upon the vital energies of the working man.'

The men also used the complicated pay system that operated at the time to press their case. A team leader, known as a piece-maker, received a contract from a foreman and was paid by him; the piece-maker in turn employed semi-skilled men and labourers from Armstrong's workforce and paid them himself. The men argued that, given the continuance of the contract system, a shorter working week need not involve a comparable rise in the cost of labour. Unconvinced, the employers again turned down the offer of talks. By now, a strike was inevitable.

From the start, the Nine Hours' League drew great benefit from the support of Joseph Cowen, who insisted in the columns of his newspaper that the men's demands were 'perfectly legitimate and even reasonable'. As well as backing their cause in the *Chronicle*,

Cowen advised the league leaders on tactics and offered them financial support; later, he would play a crucial role in mediation. With the encouragement of Cowen, Burnett and his colleagues set out to maintain an image of restraint and moderation, in contrast to what seemed the intransigence of the masters.

It was Cowen's view that the employers favoured a strike because they thought it would teach the men a lesson. Putting thoughts into the masters' minds, he wrote that, in recent years, the men had had things far too much their own way and had become too independent: 'They have got political and now they want social and trade power. In a short time they will, if not checked, become both masters and workmen. If they were turned adrift for a few months and made to feel their position they would be more submissive when they resumed work again.'

But, Cowen argued, by adopting this approach, the employers were playing with fire, apparently blind to the consequences: 'A strike is a dangerous business, and it is more than probable that when many of the men have once left their workshops they will not return to them.'

When the men's notices expired on Saturday, 27 May, the dispute began in earnest. It involved 12 engineering companies and 7,500 men, some 2,700 of whom were employed by Armstrong.[5] Most of the engineering workers at Elswick downed tools – but Armstrong immediately raised the stakes, and provoked even greater hostility, by locking out more than 200 who had not signed up to the action. According to John Burnett's later account, 'A great many who did not give their notices were kindly informed that, as many men had given notice, their services would no longer be required.'[6] For the first time in his life, Armstrong found the balance of public opinion moving sharply against him.

Early in June, a couple of the smaller firms capitulated to the league's demands and reopened on the basis of a 54-hour week, but the larger players remained determinedly resistant. On 6 June, the league made its first distribution of strike pay. The leaders had been worried about how long their limited funds would last, but contributions soon started to arrive from local trade unions and individuals – indeed, Cowen told Burnett that he was prepared to guarantee the continued issue of strike pay from his own resources. (In contrast, the Amalgamated Society of Engineers, the national body, was very slow to react.) By 19 June, when the league held its first rally on Newcastle's Town Moor, its financial problems were beginning to ease. The main reason for this was that about half of the strikers had already found work elsewhere. By the end of the strike, fewer than 2,000 men were dependent on the league's funds for their livelihood.

Public support was also judged critical for the league's hopes of success. Most local newspapers, apart from the *Newcastle Chronicle*, were hostile to the strike, so a series of mass meetings was organised to stir up popular feeling in the workers' cause, one of which was arranged for 1 July, to coincide with the end of the local holiday season known as Race Week. Some elements of the national press were more positive about the Nine Hours' Movement, however. 'In itself this demand is perfectly reasonable,' said the *Pall Mall Gazette*. 'Nine hours' continuous labour in the engineering trade is probably as much as can be maintained without a degree of exhaustion which is physically and morally injurious.' The *Spectator* was more outspoken in its criticism: 'Masters who reply cavalierly by lawyers' letters to the demands of their men, refuse personal discussion, and act as nearly as they can like despotic governments against revolutionary bodies can hardly expect their moral claims on the sympathy of the public to be conceded.'

Meanwhile, disappointed in their hopes that the dispute would be over by Race Week, the employers were discussing plans to draft in substitute workers from other parts of Britain and abroad. 'Every day this week we have had long masters' meetings,' wrote Noble to Stuart Rendel. Before these plans could be implemented, another attempt at mediation took place at the instigation of Charles Mark Palmer, whose more subtle handling of the nine hours' issue had kept his Jarrow works out of the strike. On 19 July, having consulted his fellow employers, Palmer held a long conference with a delegation from the league at his Newcastle home, but the talks got bogged down in procedural wrangling.

Still rejecting direct contact with Burnett and his team, the employers distributed printed notices to the workmen announcing that on Thursday, 3 August, the factory gates would reopen and employment would be offered on the basis of a 57-hour week – a reduction in hours, but not the 54 the league was demanding. This offer was treated with general contempt by the strikers, and on 4 August the *Chronicle* reported that no more than 20 men in total had returned to work.

'We are now determined to break this strike by importing foreign labour,' wrote Armstrong to Stuart Rendel. 'We have had a long and anxious meeting of employers this morning and numerous committees are appointed for various duties... Altogether the situation is grave.' Agents were sent to various cities in Britain and other countries in Western Europe offering generous terms and free transport to workers prepared to come to Tyneside to take the place of strikers. Meanwhile, Burnett visited the London headquarters of the International Working Men's Association, known as the First International, to seek help in preventing foreign workers from enlisting as blacklegs. Eventually, however – at great expense to the employers – more than a thousand workers were imported from Belgium, Germany, Denmark, Norway, and Sweden.

Armstrong courted further unpopularity by closing the schools attached to the Elswick Works in order for them to be used to house foreign workers. When the schools reopened, he said – in a highly controversial move – that they would be available only to the children of men who were then employed at the works. John Burnett was prompted to vent his anger in the *Chronicle*. 'I hope the working men generally of this district will note the full significance of this combination of masters,' he wrote. 'It is a combination of the masters of all kinds of trades to defeat all efforts of the English workmen to better their condition, whether in seeking higher wages or shorter hours. They also seek to accomplish this end by a most objectionable form of action, viz. the wholesale importation of foreign labour, thereby increasing the surplus labour of an already over-burdened labour market.'

By this time, according to Burnett's later account of the strike, large numbers of replacement workers had arrived from the south of England and 'new arrivals came with almost every boat from the continent'.[7] It was impossible to find lodgings for such large numbers of men, and they were consequently put up in the various factories. 'Tenants living in Sir William's property received notice to quit if they did not return to work,' wrote Burnett. 'The foremen and clerks who would consent to the operation were sworn in as special constables, and preparations were made to guard the different factories much the same as if they were convict establishments – or, as though the foreigners were lambs and the men outside were wolves.'

The importation of foreigners had its paradoxical aspects. On 1 September, *Engineering* magazine reported a mutiny among 120 of Armstrong's imported German workers, who had themselves struck in favour of the nine-hour day. 'All the efforts of the heads of the firm were insufficient to quell the disturbance,' according to Burnett. 'They promised that the Germans should be allowed to smoke when they chose; that, in fact they should have anything but the nine hours, which the Germans had by this time begun to shout for.' Taking advantage of this state of affairs, the Nine Hours' League next day 'shipped off' almost all the foreign workers involved. 'This batch of Germans left Newcastle Quay amid such a scene of excitement as is seldom witnessed.' When the Amalgamated Society of Engineers finally threw its hat into the ring, it provided a useful service – with financial help from Cowen – in persuading some of the other foreign workers to go home.

The Tyneside dispute burst on to the national stage on 11 September, when *The Times* published a long article on the strike, giving qualified support to the strikers: 'The engineers are probably the most prosperous, intelligent and closely organized body of working men in the United Kingdom, and they have in consequence enjoyed for several years a comparative immunity from strikes ... After fourteen weeks of determined resistance on the one side, and energetic endeavours on the other, the workmen still hold out, and the masters are finding one source of supply for their empty workshops cut away after another.'

Formerly a supporter of Armstrong, *The Times* went on to condemn the employers' moves to import foreign labour. 'Every contingent of imported workmen complains of being deceived, throws up its contracts with Sir William Armstrong and his confederate employers, and leaves the manufacturers to fight the battle out on the old terms with the men on strike,' declared the newspaper in forthright terms. 'If Sir William Armstrong could have retained his Prussian and Danish labourers, he might have laughed at the strike; but Prussians, Danes and English have all succumbed to the pressure of working-class opinion in the North or to the secret mandates of the International.'

This was a devastating blow for Armstrong – coming from the pen of John Delane, an editor who had once been one of his staunchest advocates. And Delane had more arrows to fire. 'We are inclined to consider the conduct of the employers throughout this dispute as imprudent and impolitic,' he wrote. 'We do not approve the general policy of trade unions, and are decidedly opposed to their methods of action; but we could wish to see some other ground chosen for resisting the aggression of the unions than a bare opposition to the Nine Hours' Movement.'

The next day, Armstrong told Stuart Rendel that he had sent a letter to *The Times* in reply to their 'shameful' article. Published on 14 September, it recounted in detail the course of the dispute from the employers' point of view and the attempts at mediation, rebuffing the claim that the policy of importing foreign labour had failed. 'Our efforts at conciliation having been not only rejected but turned to account against us as proofs of weakness, we had no alternative but a recourse to imported labour,' Armstrong insisted. 'We adopted that alternative as a necessity, and not even our most violent opponents will dispute our perfect justification in so doing. Ten weeks had elapsed before we commenced this course of action, and by that time about two-thirds of our old hands had obtained employment elsewhere, as was persistently boasted by the League. The result has been to place us in the comparatively easy position which we now occupy. We were amazed to see ourselves described in your article as being in a condition of helpless difficulty.' The simultaneous appearance in the *Spectator* of an article criticising the employers had inflicted a further wound, as Armstrong made clear: 'We had imagined that a determined effort to wrest concessions from employers by sheer force of combination was not a thing which found favour with the more educated and intelligent classes whose opinions generally find expression in the columns of *The Times*.'

Armstrong divulged some of his personal views on the matter, suggesting a possible resolution to the impasse. 'Had our men applied for an increase of wages instead of a reduction of time, the dispute might easily have been adjusted,' he wrote. 'Wages fluctuate with demand, but shortened hours of work do not alter, and, therefore, there is less objection to increase wages than to decrease time. Shortened time also involves loss of interest on capital; for when men cease work machines stand idle; and the whole establishment becomes unproductive, thus damaging employers without benefiting the men.'

He set the conflict in a national and international context. 'The hours of work which were general in our district at the time of our strikes were 59 a week. That number we have reduced to 57, which is the time worked on the Clyde. On the Continent, in places where equal advantages are possessed to those of the North of England in regard to coal, iron, and railway communication, the common hours of work are 66 a week, and the wages are less than in England.' He then went on to explain publicly, for the first time, why the employers had refused the demand for a 54-hour week. They believed that, if they had conceded, 'the district in which our factories are located would be laid under permanent and most serious disadvantage in competing with other localities in the kingdom, or if the system were to extend to those other localities, then the whole country would be placed at a like disadvantage in its competition with foreign producers of machinery'.

Armstrong then revealed his scepticism about the strikers' position. 'The men ostensibly base their claims to the "nine hours" upon the alleged social and educational advantages which would attend the change. But is this really the object they have in view? Is not the chief burden of their speeches their claim to higher wages? And do they not believe that it is their pecuniary, rather than their social, advantage that would follow the attainment of their demands?' He pointed out that the only effect of the reduction of hours at Sunderland was overtime – at the higher rate – starting one hour earlier than before.

The country gentleman at home: Armstrong in the dining-room inglenook at Cragside, painted by the local artist H. H. Emmerson.

A scientist in ermine: his lordship's right hand rests on a proposed plan for the restoration of Bamburgh Castle.

August 1884: Margaret, Lady Armstrong (centre) entertains a clutch of princesses in Cragside's drawing room.

The Prince of Wales and his two sons enjoy a relaxed conversation with their host during the royal visit of 1884.

Although Armstrong spent more time at Cragside as he grew older, and lessened his ties with Elswick, his pace of life was as hectic as ever.

In 1889, Winnie Watson-Armstrong, who had recently married Armstrong's heir, officiated at the launch of the Australian cruiser *Pandora*.

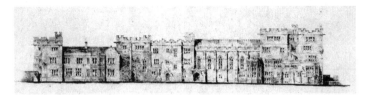

A sketch of proposed restoration works at Bamburgh Castle by the architect Charles J. Ferguson.

Bamburgh Castle as it appears today from the landward side.

Scaffolding at Bamburgh in the late 1890s indicates the extent of the renovation enterprise.

Launched in 1899, the cruiser *Albany* was the only warship built at the Elswick shipyard for the American navy.

Ceremonies at Elswick were commemorated by the production of decorative launch cards.

The Japanese armoured cruiser *Tokiwa*, launched in 1898, was one of seven Elswick-built warships to play a vital role in the 1905 defeat of the Russians at Tsushima.

Asama, completed in the same year as *Tokiwa*, also featured prominently at the Battle of Tsushima. Damaged early on by Russian guns, she later rejoined the fighting.

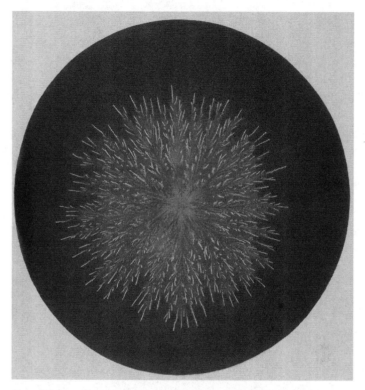

One of a series of spectacular images published in *Electric Movement in Air and Water* (in 1897 and 1899) showing electrical discharges produced by Armstrong with the help of a Wimshurst machine. The experiments were photographed by John Worsnop, and some of Worsnop's images were then coloured using a new process.

The hydraulic machinery and accumulators used to operate the giant bascules of London's Tower Bridge were designed and built at Elswick in the 1890s under the direction of Hamilton Rendel.

The Armstrong Mitchell crane in the Venice Arsenale, the last surviving example of its type, has been adopted as a restoration project by the British charity Venice in Peril.

In his own account, published in *The Times* a few days later, John Burnett accused Armstrong of 'either gross ignorance of the facts or a culpable suppression of the truth', and described the strike 'one of the worthiest movements which ever engaged the attention of the working classes of this kingdom'. He disputed Armstrong's figures about the number of men working and went on to refute many of his other claims. '[The employers] kept us out on strike ten weeks, and then offered us the same terms as the men on the Clyde have enjoyed, and as were rejected by Mr Stephenson's men at the commencement of the strike,' he noted contemptuously. 'Our employers never condescended to give us *any reasons whatever* for their refusal [to concede the nine-hour day].'

As the animated correspondence between the main protagonists continued in the columns of *The Times*, demonstrations of public sympathy for the league multiplied. On 15 September, *Engineering* magazine reported mass rallies in support of the strikers in London, Liverpool, Manchester, Leeds, Birmingham, Sheffield, and Glasgow. Two weeks later, the journal noted, 'All the chief towns in the United Kingdom continue to subscribe liberally to the Newcastle men. Batches of foreigners are leaving the works and returning to Rotterdam, Hamburg and Brussels.'

Armstrong's longing for an end to the strike was made plain in a letter published on 22 September. 'No one would more rejoice than I to see the present contest terminated by a dispassionate and rational compromise,' he insisted. But he lamented that it would be impossible to re-employ many of the men who had left their posts: 'The masters have been compelled by stern necessity to embark in the enterprise of manning their shops as best they can with strangers, engaged by contract for fixed periods of service. Already more than half the places are filled, and the masters have neither the power nor the will to dismiss from their employment the men who have come to their relief.'

All the engineering firms involved in the strike were by now feeling the pressure from the loss of orders, and some of the masters whose financial position had been weak from the start, such as Benjamin Browne of Hawthorn's, were suffering personally. 'It was a time of terrible strain and anxiety from every point of view,' wrote

Browne's daughters, 'and it put an end to his youth once and for all.'

Then, in a dramatic development, John Burnett offered, on his own initiative, to accept a reduction in wages in return for a shorter working week. Published in *The Times* on 28 September, the offer provoked heated criticism from his colleagues in the league before they were persuaded to fall into line. Simultaneously, a new player appeared on the scene, bent on reconciling the warring factions: Anthony John Mundella, Liberal MP for Sheffield. A successful entrepreneur with an enlightened interest in industrial relations, Mundella seemed ideally suited to the role of mediator. On 29 September, he told the masters that the men would accept a pay cut equivalent to the price of three hours' work as long as the masters would move from the 57 hours they had already offered and concede the demand of 54. The following day, a Saturday, a vast crowd, perhaps 25,000 strong – the greatest show of support for the strikers since the dispute began – marched behind bands and banners to a mass meeting on the Newcastle Town Moor in support of the Nine Hours' League.

It was a critical moment. If the employers had seized the opportunity unexpectedly presented to them, they might still have emerged from the dispute with some credit. As it was, they were disunited and in disarray. Even the dictatorial Noble was irritated by the behaviour of some of his fellow employers, such as F. C. Marshall of Hawthorn's, whom he blamed for bolstering the management's intransigence. 'In fact, Marshall has ruined us,' wrote Noble later to Stuart Rendel.

Even worse, Armstrong misjudged the situation and made a clumsy appeal to reason instead of seizing the tactical advantage. Apart from his scepticism about the men's motives, his personal opposition to a cut in hours was based largely on the argument that it would leave expensive machinery idle for longer periods, leading to a poor return on investment – which would ultimately be to the detriment of the workers as well as the employers. He therefore proposed that, rather than the masters' conceding the remaining three hours and cutting pay, the men should take a proportionate *increase* in wages for continuing to work the three hours. 'The condition of trade justifies an advance of wages,' he wrote to

Mundella, 'so that the proposed advance, unlike the proposed reduction, does not conflict with the laws of supply and demand.' While this esoteric reasoning carried little weight with the strikers, a deal seemed to be edging closer. But Mundella interpreted the letter as a sign that his mediation had failed and returned, disappointed, to Sheffield. The employers emerged badly from the affair. Seen as having rejected a workable compromise, their conduct was savagely attacked in the press. 'Generally speaking, the best of the London and provincial papers took the side of the men,' wrote Burnett.

Despite the continuing public disagreements, the gap between the two sides was narrowing – and the logjam was finally broken early in October on the intervention of Joseph Cowen. Cowen held talks with Ralph Park Philipson, an industrialist and coal-owner who was also Newcastle's town clerk and a prominent local Liberal, and between them the two men drafted the terms of a proposed settlement. First and foremost, the employers had to concede the 54 hours. The men had to agree to work overtime when and to the extent required by the employers; wages would stay the same as before the strike; and the men would return to work on the arrangement then existing in the factories (57 hours), with the new terms (54 hours) introduced from 1 January 1872.

Welcoming the peace formula when it was presented it to him by Philipson, Armstrong – worn down by the long weeks of wrangling and public exposure – agreed to recommend its endorsement by his fellow employers. Meanwhile, Cowen approached the league leaders. On 5 October, Burnett and his colleagues assented to the terms, subject to ratification by the men. At a mass meeting that evening, a large majority voted to accept the settlement, although some wanted immediate implementation of the 54 hours. In the event, within a few weeks – despite Armstrong's predictions to the contrary – almost all the old hands were back in their former jobs.

The strike ended on 7 October after 20 weeks. It had proved a victory for the men – and it was, in the end, the masters as much as the men who had been taught a lesson. Two days later, Noble wrote to Stuart Rendel, 'We have made the best of a hard job but you must not forget, my dear Stuart, that we pay a fearful price for it. The wages are practically raised 11.6% and this is very heavy.' In the wake of the settlement, the big firms that had managed to keep their workers out of the conflict, Palmer's and Stephenson's, also introduced the nine-hour day – and, by the end of 1871, in response to pressure from workers all over the country, the 54-hour week had been generally implemented throughout the engineering industry.

Chroniclers of the strike have described the employers as 'the architects of their own defeat' and condemned Armstrong for his 'stubborn, inflexible' leadership.[8] The masters' persistent unwillingness to hold direct discussions with the league was interpreted as 'a wounding refusal to concede that the men had a right to be heard and considered in the taking of decisions which vitally affected them'. John Burnett saw a wider significance in the outcome. 'The principal lesson which this strike ought to teach the men is that the working-man by himself is weak, but that when combined with his fellows he is almost irresistible,' he wrote.[8] 'It is to be hoped that the men of Newcastle will profit by the stern lessons of the past six months and, by becoming members of trade societies, prepare for the next great trade storm which may arise.' He went on to make a prophecy: 'The day will assuredly come when eight hours shall be fixed as the standard length of the working day.'

As well as enforcing a reduction of the basic working week in the engineering industry, the 1871 strike on Tyneside marked an important stage in the development of industrial relations in Britain. It came to be regarded as a major confrontation of national importance, 'involving such basic opposed concepts as the right of employers to untrammelled freedom of action in the conduct of their businesses, and the right of the workers to ensure that their interests received due consideration in the decisions taken by employers in the conduct of their businesses'.[10]

The damage to Armstrong's reputation as an employer coincided with a widespread trend towards replacing paternalist management by a more organised approach to industrial relations. In the old days Armstrong had stored up a large reserve of goodwill among the workers, building them schools, libraries, and reading rooms; he had hosted feasts for them and attended their social gatherings. After the strike, relations became far more formal and distant. 'A suppressed antagonism seemed to be present, even in the most peaceful interludes,' according to Alfred Cochrane, who became an Elswick manager in the early 20th century.[11] 'Everything had to be laid down by rule of thumb; and a kind of similarity, which was bound to arise between the methods of different engineering works, made any concessions on the part of an individual employer impossible.'

The antagonism of 1871 may have been stoked by the huge difference between masters and men in rewards for their toil, wrote Fairbairn. 'While the employees saw the rising ground north of the works covered by the spreading bricks and mortar of that abomination, the Newcastle flat, till not a green thing was left ... they contrasted that with the legendary story of Cragside, where Armstrong's house was being almost continuously extended and where his 1,700 acres was reputed to employ 70 gardeners.'

The lack of empathy shown by Armstrong's lieutenants was also an issue. While the founder of Elswick knew many of his employees and their families personally, George Rendel, a brilliant but ambitious individual, had joined the firm straight from public school and soon developed 'a thrust which enabled him to face any problem', as Fairbairn put it; Andrew Noble's military training had apparently made him 'impatient of everything except immediate response to orders'.

There were occasional outbreaks of industrial unrest during Armstrong's remaining tenure at Elswick, although none would prove as prominent and far-reaching as the strike of 1871. One of the more memorable – occurring two years before the founding of Newcastle United football club – was the 1890 'Football Strike'.[12] At a time of expanding output, engineering workers on the Tyne submitted a number of demands to their masters, including a two-shilling increase in wages, the abolition of systematic overtime, and a cut in hours from 54 to 53. The employers would concede no more than a wage rise of one shilling. While the men were persuaded to withdraw the other items, they were adamant about the one-hour reduction, and on 17 March 1890 they went on strike to enforce this demand. The strikers' case was that in other trades the men stopped work at noon on Saturdays, whereas the 1pm finish in the engineering industry prevented them from attending football matches, unless they went straight from work. After a series of meetings, during which concessions were made on both sides, the change was agreed to and, after eight days, the strike came to an end – with 12 o'clock established as the Saturday finishing time.

A demand for reduced working hours was at the heart of a later dispute in the engineering industry that affected the whole nation. Encouraged by the bold action of William Allan, later Liberal MP for Gateshead – who in 1892 had implemented an eight-hour day at his Scotia Engine Works in Sunderland – engineering workers began to agitate for the general introduction of eight hours. In July 1897, the increasingly powerful Amalgamated Society of Engineers called its members out on strike in support of the claim. Armstrong made his last visit to Elswick that year, during the visit of the King of Siam, but he was too old to play any effective role in the dispute. The Tyne was again at the heart of the action, however, since the president of the Federated Engineering Employers was Colonel Henry Dyer, manager of the Elswick Steel Works. This time, the masters were much better organised. At the end of an intensely bitter fight that dragged on over six months, the men withdrew their demand for an eight-hour day and reconciled themselves to a peacetime working pattern that, in the event, would prevail until the 1920s.

15

Egyptian Interlude

William Armstrong travelled out of Europe only once during his long life – to advise Egypt's supreme ruler on improvements to the navigation of the Nile. His travelling companions were Sir John Fowler, made engineer to the Khedive on the recommendation of the Prince of Wales, and Stuart Rendel, who later explained the circumstances of the trip: 'The engineering enterprise which the Khedive had most at heart was that of establishing communication between Lower and Upper Egypt, including the Soudan. The Nile was, of course, the natural channel of communication, but the Nile cataracts, or rapids, were almost an insuperable obstacle.'[1] Fowler had invited Armstrong to visit the cataracts at Aswan and concentrate his engineering genius on finding a solution to the problem. Since neither Armstrong nor Fowler spoke French, Rendel acted as interpreter.

'Everything in Egypt is unique. There is no river in the world like the river of Egypt; no monuments in the world like those of Egypt; no land in the world like the land of Egypt; and no ruler in the world like the ruler of Egypt,' said Armstrong on his return to Newcastle. Indeed, the expedition had made such an impression on him that he was induced to relate his experiences, and his reflections on them, in four lectures at the Lit & Phil. His only aim in doing so, he said, was 'to enable my friends and townsmen to share with me the natural impressions of a tour in one of the most interesting regions of the world', but – from his views on the Islamic religion to his studied nonchalance after falling off a donkey – his account provides unparalleled insights into the mind and character of the man, as well as into the country of his travels. Two years later, the lectures were published as a collection entitled *A Visit to Egypt in 1872* – one of the very few books ever to appear under Armstrong's name.[2]

They arrived at Alexandria on 17 January 1872, having previously travelled from London to Brindisi via Paris, Turin, Rome, and Naples. 'It was like entering upon a new life to be suddenly brought in contact with camels and turbans, and palm trees, and dark-skinned men, clothed in many-coloured garments,' he wrote. 'Alexandria possesses none of its ancient grandeur. It is essentially a seafaring place, reminding one, in many ways, of Wapping; and one looks in vain for any remnants of that love of philosophy and literature for which it used to be so famous.'

In Cairo, it was people's clothing that intrigued him. 'The quantity of apparel varied from almost nothing at all to such a reduplication of garments as would oppress an Englishman, even in his own cold climate,' he wrote. 'In the colour of dress, equal variety was displayed. In the East, colour is always used with skill and good taste, and the crowd before me looked like a bed of sober-coloured flowers harmoniously mixed, to please an artist's eye. Donkeys are the favourite means of locomotion for those who can afford to use legs other than their own.'

He found the 'native city' of Cairo much more interesting than the French quarter. 'On entering it, you plunge at once from wide open spaces and Frenchified buildings into narrow streets and Saracenic architecture. The city is very large, containing fully twice the population of Newcastle and Gateshead. Narrow as the streets are at ground level, they are reduced to a mere slit at the top, for the houses jut out at each storey until they almost meet at the roofs, thus affording the comfort of shade, which, under a burning sun, is a most important advantage. The windows are unglazed, being closed only with a fret-work of wood, which admits the air while it excludes the view into the room from the outside.'

The streets and bazaars seemed oppressively crowded. 'The women mix freely with the men in the streets, and so long as they keep their faces veiled below their eyes, they care not for being jostled by the crowd. In fact, I think they rather like it. Neither are they at all particular about exhibiting their bare feet and ankles, or even a little more, for I frequently saw them trying on stockings at the shop doors; but, as to showing their faces, Oh no! anything rather than that indecency.

'The variety of the human genus that one sees in the bazaars is most striking – Arabs, Syrians, Persians, Nubians, Turks, Jews, Copts and Negroes are all presented in their most typical forms, besides Greeks, Levantines and other Europeans. Drunkenness one never sees. Tobacco and coffee are the only stimulants used, and amongst the poor are the only luxuries. They look upon unbelievers with indifference rather than hatred.'

He was fascinated by the Islamic religion, especially the way it was taught in schools. 'Peeping through the door you will see rows of little boys, all repeating their lessons in their loudest voice. The Koran seems to be the only school book. Cairo is full of mosques, but they are not so much frequented as might be expected considering the religious spirit of the people. One sees and hears very little of priests in Egypt. Mahomedanism is the religion of a book, and it is surprising what a hold that book has upon the people, irrespective of priestly influence. The Koran appears to be riveted on the nation, and I doubt whether anything would displace it, short of a change of race. It came by force, and it will probably never go away unless by the same agency. The domes and minarets of the numerous mosques give great beauty to the city, when viewed from the adjacent heights.'

One Friday he accompanied a small group of English people to a religious service at the mosque of the Howling Dervishes in a Cairo suburb. 'The ceremony culminated by the whole party of Dervishes suddenly ceasing to articulate and beginning in a wild excited manner to gasp out "Allah" in a sort of spasmodic whisper. This part of the performance is, I presume, what has given rise to the term "howling", but the word is quite misapplied – there is neither howling nor anything like it in the case. The whole performance, from beginning to end, appeared to me to be simply intended to excite a religious fervour, by the constant repetition of religious phrases or sentences, aided by musical rhythm, and concurrent gesticulations.' He witnessed another example of ecstasy at the mosque of the Dancing Dervishes, where the performer 'looked as if he was floating in the air, or rather, I may say, as if he were suspended by an invisible wire from a concealed roasting jack in the roof. The action was accompanied by a plaintive strain from a flute, and by the ejaculations of the surrounding devotees. Many of these became so excited that they could not pull up when the dancer stopped, but continued to heave and gasp in a most spasmodic manner for several minutes afterwards.'

Armstrong's reluctance to comment on religious practices was revealed later in a note to Stuart Rendel, written while preparing his book on Egypt for publication. 'I had already struck out a good deal about the bible difficulty,' he explained. 'I don't think there is much harm in saying "any religion is better than none", which in my opinion is perfectly true of all the great religions of the world.'

He was happier making observations about domestic mores, which he was provided the opportunity to do when the party was invited to share a meal at the home of an Egyptian Pasha. 'We were received by the Pasha, but not by Madame. She sent kind messages, saying how much she would have liked to meet us, but that in her own country she could not do so without exciting unpleasant gossip. The Pasha, who is a very enlightened and intelligent man, and always free in condemning the usages and superstitions of his country, declared this action of his wife to be great humbug.'

Equivocal about the food served to the English guests, Armstrong was more enthusiastic about the quality of the wine. 'The injunctions of the Koran against the use of alcoholic liquor did not deter any of the party from partaking of it,' he noted, 'though only to a very moderate extent. The evening terminated with coffee and cigarets, and pleasant conversation. It was admitted that our excellent dinner had been prepared under the personal directions of Madame; and I infer that Egyptian ladies do not consider it derogatory to exercise minute supervision of household affairs. All honour be to them for so doing. The Pasha had but one wife, and it is not by any means common in Egypt for a man to have more.'

The fact that the Pasha's domestic servants were slaves prompted him to consider the institution of slavery in Egypt. 'Nominally, the traffic in slaves is illegal, but, practically, it is carried on without restriction,' he said. 'There is scarcely a house in Cairo without one or more slaves; but, in general, they are kindly treated, moderately worked, and become much attached to the family in which they are placed. The manner in which the poor creatures are kidnapped is atrocious, and is by far the worst part of the business. There are gangs of ruffians on the White Nile who do this horrible work, and their mode of proceeding is to make incursions into adjacent lands, and there, surrounding the villages, they set fire to everything that will burn. When the people rush out of their houses, the men are shot down, the children captured, and the women left to starve or provide for themselves.

'Under the head of slavery, I may properly notice the system of forced labour which, from time immemorial, has afflicted the Fellaheen or agricultural classes of Egypt. All skilled labour is in that country free; but all common labour, required for the maintenance of public works, and for the execution of new ones, is forced. I believe also that this applies, in a great measure, to all or most of the private undertakings of the Khedive. The labourers are paid, but it is only at a very low rate. In general, each set only works about six weeks at a time, after which they return to their homes, and are replaced by a new set from another locality.'

Armstrong made plain his disgust at this state of affairs, noting that the injustices of the system were fully recognised by the Khedive and his government but regarded as a necessary evil. He heard one minister argue that, without it, labour could not be procured for the maintenance of the canals and the great irrigation works on which Egypt depended for its very existence.

The Khedive himself was not only supreme ruler but also 'a land-owner, ship-owner, manufacturer and trader, all upon an enormous scale'. He was said to own one-third of all the land in Egypt. 'The whole fleet of steam vessels plying upon the Nile belong to him, as also the large sugar factories, and all the other factories which are seen on the banks of that river,' wrote Armstrong. 'His palaces are everywhere, and one sees none other but his. There is no aristocracy outside of his own family, and of his ministers of state. Below them there is nothing until you descend to the citizens of Cairo and of the other cities of Egypt, and after them come the

Fellaheen. As prince, proprietor, and trader, his position is altogether unique.'

Armstrong and Fowler had several interviews with the Khedive, who proved an urbane and generous host. On one occasion, they were invited to the palace of Abdeen in Cairo, where an attendant was ordered to bring cigars. 'The Khedive helped himself to one and motioned all to do the same,' noted Armstrong. 'Nubar Pasha, in taking one, deprecated his smoking it in the presence of his Sovereign, but the Khedive put aside his objections in a courtly and playful manner which set us all at ease. We sat smoking and talking for more than an hour.' They had serious matters to discuss, but the Khedive often cracked jokes and then laughed heartily at his own wittiness. He paid little attention to etiquette, talking more like a businessman than a head of state. 'My friends know that I am no smoker,' admitted Armstrong ruefully, 'and will probably ask how I got through my cigar without experiencing effects which would be extremely embarrassing in the presence of royalty. I have to inform them that I smoked half of it, and smuggled the rest into my pocket. The tobacco being very mild, I thus succeeded in satisfying good manners without inconvenient results.'

Few people knew anything about the Egyptian Royal Family or how many children the Khedive had. 'The babies are never heard of. The girls never appear; and the boys only come to light as they approach maturity.' However, the monarch's mother was known to have a palace all to herself, on the outskirts of Cairo. 'The wives and ladies of the Khedive are often seen in and around Cairo,' noted Armstrong, 'sometimes on the river in steam yachts, and sometimes in carriages, preceded by a couple of runners, to clear the roads and act as footmen, and defended by a mounted guard on each side of the carriage.'

The Khedive's heir apparent was Prince Teufik, aged 22, who expressed a keen interest in Britain and who mentioned that he liked to read *The Times*. A meeting with the prince involved Armstrong in another smoking trial. 'Coffee and long pipes were speedily handed to us,' he said. 'The pipes were about six feet long, and very handsome. A little silver tray was placed on the carpet to support the bowls. I found it much easier to smoke a long pipe than a cigar. The smoke reaches the mouth quite cool, and according to my experience, without any nauseating property.'

One of the most thought-provoking elements of Armstrong's adventure was his encounter with the Pyramids, which he found more imposing when viewed from afar, since many of them were far more dilapidated than he had expected. With little difficulty, despite his 61 years, he climbed to the top of the Great Pyramid at Giza (the only one of the Seven Wonders of the Ancient World to survive substantially intact), but was disappointed with what he found when he got there. Although the original Pyramid, completed more than 4,400 years earlier, had been topped by a point, its summit had since become a flat surface 30 feet square. 'All above the present top has been thrown down and taken away for building purposes,' Armstrong lamented, with the result that the summit was now 20 feet lower than it had been. 'I know of no situation more calculated than this to carry back the mind into the depths of historical time and to awake solemn reflections on the wickedness and folly of mankind.'

But the Arabs who had insisted on accompanying him to the summit gave him no opportunity for contemplation because they were so persistent in their demands for baksheesh. It was one of the rare occasions on which Armstrong's irritation was plain. 'How I should have liked, had I been able, to have tipped them over the edge one after another,' he admitted, 'but not being a Kenelm Chillingly [the hero of a recently published novel by Edward Bulwer-Lytton], I had no alternative but to abandon reflection and resign myself to the tormentors.' He later explored the interior of the Pyramid, including the sarcophagus designed to hold the body of its builder, Cheops. He did not enjoy this experience, likening part of it to a descent into a coal-mine.

After graphically evoking the vastness of the Great Pyramid, Armstrong went on to speculate about the character of its creator. 'We may assume Cheops to have been a proud, selfish monarch, who considered that his subjects were made for him, and not he for his subjects,' he said. 'His kingdom was populous and wealthy, and a large section of his people were skilled in constructive arts. He doubtless looked upon himself as the greatest king that ever reigned and resolved that his tomb should exceed all other tombs in grandeur, security and endurance. To accomplish this, he had recourse to forced labour, that cruel system which has prevailed in Egypt, probably without interruption, even from that remote antiquity and, in fact, from a still earlier date. According to Herodotus, the people were called out to work at this Pyramid in sets of 100,000 at a time, each set remaining on the work for three months being then changed for another. In this way, the Pyramid took twenty years to build.' In a final irony, the tyrant died before the monument was completed, and it is doubtful that his body ever entered the tomb prepared for it. Therefore, remarked Armstrong, the Great Pyramid exists only 'to record the monstrous wickedness of its founder'.

The next highlight was a visit to the necropolis of Saqqara, 12 miles south of Cairo. Predating the reign of Cheops by several hundred years, Saqqara was the burial ground for the ancient Egyptian capital of Memphis. Having completed part of the journey by train, the group were put on donkeys for the remainder. 'These poor little animals are generally much over-weighted when mounted by Englishmen, especially as it does not suit our dignity to sit on that part of the animal which is best calculated to carry load,' observed Armstrong. 'The consequence is they often fall; and it was my ignoble fate, on this occasion, to be, from this cause, precipitated in the dust, just as we were entering upon the site of Memphis. I quickly gathered myself up, and – adopting Mr Pickwick's policy, when running after his hat on a windy day – I tried to look as if I thought it as good a joke as the rest of the company unmistakably did. I was not hurt, but only dusted, but the dust was the dust of Memphis, and who would object to be dusted with such famous dust as that? To think of the antiquity of Memphis takes one's breath away.' Memphis is thought to have been founded around 2200BC and to have remained the capital of Egypt until its near-destruction by the invading Persians around 520BC.

'The great Necropolis of Memphis, the most ancient known burial ground in Egypt, or I may say in the world, lies on the desert, and is bounded on one side by the cultivated valley of the Nile. The space occupied by the tombs is about four miles long and, on an average, fully half a mile wide.' Its most interesting feature was the great subterranean tomb in which the embalmed bodies of sacred bulls were buried. This extraordinary sepulchre had been found only 13 years earlier by the French archaeologist Auguste Mariette, who also discovered the nearby Serapeum, a temple where the dead bulls were worshipped. 'The sepulchre of the bulls consists of subterranean galleries cut in the solid rock, at a depth of sixty or seventy feet below the surface,' wrote Armstrong. 'The galleries which we entered are fine spacious passages, several hundred yards in length, and on either side are large chambers, each containing an enormous sarcophagus of dark-coloured syenite, with a lid of proportionate size. I calculated that each sarcophagus, with its lid, would weigh upwards of sixty tons.' These sarcophagi were the coffins of the sacred bulls, but they were all empty when found by Mariette. Their lids had been thrown aside or broken by people searching for treasure, and the mummies of the bulls removed.

The ancient Egyptians believed the bull to be the earthly representative of the god Osiris – but they worshipped only one particular bull, distinguished by specific markings. When this bull died, there was 'weeping and wailing throughout the land', until a suitable successor could be found. There was then universal joy 'as if Osiris had been dead and come to life again'.

After musing on the great antiquity of many Egyptian monuments and suggesting that Egyptian civilisation must date back at least 6,000 years – about 2,000 years more than previously thought – Armstrong went on to give a typically lucid exposition of hieroglyphic writing.

Before leaving the vicinity of Cairo, he visited the site of the ancient city of Heliopolis, on the edge of the desert. 'Heliopolis is supposed to be the place where Moses planned the Exodus and Jeremiah wrote the Book of Lamentations,' he told his audience at the Lit & Phil. 'I will not vouch for the truth of these associations, but, at all events, it is certain that Plato studied there, and it is highly probable that, under a more ancient name, it was connected with the events of the Jewish captivity. The site is marked by a single granite obelisk, which is the oldest in Egypt.' At Heliopolis, as well as at Alexandria, he repeatedly wondered what had become of all the valuable materials used in building the temples and the monuments of the ancient cities of the delta, concluding that 'they were chiefly removed to Rome, to be used in the construction of the temples and public edifices of that city'.

It was time for the party to set off on its voyage up the Nile. They travelled in an English-built steamer, with engines by Stephenson's of Newcastle, and towed a *dahabeeyah*, or luxury sailing boat, provided by the Khedive. The crew consisted of 'an Arab captain, two engineers, four stokers, thirteen sailors, including eight marines for our protection. For personal attendants, and ministers to our wants, we had a portly French cook, together with three assistants, of whom one was French and two were Arabs. We had three waiters and one dragoman. Thus, in the two vessels, we had forty-three persons to attend upon, and escort, just four Christian gentlemen. Our stores of provisions were boundless. Truly, the Khedive is no niggard provider.'

They made slow progress, disembarking occasionally to visit the Khedive's sugar factories or to watch the thousands of people at work on the restoration or excavation of canals. On the third day, they reached the town of Siout, from where they climbed a rocky slope to visit some ancient tombs and enjoy a view that in Armstrong's opinion embraced the essence of Egypt in all its changeless majesty. 'Conceive yourself standing on a high cliff, looking down upon the flat valley of the Nile, as on a green sea sharply defined against a beach of yellow sand,' he said. 'Observe the opposite side, seven miles distant, bounded by a bolder coast, equally yellow, though consisting chiefly of rock; then, imagine a number of dark brown mounds, rising like islands out of the green surface, each surmounted by an Arab village, enveloped in palm trees. Turn your mind's eye downwards, upon the city of Siout, composed of low, flat-roofed, clay-coloured houses, with palm trees and white-washed minarets rising high above them. Finally, picture to yourself the glistening, tortuous streak which marks the Nile, flowing through the midst of the valley, and extending north and south as far as vision can reach. If you can do all this, you will see the land of Egypt as it is; and also as it used to be in the age of the Pharaohs.'

Six more days sailing and steaming would bring them to the magnificent tombs and temples of Thebes (Luxor), where Armstrong resumed his account, warning his audience about the vicious dogs that patrolled the ancient sites at night. 'Having arrived at the Great Temple of Karnak, I found myself in the midst of the most imposing ruins I had ever seen. For extent and massive grandeur there is nothing to equal them. The space they cover is fully a mile and a half in circumference, and so enormous are the blocks of stone employed, and so numerous are the colossal monolith figures and obelisks, that they look like relics of an age of Titans ...

'I visited the ruins of Karnak three times, twice by day and once by moonlight. The ruins are, in many parts, so tumbled about that it is difficult, without repeated visits, to get an idea of the original arrangement. The pictorial effect of the ruins is much finer by the light of the full moon than by that of the sun; but, if any of my hearers should ever have an opportunity of visiting Karnak by moonlight, let me tell them to beware of the dogs. It is, in fact, absolutely necessary to go in company, for defence against these animals; and if any should return from such an expedition without having applied other names than proper names to these troublesome brutes, I will readily acknowledge his command of temper to be greatly superior to my own' – a frank admission by a man who was known to have an intense dislike of swearing.

After exploring all of the major Theban temples, Armstrong was drawn to the remains of a sacred lake, across which the bodies of the dead, including those of the Pharaohs, had to be conveyed before burial. 'After passing the sacred lake of Thebes, the bodies of the Pharaohs were conveyed to a necropolis of their own, that is to say to the valley of the tombs of the kings,' he explained. The valley could be reached either by a gorge through the mountains or by a path across the ridge. 'In visiting the place, we went by the mountain path, and returned by the gorge. The ascent of the mountain on one side and its descent on the other are both exceedingly steep, and cliffs of great height occur on both sides. Nothing can be more solemn than the descent into this valley of death. So sternly desolate is the scene that the visitor might imagine himself in one of those lifeless, waterless valleys which our telescopes reveal to us as characterizing the surface of the moon. Nothing is to be seen but yellow rocks and yellow sand reflecting the fierce rays of the sun, and presenting the same colour, and the same shining surface, that the moon presents to our view.'

Many of the tomb interiors were covered in pictorial hieroglyphics that have thrown a great deal of light on the manners and customs of the people, and the state of the arts in ancient Egypt. There was plenty of feasting, music, and entertaining. 'Both wine and beer were manufactured in the country and freely used,' remarked Armstrong. 'In fact both men and women are sometimes represented as being what is commonly called "the worse of drink". The houses of the wealthy were luxuriously furnished with tables, chairs, ottomans, vases and various articles of what Mrs Malaprop calls "bigotry and virtue",' he went on. 'The ladies went unveiled and were not subject to hareem seclusion. They spent their time much as ladies in England do – in household duties, visiting, and walking in gardens. The wife was treated as the lady of the house and her husband's equal ... Throughout all classes great respect appears to have been shown to old age. In short, by an examination of the pictorial hieroglyphics on the walls of the tombs at Thebes and elsewhere, a very complete idea may be formed of how the people lived and spent their time.'

The ancient Egyptian text known as *The Book of the Dead* did not impress Armstrong. 'Except that this extraordinary book contains a very wholesome code of morality, enforced by the doctrine of a future state, it has not much to recommend it,' he said. 'It is a strange collection of prayers, spells and charms to be used by the deceased, and bears no sort of comparison with the sacred volume of the Jews, which commends itself to human nature by its noble simplicity, its warm glow of human passion and emotion, as well as by its poetic imagery based on natural objects.'

What did interest him, however, was the worship by the Egyptians of animal life in nearly all its forms. Among birds, the sacred ibis was an object of special veneration, and the tombs of Thebes and Memphis were full of the embalmed remains of these birds. 'I brought one of these ibis mummies from the necropolis of Thebes,' said Armstrong, 'and gave it to my friend Mr John Hancock, who skilfully separated the bones and set them up as a perfect skeleton, and here it stands upon the table – an ibis of 3000 years ago.'

Even insect life formed an important part of Egyptian worship, particularly the scarab, or common beetle, which was held to be an emblem of the sun and associated with resurrection. The sun was not only worshipped per se by the Egyptians, he pointed out, 'but was regarded as the chief manifestation of their Jupiter, the king of gods, whom they called "Amun". The word "Ra" means the sun, and the compound Amun-ra may be translated as Jupiter manifest in the sun.' In this way, the scarab became mixed up with religious belief and the hopes of a future life.

After considering the laws and social structures of ancient Egypt, Armstrong launched into a gripping account of the history of a country that, according to recent research, he said, had been united under Menes more than 6,500 years before the present. By the time of Menes, Egyptian civilisation was already well developed. 'It is like the Nile,' he said, 'which gets no smaller as we follow it to the limit of Upper Egypt; and the supposition that a highly civilized race started suddenly into existence, on the confines of history, is just as incredible as the foolish story told to Herodotus of the Nile bursting from the earth as a fully developed river on the frontier of Egypt.'

He speculated on the origins of the ancient Egyptians, suggesting that they were closer in terms of race to the English people than to 'their immediate neighbours, the Hebrews, the Syrians, and the Arabians', and going on to tell his audience about the various Egyptian dynasties, their high points and low points, their wars and triumphs, and their ultimate subjection by the Persians under Cambyses. 'Egypt was held by the Persians for about two centuries, at the end of which Alexander the Great overthrew the Persian Empire and took possession of Egypt, which, down to the commencement of the Christian era, was ruled by his successors, the Ptolemies. After that, Egypt became a Roman province.'

Having concluded this whirlwind tour of Egyptian history,

Armstrong returned to the task in hand: his voyage up the Nile. Throughout the journey, he took note of the materials and technology used in Egypt in the present and the past, speculating at one point on whether the ancient Egyptians might have been in the habit of using steel tools. The expedition's next port of call was the remarkably intact temple of Edfu, recently cleared by Auguste Mariette of the sand and rubbish in which it had been buried. They sailed on to Silsilis, past the great quarries of sandstone from which nearly all the temples of Upper Egypt were built, and the features of the landscape prompted Armstrong to turn his attention to the annual Nile inundation.

'Herodotus has justly said that Egypt is the gift of the Nile,' he said. 'Without the Nile, Egypt would be a scorched and lifeless desert; but with the Nile it is a land of unmatched fertility. Every year the Nile comes down in flood from the region of tropical rain, charged with fertilizing matter, which spreads over the surface of its valley, and then it retires to its bed to enable man to utilize the rich deposit ... As soon as the flooded Nile has so far retired as to give access to the land, the labours of the husbandman commence; but the sun soon dries up the surface, and then, if there be no renewal of moisture, begins to destroy that which has previously quickened. Hence, constant irrigation, in the nearly rainless land of Egypt, is indispensable for realizing the crops.'

Irrigation depended partly on canals and reservoirs, but mostly on water lifted from the river by an ancient device called a shadoof. 'It consists of a vertical pole stuck in the ground at the edge of the river, and a cross pole lashed to the top, in such a manner as to be free to oscillate up and down like a see-saw,' explained Armstrong. 'From one end of this cross pole is suspended, by a rope, a bucket or large earthenware jar, and to the other end is attached a counterpoise nearly equal to the weight of the bucket when full of water.' To operate the machine, a man stood beside the river and took hold of the rope, pulling it down until the bucket entered the water. 'By this downward action at the bucket end of the pole, the counterweight at the opposite end is lifted and thus becomes available for helping the operator to raise the bucket when full of water.' Very little effort was needed to lift the bucket to the required height, at which point 'the man, by a rapid and easy movement, empties the vessel into the channel by which the water is conveyed over the land'.

Armstrong enjoyed watching the shadoof operators at work – even though it made him self-conscious about the colour of his own skin. 'The swinging action is very graceful, and admirably adapted to improve muscular development, every part of the body being brought into movement,' he said. 'I have seen men of beautiful forms engaged in this work – not of herculean mould, but models for a Mercury. I have watched with admiration the graceful movements of their lithe, wiry frames, and the clearly marked play of their tight strung muscles; and as I looked upon their olive skins, tinted with the red glow of exercise, I became rather disgusted with my own colour, and thought what a fright I must look in the eyes of these people.'

At Silsilis, they were only 35 miles from their destination: the cataracts, or rapids, at Aswan. Getting to the other side of this awesome obstacle involved unloading boats at the top or bottom of the cataracts, and transporting their cargoes by camel for three miles between the upper and lower ports. The main purpose of the English expedition was to find a way to overcome this interruption to the river traffic. 'The Nile, at that part of its course, has forced a passage through a barrier of protruded igneous rocks, and in so doing has become divided into a multiplicity of channels through which the water rushes with great rapidity and violence, but without any actual cascade,' explained Armstrong. 'The islands formed by these numerous channels are all naked rocks, none of which are more than fifty feet in height.'

After surveying the lower cataracts, Armstrong and Fowler went on to Mahatta, the higher shipping place, from where they were taken by boat to the upper rapids. It was a thoroughly unnerving experience. The crew paddled the boat down to the crest of the first rapid, where they paused for observation. 'I thought we were getting rather too near, and expected every movement that the crew would use their oars to keep us further off,' Armstrong recalled. 'Instead of that, without the slightest warning, they launched us right down the surging current. The next moment we were in the midst of waves, whirlpools and broken water, and our little boat was tossed about in a most alarming manner.' Surviving the initial ordeal bolstered the visitors' spirits, however, and they volunteered to descend the next rapid in the same way.

'After that, no rush of water was too violent to restrain us,' said Armstrong, who was now in his element. 'We spent two days amongst those rapids, in the course of which we passed down every channel and visited every island,' while encountering many more hair-raising adventures along the way. 'I never fully appreciated the volume of the Nile until I saw it divided at the cataracts into many separate course,' admitted Armstrong. 'One sees that every channel contains as much water as would make a first-class English river, and thus an idea is formed of the enormous magnitude of the aggregate quantity.'

Before setting out on their return journey, the group visited Philae, a sacred island believed to be the burial place of the god Osiris, whose story carries many echoes of Christianity. The mission of Osiris on earth was supposed to have been to teach human beings all good things, and his great adversary was Seth, the principle of evil. Osiris was killed by Seth, but was raised from his tomb and became the judge of the dead. The main temple on Philae was dedicated to Isis, the sister and wife of Osiris, who was also held in the highest esteem. Osiris and Isis were the only two gods universally recognised in Egypt, according to Herodotus.

Having retraced their steps to Cairo, Armstrong, Fowler, and Rendel took a trip to Suez and Ismailia, prompting Armstrong to make some dismissive remarks about the newly opened Suez Canal, which he regarded as 'more remarkable for its situation than its magnitude'. He said he had been told on reliable authority that 'the quantity of material removed in carrying out the improvements of the Tyne already exceeds the quantity which has been moved in the execution of the Suez Canal'. In fact, he believed that the Egyptians had made a great mistake in promoting the case for a new canal, 'which has already deprived the Suez Railway of nearly all its traffic'. If, on the other hand, the ancient canal linking the Nile with the Red Sea had been restored and extended to Alexandria, 'the result would have been highly beneficial to Egypt in regard both to commerce and irrigation'.

After an intriguing desert encounter with a group of Bedouin, Armstrong returned to Alexandria, where he embarked with the rest of the party for Brindisi: 'Thence we proceeded rapidly to England, arriving there in snow and fog, which made me feel that, if any form of idolatry be excusable, it is the worship of the sun.'

As the result of the British expedition to Egypt, plans were later devised at Elswick for the construction of a 'ship railway' across the Nile cataracts, worked through turbines driven by the cataracts themselves. The idea was that the vessels would be drawn up an incline by hydraulic power and let down slowly on the other side – but this theory was never put to the test. 'The whole scheme was perfectly practicable, and I dare say might be carried out with the more ease now that the new and successful barrage has been erected on the same spot,' wrote Stuart Rendel some thirty years later[3] – by which time the first Aswan Dam had been built to control the flooding of the Nile and regulate the supply of water.

Armstrong's connection with Egypt did not end there, however. Indeed, he appears to have forged a lasting relationship with the Khedive and his family, and it was not long before the Khedive's son Hassan, a student at Oxford, came to stay with the Armstrongs in Jesmond. The Nobles were among those who entertained Hassan during his visit. Among other things, they organised a game of croquet for him. 'The Prince seemed interested in playing games with our young friends,' recalled Marjorie Noble.[4] 'As Lady Armstrong was driving him home to her house, he asked if he might get out and walk back to continue his games, at which we were much flattered.' Marjorie Noble was charmed by Prince Hassan, noting his 'admiration for English ways and manners', and he in return took her into his confidence. 'I fear when I go back they will marry me to someone I have never seen or known,' he told her – which is indeed what happened, wrote Mrs Noble in her memoirs.

16

Natural Forces

Armstrong's mystical love affair with water had lost none of its potency over the years and continued to exert a profound influence on his spiritual as well as his professional life. It was a spur to the great debate he had started about harnessing the forces of nature for the generation of power, but it was also a key to unlocking the mysteries of his heart. Alexander Munro's white marble statue of the water nymph Undine, prominently displayed at Cragside, is an embodiment of this personal response. She is shown dancing through the bulrushes, with her hair and draperies floating in the wind – beautiful and seductive, but ultimately free and unknowable.

Undine, from the Latin *unda*, 'wave', was the name given by the medieval alchemist and writer Paracelsus to the elemental spirits of water, which were female. Of the various orders of elemental spirits, undines intermarry most readily with humans, and the undine who gives birth as the result of such a union receives with her child a human soul. But, according to legend, the man who takes an undine to be his wife must be careful not to go on water with her – or at least not to anger her while on water – for in that case she will return to her original element.

Energy and its creation was the theme of Armstrong's speech at York in 1881 to the British Association – a meeting that prompted *The Times* to speculate that the human race was on the brink of one of 'the great conquests of science'. The big challenge, he said, was how to produce electricity in such a way that it was cheap and abundant enough to replace heat as a motive power.[1] 'We have firstly the direct heating power of the sun's rays, which we have not yet succeeded in applying to motive purposes. Secondly, we have water power, wind power, and tidal power, all depending upon influences lying outside of our planet. And, thirdly, we have chemical attraction or affinity. Beyond these there is nothing worth naming.' It was only the lack of an efficient device for converting heat into electricity, he said, that prevented the direct heating action of the sun's rays being used to generate energy. 'In our climate, it is true, we shall never be able to depend upon sunshine for power,' he admitted, but people in cool climates would have no need to worry as long as they had 'preserved sunbeams' in the condensed and portable form of coal.

The enormous power of the sun's rays was reckoned equal to melting a crust of ice 103 feet thick over the whole earth in a year. In tropical regions, the power would be much greater than elsewhere, although a large deduction would have to be made everywhere in order for absorption of heat by the atmosphere. Even so, his calculations had led him to conclude that: 'The solar heat operating upon an area of one acre in the tropics would exert the amazing power of 4,000 horses acting for nearly nine hours every day.' Transporting electricity over long distances would be expensive and problematic, but in the case of solar energy there would be no problem about waste. 'Waste of coal means waste of money and premature exhaustion of coal beds,' he said, 'but the sun's heat is poured upon the earth in endless profusion.'

In championing the potential of solar energy, Armstrong had lost none of his faith in the power of water, however. 'Whenever the time arrives for utilizing the power of great waterfalls, the transmission of power by electricity will become a system of vast importance,' he said. The first hydroelectric power plant of the kind Armstrong had in mind would be built by Nikola Tesla and George Westinghouse 14 years later at Niagara Falls.

Knowledge of electricity had made great strides since Armstrong's early experiments in the 1840s with his hydroelectric machine, and the recent introduction of the Fauré battery was identified as a crucial step in the wider use of electricity. (It led eventually to the industrial manufacture of lead-acid batteries, now used for starting automobile engines.) 'It will enable motors of small power to accomplish by uninterrupted action the effect of much larger machines acting for short periods, and by this means the

In 1880 the 'magician's palace' of Cragside in Northumberland became the first house in the world to be lit by hydroelectricity. An illustration of April 1881 in the *Graphic* newspaper shows the iron footbridge over the Debdon Burn (the source of the electrical power) and three illuminated interiors: the dining room, the library, and the staircase hall.

value of very small streams of water will be greatly enhanced.' Batteries would be especially useful where the power of a stream or river was required for electric lighting. 'Even the fitful power of wind, now so little used, will probably acquire new life when aided by a system which will not only collect, but equalize, the variable and uncertain power exerted by the air.'

It would greatly add to the usefulness of a Fauré battery if its weight and size could be much reduced. 'We may easily conceive of its becoming available in a lighter form for all sorts of carriages on common roads,' said Armstrong, which would vastly reduce the labour required of horses. 'Even the nobler animal that bestrides a bicycle, or the one of fainter courage that prefers the safe seat of a tricycle, may ere long be spared the labour of propulsion,' he remarked. 'And the time may not be distant when an electric horse far more amenable to discipline than the living one may be added to the bounteous gifts which science has bestowed on civilized man.'

Armstrong had been experimenting on his own territory with the generation of energy by natural forces. Soon after taking up residence at Cragside in 1865 he had begun, with the help of hundreds of workmen, to create a series of lakes – reservoirs that could also be used to drive hydraulic machinery.[2] The first two, Tumbleton and Debdon, were made by damming the Debdon Burn. Tumbleton provided a 35-foot head of water for a pumping station, from where a hydraulic engine distributed water to the house for drinking, bathing, and working labour-saving devices such as a passenger lift. A waterfall in Debdon Burn almost a mile from the house, above Debdon Lake, was the source of energy for Cragside's first hydroelectricity; in the early days, a turbine was installed here to operate, among other things, the estate sawmill. Two more lakes would be constructed in 1886 on a plateau above the house known as Nelly's Moss, along with a new power house at Debdon Burnfoot. Water for these was diverted from Black Burn, which had its source high up on the moors. The same burn was dammed lower down to form Blackburn lake, the largest of the five, which provided hydraulic power to Cragend, one of the estate farms, as well as a boating and fishing retreat. (Blackburn Lake was drained in the 1940s.)

Speaking in Coventry in October 1882, the pioneering electrical engineer William Siemens described how, on a recent visit to Cragside, he had been fascinated to see that Armstrong had 'placed one of our dynamo machines a mile from the house under a waterfall', where the water pressure was strong enough to drive a 6-horsepower turbine (which in turn operated the dynamo). By this means, said Siemens, 'his house was lighted by electricity'. During the daytime, when artificial light was not required, 'the same electric energy produced from the waterfall is made available for turning a lathe and other mechanical purpose'.

In 1878 the natural illumination from skylights in the first-floor gallery at Cragside had been supplemented by arc lights powered by the Siemens dynamo, creating the first domestic electric lighting in the world. However, the quality of the illumination was harsh and unsatisfactory – and it was not until December 1880, when Armstrong's friend the chemist Joseph Swan persuaded him to try out his new invention, that the real miracle occurred.

'As far as I know, Cragside was the first house in England properly fitted up with my electric lamps,' Swan later told the Rothbury photographer John Worsnop. The arc lights had been replaced by Swan's incandescent lamps, or light bulbs – the fruit of many years' experimentation. 'It was a delightful experience for both of us when the gallery was first lit up,' said Swan. 'The speed of the dynamo had not been quite rightly adjusted to produce the strength of current required. It was too fast, and the current too strong. Consequently, the lamps were far above their normal brightness – but the effect was splendid, and never to be forgotten.'

Swan had already demonstrated the workings of the new electric light at the Lit & Phil on 3 February 1879, with Armstrong in the chair, and would do so again on 20 October 1880.[3] On the second occasion, immediately after he had finished speaking, Swan gave the signal for the 70 gas jets that usually lit the room to be extinguished. 'Then – with a suddenness which in those days seemed quite magical – he transformed darkness into light by switching on 20 of his own lamps, producing an illumination which, as compared with gas light, had a very brilliant effect.' The occasion was of historic interest, for it was the first time that the interior of any public building, in Europe at least, had been lit by incandescent electric lamps. Swan later formed a company with his great American rival, Thomas Edison, to provide electric lighting on a commercial scale to the world's most advanced countries.

In a letter to the *Engineer* published on 17 January 1881, Armstrong expressed his delight at the experiment's success. 'The case possesses novelty, not only in the application of this mode of lighting to domestic use, but also in the derivation of the producing power from a natural source – a neighbouring brook being turned to account for that purpose,' he wrote. 'The brook, in fact, lights the house, and there is no consumption of any material in the process.' Since the distance from the house of the turbine and dynamo was 1,500 yards, the electric current had to pass through 3,000 yards of copper wire to complete the circuit. 'The number of lamps in the house is 45, but as I can switch off the current from room to room, I never require to have more than 37 in light at once,' he explained. 'For this number of lamps, 6 horsepower proves to be amply sufficient, notwithstanding the great length of the conducting wire.'

The final and most ambitious energy-generating scheme instigated at Cragside – drawing on resources from Black Burn and the lower lake at Nelly's Moss – was to provide a 340-foot head of water to a turbine in the power house erected at Debdon Burnfoot in 1886. This offered much improved power supplies to the main house and other buildings on the estate. (Eventually, each farm on the wider Cragside estate had its hydraulic pump to provide water or a turbine to drive agricultural machinery.) A second dynamo was added in 1895 to charge Fauré batteries in a dedicated room attached to the power house. To overcome the occasional lack of water, Armstrong extended the power house for a second time and installed a gas engine that would power the dynamos when the turbine lacked water pressure.

The scientific innovations at Cragside had global consequences in addition to the introduction of electric lighting, as illustrated in the account of Andrew Richardson, a native of Rothbury who contributed in his youth to the building and shaping of the Cragside estate. In 1931, Richardson, by then aged 70, reminisced about helping to dam the Debdon Burn and to lay a pipe from the brook to the original power house. A turbine, made at Kendal in Westmorland, was installed in the power station and cables were laid to the house. 'Then Mr Swan came with his newly invented lamps – and in the end the little brook came to supply the electricity for 45 lamps in the house,' he said.[4] The Scottish electrical engineer Alexander Muirhead – 'one of those largely responsible for the Niagara scheme', according to Richardson – had twice visited Cragside to inspect the hydroelectric experiments there. 'He told me himself,' said Richardson, 'that it was from Cragside that he got the idea of using the gigantic power of the Niagara Falls to produce electricity.'

As the years went by, the development of Cragside allowed Armstrong to devote more and more time to his favourite occupations: planting, building, and doing electrical experiments. The massive planting programme in the grounds – starting from the area immediately around the house and gradually working outwards – was reckoned eventually to embrace more than seven million trees and shrubs, including countless thousands of rhododendrons and azaleas. It is now believed to have changed the climate in this corner of Northumberland for all time, raising the average temperature by about 1°C and making it noticeably wetter in winter.

By radically transforming the landscape, Armstrong aimed to replicate a rugged Himalayan scene of rocks, streams, and cascades – a damp valley environment that, as it happened, was well suited to conifers. The species he planted included Douglas fir, Caucasian fir, Low's fir, and western hemlock; they would have all been quite unfamiliar to most of his countrymen at the time. 'Many beautiful trees are to be found, not the least surprising part of their history being the rapidity of their growth,' noted Thomas Sopwith in 1873. Some have since reached such a great height that, being the tallest in the country, they are described as champion trees.

Sopwith later tried to encapsulate the attractions of the Cragside estate: 'The fisherman is in the very paradise of trout fishing. The antiquary may study tumuli and ancient roads and houses. The artist may find inexhaustible materials for the pencil, and the lover of landscape gardening will in this vicinity find some of the boldest works achieved by the skill of the highly gifted owner.' But it was the ambitious nature of the endeavour that most impressed the diarist: 'Here are no namby-pamby fripperies or playthings, no mock waterfalls, no merely ornamental pieces of water, no grottoes nor artificial rockeries. All is on a great scale – no less a scale than that of nature in as bold a form as is to be met with in this country. The rock work is partly arranged by hand labour but is essentially the rock work of a mountainside. The waterfalls in wet weather recall Norwegian torrents.'

Building and landscaping on such a scale needed a large workforce. The 1881 census records 23 staff at Cragside, including two gardeners, two coachmen, a gamekeeper, and a rabbit-catcher, but there would have been many more workers living either at Rothbury or further afield. By 1891, the number of live-in staff had risen to 44, including a freestone quarryman and a 'caretaker of electric light' called John Mavin. This number had changed little by the time of Armstrong's death, but had fallen to 21 in 1911, by which time his great-nephew and heir had lost a large part of his inherited fortune.

At the busiest times, such as the tree-planting season, there were some 150 employed on the estate, many brought in from Elswick. When Lady Armstrong was laying out the 5 acres of rock garden, she would pay local people to bring buckets of fertile soil from the glen and the surrounding fields in order to fill up planting pockets among the boulders. By the turn of the century, some two dozen people were assigned to tend the Italian-style formal gardens, where a grand terrace of roses overlooked various ornamental trees and palms, complemented by a wonderful variety of shrubs, climbers, and flowering plants. The formal gardens included six conservatories, each serving a different purpose, including temperate and tropical ferneries and an orchard house. Meggie Armstrong, who had also built glass-houses at Jesmond Dene, may have been inspired by the conservatories at Kew Gardens, which she had visited with the Sopwiths. Dwarf fruit trees in large pots in the orchard house could be revolved on their bases with the aid of a hydraulic device to allow the trees a fair amount of sun on all sides, and Thomas

Sopwith saw 'a most ingenious contrivance' by which all the contents of a greenhouse could be moved into the open air by means of hydraulic machinery. Many different types of vegetables and fruit were grown on the land, which meant that, when combined with the plentiful supplies of sheep, cattle, fish, and game, the estate would have been more than self-sufficient.

A hydraulic ram was used to supply water to Cragside and its grounds from a lake above the Debdon Burn. Armstrong also installed labour-saving devices that must have done much to improve the lives of the permanent staff, particularly the estate laundry at Tumbleton, and the two hydraulic lifts, one of which linked the two kitchen levels and the other which carried coal scuttles, washing paraphernalia, and other necessities to the upstairs rooms. The spit in the kitchen was hydraulically operated, and a system of electric gongs was introduced to summon guests to meals and servants to all parts of the house. The central heating system was driven by a hydraulic engine, with the pipes being hidden behind grilles around door frames and as parts of cupboards as well as along corridors. A pioneering telephone system made it possible to talk to someone in a shooting lodge on the moors as well as allowing communication between people in different rooms. Staff were provided with a common room as well as their own bedrooms, and there were books available to encourage self-education.

Although there was muttering about Lady Armstrong's high expectations – she kept a meticulous record of her servants' activities and the payments made to them – the Armstrongs generally inspired great loyalty among their employees. When Armstrong died in 1900, his head gamekeeper, William Avery, had been at Cragside for 25 years, and the head gardener, Henry Hudson, for 35 years. The foreman William Crosby, the stonemason Willie Mavin, and William Bertram, the estate manager, had all been at Cragside as long as Armstrong himself, and would continue to be employed there after his death.

The most remarkable story was probably that of Andrew Crozier, who was born in 1871 at Longframlington, a few miles from Rothbury. Crozier entered service at Cragside in 1881 as a page boy. Ten years later he had become a footman and eventually rose to be butler. Andrew Crozier would serve all four Lords Armstrong, although the fourth had not yet acceded to the title when Crozier died in 1957 at the age of 86.

Despite the love and attention she lavished on Cragside, Meggie Armstrong continued to regard Jesmond Dene as her true home and spent much of her time there. Lively and gregarious by nature with a strong interest in the arts, she liked being within easy reach of vibrant Newcastle as well as making frequent trips to London to attend concerts, exhibitions, and lectures. And the house and garden in the dene were absorbing projects in themselves – even before the Armstrong estate there had reached its full extent.

Since inheriting Armorer Donkin's fortune in 1851, Armstrong had been steadily extending the original 16 acres of land acquired by his father-in-law, William Ramshaw, by purchasing neighbouring property as it became available. By 1860 he owned most of the land on the west bank of the Ouseburn, and it was then that he embarked on the first stage of the banqueting hall – whose original intention, according to Thomas Sopwith, had been for 'occasional soirées, assemblies of workmen, members of the Mechanics Institute from Elswick and similar meetings'. On 5 July 1862 Armstrong paid Sir Matthew White Ridley £6,450 for Heaton Dene, and by November 1868 he had acquired the remainder of the High Heaton estate from the Ridley family.

Heaton Park was created in 1878, when Addison Potter, Armstrong's first cousin, sold 23 acres of his Heaton Hall estate, excluding the hall itself, to the Corporation of Newcastle for £12,000. Soon afterwards, Armstrong signalled his wish to give the corporation 29 acres immediately north of the new park – part of the Donkin legacy. This area would be added to a few years later, as outlined in Armstrong's letter of February 1883 to the mayor of Newcastle. 'It is my intention to increase my grant of land for the purposes of a public park by the addition of the remaining portion of the pleasure grounds of Jesmond Dene,' he wrote, with the proviso that he and Meggie would retain complete control over the park as long as they lived.

The dene had previously been open to the public on payment of an annual subscription of five shillings (donated to Newcastle Infirmary), but Armstrong now offered free admission on Saturdays and Sundays, 'subject to orderly conduct being maintained', with the understanding that the park would pass freely to the people on his death. In return he asked the city corporation, among other things, to take steps to divert 'the ever-increasing sewage of Gosforth and Bulman village from the burn which flows through the grounds' and not to alter the layout of the grounds in such a way as to make them more artificial than their current state.

Armstrong's gift of Jesmond Dene was the subject of a literary anecdote by Evan R. Jones, the American consul in Newcastle, who observed Armstrong at the height of his powers. Jones's account captures the contrast between the self-effacing donor and the self-important bureaucrats with whom he was obliged to deal:[5]

'"Mr Councillor Hardingford's carriage!" cried the police officer, standing without the archway of the Banqueting Hall at Jesmond Dene, upon a dark and memorable night. The entrance hall was crowded by departing guests, awaiting cab or carriage. Egress was difficult; Hardingford was not forthcoming. Back towards the head of the staircase stood a tall figure, in a grey overcoat, with a clean-cut face of the John Stuart Mill type. He made several quiet efforts to depart; but the throng was wedged in the arch and he withdrew. At last, however, he edged his way through and quickly disappeared into the night. Keep your eye on him.

'At length came Hardingford, with the swagger of offended majesty. A seat at the "cross table" had not been vouchsafed him: a storm was raging in his breast. He had been confiding his grievances to some friends after the company had left the hall; hence the block of vehicles and the crush of aldermen and notable personages. This was no ordinary occasion. The Mayor of Newcastle upon Tyne had invited a numerous and important company to dine with him. During the evening, he announced that Sir William Armstrong had upon that day executed a deed of gift of the hall in which they were assembled, and the park in which it stood, to the city of Newcastle – for ever.

'The banqueting hall will accommodate 300 guests. Its staircase, reception-hall, gallery, and appointments are on a grand scale. The park is even more magnificent. It spreads along sloping sides to the running stream below, covering nearly 100 acres. It is original in design and treatment – picturesque and beautiful. Mountain gorse and yellow primrose flourish amid shrubs and plants culled from the gardens of the world. The serpentine walks lead you by stately trees and fragrant branches to shady nooks and sweet surprises. It is a quaint, bewitching scene of beauty: I have seen nothing like it. And all this has been handed over to the city of his birth by Sir William Armstrong – the man who, unheralded and unobserved, on foot and alone, walked out into the darkness and disappeared homeward, through the cabs and horses, while Mr Councillor Hardingford's carriage "stopped the way".'

Earlier that day, during the handing-over ceremony, Armstrong had explained that the gift had already brought its own reward. He said that it had made him happy to see the dene used for recreation by thousands of people who could only rarely take a holiday – and he now had the satisfaction of feeling that it was permanently devoted to this purpose. It was a hopeful sign of the age in which they lived, he went on, that there existed a desire for parks and recreation grounds, because it showed that the great mass of the people were starting to appreciate pursuits that were healthful and refining. It was a great pleasure to him to think he had been the instrument of saving that almost unique piece of suburban scenery from desecration – and he hoped it would in future bring great pleasure and enjoyment to his fellow citizens.

The Armstrongs had stamped their character on Jesmond Dene from the early days – not only by shaping and improving the landscape but also through their shared enthusiasm for enjoying life to the full. As at Cragside, Armstrong took an interest in every development on the estate, whether it concerned new farming practices or the study of nature that had absorbed him since childhood. Meggie had an equal passion for the natural world, and the Armstrongs together did much to promote general appreciation of the subject by providing a large sum of money for the establishment in 1884 of the Museum of Natural History (later the Hancock Museum).

Meggie Armstrong also had a strong appetite for pleasures of the mind, as repeatedly noted by Sopwith in his diary. Her houses were full of the latest books and paintings and examples of fashionable interior design, and she frequently visited London, with or without her husband, to attend concerts, exhibitions, and the opera. During a few days in London in 1860, Sopwith recorded several events where she made her presence felt, including an evening at the South Kensington Museum, 'where a conversazione was given by the Society of Arts and between 2,000 and 3,000 persons were present'. The following day, a Sunday, the Armstrongs attended a lunch party given by the Sopwiths for the meteorologist James Glaisher (who became a celebrated balloonist). 'We had a pleasant conversation on several subjects and more especially on the Whitworth Gun and on some meteorological matters,' wrote Sopwith. Afterwards they walked in Kensington Gardens and Hyde Park.

Later that year, on 12 December, Sopwith recorded a riotous party at Jesmond Dene during Armstrong's absence in London. 'Lady Armstrong entertained a party of friends all well known to each other and the evening was therefore one of hilarious enjoyment, music, dancing and games, etc.,' he wrote. 'Mrs and Miss Potter, the three sisters of that family, two Mr Hancocks (Albany and John), two Miss Hancocks, two of the daughters of the far-famed Bewick the engraver, and Dr de Mey were among the guests – and our reminiscences of pleasant evenings of former times were in some measure realized by the hearty and unrestrained spirit of festivity which prevailed.'

It was not only the Armstrongs themselves, however, who moulded the late 19th-century character of the dene. Carrying on a tradition that had been laid down by his father and Armorer Donkin, and James Losh before them, Armstrong gathered about him an affluent social set that included the families of some of the most powerful men in Newcastle, among them his business associates Andrew Noble and Charles Mitchell.

In contrast to the lack of children in the Armstrong household, the Noble family had been growing apace, and by the early 1870s

Deep Dene House had become too small for them. The Nobles bought another property, Jesmond Dene House, a short distance to the north, and had it enlarged by Richard Norman Shaw, who had started working for the Armstrongs at Cragside. Andrew Noble later had a real tennis court built on his land there. 'Our additions were hindered by the great strike that took place then,' commented Margery Noble, 'but we got into the new house in 1872.'[6] Although Margery was somewhat in awe of Meggie Armstrong, who was 20 years her senior, she appreciated the older woman's gift for hospitality and her curiosity about new people and unfamiliar experiences.

Charles Mitchell, meanwhile, was engaged in building projects of his own, having bought an old house called West Jesmond, together with 60 acres of land, in the north of the dene. Although the house had been largely rebuilt in the 1830s by John Dobson, Mitchell commissioned another local architect, Thomas Oliver, to draw up plans for enlarging it.[7] Oliver added a new wing in the neo-Gothic style and in 1870, when the Mitchells moved in, the house's name was changed to Jesmond Towers. Mitchell rented out a smaller house on the estate, called North Jesmond, to his partner and brother-in-law, Henry Swan, with the result that the Mitchells and the Swans then lived within 100 yards of each other – and within half a mile of the Armstrongs and the Nobles.

Both Armstrong and Mitchell were keen art collectors. By the mid-1870s, Armstrong was collecting Turners and Pre-Raphaelites to adorn the walls of his gallery at Cragside, and in 1878 he became the first chairman of the Newcastle Arts Association, which mounted exhibitions in the town's Neoclassical Assembly Rooms. Mitchell commissioned the Yorkshire architect Thomas Ralph Spence to design and build a gallery extension to Jesmond Towers, where he displayed works by, among others, his own son, Charles William, a talented artist who first exhibited at the Royal Academy in 1876.[8]

Charles Mitchell's most conspicuous and long-lasting contribution to Jesmond, however, was St George's church at the northern end of the parish, designed by Spence and built at the sole expense of its sponsor. Mitchell laid the church's foundation stone on 8 January 1887 and decreed that stone for its building should come from North Brunton quarry near Gosforth. Spence had drawn plans for a building 150 feet long and 58 feet wide, with a detached tower modelled on the campanile of St Mark in Venice; the main tower was 254 feet high, and an iron cross on top of it (since replaced) added a further 30 feet of height.

The fabulous stained glass and mosaics by James Brown adorning St George's recall the churches of Ravenna that had impressed Mitchell in his youth. Mosaics on the chancel walls include life-size representations of the Apostles, while the three mosaic figures over the altar – Archangel Gabriel, Christ, and St Michael – were designed by Charles William Mitchell. The altar and steps are made of white Carrara marble and red jasper. Among the many glories of St George's is the organ commissioned by Mitchell and built by Lewis of London in 1887; its original conducting tubes were over 3 miles long. To provide air for the organ, Armstrong supplied two powerful hydraulic engines sited under the tower. On the north wall of the church is a memorial to Charles Mitchell by George Frampton, who sculpted the bronze of Peter Pan in Kensington Gardens and the statue of Queen Victoria that stands outside Newcastle's Royal Victoria Infirmary.

The cost of the church and nearby vicarage was said to be over £30,000, but Mitchell was apparently unconcerned at the expense, telling the vicar, Reverend Edward Somerset Pennefather, 'It is not what it costs but what is best. I have built a great many ships and have made it a rule to put in the best material from end to end of them. I am building one house for God and I shall put the best material in it from east to west.'[9]

Meggie Armstrong continued to enjoy party-going even in later life, as revealed in a letter of January 1874 from Armstrong to Stuart Rendel in which he asks advice on his wife's dress for a 'fancy ball' in aid of the Newcastle Infirmary. 'Lady Armstrong thinks it will be the only chance of her showing off the gorgeous cloak that Efflatoun Pasha gave her,' wrote Armstrong. 'She is therefore proposing to go as an Egyptian lady. She has no difficulty about anything except the headdress. Can you give her an idea as to what she might wear to be in keeping with the character – should it be turban, cap or bonnet?' His wife's energy seemed to have diminished little over the years. 'Enjoying good health – her good looks and active habits are remarkable,' wrote Sopwith after a visit from Meggie in the late 1870s, by which time she was 70.

Always a loyal friend, Meggie Armstrong retained her close relationship with the Sopwiths and continued to see them regularly in London. There was always something new to report. 'In the evening Lady Armstrong called and sat some time with Annie and me in my library,' wrote Sopwith in February 1875. 'We were glad to hear of consuming matters relating to progress at Cragside ... the telescope is mounted and the picture gallery is a useful addition to the numerous attractions of the mountain residence.'

Sopwith maintained an interest in his old friends' activities until a few weeks before he died. 'Last evening Lady Armstrong spent an hour or two with us,' he wrote on 16 November 1878. 'Sir William has introduced electrical light in his picture gallery with highly satisfactory results and proposes to light the library and drawing room (also at Cragside) in the same manner. Lady A. thought me much improved in outward aspects of health since the summer.'

Behind these outward shows of gaiety, however, the Armstrongs' childlessness remained a source of deep regret. Time and again in both their lives incidents occurred to illustrate their fondness for young people and their longing for offspring of their own. Armstrong – who himself in some ways remained a child at heart – cultivated close relationships with the children of friends or relatives, in particular the Rendels and, to a lesser extent, the children and grandchildren of his nephew, Johnny Watson. As well as reaching out to all the children she met, Meggie immersed herself in charitable work and fund-raising, especially for causes of benefit to young people, such as schools and children's hospitals. Both of them clearly nurtured a desire to give. As early as August 1859, when he was still only beginning to establish his fame and fortune, Armstrong had been thinking of useful ways of spending his money. 'I should like to give a pleasure trip to the Blind Asylum and the Deaf & Dumb Asylum and the Ragged School – I mean a separate trip to each,' he wrote to Meggie from London. 'I don't know what it should cost but I should suppose about £10 each would give them a nice run out and a tea or other refreshment as well. Will you call and see the head of each institute and arrange the matter.'

The lack of children could be seen as having contributed to the worldly success of this remarkable pair – encouraging them to pursue their goals with single-minded determination and to give free rein to their exceptional creative instincts. But only someone who fully understood the extent of their sorrow could have been cruel enough to place the notice in the *The Times* of 3 April 1883. When it was published, there was only one Lady Armstrong living at Cragside, and she would have been 75 years old at the time. The notice appeared in the newspaper's Births column and read as follows: 'On the 1st April, at Cragside, LADY ARMSTRONG, of a son and heir.' No satisfactory explanation has yet been found for this strange announcement.

17

The Rising Sun

Soon after George Rendel had perfected his groundbreaking *Staunch* gunboat at the end of the 1860s, orders from foreign customers began to arrive with almost every post. Near the front of the queue was the government of China, which urgently needed small armed vessels to protect its coastal waters against pirates. Eventually, Elswick ships and guns would be sold all over the globe, from Canada to Argentina to New Zealand, but in the closing decades of the 19th century, and for a few years beyond, the Asian Far East would prove to be one of the firm's most lucrative markets.

During the 1870s, Elswick built 11 gunboats for China, all named after letters of the Greek alphabet. Small, unarmoured cruisers were also built during this period; the first was *Tsukushi-kan* for Japan, swiftly followed by *Chao Yung* and *Yung Wei* for China. An early gunboat order from Chile was replaced in 1882 by *Esmeralda*, the revolutionary vessel that would become the prototype of cruiser development for the next 20 years.

Two cruisers built for Spain and launched in 1886 were *Isla de Luzon* and *Isla de Cuba*, both of which were sunk by the Americans in the Philippines during the Spanish–American War of 1898.[1] However, after that war, the two ships were raised, repaired, and incorporated into the American navy. They survived, respectively, for another 30 and 40 years.

'I remember, as a boy, looking upon Japan as a strange, mysterious land, inhabited by an unknown people who might as well have come from another planet,' Armstrong admitted to a group of Japanese visitors to Newcastle in March 1885.[2] He little thought then how much he might eventually have to do with Japan, he said, but now that he had had many direct dealings with the Japanese people he had come to regard them as 'one of the most interesting nations on the face of the earth'.

Armstrong's comments followed the launch of *Naniwa-kan*, an exceptionally fast cruiser built by Armstrong Mitchell at Low Walker for the Japanese imperial navy. Proposing a toast to the Emperor of Japan at a dinner attended by Prince Yamashino and a group of high-ranking Japanese engineers and officials, Armstrong said he was pleased that the ship had been created for a nation that was 'likely never to come into collision with our own peace-loving country'.[3] *Naniwa-kan* was an impressive achievement. 'She is the largest of the class that this firm has built,' reported *The Times*, 'and will be the most powerful warship in the navy of Japan, and one of the fastest-going ships in the world. When complete, she will have on board eight Armstrong guns of the new type. Another ship of the same class and for the same government is rapidly approaching completion.'

Both vessels would carry a truly amazing complement of weapons, including two 28-ton 10-inch guns worked and loaded by hydraulic machinery. On each broadside were three 5½-inch guns, each weighing 5 tons, ten 1-inch machine guns and two rapid-fire guns, while mounted at the top of two 'military masts' were four of the improved Gatling guns made at Elswick. In addition, each vessel had a complete set of 'locomotive torpedoes' ejected from four stations, two on each broadside, situated just above water level.

Delivery of *Naniwa-kan* and her sister ship, *Takachiho-kan*, marked a critical stage in the naval revolution taking place in Japan – an outward manifestation of the huge changes under way generally in the country as the Japanese threw off long years of feudalism under the shoguns to take their place as one of the most powerful nations on earth. Described by Armstrong himself as 'unique in the history of the world', Japan's emergence had begun in the mid-1850s, when an American expedition under Commodore Matthew Perry had sailed halfway around the globe to encourage the Japanese to end their centuries of isolation and re-establish trading links with the West.

The pace of change quickened in 1868 with the ousting of the feudal Bakufu government and the restoration of imperial rule under the 15-year-old Emperor Meiji – followed eventually by a huge increase in defence spending. Indeed, the Meiji administration had paid a total of £546,980 for the two Elswick cruisers, whose engines and other vital parts were protected in a steel deck below the waterline, although the ships had no armour.[4] Designed by William White, a new recruit to Armstrong Mitchell, the vessels were modelled on the fast cruiser *Esmeralda* and reflected Armstrong's belief that a warship's speed and agility should not be sacrified to the need for heavy armour.

A year earlier, the Japanese had bought a smaller unarmoured cruiser from the Tyneside firm, originally destined for Chile, and renamed it *Tsukushi-kan*. 'These three cruisers, with their high speed and heavy armaments, will constitute very important additions to Japan's naval strength,' commented the *Newcastle Courant*, 'and enable that country to make its influence felt in any complications which may in future arise in the Eastern seas.' A decade later, the original *Esmeralda* – another Chilean commission – was sold to the Japanese and renamed *Idzumi*.

William Armstrong had long been held in high regard by Japanese visitors to Britain – and their admiration for him would only increase as the years went by. During the first official visit by Japan's feudal government, the Bakufu, in May 1862, Armstrong was superintending the Royal Gun Factory at Woolwich and during a tour of the works the guests witnessed the casting and fitting of Armstrong guns. According to *The Times*, the visitors 'lingered over the operations in the gun-factory as if under some spell, wholly regardless of the fierce heat from the furnaces to which they were often exposed, and they left the place with evident reluctance'. Described by the *Illustrated London News* as 'dark-haired sons of the mysterious East', the Bakufu envoys had come to Britain ostensibly to discuss international trade, but they were also keen to inspect shipyards and arsenals, 'signifying the growing awareness in Japan of the importance of military advancement'.

On 26 May, they travelled to Newcastle to learn about mining technology in the capital of coal. Before their departure from Britain, they signed an agreement with the British government postponing until January 1868 the opening of 'treaty ports' at Edo

(Tokyo), Osaka, Hyogo, and Niigata. (A phenomenon of East Asia, the system of treaty ports was highly controversial. It originated in the 1840s with Western encroachment into China.)

Little more than a year after the Bakufu mission, the Japanese had a chance to see Armstrong's guns in action on their own territory, during a confrontation at Kagoshima, on the south-western tip of Kyushu island – the consequence of a classic example of gunboat diplomacy.[5]

Ignited by the killing of Charles Richardson, a British merchant, by retainers of the *daimyo* (lord) of Satsuma, the incident culminated in the arrival at Kagoshima on 12 August 1863 of a British naval squadron under Rear-Admiral Augustus Kuper. Kuper's seizure of three Satsuma steamers prompted the Japanese to open fire from their land bases, and a three-day battle ensued, with the British eventually gaining the upper hand. Ernest Satow, an interpreter on board Admiral Kuper's ship *Euryalus*, was dismayed by 'the unnecessary severity in bombarding and destroying large parts of the town by the newly developed breech-loading Armstrong guns and by rockets'.[6] The outcome was not clear-cut, and the Satsuma contingent claimed that they had driven back the intruders, but a month later they acceded to the original British demands.

Armstrong's 40-pounders and 110-pounders were both put to the test at Kagoshima. Although the 40-pounders performed well, there were reports that some of the vent-pieces on the 110-pounders had blown out, giving fuel to Armstrong's opponents in Parliament. Armstrong breech-loaders were 'a dead failure', according to Ralph Bernal Osborne MP, who called for the government to reconsider adopting the guns made by Whitworth, Blakely, and others.[7] In a later exchange of letters with Lord Clarence Paget, the secretary to the Admiralty, Armstrong fiercely defended the 110-pounder, describing it as a 'very valuable shell gun, throwing the most destructive projectile now in use'.[8] Although he admitted that its vent-piece was not perfect, he insisted that the publicity about the gun's poor performance in Japan was full of inaccuracies.

A few months later the 110-pounder was again used in Japan, in a concerted attack on groups of the Choshu clan who had been blockading the narrow straits of Shimonoseki, between Honshu and

Kyushu. For four days in early September 1864, British, French, American, and Dutch warships pounded the Japanese bases overlooking the straits, eventually destroying them. All the British ships involved in the battle were carrying Armstrong guns.

The shortcomings of some of the 110-pounders were described by Ernest Satow, who later became Britain's resident minister in Japan. 'We anchored about 2,500 yards from the enemy's batteries, and consequently near enough to reach them with our 110-pounder breech-loading Armstrong gun on the forecastle,' he wrote.[9] 'The *Euryalus* fired only sixteen rounds from her 110-pounder, which was pretty good work, considering that the vent-piece got jammed once and a considerable time was lost digging it out with handspikes. Another time the vent-piece was blown up into the fore-top owing to its not having been screwed in tightly enough.' As Armstrong had suspected, some of the problems may have been caused by the fact that the gunners had been poorly trained. But, although the overall performance in the battle of the Armstrong breech-loaders was praised, continuing doubts about the 110-pounder would prompt the Admiralty to recommend its withdrawal – a step that led to the temporary abandonment by the armed forces of all breech-loading guns.[10]

The gun controversy raging in Britain's Parliament made little impression on the Japanese who had fought in the battle of Shimonoseki. In its immediate aftermath, the defeated Choshu fighters were allowed to inspect the British ships that had fired on them – and they were deeply struck by the sophistication of the weaponry they saw, particularly since most of their own guns were made of brass or bronze, and in some cases even from wood. 'These future leaders of Meiji Japan were to see in Armstrong's firm a source for the technology that would transform their country in the years to come,' wrote the historian Marie Conte-Helm.[11]

Elswick soon began to receive covert orders for guns and ammunition from Satsuma and Choshu rebels plotting to overthrow the Bakufu government. The arms deals were arranged by Thomas Glover, a British agent for the firm of Jardine Matheson, based in the southern port of Nagasaki.[12] Glover had earlier helped to smuggle five young Choshu men to England so that they could study Western industrial and technological facilities and take crucial technical information back to Japan.[13] He was prominent among the large network of agents that the Elswick firm was starting to build up around the world.

Of even more significance to the relationship between Armstrong and Japan was the high-level Meiji mission to Europe and America led by the foreign minister Iwakura Tomomi, which arrived in Newcastle on 21 October 1872.[14] The declared aim of the Iwakura mission was the revision of the 'unequal' trade treaties signed with America, Britain, and various other European nations in the 1850s – but the visitors were also intent on finding out more about Western institutions, industries, and culture. The Japanese envoys were taken on a tour of Elswick Works by Armstrong himself, who introduced them to his chief lieutenants, Andrew Noble and George Rendel, as well as showing them the hydraulic machinery, the engineering shops, the erecting and fitting departments, and the guns in various stages of construction. Armstrong also took them down a coal-mine in Gosforth, and entertained them in the evenings at his home in Jesmond. They were particularly struck by a visit to Newcastle's recently erected observatory. 'The great telescope was housed inside a circular chamber which had a domed glass roof supported by semi-circular ribs of iron,' wrote the mission's chief secretary, Kume Kunitake, in his later account of the expedition.[15] 'The telescope could be tilted up and down and rotated to left and right by machinery. A device projected the images of the stars onto a mirror behind the telescope.'

Their host cut an impressive figure, being described by Kume as 'taller than seven *shaku* and of mild demeanour'. (A *shaku* is a measurement slightly less than one foot.) It was not simply Armstrong's physical bearing and courtesy that charmed the Japanese, however. They apparently saw in him traits of character that seemed familiar and admirable to them, both on a personal level and in regard to his business dealings and the highly efficient way in which he ran his company. To show their gratitude for his hospitality, the envoys later presented Armstrong with what he described to Stuart Rendel as 'two large and remarkably fine Japanese porcelain vases – the finest by far that I have ever seen'.

From the late 19th century, the Japanese began to challenge Chinese and Russian supremacy in south-east Asia. Japan's resounding defeat of Russia at the Battle of Tsushima on 25 May 1905 was regarded as the greatest naval victory since Trafalgar a century earlier.

By the early 1880s – after Japan's Navy Expansion Bill had provided for a massive increase in defence spending – Elswick was starting to receive serious enquiries from Japan about warships and guns. According to Marie Conte-Helm, it was the start of a period of 'intensive technology transfer', in which Britain would be a leading inspiration and model for the development of the Japanese navy.[16] An early high-profile visitor to Elswick, in November 1883, was Rear Admiral Ito Shunkichi, the first president of the KUK (Kyodu Unyu Kaisha) shipping company (later NYK, or Nippon Yusen Kaisha), who was accompanied by Major S. T. Bridgford, Elswick's agent in China since 1880. Ito placed orders for two fast protected cruisers modelled on *Esmeralda*, in which the Japanese had already shown great interest – these were the vessels that, within 18 months, would be launched as *Naniwa-kan* and *Takachicho-kan*. Bridgford was paid £4,000 commission on the sale, and two years later – on the recommendation of Elswick contacts at Jardine Matheson – he was confirmed as Elswick's agent in Japan.[17] Models of *Naniwa-kan* and *Takachicho-kan* were displayed at the international exhibition held in Newcastle to celebrate Queen Victoria's golden jubilee in 1887. Among other leading attractions at the exhibition was a full-sized model of the Armstrong 110-pounder that had made such an impression on the Japanese at Shimonoseki.

Following the opening of a shipyard at Elswick in 1884, Japan's interest in Armstrong Mitchell warships assumed greater importance in the eyes of the Tyneside firm, and over the next two decades a steady stream of high-ranking Japanese officials were royally entertained in north-east England – by Armstrong at Cragside and by Andrew Noble at Jesmond Dene House. Noble, by then managing director of Elswick, and his wife, Margery, provided lavish hospitality for many Japanese and other foreign business associates at their Jesmond home, and their sons Saxton and John soon became involved in the trade with Japan. One early consequence of this relationship was the decision, brokered by the weapons expert Yamanouchi Masuji, to arm the Japanese navy with 12-inch Armstrong guns. The yoking together of warlike equipment and sentiments of harmony and peace was a constant thread running through the long association between Elswick and Japan.

Japan's first real opportunity to put the Elswick-built ships and arms to the test came in 1894, during a war with China over the control of Korea, when the Japanese fleet included the cruisers *Yoshino* and *Naniwa-kan*. Designed by Philip Watts, another new Elswick recruit, and launched in 1892, *Yoshino* had been hailed as the faster cruiser in the world after exceeding 23 knots in trials, and later performed outstandingly well in battle against the Chinese. The ship's launch inaugurated what some people later called a Japanese period at Elswick, but, according to the Elswick historian A. R. Fairbairn, 'It was Japanese only in that Japanese ships were the most numerous on the stocks or alongside, for in the same period a Chinese, a Chilean, a Brazilian and an Argentine navy was also being built at Elswick, while the yard was never without a British ship in building.'

Armstrong Mitchell also kept Japan well supplied with guns throughout the Sino-Japanese War and were credited with having played a crucial role in securing a Japanese victory.[18] In recognition of this role, William Armstrong and Andrew Noble were each presented with the Order of the Sacred Treasure of the Rising Sun. However, Japan's sense of triumph was short-lived. Within a few days of making peace with China, the Japanese were humiliatingly forced to give up their claims to the Liaodong peninsula in southern Manchuria, including the strategic base of Port Arthur (Lüshun), by a triple alliance of Russia, France, and Germany. The Russians' increasing control over Port Arthur – where they sought to set up an alternative Pacific base to Vladivostok, which was ice-bound in winter – would eventually lead to another Japanese war.

The wisdom of arming foreign countries would later come under severe scrutiny but, as Fairbairn points out, all such arrangements had to be sanctioned by the government. 'Not a ship, not a gun, not a shell or fuse could be put in hand without the prior permission of the British authorities.' They were willing to grant approval because such work 'increased the capacity and efficiency of the country's armament production' and it made the foreign countries dependent on Britain for their warships and arms.

In the meantime, drawing on their success against China, the Japanese embarked on a ten-year naval reinforcement programme, which included the construction of 4 battleships, 12 cruisers,

63 torpedo boats, and 23 torpedo-boat destroyers.[19] Most of the orders went to British shipyards, with Armstrong Mitchell taking a substantial share.

The first battleship built at Elswick for the imperial Japanese navy was *Yashima*, designed by Philip Watts and named on 28 February 1896 by Madame Kato, the wife of the Japanese minister in London.[20] Armstrong's speech at the launch ceremony, which made reference to the Japanese victory, reflected the feelings of many people in Britain towards Japan at the time: 'Whatever may be the destiny of this splendid ship, we may be sure that she will be handled with the ability, the skill, and the courage recently displayed in the Japanese navy, and that she will prove worthy of the highly civilized and progressive nation to which she belongs.'

Soon after the launch of *Yashima*, Noble and Watts embarked on a tour of Japan and China lasting several months, during which they secured major orders for Elswick ships while boosting the Newcastle firm's already high standing in the East. As it happened, the company was reorganising after the sudden death of Charles Mitchell in August 1895, but the Japanese orders were fulfilled on time. Indeed, 1896 would prove to be one of the busiest and most successful years for the firm, with no fewer than 20 warships of different classes at various stages of completion – 15 at the Elswick yard and five at the Walker yard – amounting to a total displacement of 98,000 tons. Between May 1897 and March 1900, six ships were built for Japan: the protected cruiser *Takasago*, the first-class battleship *Hatsuse*, and the armoured cruisers *Asama*, *Tokiwa*, *Idzumo*, and *Iwate*.

Launched on 27 June 1899, *Hatsuse* was 400 feet long and more than 76 feet wide, with a displacement of 15,000 tons – up until that point, the largest warship ever seen on the Tyne.[21] The ship's armaments included four 12-inch guns, twelve 6-inch guns, twenty 12-pounders, and five torpedo tubes. The launch ceremony was performed by Madame Arakawa, the wife of the Japanese consul-general in London, watched by representatives of the navies of the United States, Chile, Portugal, and Norway, as well as a large number of Japanese embassy staff and high-ranking navy officials. It was a hugely important symbolic moment – a timely reminder of Japan's emergence on the world stage.

William Watson-Armstrong spoke on behalf of his 88-year-old great-uncle, reminding his audience that the master of Cragside had always take a keen interest in Japan and the Japanese people.[22] Armstrong had watched with deep admiration, he said, how the Japanese 'had built up out of a remarkable ancient and picturesque civilization a might and formidable power until, within a comparatively short space of time, [there had] evolved a glorified Japan, the greatest naval power of the East'. Completed in January 1901, *Hatsuse* was one of the many warships from foreign nations to take part in the ceremonies at Portsmouth to mark Queen Victoria's death, before steaming out to Japan to add strength to the imperial navy.

Britain's support for the swift modernisation of Japan took on a political aspect around this time when the two nations joined an international coalition to quash the anti-imperialist Boxer Rebellion in China – and warming relations were cemented in January 1902 by the sealing of an Anglo-Japanese alliance. The two countries agreed to remain neutral if either became involved in an international conflict; they also agreed to come to the assistance of the other should either nation be confronted by the opposition of more than one hostile power. Both explicitly disclaimed aggressive tendencies towards China or Korea.

The vast Japanese investment in warship construction would bear fruit two years later when tensions with Russia over competing interests in southern Manchuria and Korea boiled over into war. Japan's diplomatic and military position had been strengthened by its formal alliance with Britain, emboldening Japan to demand clarification from Russia about its intentions in the region. On 8 February 1904, negotiations having broken down, the Japanese surprised the Russians by launching a torpedo-boat attack on their fleet at Port Arthur, declaring war on Russia the same day.

In command of the imperial Japanese Navy during the 15-month campaign was Admiral Togo Heihachiro, whose flagship, *Mikasa* – one of the four battleships commissioned under Japan's ten-year expansion programme – had been built by the British company Vickers, Sons and Maxim of Barrow-in-Furness and launched in November 1900. While *Mikasa* was a Vickers ship, it was, like the rest of the Japanese fleet, armed entirely by Elswick guns.

For both Japan and Tyneside, the most disastrous day of the Russo-Japanese War was 15 May 1904, when three Elswick-built ships were all sunk.[23] The battleships *Hatsuse* and *Yashima* were both hit by mines while patrolling the entrance to Port Arthur harbour. *Hatsuse* had survived an initial strike and was being towed to safety when she collided with a second mine, setting off a series of explosions; the former pride of the Tyne sank within a few minutes, taking more than 500 men with her. Despite being holed by two mines, *Yashima* stayed afloat for several hours, allowing most of her crew to escape before she capsized. Later in the day, the cruiser *Yoshino* was fatally damaged in a collision with another Japanese vessel while steaming towards Port Arthur in dense fog; some 320 lives were lost in the calamity.

The decisive naval engagement of the war took place on 27 May 1905 in the straits of Tsushima, the eastern part of the channel between Korea and Japan. And it was at Tsushima – hailed as the greatest naval battle since Trafalgar a century earlier – that the Armstrong vessels made their most dramatic impact. Indeed, almost half of Admiral Togo's fleet on this occasion consisted of Armstrong ships: *Asama*, *Iwate*, *Idzumo*, and *Tokiwa* were built at Elswick, while *Idzumi*, *Naniwa-kan*, and *Takachiho-kan* had originated at Low Walker. *Asama* was damaged in the fighting, but later rejoined the action; *Iwate* was hit 16 times but sustained only minor damage; in all, the Japanese lost 117 men and three torpedo boats. By contrast, Russia's Baltic Fleet was virtually annihilated: eight battleships, four cruisers, and five destroyers were sunk, with nearly all the other Russian ships being wrecked or captured; 4,380 men died and more than 5,900 were taken prisoner.[24]

It was generally acknowledged that superior ships and guns, combined with Togo's inspired and intelligent leadership, had been responsible for the overwhelming Japanese triumph – which led to an immediate Russian surrender. Under a peace treaty signed later that year, Russia agreed to cede control of Port Arthur and the Liaodong peninsula to Japan and to recognise Japanese interests in Korea. There was disquiet among the Japanese people about some of the treaty terms, but the defeat of Russia caused a great surge of national pride. 'Japan had achieved Great Power status through the

Russo-Japanese War,' wrote Marie Conte-Helm more than 80 years later, 'and the contributions of British advisers and firms like Armstrong's to her naval victory would not soon be forgotten.'[25]

Admiral Togo's flagship, *Mikasa*, has since become a national monument – the Japanese equivalent to HMS *Victory*, Nelson's flagship at Trafalgar. Moored permanently at Yokosuka, near Tokyo, *Mikasa* is the last remaining example of a pre-Dreadnought battleship anywhere in the world. The outcome of Tsushima also had far-reaching consequences in Russia, in that the humiliation inflicted on the country's Tsarist rulers by the unexpected defeat fuelled the dissent that sparked off the Russian revolution of 1905.

Worsening relations with Russia at the turn of the century had prompted Japan to rush through a supplementary naval construction programme that included three more battleships. One of these was *Kashima*, whose building had got under way at Elswick in mid-April 1904, two months after the outbreak of the Russo-Japanese war. One of the last major battleships to be built outside Japan, *Kashima* was launched on 22 March 1905, but was not completed until a year later. When Japanese naval officers arrived on Tyneside to collect their ship in April 1906 – seven months after the conclusion of peace with Russia – they were welcomed as 'Togo's Heroes'.[26]

On the evening of 24 April, after feasting and speeches, some 150 members of *Kashima*'s crew and a group of officers were taken to a football match at St James's Park, where they watched Newcastle beat Stoke 5–0. As the Japanese guests took their seats on the stand, they received 'a hearty cheer', according to the *Newcastle Weekly Chronicle,* and the crowd cheered again when the officers stood to attention during the playing of the Japanese national anthem.[27]

The evident friendship between the Japanese visitors and their British hosts was rooted in something more than the desire for military supremacy or commercial advantage. As Armstrong himself had recognised, there was a natural empathy between the two island races, which found expression in their shared interest in ships and the sea. The master of Cragside had inspired respect in the Japanese from the early days, and they had been impressed by the highly efficient management of his business enterprise, as well as by the sophistication of his scientific and technological achievements –

the very same qualities that would distinguish Japan's commercial investment in Britain in the second half of the 20th century. There was also a shared understanding about the elusiveness of true knowledge. The comments of a contemporary Japanese philosopher bear an uncanny resemblance to the remarks with which Armstrong concluded his speech to the British Association in 1863: 'We have sounded the depths of speculation only to find that there are depths unfathomable below those depths; we have voyaged to the farthest limit that thought may sail, only to find that the horizon forever recedes.'

Traditional English styles of living, especially 'country house' mores, also stirred interest among the visitors from Japan – as exemplified by the regular flow of Japanese to Jesmond Dene and Cragside during the last two decades of the 19th century. Their trips would often coincide with the final stage of contract negotiations or the times when ships were due to be officially handed over to the Japanese navy, but some of the guests had a more long-term interest in Tyneside. A journalist who visited Cragside in 1893 learnt that 'some forty or fifty young Japs of high social position have been articled as pupils to Sir William Armstrong, Mitchell & Co.'[28]

As it turned out, the north-east of England became a place of pilgrimage for the Japanese in the years that followed their defeat of Russia. From the mid-1880s onwards, the signatures of many Japanese ministers and naval officials, including two future prime ministers, Kato Takaaki and Saito Makoto, appeared in the Cragside visitors' book. Such guests revelled in the chance to experience for themselves life in a traditional English country house – and Armstrong and his heirs took equal pleasure in entertaining them. Among the most illustrious were members of the Japanese Royal Family. The Marquis and Marchioness Tokugawa Yorisada, uncle and aunt of Princess Nagako, who became Empress Consort of Japan in 1925, visited Cragside in 1916, 1929, and 1951 – and the Japanese Room there still contains gifts and memorabilia associated with them.

Crown Prince Akihito, who would succeed his father, Hirohito, to the imperial throne of Japan in 1989, spent a week at Cragside in 1953 before attending the coronation of Queen Elizabeth II. The following account, published by the Japan Society of London,

During a visit to England in 1911 Admiral Togo Heihachiro (seated) – dubbed 'the Nelson of Japan' – and his retinue stayed with Sir Andrew and Lady Noble at Jesmond Dene House.

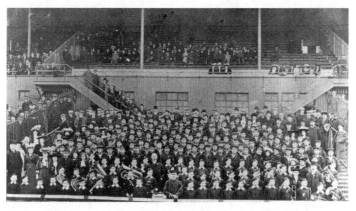

When Japanese sailors arrived in Newcastle in 1906 to collect a new battleship, they were greeted as 'Togo's heroes' and taken to watch a football match at St James's Park.

captures the peculiar attractions of Cragside – and, by extension, its creator, a former vice-president of the Japan Society – in the eyes of the Japanese prince. (The master of Cragside at that time was the second Baron Armstrong of Bamburgh and Cragside, the great-great-nephew of the founder of Elswick.)

'The deep bow and full curtsy [of the hosts] showed that this was no ordinary guest. The heir to the ancient throne of Japan had come to an English country-house, closely associated in bygone years with his own people, to stay for eight days' rest and recreation. Prince Akihito had travelled 250 miles to join with other Japanese and English friends a typical English country-house party. Every bedroom was occupied, and some 20 persons sat down in the dining room to each meal. The tennis-court was ready; the horses were in the stable; fishing-rods awaited those who wanted to sample the lakes for trout. The billiard-room invited on wet days and in the evenings. The grand piano stood open, and a singer and accompanist were expected; it was rumoured that the carpet in the Long Gallery would be rolled back one or two nights for dancing.'

The programme for the prince's stay would include a grand dinner-party for the 'county set', a garden party for neighbours and local voluntary organisations, and an expedition to Bamburgh Castle and the Farne Islands. The overriding concern, according to the Japan Society, was that the prince should feel at home, 'and so fulfil the representative duties required of him from a background of ease and comfort reminiscent of those distant Victorian and Edwardian days when his country and ours were the closest friends and allies, and when many of her famous statesmen, ministers, admirals and merchants had stayed in this historic house'. During his stay at Cragside, Prince Akihito apparently caught his first trout outside Japan, and he told Lady Armstrong that the pine trees, lakes, and flowering shrubs reminded him of his native land. Crown Prince Naruhito followed in his father's footsteps by visiting Cragside in 1991.

Apart from the Armstrong family, the person who did most to foster good relations with Japan in north-east England was Andrew Noble, the management chief at Elswick during the busiest period of warship-building. Noble was renowned for the imaginative entertainments he laid on for his guests – during a visit to north-east England by the naval weapons expert Yamanouchi Masuji, Noble arranged a deer-shooting expedition in Redesdale to demonstrate the efficacy of the quick-firing breech-loading gun. According to Marie Conte-Helm, Yamanouchi later wrote that, while contact had initially been made with France and Germany for the provision of guns, 'the Japanese came to prefer their dealings with the English'.[29]

Andrew Noble's sons Saxton and John, who joined their father in what was by then Armstrong Whitworth, were also deeply involved in business dealings with Japan. During the Russo-Japanese War, John Noble was responsible for maintaining close links with the Japanese navy and became virtually resident in Tokyo. In the years that followed, he would play a key role in the establishment of the Japan Steel Works at Muroran on Hokkaido.[30]

In July 1911, after attending the coronation of King George V in London, Admiral Count Togo Heihachiro – dubbed 'the Nelson of Japan' since his victory at Tsushima – arrived in Newcastle to fulfil what he called his 'long-cherished' desire to visit the city and the Elswick shipyard.[31] He and his entourage stayed with the Nobles in Jesmond. Togo had strong personal links with Britain, having come to the country in 1871 as a naval cadet, attended Cambridge University and then studied naval engineering at Greenwich. His first direct experience of Armstrong's ships dated from 1890, when he was given command of *Naniwa-kan*. On 19 July 1911, at a lunch at the Mansion House hosted by the Lord Mayor of Newcastle, Togo paid tribute to Elswick and Armstrong:

'It is a well-known fact that the name Newcastle is inseparable from the pages of the history of the Japanese navy, so many men-of-war have been either built or armed by the famous works of Elswick, which the city of Newcastle is very proud to possess. A great number of our officers and men have studied in this city how to build ships and how to make guns. I believe I am not flattering you too much if I say that, but for the kind help of your people, the history of the growth of the Japanese navy might have been written in a different way.'[32]

18

Baron Armstrong of Cragside

'Please put this note in the fire,' wrote Armstrong at the end of a hastily scribbled letter to Meggie of 23 April 1875 revealing his decision to bid at a Christie's auction for two paintings by the fashionable Pre-Raphaelite painter John Everett Millais. The reason for such furtiveness is not clear – perhaps it was a fear of failure – but it was a rare occasion on which Armstrong acknowledged that others might have an interest in his private correspondence.

In the event, he need not have worried. 'I have bought *Chill October* and *Jephthah* for 900 guineas – a big price but much less than they were expected to bring,' he wrote to Meggie after the auction, displaying evident confidence in his own artistic judgement. 'The one [*Jephthah's Daughter*] is unquestionably the finest figure painting and the other the finest landscape that has been produced in the present generation. I was also induced by strong advice but rather against my will to buy a very fine early Turner.'

By this time, Armstrong was fully engaged on a mission to acquire beautiful objects to furnish and adorn his growing palace at Rothbury, where he was gradually reinventing himself in the guise of English country gentleman – and where Richard Norman Shaw continued to invest a great deal of creative genius. The relationship between the two men was sometimes strained – Shaw reputedly resented the owner's repeated interference in his plans for Cragside[1] – but, like so many of Armstrong's professional and personal relationships, it was also dynamic and highly productive.

Shaw was given a relatively free hand in designing the interiors and commissioning craftsmen to work on the decorative features of Cragside, and Armstrong held his opinion in high regard. 'Mr Shaw is immensely struck with the pictures, especially the *Jephthah*,' he wrote to Meggie soon after the triumph at Christie's. On this occasion, the opinion of the artist was even more important. 'Millais has been to Agnew's to see once more the *Chill Oct.* and the *Jephthah*,' he wrote. 'He says they are his two best pictures and that he is very glad they have passed into my hands.'

Exterior building work at Cragside was carried out by local masons under the supervision of Armstrong's managing agent, William Bertram. Skilled workers were also imported from Elswick, bringing with them heavy-engineering materials such as steel girders and rivets, which were incorporated into the fabric of the house or used to make structures such as the footbridge over the Debdon Burn, an elegant addition to the landscape.

The startling differences in style that can be seen between the library and dining room begun in 1870, and that of the picture gallery of 1873–74 – originally intended as a museum where Armstrong could keep his scientific, geological, and natural history specimens – and that of the classical Renaissance drawing room of a decade later reflect Shaw's changing aesthetic priorities. The character of Cragside, however, was also moulded by Armstrong's determination to integrate his inventions into the house and grounds, thereby 'adding the magical dimension to this dramatic composition',[2] and for a need for Cragside to be grand enough and amazing enough to impress his high-powered business clients from around the world.

Shaw's first extension to the shooting lodge, begun in 1870, was the library and dining-room wing, with its striking Pre-Raphaelite features, including the luminous stained glass by William Morris and Dante Gabriel Rossetti. In 1873 the new south entrance front was built, incorporating the gallery that led to the Gilnockie Tower and Armstrong's glass-domed observatory. Next was an extension beyond the dining room incorporating the north tower. At the far end of the gallery, a spectacular toplit drawing room was completed in time for the royal visit of 1884. The last major additions, in 1895, were the billiards room and an electricity room designed by a quite different architect, Frederick Waller of Gloucester, in a Jacobean revival style with panelling and classical columns.

This process of evolution was captured in a tribute by the broadcaster June Knox-Mawer: 'Year by year the house grew, from the magician's laboratory in the tower to the Turkish baths in the basement, with Armstrong himself urging on his workmen and sometimes joining them, hammer and trowel in hand. As if keeping time with the house, his industrial empire was also expanding, to include huge shipyards, where foreign potentates came to order the latest designs in battleships and cruisers.'[3]

Both the exterior and the interiors of the somewhat anarchic building have long held a strong fascination for architects and architectural critics. Writing in the early 1970s, Mark Girouard described the library as 'one of the most sympathetic Victorian rooms in England'.[4] Its beamed and coffered walnut ceiling, relatively low in height, is complemented by the oak-panelled bookcases and shelves around the walls, creating a feeling of intimacy; the chimneypiece incorporates slabs of onyx inspired by Armstrong's visit to Egypt. The room basks in an abundance of light from a stone-mullioned bay window overlooking the glen. Much of the decorative carving is by one of Shaw's favourite craftsmen, James Forsyth.

Cragside was never meant to be a mere showpiece, however. Its owners were genial hosts who liked nothing better than sharing their pleasures with friends. In September 1873, Thomas Sopwith and his wife Annie were invited to one of many house parties, where they found among their fellow guests 'Mr and Mrs John Watson, Mr and Mrs William Cruddas, Mr and Mrs Stuart Rendel, Colonel Campbell and Captain Andrew Noble of the Royal Artillery'. The morning after their arrival, they awoke to 'a most clear, lovely, bright day – all the beautiful scenery bathed in sunshine', recorded Sopwith in his diary.

After breakfast, they set off on an arduous trek, 'the chief points of destination being a lofty and rocky eminence at Keigh Heugh and the still loftier and more extensive range of the Simonside hills', wrote Sopwith – the second of which proved too much for him and some of the others. Among the less robust on this occasion was Johnny Watson's wife, Margaret, who had recently given birth to a daughter, Susan Dorothea. A few days

Cragside library, taken in 1891 by the architectural photographer Bedford Lemere. On the long wall hangs *Follow My Leader*, which Armstrong commissioned in 1871 from Albert Moore.

Cragside's magnificent drawing room with its domed glass ceiling, also photographed by Bedford Lemere. J. E. Millais's paintings *Chill October* and *Jephthah's Daughter* are both visible.

later they walked to Cragend Farm to see the herd of shorthorn cattle recently acquired by Armstrong, who told Sopwith that farming was one of his favourite occupations.

However, the good weather did not last, and much of the time was spent indoors. Sopwith, for one, was not dismayed by this turn of events because it gave him a chance to explore the 'abundance of resources' on offer. 'The library alone furnished ample treasures and I read in a splendid edition of large type Shakespeare's play of *Antony and Cleopatra*. I also re-read part of *Barchester Towers* and portions of scientific works, of which there are many, including the best magazines and the most recent publications.' One aspect of life at Cragside that irritated the Sopwiths, however, was Armstrong's insistence on punctuality. 'An exact routine prevails in the arrangements of the house from which there are few deviations,' wrote the diarist. 'Breakfast is on the table at 8 to a second! Luncheon at ½ past 1, tea at 5, and dinner at from ½ past 7 to ¼ past 8, according as the early or late arrival of visitors or return of sportsmen from the moors may require.' This complaint was somewhat disingenuous, however, since Sopwith himself was renowned for an obsession with timekeeping.

Before leaving, Sopwith felt inclined, as he often did, to reflect on his friend's worth and integrity. He remembered the surprise and pleasure of the radical politician Richard Cobden when he told him that 'the inventions and useful appliances brought into operation by [Armstrong] in connection with peaceful acts and commercial prosperity were quite equal, and in my view far superior, to those semi-military achievements by which his popularity was most largely achieved'.

Measuring 20 by 33 feet with a large recess at one end, Shaw's library at Cragside was one of the first rooms to be lit by Joseph Swan's filament light bulbs. As Armstrong himself explained in January 1881, eight lamps were needed to provide the desired brightness: 'Four are clustered in one globe of ground glass, suspended from the ceiling in the recess, and the remainder are placed, singly and in globes, in various parts of the room, upon vases of enamelled copper set on a base.'[5] These decorative vases had originally been designed by Shaw as oil lamps. The electric current was introduced through a wire to a small cup of mercury in the detachable base of each vase, and was then 'carried forward by a piece of insulated wire which passes through a hole in the bottom of the vase and thence through the interior to the lamp on top'. When the vase was put down on its base, the protruding end of the wire made contact with the mercury in the cup. In this way, the lamp could be extinguished and re-lit simply by removing the vase from its base and setting it down again.

The dining room next door is dominated by a monumental stone-arched inglenook that was based on a medieval kitchen fireplace at Fountains Abbey in Yorkshire. 'The fireplace is quite a gem of Old English expression,' wrote Sopwith. 'It forms a large recess with small sofa seats at each end and a bold archway with richly ornamented mouldings is over the front.' Over the fireplace is the cosy inscription *East Or West Hame's Best* – which Shaw's partner, W. Eden Nesfield, had earlier used at Cloverley Hall in Shropshire.[6] A carved frieze by James Forsyth of birds, hunting dogs and other wildlife among the foliage surmounts the stone panelling above the inglenook arch, while either side of the chimneypiece are two stained-glass panels by Morris and Company, each panel illustrating one of the four seasons. Some of the earliest Morris stained glass, of sunflowers and other floral designs, can be seen in the Elizabethan-style window lighting the staircase to the picture gallery. William de Morgan, Philip Webb, Ford Madox Brown, and Edward Burne-Jones are among the other fashionable craftsmen whose work adorns this part of the house. And behind all these details was Shaw's guiding hand.

In addition to his highly developed aesthetic tastes, Shaw was an excellent technician with a fascination with how things worked. According to his biographer Andrew Saint, Shaw once told a friend that he ought to have been an engineer rather than an architect. 'A shared practicality, I suspect, is the secret to what seems to have been a very good relationship between Shaw and Armstrong,' said Saint, while acknowledging that Shaw was frustrated by the piecemeal way in which Cragside had developed.[7]

Armstrong's ever-growing picture collection, including paintings by Constable, Leighton, Bonheur, Fantin-Latour, and Landseer, was on show principally in the long gallery, along with display cabinets, designed by Shaw, containing collections of fossils, minerals, and shells. A separate watercolour room leading off the gallery included J. M. W. Turner's *Dunstanborough Castle* and *Lake of Lucerne*, along with works by David Cox, Copley Fielding, and Clarkson Stanfield.

The lighting in the gallery, a room which before 1884 was also used as a drawing room, consisted of 12 overhead lamps, but, as Armstrong himself explained, 'when the eight lamps in the dining room are no longer wanted, the current supplying them is shunted to the gallery for lighting eight additional lamps, making twenty in all', which allowed the pictures to be seen at night as distinctly as in daylight. The illumination in the library could also be 'raised to the utmost brilliancy or depressed to almost twilight dimness by the simple turning of a tap'. The quality of the light given off by his various devices was clearly important to Cragside's owner: 'In the passages and stairs the lamps are for the most part used without glass shades and present a very beautiful and star-like appearance, not so bright as to pain the eye in passing, and very efficient in lighting the way.'

In the last few years of his life, Thomas Sopwith made an annual pilgrimage with Annie to Cragside, and with each visit he became more intrigued by the place he described as 'a palace of intellectual luxury and a home of comfort' – but what he most enjoyed was the stimulating company of the Armstrongs and their friends. In September 1875, for example, among the Sopwiths' fellow guests were Professor Thomas Henry Huxley, 'one of the most distinguished men of science of the time', his Australian-born wife, Henrietta, and their six children. The Nobles, the younger Charles Mitchell and Johnny and Margaret Watson were also among the guests. Sopwith strolled daily around the estate with Johnny Watson, and spent an enjoyable afternoon boating on Tumbleton Lake with Johnny, Charles Mitchell, and the Huxleys' eldest daughter, Jessie. (Two years later, Jessie Oriana Huxley married Frederick Waller, the architect who made additions to Cragside in the 1890s.) An autumnal glow seemed to have settled over proceedings. 'Whether in fine weather or otherwise, time passes very pleasantly at Cragside,' he wrote. 'The walks are so varied and full of interest that there is no end of agreeable exercise. When in the house the hours pass swiftly away in reading, writing, the observation of paintings and sculpture, drawing, music.'

The hosts took great pains to ensure that their guests had every comfort, as revealed in Armstrong's personal correspondence with Stuart Rendel. 'Could you or Nellie without much trouble make out a list of good and popular music by all the best composers for the use of visitors at Cragside,' he asked on one occasion. 'People don't always bring their own music and it requires a rather large collection to meet all tastes and all wants.' He also enlisted Stuart's help in acquiring a grand piano, which had to be black to match the 'ebonised' furniture introduced by Shaw.

Another of Stuart Rendel's tasks was to attend wine sales in London on his friend's behalf. 'Could you call at Willis's rooms and enquire the price of the Steinberg cabinet served at the engineers' dinner on Saturday last,' wrote Armstrong in March 1874. 'I thought it the finest wine I ever tasted and everybody remarked upon it. I dare say it will be very high priced but I should like to have a couple of dozen for special occasions.'

When the Sopwiths returned to Cragside in October 1876, the most conspicuous change was 'the very great and rapid progress of the vast number of trees which have been planted between the rocks', which gave the appearance of continuous plantations – but there was still areas of bare moorland, where 'masses of enormous blocks of stone assert their native supremacy'. On that occasion, Isambard Brunel (a son of Isambard Kingdom Brunel) was also staying at the house. After a visit to the local studio of the painter Henry Hetherington Emmerson, another friend of Armstrong, the guests heard Brunel play Handel on the grand piano in the picture gallery.

Perhaps increasingly aware of his own mortality, Sopwith felt impelled to put down on record the details of his long association with Armstrong, dating from the 1830s. 'I witnessed some of his early experiments with hydraulic apparatus and actively assisted in the publication of his researches,' he wrote. 'I accompanied him on the first occasion of his seeing electricity developed from steam, and I wear daily in my pocket a gold pencil bearing the name of the only other person present on that occasion, namely the late William Daniel Anderson.' He remembered that he had taken Robert Stephenson to Jesmond to see Armstrong's 'marvellous electric machine' and later promoted its exhibition in London.

Sopwith's powers of observation were as acute as ever on his last visit to Cragside, in October 1878, when he was again amazed by the swiftly burgeoning woodland. 'In the midst of these rocky hills and richly wooded dales are many well-laid-out walks, some leading to a lofty iron bridge and to admirably laid-out gardens. A great part of the surface has been made into a sort of botanical museum in which the varieties of heather present a very charming aspect,' he wrote. 'I know not any place that can be compared with Cragside as a magnificent example of landscape gardening.' He was critical, however, of the way in which the design of the house had evolved. 'Handsome and stately as it undoubtedly is, it nevertheless seems to me somewhat wanting in a quality which the old fathers designated "the grace of congruity".'

There was more of the same the following year, but more poignant is the diary entry for 14 December 1877, when Sopwith recorded a visit to his London home by Meggie, then aged 70. 'Lady Armstrong dined and spent the evening with us and it gave me great pleasure to see so highly valued a friend,' he wrote. 'We always find abundant interest in talking of old times and of our first meeting on a journey to Darlington on my way to London in spring of 1835 – no less that 42½ years ago.' Sopwith spent the remaining few weeks of his life at his home in London with his beloved Annie. He deliberately finished writing the 168th volume of his sparkling diary on his 76th birthday, and died two weeks later, on 16 January 1879.

By the time of the royal visit in 1884, Armstrong was able to hang some of his favourite paintings in the new drawing room. Prominent among these were the two works by Millais that he had acquired almost a decade earlier. The appeal of *Chill October* was enhanced by the fact that attached to the back of the canvas was a rare inscription, written and signed by the artist, explaining that the scene had been painted from a backwater of the Tay near Perth. 'The scene, simple as it is, had impressed me for *years* before I painted it,' wrote Millais. 'The traveller between Perth and Dundee passes the spot where I stood. Danger on either side – the tide which once carried away my platform, and the trains which threatened to blow my work into the river.' He had chosen the subject for the emotions that it aroused in him, wrote the artist, but admitted that many of his friends had been at a loss to understand what he saw to paint in such a scene. 'I made no sketch for it but painted every touch from Nature on the canvas itself, under irritating trials of wind and rain. The only studio work was in connection with the effect.'

The Dutch artist Vincent van Gogh would later repeatedly insist in letters to his brother Theo that *Chill October* was one of the works that had done most to influence his development as a landscape painter.

Created by Shaw between 1883 and 1884, Cragside's drawing room has a number of remarkable features, including its half-elliptical, top-lit ceiling. Some 60 feet long by 25 feet wide, the room is dominated by a massive two-storey inglenook fireplace – virtually a room in its own right – extravagantly decorated with putti and swags of fruit, which fills most of the south wall. Carved from Italian marbles by the firm of Farmer and Brindley, the 10-ton fireplace was designed by W. R. Lethaby, Shaw's chief assistant, whose sketch for the extraordinary structure was used to illustrate an editorial in the *Architect* magazine of 7 July 1883. Among the many beautiful artefacts adorning the room was (and remains) a sublime marble statue of the water nymph Undine by Alexander Munro – a representation, some would say, of Armstrong's ideal of womanhood.

The completion of this stage of the building works also marked the end of Shaw's professional involvement with Cragside – an episode that had firmly established him in the premier rank of British architects. By the end of the 1880s, wrote Nikolaus Pevsner,

'Morris was the leader in design, Norman Shaw in architecture.'[8] Shaw also had a far-reaching influence in architectural trends, for, in the words of Jeremy Blake, 'his office produced an impressive band of pilgrims whose independent approach to architecture was unmatched in Europe in the late 19th century'.[9]

The fireplace and the drawing room form the backdrop of one of an evocative series of paintings by H. H. Emmerson of the 1884 visit to Cragside by the Prince and Princess of Wales and their entourage, during which the Armstrongs cemented their already close ties with the royal family. A fortnight after the royal visit, a letter addressed to 'My dear Sir William' arrived from the Hon. Charlotte Knollys, lady-in-waiting to the Princess of Wales. 'The Princess is perfectly delighted with the books and desires me to tell you she is very much touched by all the trouble you have taken,' she wrote. 'HRH immediately recognized the likeness of the Queen.' On behalf of the Prince of Wales, she reminded Armstrong of his promise to send some seeds or cuttings to the gardener at Sandringham.

The extravaganza of 1884 marked the start of a succession of visits to Cragside by monarchs and magnates from around the world, all seeking to do business with Armstrong. Some of the exotic guests provoked curiosity among local observers. The culinary habits of the Crown Prince of Afghanistan, for example, were a source of fascination when he came to Cragside in 1895 accompanied by a retinue of more than 50, including several cooks. The catering staff were provided with special charcoal fires for the preparation of food – 'everything in the shape of flesh meat having to be brought to them alive to be killed as well as cooked by themselves', according to the *Newcastle Daily Journal*. On this occasion, the royal guest preferred to dine alone in his room. Next day, however, Armstrong showed the Afghan prince some of his electrical experiments, 'in the course of which a slight shock was administered to His Highness, which greatly amused him'.

The year 1887 saw the 50th anniversary of Queen Victoria's accession to the throne, which was marked all over the British Empire with commemorative events and lavish celebrations.

In Newcastle, the launch of the battleship *Victoria* on 9 April was followed by the opening a month later of the Royal Mining, Engineering, and Industrial Exhibition.

Occupying a newly created park on the edge of the Town Moor, the event was a showcase for the city's greatest achievements and would be attended by more than 100,000 people. Displays included a complete and full-sized working model of a coal-mine and a reproduction of the medieval bridge over the Tyne, swept away in the great flood of 1771; dating from the 13th century, the old bridge had been lined with shops, houses, and other buildings, including a prison.

The *Illustrated London News* devoted a special issue to the Newcastle exhibition, praising it as a compelling demonstration of the ways in which 'the ingenuity of man has utilized the natural advantages and products of this district'. Pride of place in the armaments section was taken by the Elswick 111-tonner, the largest – and most astonishing – gun in existence. The gun had a calibre of 16.25 inches, a total length of 43 feet 8 inches, and an effective range of 8 miles; its 1,800-pound projectile could attain a speed at the muzzle of 2,020 feet per second and penetrate wrought iron to a depth of 30.6 inches at a distance of 1,000 yards. Also on show at the stand were models of warships built at the Elswick shipyard for the British, Spanish, Italian, and Chinese governments, and a gun with a 'disappearing' hydraulic carriage, which could be raised for firing and quickly lowered again afterwards – 'a marvellous adaptation', remarked the *Illustrated London News*, 'of the long-unsuspected power of water for the storage of force'.

On 20 June, the date of the anniversary itself, Lady Armstrong presented every child in Rothbury with a story book. The news that the Cragside grounds would be open to the public in the afternoon had attracted a large number of visitors to the town. Armstrong had granted a day's holiday to all his workers in the district, and given each a railway pass to Newcastle, a ticket of admission to the exhibition, and an allowance for refreshments. That very morning, a handwritten letter was delivered to Cragside from Robert Cecil, 3rd Marquess of Salisbury, the prime minister:

My dear Sir William

Her Majesty has been previously pleased to command that in celebration of Her Majesty's jubilee, your name shall be included in the list of a small number of Peers which she proposes to create on that occasion.

It gives me great pleasure to be the instrument of conveying this information to you, which I trust will not be unacceptable to you. I am sure that it will be gratifying to very many of Her Majesty's subjects that this creation should take place.

Believe me

Yours very truly

Salisbury

Armstrong was one of six men to receive such a letter in Queen Victoria's golden jubilee year. In accepting the honour, he became the first engineer – indeed, the first scientist – to be raised to the peerage. (The second scientist to go to the House of Lords was William Thomson, who became Baron Kelvin of Largs in 1892.)

As news of his ennoblement spread, messages of congratulation poured in from around the world. At the end of August an adulatory letter arrived from Tseng Chi-tse, popularly known as Marquis Tseng, who had recently returned to Peking (Beijing) after eight years as Chinese ambassador to Britain and France. To the dismay of Chinese conservatives, during his service in Europe, Tseng had become a keen admirer of the West and an advocate of Westernisation. He described Armstrong's elevation as 'a credit to your Sovereign and the country', and lavished praise on a system in which 'party claims are laid aside and invention, ingenuity, skill, perseverance, the advancement of science and the material and industrial development of one's own country and that of the world meet with such recognition'.

A letter of quite different tenor came from Armstrong's sometime adversary Joseph Cowen, veteran proprietor of the *Newcastle Chronicle*, written from his home at Blaydon-on-Tyne. 'You will find the House of Lords more agreeable than the House of Commons would have been,' wrote Cowen. 'A seat in the former assembly has always been regarded as a reward for great national service – and on no Englishman could one have been more appropriately conferred than on your Lordship. It is melancholy to witness how the House of Commons is losing both its reputation and authority.' Cowen himself had recently retired from Parliament after 13 tempestuous years as Liberal MP for Newcastle, and he was referring to Armstrong's own failed attempt to be elected to the Commons the previous year.

Despite his well-known wariness about politics, Armstrong had been invited in 1884 to stand for election to Parliament, as a candidate acceptable to both Liberal and Conservative interests. In turning down the offer, he insisted that he would be too advanced for one party and not advanced enough for the other. One issue that troubled him deeply, however, was home rule for Ireland, and after Gladstone introduced his first Home Rule Bill, he was persuaded to stand as a Liberal Unionist in the election of 1886.

The political tide was running in favour of maintaining a United Kingdom of Great Britain and Ireland, seen by many as the best way to preserve free trade, the rule of law, and freedom of religion – but, even though the pro-union Conservatives won the national election, Armstrong was defeated in Newcastle by the Gladstonian candidate, John Morley. The loser was probably more deeply affected than he cared to show. 'That Sir William did not obtain the coveted seat in the greatest representative assembly in the world must be described as his one failure in life,' wrote a London journalist later.[10] A recent dispute at the Elswick Works was also thought to have played a part in the result.

The correspondence between Cowen and Armstrong that followed the election throws a rare light on Armstrong's political beliefs. 'I don't agree with your views about the government of Ireland,' wrote Cowen on 7 July, 'but in common with all Tynesiders who have not allowed political partisanship to destroy their sense of local patriotism and gratitude, I grieve at your defeat.'

'Your note has gratified me much,' replied Armstrong. 'Though I have often differed from you before, yet there has generally been an affinity of opinion between us, our differences being more matters of degree than of principle.' Betraying no hint of regret at the outcome, he suggested that it must be a comfort for Cowen to 'escape' from London parliamentary life. 'With the *Newcastle Daily Chronicle* at your command, you may continue to exercise great weight in the political world. I know of no finer thing for a man of ability, independence and patriotism to do than to use such an organ as yours for leading the public mind in the ways of justice, moderation and common sense.' Cowen was, like him, 'a votary of liberty', he said, 'but I think you must be of my opinion that liberty and democracy do not go hand in hand'.

A few months after the election – in a reaffirmation of the esteem in which he was held by his fellow citizens – Armstrong was presented with the Freedom of Newcastle upon Tyne. In making the award, the mayor, Benjamin Browne, pointed out to his audience that one quarter of the entire population of the city was now dependent on the master of Elswick for a living.

On his elevation to the peerage in 1887, Armstrong remarked that the calmer atmosphere of the Upper House would suit him much better than the Commons – but his career in the House of Lords did not begin in tranquillity. When the new parliamentary session opened the following February, he was invited to second the motion in the Lords for the adoption of the Queen's Speech. In accepting this traditional honour, he did not shirk from addressing two of the most contentious issues of the day: the preservation of the union of Great Britain and Ireland (in force since 1800), and the condition of the nation's defences. Armstrong's speech on this important state occasion offers rare insight into his views on politics, international relations, and the rule of law.

The Liberal Unionists (his party) had been accused of supporting an authoritarian policy in Ireland, he said – but it was his belief that coercion used to restrain tyranny, including the kind of tyranny rife in Ireland at the time, should be applauded. People could only experience true liberty if they were protected by law – and law without coercion was worthless.

When it came to foreign policy, Armstrong continued, many people thought that Britain should not intervene in other countries' affairs. But how should we respond to those who were prepared to use aggression in pursuit of their ambitions? It was folly to talk of treaties alone as the answer to resolving disputes. Just as effective law enforcement depended on the threat of coercion, treaties would only work if backed by the threat of force. And Britain was particularly vulnerable at the present time. 'There is no nation in the world less disposed to break the peace of Europe than our own,' he said, 'but our great wealth, the vulnerability of our commerce, and our absolute dependence on it, present the greatest possible temptation for an aggressive power to make war upon us.'

He painted a stark picture of what it would be like if Britain failed to maintain and expand its navy: 'If we lose our ascendancy on the oceans, our nation will be like a beleaguered city, with a community living on half-rations, and with the certainty of being starved into submission.' An unequivocally dominant navy would be the most effective way of preventing war, and the way to achieve this was to build swift unarmoured vessels capable of carrying more arms, more powerful engines, and more fuel than their ironclad counterparts. He argued that speed and nimbleness combined with great offensive power were the qualities that would be most valuable in the naval warfare of the future.

The cost of expanding our defences would be great, Armstrong admitted, but Britain was, after all, a very rich country. Besides, such expenditure would boost the national economy, creating many thousands of jobs. The benefit would not be confined to particular industries, for an increase in the spending power of one sector indirectly increased that of others which supplied its needs – and this process went on in an ever-growing circle until the money was diffused through the entire economy.

Finally, Armstrong turned his gaze on the British Empire. The kingdom of Great Britain and Ireland held a foremost place among the nations of the world, he said, ruling over something like one-fifth of the entire human race. To maintain that sway and our influence among nations generally, we must maintain our prestige, and in order to do that we must maintain our power. 'It is human nature to despise the impotent,' he said, 'and if we once exhibit feebleness, this great empire, of which we should be so proud, will break up and dissolve.' He hoped that under the present (Conservative) government the subject would be treated more seriously than it had been so far – 'especially as our great Australian colonies are showing a willingness to cooperate with the parent country in giving strength and security to the empire'.

Armstrong's emphasis on the power of deterrence must have resonated with the naval strategist John Fisher, who had consistently argued that the best hope of peace lay in preparing for war, and his speech no doubt did much to influence the passage of the 1889 Naval Defence Act, which provided £21 million for the expansion of the navy – giving it the resources to expand to twice the size of its two greatest rivals, France and Russia. Admiral Fisher, appointed first sea lord 15 years later, was the mastermind behind *Dreadnought*, the first of a new class of superlatively fast, heavily armed battleships, whose launch in 1906 would ignite a new arms race – this time, with Germany.

19

King of the Castle

Meggie died at Jesmond Dene on 2 September 1893 at the age of 86, just six years after becoming Baroness Armstrong of Cragside. A serious fall the previous autumn had taken a heavy toll, and after suffering a stroke in mid-August she did not regain consciousness. Although always overshadowed by her husband in the public eye, Meggie Armstrong had been a much admired figure in her own right, if rather commanding and, occasionally, alarmingly stern. 'She was a lady of great force of character and generosity,' wrote William Watson-Armstrong, 'and for more than 50 years of married life her chief source of pride was her husband's success.'[1] The pair had actually met 67 years earlier, in Bishop Auckland, and married in 1835.

Meggie Armstrong's original mind was perhaps most evident in her gift for gardening. 'The idea that runs through both Jesmond Dene and Cragside – of making art the handmaid of nature – and preserving the wild contour [of the landscape] and the natural condition of trees and plants was thoroughly understood by Lady Armstrong,' said the *Newcastle Journal* in its obituary. A keen botanist, Meggie had also collected numerous species of rare local and British plants and introduced them to her gardens at Cragside.

Rather than dwelling on her own childlessness, Meggie had lavished affection on the children in her immediate circle, in particular Johnny Watson and his family. She gave money and support to all sorts of organisations, but especially those connected with children – not only schools and hospitals, but also bodies promoting the arts and recreational activities. She funded, for example, several scholarships for the National Training School for Music, set up in 1876, which evolved into the Royal College of

Music. 'Nearest to her heart, perhaps, was Newcastle's old Hospital for Sick Children in Hanover Square, to which she rendered invaluable assistance when its need was sore,' remarked the *Evening Chronicle*. Shortly before her death, she bought some property in Tuthill Stairs, Newcastle, with the idea of converting it into almshouses for elderly people, a project she did not live to see carried out.

Her patience and talents as a hostess must have been tried to the limit by the endless stream of foreign diplomats, businessmen, and royalty who arrived at Cragside expecting comfort and entertainment, but, according to the *Journal*, all visitors received a warm welcome: 'Even passing strangers who merely called to behold the attractions of that marvellous spot, and to admire the works of art and tastes that are to be found in the rock-built mansion, will not soon forget the assiduous kindness shown to them by Lady Armstrong when she was in the vigour of her health.'

Crucially, Meggie remained involved until death with all aspects of her husband's work. William's intense single-mindedness and obstinate determination to persevere with every challenge cannot have made him easy to live with, but there seems to have been no subject about which he did not confide in her, and, despite the tensions, they made a remarkable team. 'She took a keen interest in the scientific matters to which Lord Armstrong has given his attention, and many institutions, notably the Natural History Museum, are largely indebted to her liberality,' said the *Evening Chronicle*. 'Lady Armstrong was esteemed by all who knew her.'

After a simple ceremony at Rothbury parish church, she was laid to rest in a secluded part of the churchyard near the river, in a grave lined with ivy leaves. Armstrong remained at the graveside for a while after the crowd of mourners had departed. 'His lordship was naturally deeply affected,' noted an observer. His tantalising Undine had finally eluded him.

After the loss of Meggie, Armstrong seemed preoccupied by his legacy to the world. His advancing age had brought some physical infirmity, but his energy appeared undiminished – and his mental acuity remained razor sharp. Indeed, he was about to embark on one of his boldest ventures. Before the year 1893 was out, he had offered to buy and restore a dilapidated medieval castle at Bamburgh on the Northumberland coast. Since the scheme surfaced so soon after his wife's death, it is probable that the Armstrongs had discussed the idea between them – and his plans for the ancient citadel would surely have met with her approval.

For more than 170 years, Bamburgh Castle had been in the care of the trustees of Nathaniel, Lord Crewe, a former bishop of Durham, who had died without heir in 1722, leaving his estate in trust to charity. The Crewe trustees had faced an almost impossible task at Bamburgh since serious damage inflicted in the 15th century, during the Wars of the Roses, had never been repaired, and the castle had suffered severe neglect during the tenure of the profligate Forster family. (Having proved impregnable over several centuries to every kind of armed assault, Bamburgh had become in 1464 the first castle in England to succumb to gunfire, when it was attacked by the army of the Yorkist king Edward IV.[2])

Lord Crewe's interest derived from his marriage to Dorothy Forster, whose ancestor, Claudius Forster, had been installed there as royal constable by James I of England and VI of Scotland following the 1603 union of the crowns. For a century afterwards, the Forsters held Bamburgh under the crown, but did little to maintain it. When Crewe bought the estate in 1704, and paid off the Forsters' debts, he found the castle a mere ruin almost buried in blown sand. A vastly wealthy landowner with many other concerns, Crewe continued the tradition of neglect – and, despite the later endeavours of Dr John Sharp and other trustees, by the end of the 19th century a financial crisis loomed.

There was initial public suspicion about Armstrong's intentions as a prospective purchaser of Bamburgh Castle, but in the end the trustees had little option but to accept his generous offer. (Armstrong later told the King of Siam that he had paid £60,000 for the estate.) As well as promising to preserve and restore the ancient character of the property, Armstrong said that he intended to establish there 'a home for people who had seen better times'.[3] He was also keenly aware of the historical significance of Bamburgh, whose outstanding site and location – on a high rocky promontory some 50 miles north of Newcastle and 20 miles south of Berwick – had made it a natural fortress from earliest times.

There is evidence of human settlement at Bamburgh during and before the Roman period, but it was in the sixth and early seventh centuries AD that the place really came to prominence and, according to the Anglo-Saxon chronicles, was first acknowledged as a royal fortress. 'The castle-rock of Bamburgh may be justly regarded as the very foundation-stone of England,' claimed Cadwallader John Bates, a historian of Northumberland.[4] 'It was the ascendancy of the English kings whose throne was firmly established on the basalt ramparts of Bamburgh during the most crucial period of our national history that gave the English name to the land that was already being called a new Saxony.' Bates was referring to the period that began in 547, when the English chieftain Ida established a power base at this strategic point on the northern coast. Ida's grandson Aethelfrith – an ambitious warlord characterised by Anglo-Saxon chroniclers as 'a ravening wolf' – gave the stronghold to his wife, Bebba, who after her husband's death saw off rivals to secure pre-eminence in the region. It was during Bebba's tenure that the castle-rock acquired the name Bebbanburgh, or Bamburgh.

From that time, royal claims on Bamburgh would be pursued with more or less vigour for well over a millennium – and its proximity to Lindisfarne and the Farne Islands, where the early saints Aidan and Cuthbert once lived and prayed, earned it an important place in the history of Christianity in Britain. Often associated with Joyous Gard, the legendary retreat of the Arthurian knight Sir Launcelot, Bamburgh has also inspired generations of writers, artists, and film-makers.

To Armstrong, coming to Bamburgh Castle felt in a peculiar way like coming home. He told interested enquirers that he had family connections with Bamburgh. By this he meant not the Armstrong clan but the family of his late sister's husband, William Watson, who had been his legal mentor in London 65 years earlier. Watson was descended on his mother's side from the Greys of Shoreston, a settlement that had long formed part of the royal demesne land of Bamburgh Castle. The Greys could trace their local lineage back to Stuart times and had intermarried with the Forsters. Armstrong reportedly recognised a need to atone for the Forsters' sins of omission in the 17th century by restoring Bamburgh to its former glory. In doing so, he was identifying himself ever more strongly with the Watson family.

The living reminder of this heritage was the family of Armstrong's nephew, Johnny – especially his children, William and Susan Dorothea, known as Willie and Tottie. In 1889, Willie had married Winifreda Adye, the beautiful daughter of General John Adye, one of Armstrong's old adversaries in the military establishment. By then, Willie was ensconced as Armstrong's amanuensis and universally acknowledged as his heir. After his marriage, with his great-uncle's encouragement, he changed his surname by royal licence to Watson-Armstrong, becoming William Henry Armstrong Fitzpatrick Watson-Armstrong. In doing so, he was both acknowledging his destiny and blurring his line of descent.

Armstrong's purchase of Bamburgh involved not only the castle but also several hundred acres of land, including three farms, and a share in the Farnes, a group of 25 small offshore islands that provided a haven for seabirds and seals. The Farnes were renowned as the site of both St Cuthbert's hermitage and the Longstone lighthouse, from where Grace Darling, the lighthouse-keeper's daughter, set out on a daring rescue of shipwrecked sailors in 1838. Armstrong also acquired Adderstone Hall, a former Forster property a few miles from the castle, and its accompanying 150 acres. As the restoration of Bamburgh Castle got under way, Johnny Watson, who had retired from legal practice, was installed at the 18th-century hall with his wife, Margaret Godman Fitzpatrick. Both would live there until their deaths in, respectively, 1909 and 1922, and both are buried in nearby Lucker churchyard.

Before Armstrong's arrival, the great champion of Bamburgh had been a Crewe trustee by the name of Dr John Sharp, archdeacon of Northumberland, who carried out a huge amount of work at the castle over a 35-year period, largely at his own expense, and inspired other trustees to follow his example after he died.[5] The centrepiece of Sharp's project was the restoration of the majestic Norman keep, measuring 70 by 77 feet at its base. Built to withstand ferocious attack, the walls of the keep were from 10 to 13 feet thick, and its bottle-shaped doorway was designed to allow defenders on horseback to enter at speed without dismounting. The entrance passage led to a vast hall with a high vaulted ceiling. Comparable with the 12th-century keeps at Dover and Newcastle, the Bamburgh keep is thought to date from the reign of Henry II (1154–89).

Sharp began restoring the keep in 1757, with the idea that he and his family would live there, but he also had more ambitious ideas for the building. A new, stone-tiled roof was added, and new floors were installed in the rooms that originally had timber floors; one of these, over the Court Room, was at a higher level to provide extra headroom, and was used as a library for Sharp's famous collection of books. Fireplaces were added to most of the rooms. The upper part of the keep was used for grain storage. The archdeacon also built a windmill and a 200-feet-long granary, where provisions were stockpiled and sold cheaply to local people in times of scarcity.

Ever aware of the hazards posed to shipping by the treacherous Northumberland coastline, Sharp decided to reserve part of the keep for the care of shipwrecked sailors, setting up beds for 30 people. He arranged for a gun to be fired and a bell to be rung at intervals from the top of the keep in foggy or stormy conditions, and laid in massive chains for rescue and salvage work at sea. Outside was a cannon that could be sounded to alert local people to a vessel in distress. By these measures, Sharp won a reputation as a pioneer of Britain's coastguard service.

Sharp's most adventurous project was to transform buildings in the inner ward into a free school for up to 300 boys and girls. What had been the Great Kitchen was used as a classroom for boys, while the girls were taught on an upper floor. The area originally occupied by the King's Hall, or Great Hall, was reconfigured to contain a pantry and dairy and children's washing yard, with bedrooms and living rooms on the three floors above. Other buildings were altered to make room for, among other things, a medical dispensary and an infirmary for the poor.

Although the institutions established by Sharp at Bamburgh continued to play a vital philanthropic role for a century after his death in 1792, and were highly valued by local people, his architectural interventions did not attract praise. The antiquarian William Gibson, for example, described them as being 'in the worst possible taste' and made a heartfelt plea for the restoration of the castle's medieval character.[6]

When Armstrong – perhaps spurred on by the comments of Gibson and others – offered to buy Bamburgh Castle, there were concerns that Sharp's mistakes would be perpetuated or repeated. But the Crewe trustees who had tried to sustain the archdeacon's good works had reached the end of the line. Rental income from the Bamburgh estate had fallen dramatically in recent years, with the result that the charities dependent on the rents had been forced to rein in their activities. Notably, the girls' school (as it had become) had been forced to close, and the other charitable concerns based at the castle had been scaled down. The trustees made clear their reluctance to part with the property and their fear that, if it were sold at auction, the highest bidder might be 'a speculative builder or an adventurous hotel-keeper'.[7]

In the event, Armstrong approached the trustees privately, reassuring the doubters that he would restore something of the 'ancient grandeur' of the castle.[8] With his usual wily tact, he said that he wanted the trustees to maintain contact with the castle – and, to that end, promised to provide them with a space in the restored citadel for 'their library, pictures and other treasures', as well as making available two bedrooms for their exclusive use in case any of them wanted to stay a few nights at Bamburgh. The deal was sealed with little further discussion.

Soon after taking possession of the castle in June 1894, Armstrong engaged the Carlisle architect Charles Ferguson to carry out a hugely ambitious programme of renovation and building, which took nine years to complete and would eventually entail an investment of more than £1 million – some £57 million in today's money. Ferguson's work at Bamburgh upset some critics, being dismissed by Henry Avray Tipping of *Country Life* magazine as 'the acme of expenditure with a nadir of intelligent achievement'.

But, as the architect David Ash pointed out some 50 years later, had it not been for Armstrong and Ferguson, 'Bamburgh Castle would no doubt be in a ruinous state like Dunstanburgh is today, and no longer "living".'[9]

Before starting work at Bamburgh, Ferguson took numerous photographs of the existing buildings in their various stages of dilapidation and made many detailed drawings of proposed alterations and additions for submission to his client. He kept in close contact with Armstrong by letter throughout the project, involving him in every decision, large and small. Dark grey sandstone from the moors around Cragside was chosen for most of the renovation work; this was quite distinct from the pinkish local sandstone previously used at the castle, and had to be transported almost 30 miles from Rothbury in horse-drawn carts. Although he had no hesitation in demolishing most of Sharp's additions and alterations, Ferguson kept the lower walls of the medieval kitchen and adjoining buildings, and built them up in warm local stone, reserving the darker stone for the new King's Hall and residential block.[10]

The buildings in the inner ward that had been used for the school and dispensary were transformed into the Crewe Lodging, the Captain's Lodging, and a reincarnated King's Hall. The Crewe Lodging included the Great Kitchen, which was left intact, while the original buttery and pantries were converted into rooms for Armstrong's agent at the castle, Colonel J. G. Hart. A block of buildings at the eastern end of the King's Hall was earmarked for conversion into 'a convalescent home for persons of superior bringing up [who were] unable to afford the advantages of a change to the seaside' with an endowment of £20,000.[11] Armstrong was determined to ensure that the charitable uses to which the castle had been bequeathed by Lord Crewe would not lapse. A further plan was that the King's Hall, when restored, would be available for 'the exercise and recreation of the hospital inmates in bad weather'.

In reconstructing the King's Hall – by then, little more than a ruin – Ferguson aimed to replicate the exact lines and character of the ancient building, dating from the mid-13th century, which had been a foot wider at one end than at the other.[12] The floors inserted when the building was used as a school were removed, and the walls were totally refaced. 'One part of the work of Archdeacon Sharp was the entire removal of the facing of the old walls of the King's Hall above the floor level,' wrote Ferguson in October 1898. 'He probably robbed them of 2 feet of their original thickness and refaced the reduced wall with a soft local stone, leaving the walls 12 inches or 13 inches thinner than they originally were.' The solution was radical: 'We underset the whole length of ancient wall for a depth of from 10 to 16 feet, we re-faced the front of Sharp's facing to its ancient thickness, and we built three or four buttresses on the land side to ensure the stability of the old walls.'

Interior walls were panelled in teak from Siam (Thailand), and the same material, carved over several years by a Cragside craftsman, was used to make the spectacular hammerbeam ceiling, modelled on that of St George's Hall at Windsor Castle. Separated from the King's Hall at the north end by a vast round-headed stone arch is the Cross Hall, again panelled in teak, with a carved-teak fireplace. When the King of Siam visited Bamburgh in 1897, the *Newcastle Daily News* reported his surprise at seeing wood imported from his own country – and his admiration that it was being wrought by hand rather than by machinery.[13] The king reputedly made a few chisel-marks on the panelling as a sign of Anglo-Thai friendship. A minstrels' gallery was constructed with a stained-glass window incorporating many of the figures associated with the castle's history.

Restoration of the keep was largely confined to the ground floor and involved opening out the main hall into its original six bays and exposing in the west corner a well dating back to the Saxon period. A startling feat of early engineering, the well had been sunk through solid rock, including 75 feet of hard whinstone, to a depth of 145 feet, to provide a reliable source of clean water for the castle's defenders. Part of the defensive cross-wall that had been removed by Sharp was rebuilt, and two bays that had been filled in were reopened. One side of the basement was turned into a housekeeper's room, a staircase with lift to the floors above, and a kitchen.

The Armoury occupying most of the first floor of the keep remained unchanged. Its fearsome array of weapons and armour, acting as a constant reminder of Bamburgh's turbulent history, ranged from ballistas – the forerunner of crossbows, used for hurling stones and bolts – to pikes, halberds, and flintlock muskets issued to local militia in anticipation of a Napoleonic invasion.

Among other innovations, a terrace was created in front of the keep with expansive views of the sea and surrounding countryside. The Vale Tipping Tower, opposite the Porter's Lodge, was restored and two storeys added; it was renamed the Constable Tower after the original Royal Constable and live-in keeper, Claudius Forster. The 18th-century granary was rebuilt to house Sharp's library as well as to accommodate lodgings, coach houses, and stables. A gas works was constructed half a mile to the south-west of the castle, from where gas could be piped to the castle to supply lighting and heating.[14]

In the event, however, the convalescent home in the castle would never materialise. After Armstrong's death, his heir, Willie Watson-Armstrong, decided to keep the castle as a family home, and only some 25 years later did he commission instead the building in Bamburgh village of a home for retired people, which survives today as Armstrong House. When Armstrong House opened in June 1927, the heir told the *Newcastle Journal* and other local newspapers that experience of the 'severe gales' that assailed Bamburgh Castle had convinced his great-uncle that the castle was unsuitable for the purpose for which he had intended it.[15] This claim was not borne out by Armstrong's will, which made clear his unwavering desire that part of the castle should be used as a convalescent home, for which purpose an endowment fund had been set up. In one of several passages in the will that reveal a lack of confidence in his heir's reliability, Armstrong wrote: 'I desire to express to the said William Armstrong Watson-Armstrong my earnest wish that in case he should [put an end to] such use he will either pay ten thousand pounds to the trustees of the endowment fund for the purpose of providing another building for the said convalescent home or will himself provide another building satisfactory to those trustees ... though I do not mean by this my will to impose any legal obligation on any person I declare my wish in full confidence that it will be complied with.'

Although Armstrong continued to live mostly at Cragside, and occasionally at Jesmond Dene, he spent more time at Bamburgh as the castle gradually became habitable, probably occupying an apartment in the keep, so that he could keep an eye on developments. It was from Bamburgh that he launched his last great masterpiece, a spectacular book entitled *Electric Movement in Air and Water*, published in 1897 by the London firm of Smith Elder. And it was from Bamburgh that he conducted private and public correspondence about the book and its even more breathtaking supplement, which appeared two years later. A review published in *The Times* on 10 June 1897 captures some of the general amazement that greeted the publication of this volume. 'Lord Armstrong embodies [in his book] one of the most remarkable contributions to physical and electrical knowledge that have been made in recent years,' proclaimed the writer. 'It is nearly 25 years since Lord Kelvin (then Sir William Thomson) first formed his conception of matter as "the vortex motion of an everywhere present fluid". It has fallen to Lord Armstrong's to demonstrate by experimental results of surpassing beauty that, in the domain of electricity, vortex motion, in all probability, plays a hitherto unsuspected part.'

Armstrong had commissioned John Worsnop, a Rothbury photographer, to reproduce images of a series of electrical experiments involving powerful induction coils, a giant Wimshurst machine (a device for generating high-voltage electrical charges), and condensers varying from pint bottles to ten-gallon jars. These images were reproduced in *Electric Movement in Air and Water*, accompanied by descriptive text. 'It is impossible here to enter into an analysis of the marvels shown in the 40 or more plates,' commented *The Times*, but one was particularly worthy of note because of 'the astonishing resemblance it shows between the imprint obtained from electric streams ... and the growth of a tree'. Stem, branches, twigs, and roots were depicted with such 'rare fidelity' that the image suggested to the writer an explanation of how sap could rise in the giant sequoias of California to heights that seemed theoretically impossible.

Implied interconnections between apparently disparate systems in the physical and natural world were an important element of Armstrong's discoveries. Musing on the images produced by his experiments, he commented, 'Their general appearance is strikingly like pictures of physiological cells; and, what is more strange, we see them in every stage of fission, from small beginnings to complete separations, and in every case the divided form displays the same internal structure as the original from which it springs. I have already spoken of electricity as organized motion, and we have here an example of it carried apparently to the very verge of life.'

He was particularly fascinated by the relationship between matter and motion, believing that no one could speak with more authority on this subject than William Thomson, Lord Kelvin, whom he regarded as 'the greatest scientist in the world, towering above everyone else'. He quoted Kelvin as saying, 'It is scarcely possible to help anticipating the arrival of a complete theory of matter, in which all its properties will be seen to be merely attributes of motion.'

The Times alerted its readers to the 'sumptuous form' of the book, which had a beautifully designed leather cover embossed in gold leaf and a page size of 11 by 15 inches. 'The illustrations are produced in a superb manner, entirely worthy of so remarkable a monograph,' the newspaper concluded. A supplement of similar dimensions, published two years later, was put together with the help of Henry Stroud, a professor of physics at the Durham College of Science in Newcastle. Almost 50 years before the advent of colour photography, some of the photographs in this volume were hand-coloured. 'The illustrations to this Appendix, fourteen in number, have been admirably reproduced for publication by the Autotype Company, who have had great difficulties to contend with in the duplication of the colours,' explained Armstrong in his introduction. Reminiscing about his hydroelectric machine of the 1840s, he admitted that he had spent almost half a century longing to return to the study of electricity. 'It was always my intention to follow up the subject as soon as I could provide myself with a sufficiently powerful apparatus and could find leisure to devote to its use,' he wrote. Indeed, it was his firm belief that, had he applied himself to the development of electricity as he had to hydraulics, he would have been even richer and more famous than he was.

Armstrong's latest experiments had come to public attention in February 1893 during the centenary celebrations of the Lit & Phil, when he delivered a presidential address to as large and brilliant a gathering as the society had ever seen.[16] He had been president of the Lit & Phil for 32 years, and a member for 57, having joined in 1836 at the age of 25; while his father, William senior, had been a founder member of the society in the 1790s. In the audience was Alfred Cochrane, a son-in-law of Andrew Noble who would later publish a history of the Elswick Works. '[Armstrong] began by reminding his hearers that 49 years earlier he had shown his hydroelectric machine to the same society,' wrote Cochrane, 'and on that occasion so dense a crowd has collected that he, the lecturer, had to enter like a burglar through the window.'[17] The meeting room had been very much smaller in those days, of course – before Armstrong himself had financed the building of a 700-seat lecture theatre.

The lecturer admitted that the hydroelectric machine had been his 'first electrical love', and lamented that soon after its introduction he had been diverted by the hydraulic experiments that had led to the establishment of Elswick. From that time until recently, the demands of business had prevented him from electrical pursuits, 'but I remained faithful to my first love, and resolved to renew my addresses if ever circumstances permitted me to do so'. By the time he returned to electricity, however, 'I had grown old and unable to bear the necessary outdoor exposure, so I transferred my affections to a less exacting mistress that would be satisfied with indoor attentions. That second mistress was the Ruhmkorff induction coil [an electrical transformer used to produce high-voltage pulses from a low-voltage direct current supply].'

He proceeded to demonstrate how to combine induction coils in such a way as to form a battery. As before, one aspect of the show that particularly thrilled both lecturer and audience was the creation of sparks. 'The short spark with which I commence consists entirely of flame, which is due to the combustion of the nitrogen of the air in its union to form nitric acid,' he explained. 'As I gradually increase the separating distance, you will see a torrent of sparks passing between the terminals. I go on increasing up to 18 inches, when sparks still continue to pass, though in reduced numbers.' His listeners were promised the chance to see some other beautiful effects of illumination before he moved on to matters of more scientific interest.

Later in the evening, Armstrong referred to tests he had done on 'the dispersive effect of the electric spark upon dust', during which he had noticed that the disturbed dust always settled in a circular pattern. He had then embarked on an elaborate course of experimentation that yielded a rich harvest of results. Photographs of many of the 'dust figures' produced this way had already been exhibited at the Royal Society.

Armstrong then performed a series of experiments whose results were projected on to a screen behind him, including one that showed the transmission of electricity by convection. Many formidable shapes and figures were produced from the arrangement of dust on plates of glass. 'You see the dust rolls up in massive circular waves from the circumference to the centre, followed by beautiful streamers from the surrounding points,' he remarked to his audience. 'I will next put the four-pointed star already used in the centre, and proceed the same as in the preceding experiment. You see a figure widely different from the last, and not less beautiful.' The dust figures could in fact be multiplied in an endless variety of ways. Armstrong acknowledged that some of his audience would question the value of such experiments. 'I answer,' he said, 'that the more we pry into the mysteries of electricity the more we shall be able to apply it to the service of mankind – but, apart from that consideration, knowledge, for knowledge sake, is a worthy object of pursuit.'

Early in the morning of 8 February, sparks of a much less welcome kind were responsible for a fateful event at the Lit & Phil that would never be forgotten. A few hours after the end of the joyful centenary festivities, a disastrous fire broke out in the library, destroying a multitude of books and resulting in thousands of pounds worth of damage to the building. Believed to have been started by smouldering wood from a caterer's stove, the fire had caused the greatest havoc in the west end of the building, where the flames had apparently been fanned by a strong wind from the street. The floor and the glass roof collapsed, the gallery was largely destroyed, and bookcases containing many rare volumes were consumed by the flames or irreparably damaged by water. Sculptures and busts toppled over and crashed to the ground, among them a bust of James Watt, which was decapitated by a fall of slate and glass from the roof.

'Lord Armstrong, the society's president, was among the first to visit the scene of conflagration soon after daybreak,' noted the *Newcastle Courant*. 'He was the first to discover his own bust at his feet amid the extraordinary confusion of wreckage which was strewn along the floor of the library.'

Following the publication of *Electric Movement in Air and Water*, Armstrong was obliged to defend himself in the press against those who dismissed his experiments as of marginal importance and his analysis as wrongheaded. In a letter to *The Times* from Bamburgh Castle dated 14 August 1897, he said he had anticipated dissent but that his primary aim had been 'to illustrate by photography electric effects hitherto invisible and unknown'. The results had revealed facts that could not be ignored in the attempt to reach a complete theory of electricity.

'That wonderful agent has sprung upon the world like a physical revelation almost within the present century, and its operation in the service of mankind continues to increase with amazing rapidity, but we are hampered by ignorance of its nature,' he wrote. 'New facts are needed for guidance to greater knowledge of it, and, when those elicited by the pictorial illustrations I have produced are fully understood, we shall be much more enlightened concerning electricity than we are at present.'

20

The Philosopher Crab

Armstrong had distributed a number of copies of *Electric Movement in Air and Water* among his friends and colleagues in the scientific world, attracting a string of adulatory letters, including one from the iron and steel magnate Isaac Lowthian Bell, who had been invited to observe the experiments as they took place. 'Your splendid and most interesting gift will occupy a dress-circle seat among my most valued treasures,' he wrote. 'The fact that I was permitted to witness some of the wonderful changes effected under your own magic wand of course adds much to their interest.' In a later letter to his old friend, Lowthian Bell recommended that Armstrong take cocaine to relieve the pain of a forthcoming cataract operation.

Even at this late stage in life, Armstrong continued to make new friends, among them John Worsnop, the Rothbury photographer who had worked with him at Cragside during three winters, from 1894 to 1896, and had played a vital role in the genesis of *Electric Movement*. 'There was ample scope in the great field of electricity for the exercise of his mighty intellect,' wrote Worsnop in a memoir, 'and the patience, perseverance and dogged determination, the fertility of resource and intense enthusiasm with which he pursued his researches filled one with wonder and admiration.'[1]

To Worsnop's surprise, the octogenarian never seemed to get tired, and often regretted his inability to get more done. He began his working day at 9am and usually finished at 7.30pm, but when there were no guests in the house he frequently allowed himself only ten minutes for dinner and then went on working until half past nine at night. 'The work was wholly experimental,' wrote Worsnop, 'but difficulties only increased his enthusiasm and stimulated his energies; he revelled in them, and his efforts never ceased till he conquered and overcame them.'

But what most impressed Worsnop were Armstrong's marvellous powers of concentration. When trying to solve a problem, he would enter into a trance-like state that made him totally oblivious of his surroundings, as Worsnop recounted in his memoir: 'I remember his coming into the laboratory one morning at nine o'clock, and after passing the compliments of the day he sat on a chair which stood close to a large gas-stove with his legs crossed. With one hand in his pocket and his chin resting on the other, he began to work out an abstruse problem.' Worsnop and his colleague realised that Armstrong did not want to be disturbed, so they moved into another room, but returned to the laboratory every 10 or 15 minutes to see if they were needed. On several occasions they deliberately made a noise, but Armstrong apparently neither saw nor heard them. 'At last he became cognisant of his surroundings, and, looking at his watch, he said, "It is one o'clock. Come back at a quarter past two and I'll have something for you to do." During the whole of the time, as far as we observed, he never once changed his position, and though he was motionless as a statue, I question very much whether any man in the county of Northumberland worked so hard that morning as he.'

Percy Westmacott, a leading light for many years in the hydraulic machinery department at Elswick, gave another impression of what it was like to witness Armstrong having a brainwave. 'We could tell by the chief's manner of any fresh hatching in his active brain,' he wrote. 'He would enter briskly, with a fixed, intent expression and his left shoulder well forward. He would then go straight up to Hutchinson and carry him off to his little den of an office. The hands [factory workers] would lift *their* hands and wonder what new scheme was coming on.' According to Westmacott, whenever Armstrong was deep in thought or intellectually stimulated, he adopted a strange side-shuffling gait, carrying his left shoulder well forward – a trait that became more pronounced as he got older. 'This peculiar way of walking excited the chaff of the good-natured officers at Shoeburyness, who gave him the name of "the Crab",' said Westmacott.

Armstrong had a great love of children and delighted in giving them treats. 'He was devoted to Master Will and Miss Winnie, the children of Mr and Mrs Watson-Armstrong,' remarked Worsnop. They came into his study every morning and, no matter how busy he was, Armstrong found time to interest himself in their childish conversation. 'The interview always ended by his lordship saying, "Now, Will, bring the bottle," and the little fellow went to the cupboard and brought a bottle of sweets, which his lordship opened and gave one to each of them. Then he would kiss them and resume his work.'

Another example of Armstrong's natural empathy with children was observed during the cold winter of 1891–92, when the 81-year-old master of Cragside was walking through the snow to Rothbury's north lake, where many local villagers liked to skate. Several small boys were sliding too close to the edge of the ice, but when they saw 'his lordship', they stopped. 'He noticed it at once and said, "Go on with your sliding, my boys. Don't let me stop you." Apparently, the kindly suggestion only increased their shyness, so, to make them unconscious of his presence, and put them at ease, he himself began sliding, and invited them to join him, saying, "Come along, boys. We'll soon have a grand slide."'

Along with his abiding love for his mother, to whose memory he built 12 almshouses in Rothbury, Armstrong's humility and respect for his fellow man and woman were the qualities that most impressed Worsnop: 'He was destitute of pride, and unaffectedly simple in his manner, and his geniality and sympathetic nature endeared him to all who had the privilege and honour of his friendship.'

Another astute commentator who fell under the magician's spell during the last decade of his life was Frederick Dolman, a London journalist who visited Cragside and Elswick and published accounts of his experiences in *Ludgate Monthly* and *Osborne* magazines. He saw Cragside as the embodiment of its owner's struggles and triumphs. 'Above and beyond the romance of colour and form,' he wrote, 'there is the romance of science, of hard struggle with nature, of power and determination overcoming seemingly insuperable difficulties.'

Armstrong told Dolman that he now had much less energy than he used to have, and went to Elswick only occasionally, for board meetings and to keep in touch with developments. 'When a man turns eighty I think he is entitled to repose,' he remarked – a thought that prompted him to reflect on the early days at Elswick. 'For the first 15 years, I had a very hard struggle to make headway. During the whole of that time I never had a week's holiday, and many a time I stayed at Elswick all night, working on till ten or eleven when I had some important matter in hand, and then laying down on a couch for a few hours. But it is not hard work that kills – hard work never did anybody much harm; it is worry and anxiety that tell on one.'

Despite Armstrong's protestations, there was remarkably little evidence of a slowing-down in his pace of life or a narrowing in his range of interests. Apart from his business and scientific preoccupations, he had represented Rothbury on Northumberland County Council from 1889 to 1892, and in 1890 he had accepted the presidency of the Natural History Society of Northumberland and Durham – a post he would hold until his death. He continued to attend regular meetings of the Lit & Phil, which he had presided over since 1860. In 1891 he was presented with the Bessemer Medal by the Iron and Steel Institute, since described as 'the Nobel prize of the metallurgical world'. Countless other accolades in recognition of his contributions to science, engineering, and education included honorary degrees from the universities of Oxford, Cambridge, Durham, and Dublin.

Before Dolman left Cragside, Armstrong took his guest through a door beside the drawing-room fireplace to show him the scientific laboratory he had created there, containing all kinds of electrical instruments. 'I am chiefly engaged at present in experiments with high tension – the conversion of a low-tension current into one of high tension,' he explained.

'I suppose in electricity there is almost inexhaustible scope for study and experiment?' asked Dolman.

'Yes. We are little more than at the beginning of the science,' his host replied. 'No one can say what the future of electricity may have in store for us.'

At the end of their conversation, Armstrong agreed to the journalist's request that he might visit Elswick. This was not as straightforward a venture as might have been imagined. Elswick was, as the journalist would discover, 'a domain rather jealously guarded', largely because of the fear of spies. 'They are constantly on the alert for the designing engineer and the enterprising foreigner – the American being more particularly an object of suspicion,' wrote Dolman, who finally managed to penetrate the ring of steel. (The United States had long lagged behind the Old World in its naval capability, and had only recently begun to build a new navy and seek a more ambitious role on the world stage.[2]) Even then, the journalist discovered, there were several 'shops' containing important models and designs which only a few members of Armstrong's staff were ever allowed to enter.

Although the task of inspecting Elswick clearly taxed his stamina and resilience, Dolman managed to convey a vivid impression of what it felt like to be inside the secretive powerhouse of British industry:[3]

'On first entering the engineering shops one has merely an overwhelming impression of the magnitude and variety of the machinery at work, with its deafening multiplicity of noises and many different functions. Steel and iron are being cut, planed, punched and chiselled, as if it were wood, for the smaller parts of cranes, dock-gates, etc. It was in these shops that the great cranes and gates for the Bute Docks at Cardiff were made, including a crane, 280 tons, and 80 feet in height, also the gate weighing 100 tons for the harbour at Malta. As a rule, 1,500 men are employed in this department, which covers 9 acres and contains 300 machines.

'The hydraulic crane was the beginning of the great Elswick firm, but it is in the construction of ordnance, of course, that its greatest fame has been obtained. In this department no fewer than 5,000 men are often employed, some in the immense foundry (90 yards long by 70 yards wide) and the hammer-shed; others in the boring and finishing shops. The largest of their steam-hammers is of 35 tons weight, and to see it pressing a mass of red-hot metal into the shape of a gun is one of the most interesting sights in the Elswick Works. This splendid piece of mechanism, known to the workmen as "Big Ben", is considered to be the finest of its kind. It is so delicately adjusted that it will crack a nut without breaking the kernel, and this with the same power which pulverises tons of metal with a thud that shakes the floor. When the Prince of Wales visited Elswick, nearly ten years ago, he placed his hand under this gigantic tool, and it just touched the flesh, which, with equal facility, it could have crushed. The hammer is worked by three or four men, one regulating the force of the blow, and the others manipulating the burning metal with large tongs, while sparks fly around fast and furiously.

'In the ordnance department are guns in all stages of construction, and the large ones are finished in the same place as they were begun. The smaller ones are finished – polished, browned, and varnished – in a separate shop. Most of those seen being made have been ordered by the British and foreign governments, but at Armstrong's there is always kept a stock of ordnance of different kinds and sizes. It is from the specimens kept in these large galleries that the representatives of the war offices of the world give their orders.'

Although Armstrong's would remain, with Krupp's, one of the two leading armaments companies in the world until the early 20th century, by the late 1890s a new British rival was emerging in the shape of Vickers Brothers, a long-established steel-manufacturer based on the River Don in Sheffield.[4] Tom and Albert Vickers had recently branched out into the production of heavy guns and armour plate, and had prospered in the wake of the Naval Defence Act of 1889, which vastly boosted defence spending. But it was the acquisition in 1897 of a naval yard at Barrow-in-Furness on the Lancashire coast that sealed their fortunes – coupled with the purchase, later that year, of the Maxim–Nordenfeldt company, makers of machine-guns. After buying Barrow, Vickers went from strength to strength, and by 1901 they had two battleships, three cruisers, and some smaller vessels under construction at the yard. That autumn – five years before Krupp built the first German U-boats – Vickers, Sons and Maxim launched the first submarine for the Royal Navy.

Vickers' ambitions, to which the Elswick chieftains were alerted in advance, sparked fears that the Sheffield company might also attempt to buy Whitworth as part of a plot to usurp Armstrong's position as a world leader. On 8 December 1896, Noble wrote to Stuart Rendel: 'You know, I suppose, that the Barrow Naval Armaments Co. has been bought by Vickers, but it turns out that this sale is only part of a syndicate captained by Albert Vickers and backed, I fear, by Rothschild.'

Noble explained that, on hearing the news, he had gone at once to Cragside to consult Armstrong, 'who is more anxious about the matter even than I am'. Armstrong had told Noble of his long-held belief that: 'Whitworth's concern would sooner or later fall into the hands of a company desirous of acquiring gun and armour plate works, with a view of competing with Elswick.' The only answer, it seemed, was for the Armstrong firm itself to enter the fray. 'If Elswick absorbs Whitworth's there will be an end of this danger, and at the same time the present competition will be extinguished, and the prestige of the combined companies will be increased,' wrote Noble. 'There is no time to be lost.'

Far from remaining aloof from the turmoil, Armstrong took an active role in discussions, reinforcing Noble's view in a succession of letters to Stuart Rendel. 'Vickers minus Whitworth's is not to be feared,' he insisted. 'What we gain by absorbing Whitworths is the *duration* of our supremacy, and that is a thing for which we can hardly pay too much.' He also saw that Whitworth's Openshaw works outside Manchester offered good commercial opportunities.[5] Since Joseph Whitworth's death a decade earlier, the works had concentrated on the production of armour plate, for which demand was ever growing. 'The Whitworth shops are very spacious and have room for great extension of plant,' remarked Armstrong. Current overcrowding at Elswick made this particularly attractive.

With the support of Armstrong, Noble, Henry Dyer and, to a lesser extent, Josiah Vavasseur, an agreement with the Whitworth board was endorsed just before Christmas 1896, and the amalgamation was approved a month later, with Armstrong's confirmed as emphatically the dominant partner in the new concern. Although hope of preserving Elswick's industrial pre-eminence would be disappointed in the years leading up to the First World War, the merger frustrated Vickers' expansionist aims while at the same time absorbing an important rival.

The takeover of Whitworth led Henrietta Huxley, the widow of T. H. Huxley, to ask her 'dear friend' Lord Armstrong whether she could invest in the new company. 'If it is a public one, I would like to have some shares in it,' she wrote in an affectionate letter, 'for my lawyer tells me I must invest whatever money comes from the books as copyrights will fall in about four or five years & diminish my income.'

Mrs Huxley continued to take a close interest in the latest scientific developments. 'Is your book out?' she asked. 'It must be delightful for you to be still able to work at electrical experiments. That discovery of Marconi's is grand & stupendous. Surely such a power must put an end to war.' In March 1897, Giuglielmo Marconi, the inventor of wireless telegraphy, had transmitted Morse code signals over a distance of four miles across Salisbury Plain. Later that year, he sent the first ever wireless communications over the open sea.

One Elswick director who had vehemently opposed the Whitworth takeover was Hamilton Rendel, the younger brother of George and Stuart, who complained that Elswick was already too large for effective management. This and other objections were breezily dismissed by Armstrong, who, in a letter to Stuart, questioned Hamilton's qualities as a manager and characterised him as 'habitually opposed to development'. George Rendel was much more positive than his brothers about the amalgamation and wrote to Armstrong from his home in Italy to wish it every success. 'I told Stuart (who was in doubt) long ago that I agreed with your view,' said George. 'Poor Hamilton hurts himself much by his prejudice. At least, however, opposition fortifies and strengthens the right side. You must give him the benefit of this consideration and your forgiveness.'

As a consequence of the merger, Hamilton resigned from the board, ending a 30-year link with Elswick that had begun when he was apprenticed to the firm in 1866. It was only the most obvious sign of the growing acrimony between the Rendels and other Armstrong directors, while the Noble faction continued in the ascendant. But there was a peculiar poignancy in the departure of

Hamilton, who, having suffered from childhood with a debilitating stammer, lacked the social ease and self-confidence of his brothers – for he had been the Elswick engineer most closely associated with one of Armstrong's crowning achievements.

In 1888 an order had been received at Elswick for machinery to operate an 'opening' bridge on the Thames near the Tower of London. As Stuart Rendel recorded in his memoirs, the company had periodically been invited to submit plans for such a structure, but 'when the right moment and the right man coincided', the architect and engineer John Wolfe-Barry, who had succeeded Horace Jones as leader of the project, adopted Elswick's designs for a bascule bridge.[6] The man responsible for the design, building, and installation of the machinery to work the bascules, or opening sections – the most critical and groundbreaking feature of the bridge – was Hamilton Rendel.

When it opened in 1894, Tower Bridge, the largest and most sophisticated bascule bridge ever completed, was hailed as one of the engineering marvels of the age. The bascules, each weighing about 1,000 tons, were operated by hydraulics, using steam to power the gigantic pumping engines. The energy created was stored in six massive accumulators, which fed the engines that drove the bascules up and down. The bascules – which take barely more than a minute to rise to their maximum angle of 86 degrees – are still operated by hydraulic power, but since 1976 they have been driven by oil and electricity rather than steam. During its early life, the bridge used to be raised about 50 times a day, but is now raised fewer than 1,000 times a year. Elswick's original pumping engines, accumulators, and boilers form part of a permanent exhibition in the Victorian Engine Rooms.

Although Armstrong's relations with the older Rendel brothers had apparently cooled in the early 1880s, he continued to correspond regularly with both George and Stuart on both personal and business matters. Ensconced as manager of the Pozzuoli works, George lived with his second wife and young family at Posillipo, near Naples, where he had purchased the sumptuous Villa Maraval. Like Stuart, George would gain a reputation as a generous host.

In early 1897, shortly after the Whitworth takeover, it was Armstrong's sad task to attend the funeral of their sister Fanny, Lady Bowen, whom he had once treated like a daughter. Not well enough to travel from Italy, George wrote soon afterwards to thank Uncle W. for his unwavering love and support for the whole family: 'Although I am sure your old and constant friendship for her took you to her bedside and to her grave, yet I think all of us who have shared that affection owe you another debt of gratitude for such a mark of it, and I venture to tell you how much I for my part feel what you did for her.'

By this time, Armstrong's earlier fondness for Fanny had been supplanted by his interest in Winnie Watson-Armstrong, the wife of his great-nephew and heir. Soon after the couple's marriage in 1889, Armstrong had invited Winnie to officiate at the launch of an Elswick-built cruiser, *Pandora*, for the Australian government. Since then, she had given birth to two children, a son and a daughter, thereby assuring the Armstrong succession.

Winnie shared Armstrong's interests in gardening and fishing, and used to accompany him on expeditions on the Coquet, when the old man would reminisce about his days as the Kingfisher. He once told her that he had been so 'delicate' in his youth and early manhood that no insurance company would insure his life. 'He used often to smile over the money he saved to himself and lost to the insurance offices,' wrote Winnie, commenting on his remarkable longevity. 'He always said it was the pure bracing air of Rothbury that saved him.'

By the time Winnie Watson-Armstrong became mistress of Cragside in 1901, she had developed a deep and abiding love for the estate. 'At all times of the year Cragside is beautiful, but perhaps more so in the spring and autumn,' she wrote in a magazine article.[7] 'There are no fewer than one hundred varieties of rhododendron of every shade and hue, sixty varieties of hardy heathers which have spread into many acres; and in the early autumn the rich colouring of the red heathers, mingling with the white, spreading for miles, is a sight not easily to be forgotten.' She praised the five lakes that Armstrong had created on the estate, 'which gleam like silver mirrors framed with jewels', as well as 'the masses of double sweet-scented gorse, weigela, Alpine rose, and thousands of rock plants in addition to the large plantations of conifers'. More than 1,700 acres had been covered in trees and shrubs. 'Practically none of these has perished, testifying to Lord Armstrong's care in, firstly, choosing plants that he knew would be congenial to the soil and, secondly, to the manner of planting.' He took the keenest interest in the gardening and forestry work, she wrote, every detail being submitted to him for approval.

William Armstrong died at Cragside shortly after 1pm on 27 December 1900, probably from pneumonia. He had been unwell for several weeks and was nursed through his final illness by a resident nurse, Nora Ainsworth, for whom he had made generous provision in his will. Four days later, on what was then regarded as the last day of the 19th century, he was buried beside Meggie in Rothbury churchyard, in a tranquil spot overlooking the Coquet – his original 'river of pleasure'.

Despite the large crowds gathered in Rothbury for the occasion, his funeral was marked by extreme simplicity. 'The usual trappings of mourning were entirely dispensed with,' noted a local reporter, and a farm trolley drawn by two cart-horses was used instead of a hearse.[8] In the centre, on a purple cloth, lay the coffin, covered with floral tributes, and behind came another cart with upright sides about a foot high; also draped in purple, this was filled with wreaths and more flowers. The pallbearers were workers from Elswick and tenants from the Cragside and Bamburgh estates, and the service was conducted by the Bishop of Newcastle. 'Of the multitude who came to Rothbury Church from far and near, every soul seemed to feel that it had lost a friend, and that its duty was to bear itself respectfully on that eventful day,' said the reporter. 'There was not a single hitch nor a loud word, because reverence for the memory of Lord Armstrong ruled the mind of every visitor.'

The previous evening, in a service at St Aidan's in Benwell, not far from Elswick Works, the Reverend H. Bott had devoted his Sunday address to the death of Lord Armstrong. After dwelling on his subject's many qualities, Bott said that the church itself owed its existence to him. 'I am addressing many who will remember the time when all around here was fields. Then, as if with the wave of a magician's wand, that bright intellect flashed forth its wondrous rays – and forthwith sprang up streets and houses in untold and ever-increasing numbers to shelter those who worked out his plans and put into operation his researches and discoveries.' When an appeal was raised for St Aidan's, Armstrong had been the first to make a generous donation towards its building and upkeep. 'Many of you who have worked 30, 40, ay nearly 50 years in the great Elswick Works will know him far better than I, but I feel that I have lost a true friend and the parish a staunch supporter,' said Bott. 'England has lost one of her most talented sons, and Northumbria her most famous scion.'

Although the Duke of Northumberland was among the mourners at Rothbury, another local aristocrat, Sir Edward Grey, later Viscount Grey of Falloden, had been prevented by injury from attending. Grey wrote to the Watson-Armstrongs expressing regret that he had been unable to stand beside the grave of 'the Great Northumbrian' and reminiscing about the talks he had had with Armstrong over the years. Grey expressed relief that Armstrong had died with his mental faculties intact: 'I like to think of him going down with his beautiful lucid intellect still undimmed at the close too of the century to whose triumphal progress he had contributed so much.'

Armstrong left £1.4 million in his will, which in today's money would be worth about £80 million. He was reckoned to have spent another £1m on the restoration of Bamburgh Castle.

'More almost than any other man, he *was* the 19th century, epitomising in himself that age of scientific discovery, industrial development, philanthropy and liberalism – in which, while being one of its great figures, he also displayed the simple tastes of one who, throughout his long life, was always a country lover,' wrote the Elswick historian A. R. Fairbairn. 'When he died, the firm which he had founded was at the zenith of its commercial career, paying a dividend of four shillings on its £1 shares; it was really the end of an epoch. Never again will it be possible for one man to amass such great wealth, until, it may be, this civilization goes down into the dust of its predecessors, and mankind begins again the Sisyphus-task of rediscovering the arts and sciences, and some future Armstrong applies such a simple principle of power-application as hydraulics to the service of man.'

Henry Palin Gurney, the principal of the Durham College of Science in Newcastle (later Armstrong College), remarked that no man had been more closely identified than Armstrong with the utilisation of natural forces to the service of man. His fame had spread through many nations: 'Obituary notices in every language known to civilization proved that the whole world felt poorer by his death.'

21

Rise and Fall of an Empire

By the time of Armstrong's death in 1900, the small hydraulics manufacturing firm he had established on the north bank of the Tyne half a century earlier had evolved into a dominant global shipbuilding concern. In 1889 Armstrong Mitchell had been the sixth biggest builder in Britain; during the next decade it periodically occupied first place. And Armstrong's was more fully integrated than any comparable business. The firm's pre-eminence in arms production was highlighted in 1896 by the weapons expert Charles Orde Browne. 'All the war stores made in all the private establishments in England put together would be a small quantity compared with those made at Elswick,' wrote Orde Browne, who went on to identify the works as 'perhaps the only establishment in the world that will turn out a first-class man-of-war complete with all her armament, the armour and engines only being made outside of Elswick itself'.[1] In 1881 the firm had employed some 4,000 people; 20 years later the total was nearer 25,000. The profits for 1883 were £144,000; by 1900 they had grown to £664,000.[2]

As pressure on space at Elswick continued to grow after the merger with Whitworth, more land was acquired at Scotswood, a mile upriver from the original site, and new facilities were built there, including a brass foundry, shell shops, an explosives factory, saw mills and, eventually, a motor-car department. To all outward appearances, the company was flourishing – but internally it was clear that the founder's death had lifted the lid on a steaming cauldron of boardroom animosities.

Andrew Noble, knighted in 1893 in recognition of his pioneering scientific work, succeeded to the chairmanship of Armstrong Whitworth in 1901 and, with the backing of his sons

John and Saxton, set about consolidating his hold on the firm. The largest shareholder in Armstrong Whitworth was now Stuart Rendel, who became vice-chairman after Armstrong's death, but continued to feel irked that his family's position had been undermined, and may even have believed that he still had a chance of wresting control of the company from Noble. Stuart's elder brother George, the brilliant naval engineer who had won Armstrong's affection in his youth, and his younger brother Hamilton, who had engineered the machinery for Tower Bridge, both died in 1902, and soon afterwards Stuart made his hostility plain. He warned that, if the Nobles secured exclusive control at Elswick, it would be only a matter of time before the firm would be taken over by its greatest rivals, Vickers.[3]

Stuart had political interests to divert him from battles in the business world. Since entering the House of Commons in 1880 as Liberal MP for Montgomeryshire, he had championed Welsh nationalist causes and became widely known at Westminster as 'the member for Wales'.[4] An early friendship with William Ewart Gladstone was cemented by the marriage of his daughter Maud to Gladstone's son Harry in 1890. A man who liked to describe himself as 'half man of culture, half man of the workshop', Stuart lived in rather grand style, with houses in London and Surrey, acquiring the large Hatchlands estate in 1887.[5] He also bought Château de Thorenc in Cannes, which became a famous rendezvous for politicians and socialites, and spent every winter there from 1894 to 1912.

One of Gladstone's last acts before retiring had been to grant Stuart Rendel a peerage – but, although he had been linked politically with Gladstone for 14 years, and the two men were close friends until Gladstone's death in 1898, Rendel never held ministerial office under him. The prime minister once told Rendel that he thought such an appointment would have been incompatible with his interests at Elswick.[6] When Gladstone received a state funeral at Westminster Abbey on 28 May 1898, the Prince of Wales (the future Edward VII) led the ten pallbearers; among the others were the Duke of York (the future George V) and Lord Rendel of Hatchlands.

In the years leading up to the First World War, the only other surviving Rendel brother was Sir Alexander Meadows (Med), the head of the family firm founded by their father, James Meadows, in 1838. Although Stuart and Med were both dead by the end of the war, the Rendel engineering connection survived until the late 20th century through the firm of Rendel Palmer and Tritton, designers of, among many other iconic structures, the Thames Flood Barrier.[7]

Andrew Noble kept his autocratic inclinations concealed during Armstrong's lifetime and never contradicted his master, according to Stuart Rendel.[8] Meanwhile, he maintained a ferocious pace of work, as recorded by his wife, Margery, who listed his activities in London on 9 March 1898, allegedly a typical day: 'In the morning at 10.30 a clerk came with letters and telegrams; 11.30 Chinese Embassy, where he received the Order of the Double Dragon; 12 o'clock saw the Controller of the Navy; 12.15 Sir Baldwin Walker; 1 o'clock Commander in Chief; 1.30 Foreign Office; 2 o'clock American Embassy; 2.30 Physical Laboratory; 5 o'clock Sir Frederick Richards; 5.30 to see George in Curzon Street; 6 o'clock sending telegrams; 6.30 to see George Rendel; 7.15 dinner; 8.15 to Newcastle from King's Cross.'[9]

Although Armstrong apparently admired Noble's 'exclusive devotion' to the firm and was alienated by 'the comparative failure of the Rendels to live for nothing but Elswick',[10] he remained a loyal friend to the Rendel brothers, and usually respected their views on business matters. 'During [Armstrong's] lifetime, Noble established no special authority at the board,' wrote Rendel, but after Armstrong's death a complete change took place, with board meetings and company operations quickly degenerating into a 'discreditable farce'. Combining the roles of chairman and managing director, Noble was rude and bullying to his fellow managers and seemed have a shaky grip on the company's finances. 'Elswick is in a bad way, there is no mistake about it,' wrote William Cruddas, the financial director, to Stuart Rendel. 'The sums that have been recently lost by incompetence I believe you have some idea of, and Elswick cannot bear such losses much longer.'[11] The business historian Clive Trebilcock was especially critical of the Noble regime, describing it as 'a jealous and exclusive autocracy by a family interest group of definitely wayward tendencies', which should be condemned for 'costly errors in shipyard expansion' and in 'ill-judged experiments with motor-car production'.[12]

Despite the tensions inside the company, which would rumble on for a long time, Armstrong Whitworth continued to thrive in the years leading up to the First World War, and Andrew Noble was never reticent about drawing public attention to the firm's awesome manufacturing capability. 'It is not too much to say that from our Elswick yard alone we could, if need be, deliver three Dreadnoughts completed in 2½ years from the date of the order,' he asserted in April 1909, 'and could further continue delivering at the rate of three vessels each 15 subsequent months.'[13]

Meanwhile, however, Vickers were steadily gaining ground on their rivals – and, in some areas, overtaking them. The Vickers historian J. D. Scott lays part of the blame for the relative decline of Armstrong Whitworth at the door of its founder, suggesting that Armstrong's immense riches and widespread fame had diverted him from the more important task of running his business. 'To the end of his life he continued to lavish money upon his estate at Cragside,' wrote Scott, 'creating and recreating landscape like an 18th-century nobleman or one of his own American millionaire contemporaries of the Gilded Age'. Numbered among this group were Cornelius Vanderbilt, John D. Rockefeller, Andrew Carnegie and J. P. Morgan. Like these men, Armstrong had moved towards the political right in later life, according to Scott, and developed a dislike of trade unions. 'Yet, despite his heroic measures at Cragside, and despite his detestation of the unions, Armstrong was not really a figure of the Gilded Age,' wrote Scott. To the end of his life, he retained the appearance of 'romantic melancholy' captured by the painter James Ramsay in his subject's youth, and there was a remoteness in his temperament that impressed people. Scott gives a perceptive explanation of Armstrong's success in overcoming the obstacles that might have been put in his way by the British class system: 'He had the gift, so important in British public life, of not seeming to try too hard – and this contributed to the position which the Armstrong firm enjoyed of being something more than a commercial organization, something more like a national institution.'

In the early years of the 20th century, the Elswick Works occupied a frontage along the Tyne of one and a half miles and covered well over 300 acres.[14] In 1907 the number of employees was 25,300 and the annual wages bill was £1,672,000.[15] But, as the expansion in shipbuilding gathered pace in the years before the First World War, it was clear that the shipyard at Elswick would not be enough to fulfil future requirements – and that the new generation of battleships would be too wide to pass between the piers of Newcastle's Swing Bridge. So the firm decided to build a new and larger yard further down the Tyne at High Walker, near the original Mitchell establishment, where a bend in the river would allow the safe launch of ships up to 1,000 feet long.

By the time the Walker Naval Yard opened in 1912, the prosperity and fame of Sir W. G. Armstrong Whitworth & Co. had acquired legendary status. 'The works was one of the sights of Newcastle and the name of Armstrong was used almost as an incantation,' wrote Fairbairn. The company's capital was £6¾ million, and the £1 shares were valued at 45 shillings. It was recognised that this had been built up on 'the genius of its inventors, the masterly management of its chiefs, and the abiding skill of its workmen'; these things remained, and the firm was thought to be, 'as safe as the Bank of England'.

By 1918, there were 78,000 people on the payroll of Armstrong Whitworth, with a wages bill of £1,000,000 a week – but, when wartime production ceased, the demand for Elswick armaments evaporated overnight. The company was faced with a completely new set of problems, and there had been changes in top management.

After relinquishing active control of the company in 1911, Andrew Noble had died in October 1915 at Ardkinglas, the retreat he had built for himself on Loch Fyne in the Scottish Highlands. His successor as chairman was the unlikely character of John Meade Falkner, an academic and writer, who had once acted as tutor to the Noble children. Falkner is better known today for his literary accomplishments, particularly as the author of the 1898 adventure story *Moonfleet*, featuring Blackbeard's diamond. 'The ordinary Elswick man regarded him as slightly queer because he wrote novels,' remarked Fairbairn.

In the event, Falkner's tenure lasted only five years before he was replaced in 1920 by Glyn West, with John Noble as vice-chairman. That year, the dividend paid by the company fell from 12.5 per cent to 10 per cent, and the following year fell again, this time to 5 per cent. During the following three years of economic depression the dividend stood at 5 per cent, but it disappeared altogether in 1926. 'It was with a feeling of dismay that the country watched the decline of the industrial giant whose stability had for two generations been taken for granted,' wrote Fairbairn. 'The value of the shares, which had been worth 45 shillings a few years earlier, sank to precisely nothing.' Attempts to diversify into locomotive building and the manufacture of turbines for hydroelectric schemes around the world had both ended in costly failure.

Even the booming motor-car and aeroplane divisions could do little to prop up the expiring leviathan. Within a few years of its first appearance in 1906, the Armstrong Whitworth had established itself as one of the leading makes of car – based on the reputation that it was 'built like a battleship'[19] – but it was after the merger in 1919 with the Siddeley-Deasy Motor Company that this branch of the firm really prospered. Over a period of 40 years, until production ceased in 1960, a long succession of Armstrong Siddeley cars came to represent the epitome of British motoring style. During the interwar years, Armstrong Siddeley also built aero-engines and aeroplanes, and subsidiary companies were set up, such as Armstrong Whitworth Aircraft, absorbed in 1935 into the Hawker Siddeley Aircraft Company (although surviving as a separate division until 1963). In a surprising but satisfying twist of history, the founder and chairman of Hawker Siddeley was T. O. M. (Tommy) Sopwith, a grandson of Armstrong's great friend and mentor, the diarist Thomas Sopwith. In 1936 Tommy Sopwith became chairman of Armstrong Siddeley Motors.

At the end of 1927, as the economic crisis worsened, Armstrong Whitworth and Vickers – great historical rivals both fighting for survival – had no choice but to merge most of their businesses, forming the jointly owned Vickers-Armstrongs Ltd. Resurgent a few years later under the direction of two former navy commanders,

Charles Craven and, later, Robert Micklem, Vickers-Armstrongs embarked in the mid-1930s on a huge modernisation and investment programme. Armstrong Whitworth finally went into liquidation in 1941, having sold its holdings in the merged company to Vickers Ltd a few years earlier.

The astronomical output of Vickers-Armstrongs during the Second World World is illustrated in figures compiled by A. R. Fairbairn: '33,000 guns and gun barrels, 860 naval mountings, 3,500 gun carriages, 1.25 million shells and bombs, 11 million cartridge cases, 16 million fuses, 39,000 high-pressure air and oxygen cylinders, 23,000 aircraft undercarriages, and 3,500 tanks'. At the same time, with its yards at Barrow and Walker, the firm continued to ride high as one of the world's most important warship manufacturers, while also asserting authority in the air with its Wellington bombers and Supermarine Spitfires. 'It is almost certainly no exaggeration to say that without Vickers-Armstrongs the Second World War could not have been won,' said the public relations adviser Harold Evans, who wrote a history of the company.

As part of a radical consolidation of British shipbuilding in the 1960s, the Vickers Naval Yard at High Walker was absorbed by Swan Hunter Shipbuilders, a new firm combining all the shipbuilding interests on the Tyne. Swan Hunter invested £16 million in modernising their plant to produce cargo vessels, bulk carriers, oil tankers, and container ships of all sizes, as well as naval ships for the Ministry of Defence – but, on 1 July 1977, the company was nationalised under the Aircraft and Shipbuilding Industries Act, becoming part of British Shipbuilders. Although Swan Hunter was later returned to the private sector, and survives today as part of BAE Systems Submarines, the Walker Naval Yard closed down in the 1980s. A 145-year-old tradition of shipbuilding on the Tyne ended in April 2009, when the last surviving Swan Hunter cranes were dismantled at Wallsend for transport to India.

In 1960 the Vickers aviation division became part of the newly formed British Aircraft Corporation (BAC). BAC was nationalised in 1977, and renamed British Aerospace (BAe), but privatised again three years later by the new Conservative administration under Margaret Thatcher. A complicated sequence of mergers and takeovers followed. In 1999 BAe bought Marconi Electronic Systems to form BAE Systems. In the same year, Rolls-Royce acquired Vickers plc (what remained of Vickers-Armstrongs after the nationalisation of its aviation, shipbuilding, and steel interests) for its marine engines and turbines business. Rolls-Royce then sold Vickers Defence Systems (manufacturer of tanks and other military vehicles) to Alvis plc in 2002 – which then became Alvis Vickers, the largest armoured-vehicle company in the UK. Alvis Vickers was acquired by BAE Systems in 2004 and became BAE Systems Land Systems (Weapons & Vehicles) – and the once-proud name of Vickers finally disappeared from the annals of British business history.

While Armstrong's business empire rolled on after his death under its own powerful momentum, his personal legacy was left to a more unpredictable fate. William Watson-Armstrong inherited most of his great-uncle's vast fortune as well as the estates of Cragside and Bamburgh Castle, totalling more than 17,000 acres, and set out to continue his noble ancestor's tradition of philanthropy, contributing in particular £100,000 to the building of Newcastle's Royal Victoria Infirmary. Armstrong's title had died with him in 1900, but three years later Watson-Armstrong was ennobled as the first Baron Armstrong of the second creation, his full title being Baron Armstrong of Bamburgh and Cragside. The new baron, his wife, Winnie, and their two children lived for the most part at Cragside, which Winnie had grown to love, but they also spent long periods at Bamburgh, occupying an apartment in the keep, especially at Easter and during the winter-ball season.

William (Willie) Watson-Armstrong had joined the Elswick board following the merger of Armstrong and Whitworth in 1897, but it was soon clear that he was not cut out for a business career. Stuart Rendel originally had high hopes for the new recruit, but they were not fulfilled. When Andrew Noble fell seriously ill in 1906, at the age of 75, there was urgent discussion about who, if necessary, might take over as chairman. Noble's sons Saxton and John, while clearly able, were not regarded as ready to lead a mighty concern such as Armstrong Whitworth – and everyone agreed that Watson-Armstrong was inadequate for the job. (In the event, Noble recovered and continued at the helm of Armstrong Whitworth for five more years.) The new baron 'has a sadly easy command of second-rate abilities, and this he loves to exercise', wrote Stuart Rendel in a forthright correspondence with other board members.[17] He was 'a good, upright, kindhearted, excellent fellow' – but these were seen as liabilities for the leader of Elswick. 'If he were a worse fellow,' said Rendel, 'he might be less easily made use of by inferior men.' In January 1908 Watson-Armstrong wrote a letter to *The Times*, from Roquebrune in the south of France, insisting that, contrary to popular belief, he was not head of Armstrong Whitworth and had never taken part in its management. Later that year he was forced off the board, in Rendel's words, 'for the good of the company'.

More seriously, it appeared that the new Lord Armstrong's gullibility had led him into some highly dubious business ventures, and within eight years of coming into his inheritance he was spending a great deal of time in the bankruptcy courts, trying to reclaim thousands of pounds he had unwisely lent to speculators. A scheme to publish a society magazine called *The Throne*, containing contributions from 'persons of social influence and importance', soon came to grief, leaving him with debts of more than £10,000.[18] In September 1908, he was suing a syndicate for the return of £40,000 invested in a large automobile concern in France. He also lost a substantial sum in the Lemoine case, a contemporary *cause célèbre* involving a French fraudster called Henri Lemoine, who claimed to be able to make synthetic diamonds. In a similar case in December 1909 – a few months after the death of his father, Johnny – he forfeited £108,398 lent to a Brighton man called Mr Cardinall for use in 'joint undertakings relating to a process for the manufacture of diamonds'. The consequence of all this profligacy was that, within a decade of his great-uncle's death, Lord Armstrong was reckoned to have debts amounting to half a million pounds.

Urgent measures were required to raise funds, and the sale of possessions seemed the only solution. First under the hammer was the herd of shorthorn cattle that had been fondly nurtured by his great-uncle for over a quarter of a century. The sale of 48 cows and calves raised 2,500 guineas, and ten bulls were sold for 615 guineas. In the summer of 1910, the London auctioneers Christie's held two sales of 'Armstrong heirlooms', one covering Chippendale furniture and a large quantity of porcelain, including Ming vases and other gifts from grateful clients, and the other all the paintings at Cragside thought to have any real value. The second sale included two Constables, three Turners, two Leightons, and the two paintings by Millais that had been acquired with such excitement in 1875, *Jephthah's Daughter* and *Chill October*, as well as works by Landseer, Burne-Jones, Bonheur and many others. The sale of 102 lots raised a total of £28,528 15s. 6d.[20]

The large shortfall was presumably made up by sales of land – the Bamburgh and Cragside estates were both much reduced over the years – and in the event it proved unnecessary to dispose of the furniture and other interior accoutrements installed at Cragside by Richard Norman Shaw and his collaborators. The fact that almost all the original contents remained in the house proved a huge boon when it was taken over by the National Trust in the 1970s. Very few High Victorian houses complete with their contents can still be found in Britain, and Cragside is regarded by many as the most important surviving example.

The Armstrongs were struck by personal tragedy in March 1912 when their 17-year-old daughter Winifred died suddenly from meningitis. Winnie, Lady Armstrong, who had been away in France at the time of her child's death, apparently never recovered from the loss. She herself died two years later at the age of only 54. Perhaps mercifully, Winnie did not live to see her son, William John Montagu, severely wounded during the First World War, at Ypres on the Western Front.

Willie, Lord Armstrong outlived not only Winnie but also his second wife, Beatrice Cowx, a former governess to the Armstrong children who had been resident at Cragside for several years before her marriage in 1916. After Beatrice's death in 1934, Willie was married for a third time – on this occasion, to Kathleen England, 35 years his junior. His sole surviving child, William John Montagu, succeeded to his father's estates and titles in October 1941, and would eventually pass on the baton to *his* only son, who became the 3rd Baron Armstrong of Bamburgh and Cragside.

Shortly after the end of the Second World War, the third baron, popularly known as Weir, had married a glamorous Italian divorcée, Baroness Maria Teresa Chiodelli Manzoni, but since there were no children of the union, the Armstrong title again became extinct on his death in 1987. The couple's adopted children, Francis and Isabella Watson-Armstrong, acceded to the family estates.

In 1977 the Armstrong family had been obliged to transfer Cragside and much of its remaining land to the National Trust in lieu of death duties. From that time, their main residence has been Bamburgh Castle, where the last baroness lived out the rest of her life, and which is still owned by the Watson-Armstrongs. Archaeological digs are regularly conducted at the castle and in the surrounding area, and its dramatic architecture and geographical location have acted as a magnet for film directors ranging from Ken Russell to Shekhar Kapur. In recent years, parts of the castle have been let as private apartments, although other areas are open to the public, including the Great Kitchen, the King's Hall, the Captain's Lodging, and part of the keep, including the Armoury. Dr John Sharp's library has been moved to Durham, and now forms the Bamburgh Collection in Durham University Library.

When the Farne Islands, part of the original Bamburgh purchase, were put up for sale in 1924, the ornithologist Sir George Noble, a son of Andrew Noble, launched a campaign for their preservation as a bird sanctuary. He was enthusiastically supported by Lord Grey of Falloden, who argued that, as the northernmost breeding ground of the sandwich tern and the southernmost of the eider duck, the Farnes were 'one of the most remarkable and wonderful breeding places for seabirds in the British Islands'. A public appeal raised the £2,200 needed to buy the islands from the Armstrong family and their joint owner, the Reverend Charles Thorpe. They were given to the National Trust, and have since been designated a National Nature Reserve. Apart from the important colony of grey seals, producing about a thousand pups each year, the Farnes now sustain more than 73,000 pairs of breeding seabirds.

Cragside has flourished under the guardianship of the National Trust, especially because the house and grounds have been deeply loved and cherished by those entrusted with their care. In the early days, the house manager, Sheila Pettit, took great pains, with the help of the Victoria and Albert Museum, to track down the original wallpapers and furnishing fabrics chosen by William and Meggie Armstrong and have them reinstalled in the correct locations.

In more recent times, the entire house was rewired using 30 miles of cable – and some of Armstrong's original electrical fittings were found in the process. The rock gardens were gradually rescued from the vegetation that had grown up and smothered them over many years, and the cascades constructed there by Armstrong were put back into working order. The elegant iron footbridge that soars across the Debdon Burn was dismantled, repaired and reconstructed for public use. Major restoration works are being carried out on the original power house to install a new hydroelectric plant to generate power for the house and the estate. The site of the formal gardens, where the six great glass-houses once stood, came into the National Trust's possession later than the main acquisition, and this too has now been returned to its former glory.

Cragside is a hive of activity, as it was in Armstrong's day, and there is a sense in which, even though there is no family in residence, the house and gardens are thoroughly inhabited. The spirit of Cragside's creators lives on in its lakes and burns and waterfalls, in its trees and ferns, and in its electric lights and extraordinary labour-saving devices, which were so in advance of their time. Some National Trust staff, such as Anthony Adam, have hinted at a more material presence. 'Sometimes, when I'm in there on my own in the evening or at night, in the dark, I seem to hear noises – people – a lot of chatter going on in the dining room,' reported Adam.[21] 'I suppose people raise their eyebrows when I say this, but it's quite true. When I listen hard, there's nothing, but it's really very clear to me, and I even walk through the corridor behind us to have a peer into the room – I have a light on – to see if there really is something going on. It's nothing frightening. It's really very pleasant – a pleasant atmosphere.' His experience recalls Armstrong's remarks to a friend when reflecting in old age on what Cragside had meant to him: 'I feel certain that, had there been no Cragside, I shouldn't have been talking to you today – for it's been my very life.'

Why Armstrong did not become a national treasure in the mould of a Nelson or a Churchill remains a mystery. Although he never donned a uniform or became a politician, he had many of the other necessary qualities. In both life and death, he was held in the highest esteem not only by his fellow Britons but also by people of high and low estate around the globe. He was perceived above all as a patriot. It was for his patriotism in handing over his gun patents to the government, in the wake of the humiliation in the Crimea, that he was given a knighthood. And it was for his patriotism in promoting his country's industrial and commercial might, and helping to maintain its seemingly unassailable position as an imperial power, that he was invited by the Queen to join the House of Lords in 1887.

William Armstrong was never part of the British establishment, nor did he want to be. Although admitted in 1859 to the Athenaeum Club – 'brought in as one of the eminently distinguished', in the words of its president – he had none of the advantages that might have been expected of a member of the ruling elite. He had no regular Oxford or Cambridge degree, nor even a public school education, let alone an aristocratic lineage. He grew up in a world where high-ranking engineers in the army were looked down upon by 'gentlemen' officers because they were part of the non-purchase corps – that is, they had not paid for their commissions. Envy and surprise at the meteoric rise of this unconventional, non-military upstart was a major cause of the bitter battles over the first Armstrong gun.

Armstrong's typical northern reticence reinforced public perception of him as an outsider. While showing a fierce pride in their region's natural and man-made advantages when on home territory, the people of north-east England are notoriously reluctant to promote themselves to the wider world – and 'Newcastle's greatest citizen', as *The Times* described him, was no exception. Armstrong was much happier enveloped in the dust and clamour of

Elswick Works or puzzling over conundrums in his laboratory at Cragside than when exposed to the public gaze.

It was his genius as a scientist, engineer, and businessman that lifted him head and shoulders above most of his contemporaries, as well as his magnetic ability to communicate his discoveries in a way that ordinary people could understand – a quality identified after his death by Lord Grey of Falloden, who had enjoyed many philosophical discussions with the maestro. 'I remember now with the feeling of gratitude I experienced at the time,' wrote Grey, 'my delight at his conversation, in which beamed forth kindness, eagerness, tolerance for my stupidity – and the power which belongs only to the elect of making the obscure and complex appear simple and intelligible to the dullest ignoramus.'

But Armstrong came to greatest prominence at a time when science and engineering were going out of fashion in Britain. The romantic view of science which had taken hold in the mid-18th century, and gathered pace in the early part of Victoria's reign with the encouragement of the Prince Consort, had been sullied by the revelations of Charles Darwin, and scientists had come to be seen by many as subversive, even potentially dangerous. Engineers – who in the heyday of Telford, Stephenson, and Brunel had been swathed in an aura of glamour – were now ever more closely associated with the evil consequences of the industrial revolution such as mass urban deprivation and desecration of the landscape. This perception intensified in the 1920s, when Brunel and his tribe were portrayed by the literary elite of the day as among the lowest of the low.

While the reputations of Brunel, Darwin, and others were revived in the later 20th century with the help of their descendants, Armstrong had no such champion to fight his corner. His childlessness left its own legacy in the form of public forgetfulness. Indeed, Willie Watson-Armstrong's troubles with money and other family crises meant that the name Armstrong was not always one to boast about.

There was also a political aspect to this collective amnesia, for, with the inexorable rise of communism and fascism, the wisdom of Britain's long imperial adventure was coming under ever closer scrutiny. As Armstrong himself had acknowledged, the industrial giant he had created on the Tyne was intricately bound up with his country's world dominance – and, once a sense of imperial guilt took hold in the nation at large, his reputation was bound to suffer. Moreover, he was an arms manufacturer – a fact that periodically exposed him and the companies that bore his name to hatred and revulsion.

During Armstrong's lifetime and through the early part of the 20th century, the prevailing wisdom had been that the best hope of peace lay in maintaining strong defence – an argument that Armstrong himself passionately endorsed and used on many occasions to fend off attacks on his integrity. But, even before his death, there were widespread rumblings about the morality of the arms trade and the men who made fortunes from it – a situation satirised by George Bernard Shaw in his 1905 play *Major Barbara*. The critics became especially vociferous during the 1930s, when Vickers-Armstrongs was among those firms condemned as 'merchants of death' in a hugely influential international bestseller of that title by H. C. Engelbrecht and F. C. Hanigen.[22]

All these factors combined to undermine the memory of Armstrong's achievements and his lasting contribution to human civilisation, with the result that he has been subtly airbrushed out of history. All of his speeches and writings, and many of the books and articles written about him, have been allowed to go out of print, depriving readers of access to a great visionary of the 19th century. Not before time, this is beginning to change. Now, more than ever, we need to share his confidence in humanity's abiding capacity for salvation and renewal. 'As in the vegetable kingdom, fit conditions of soil and climate quickly cause the appearance of plants, so in the intellectual world fitness of time and circumstance promptly call forth appropriate devices,' he wrote in the Admirable Speech of 1863. 'The seeds of invention exist, as it were, in the air, ready to germinate whenever suitable conditions arise, and no legislative interference is needed to ensure their growth in proper season.' Only armed with such insights shall we be able to set out with any hope of success on a voyage to explore 'the immensity that lies beyond'.

Notes

Chapter 1 (pp.1–14)

1. From a BBC radio programme marking the opening of Cragside by the National Trust on 5 June 1979.
2. This and many other details of the royal visit of 1884 are drawn from the *Record of the Visit of their Royal Highnesses the Prince and Princess of Wales to Tyneside, August 1884*, compiled by the Town Clerk of Newcastle upon Tyne and published by Andrew Reid, Newcastle, 1885.
3. *Newcastle Weekly Courant*, 22 August 1884.
4. *The Times*, 20 August 1884.
5. *ibid*.
6. Richardson, John Wigham (1811) *Memoirs 1837–1908*, Glasgow: Hopkins.
7. Warren, Kenneth (1989) *Armstrongs of Elswick: Growth in Engineering and Armaments to the Merger with Vickers*, London: Macmillan.
8. Jones, Evan Rowland (1886) *Heroes of Industry*, London: Sampson Low.

Chapter 2 (pp.15–30)

1. Charleton, R. J. (1890) *A History of Newcastle-on-Tyne: From the Earliest Records to its Formation as a City*, Newcastle upon Tyne: William H. Robinson.
2. Cited in Welford, Richard (1895) *Men of Mark 'Twixt Tyne and Tweed*, London and Newcastle upon Tyne: Walter Scott.
3. Worsnop, John 'The Late Lord Armstrong, His Association with Rothbury', *Newcastle Daily Journal*, 28 December 1900.
4. Jones, Evan Rowland (1886) *Heroes of Industry*, London: Sampson Low.
5. Kemp, Laurie (1997) *Woodside*, Wreay, Cumbria: Courtyard Press.
6. Hughes, Edward (1963) (ed.) *The Diaries and Correspondence of James Losh*, London: Bernard Quaritch.

7. Watson, Robert Spence (1897) *The History of the Literary and Philosophical Society of Newcastle-upon-Tyne, 1793–1896*, London and Newcastle: Walter Scott.

8. Armstrong, Anne (junior), *To the Lakes*, an unpublished journal.

9. Welford, *op. cit.*

10. *ibid.*

11. Cochrane, Alfred (1909) *The Early History of Elswick*, Newcastle upon Tyne: Mawson Swan and Morgan.

12. Welford, *op. cit.*

Chapter 3 (pp.31–45)

1. Lamb, Charles 'The Old Benchers of the Middle Temple', one of his *Essays of Elia*, published in the early 1820s.

2. Dickens, Charles (1837) *The Posthumous Papers of the Pickwick Club*, London: Chapman and Hall.

3. Horsley, John Callcott (1903) *Recollections of a Royal Academician*, London: John Murray.

4. Watson, Robert Spence (1897) *The History of the Literary and Philosophical Society of Newcastle-upon-Tyne, 1793–1896*, London and Newcastle: Walter Scott.

5. Jones, Evan Rowland (1886) *Heroes of Industry*, London: Sampson Low.

6. Cochrane, Alfred (1909) *The Early History of Elswick*, Newcastle upon Tyne: Mawson Swan and Morgan.

7. Jones, *op. cit.*

8. Latimer, John (1846) *Local Collections, or Records of Remarkable Events Connected with the Borough of Gateshead*, Newcastle upon Tyne.

9. Morrell, Jack and Thackray, Arnold (1981) *Gentlemen of Science: Early Years of the British Association for the Advancement of Science*, Oxford: Clarendon Press.

Chapter 4 (pp.46–64)

1. Noble, George (1931) *Birds of Jesmond Dene*, London: Eyre & Spottiswoode.

2. From an article called 'Reminiscences of Jesmond' by William Gascoigne, Jesmond Dene Archives; publication and date unknown.

3. Watson, Robert Spence (1897) *The History of the Literary and Philosophical Society of Newcastle-upon-Tyne, 1793–1896*, London and Newcastle: Walter Scott.

4. Batchelor, John (2006) *Lady Trevelyan and the Pre-Raphaelite Brotherhood*, London: Chatto & Windus.
5. Howitt, William (1842) *Visits to Remarkable Places: Old Halls, Battlefields, and Scenes Illustrative of Striking Passages in English History and Poetry*, London: Longman.
6. Cochrane, Alfred (1909) *The Early History of Elswick*, Newcastle upon Tyne: Mawson Swan and Morgan.
7. Morrell, Jack and Thackray, Arnold (1981) *Gentlemen of Science: Early Years of the British Association for the Advancement of Science*, Oxford: Clarendon Press.
8. Batchelor, *op. cit.*
9. Quoted in Dolman, Frederick 'Notable Men and Their Work: Lord Armstrong and Newcastle-upon-Tyne', *Ludgate Monthly*, October 1893.
10. Scott, J. D. (1962) *Vickers: A History*, London: Weidenfeld & Nicolson.
11. Benwell Community Project, 'The Making of a Ruling Class', Newcastle upon Tyne, 1978.
12. *Dictionary of National Biography*, entry on Edwin Chadwick, online edition.
13. Rennison, R. W. (1979) *Water to Tyneside*, Newcastle and Gateshead Water Co.
14. McKenzie, Peter (1983) *W. G. Armstrong: The Life and Times of Sir William George Armstrong, Baron Armstrong of Cragside*, Northumberland: Longhirst Press.
15. *ibid.*
16. Quoted in Dolman, *op. cit.*
17. Dougan, David (1971) *The Great Gun-Maker: The Story of Lord Armstrong*, Newcastle: Frank Graham.
18. Jones, Evan Rowland (1886) *Heroes of Industry*, London: Sampson Low.

Chapter 5 (pp.65–80)

1. Rendel, Guy (2004) *An English Tapestry: Two English Families: Rendel and Rylands: How They Worked in Peace and How They Went to War 1750–2001*, Worcestershire: Perry Mill Press.
2. Hamer, F. E. (1931) (ed.) *The Personal Papers of Lord Rendel*, London: Ernest Benn.
3. Cochrane, Alfred (1909) *The Early History of Elswick*, Newcastle upon Tyne: Mawson Swan and Morgan.
4. Dougan, David (1971) *The Great Gun-Maker: The Story of Lord Armstrong*, Newcastle upon Tyne: Frank Graham.
5. *ibid.*

6.   *ibid.*

7.   Quoted in Dougan, *op. cit.*

8.   McKenzie, Peter (1983) *W. G. Armstron: The Life and Times of Sir William George Armstrong, Baron Armstrong of Cragside*, Northumberland: Longhirst Press.

9.   *The Times*, 28 December 1900.

10. McKenzie, *op. cit.*

11. Rolt, L. T. C. (1970) *Victorian Engineering*, London: Allen Lane.

12. Manchester, William (1968) *The Arms of Krupp 1587–1968*, Boston, USA: Little Brown & Co.

13. Cochrane, *op. cit.*

14. Dougan, *op. cit.*

Chapter 6 (pp.81–98)

1.   Benson, A. C. and Esher, Viscount (1907) (eds.) *The Letters of Queen Victoria*, London: John Murray.

2.   Bastable, Marshall J. (2004) *Arms and the State: Sir William Armstrong and the Remaking of British Naval Power 1854–1914*, Aldershot: Ashgate Publishing.

3.   Hamer, F. E. (1931) (ed.) *The Personal Papers of Lord Rendel*, London: Ernest Benn.

4.   Letter in Rosemary Rendel's collection that contradicts other accounts that Armstrong started work on his gun after the battle of Inkerman.

5.   Quoted in Warren, Kenneth (1989) *Armstrongs of Elswick: Growth in Engineering and Armaments to the Merger with Vickers*, London: Macmillan.

6.   Bastable, *op. cit.*

7.   *ibid.*

8.   Cochrane, Alfred (1909) *The Early History of Elswick*, Newcastle upon Tyne: Mawson Swan and Morgan.

9.   Bastable, *op. cit.*

10. *ibid.*

11. Quoted in Dougan, David (1971) *The Great Gun-Maker: The Story of Lord Armstrong*, Newcastle upon Tyne: Frank Graham.

12. Quoted in Cochrane, *op. cit.*

13. (1964) *Rendel Palmer & Tritton, 125 Years*, London: Hutchinson Benham.

14. Lane, Michael R. (1989) *The Rendel Connection: A Dynasty of Engineers*, London: Quiller Press.

15. White, Walter (1859) *Northumberland and the Border*, London: Chapman and Hall.

Chapter 7 (pp.99–114)

1. *Hansard*, 4 March 1859.
2. Bastable, Marshall J. (2004) *Arms and the State: Sir William Armstrong and the Remaking of British Naval Power 1854–1914*, Aldershot: Ashgate Publishing.
3. *ibid.*
4. Warren, Kenneth (1989) *Armstrongs of Elswick: Growth in Engineering and Armaments to the Merger with Vickers*, London: Macmillan.
5. Hamer, F. E. (1931) (ed.) *The Personal Papers of Lord Rendel*, London: Ernest Benn.
6. Bastable, *op. cit.*
7. *Newcastle Journal*, 14 May 1859.
8. Parish, Charles *The Literary and Philosophical Society of Newcastle upon Tyne: The Building and Development of its Library 1793–1986*, Newcastle upon Tyne.
9. Hamer (ed.), *op. cit.*
10. Bastable, *op. cit.*
11. *ibid.*

Chapter 8 (pp.115–34)

1. Short, Alice (1989) *The Contribution of William Lord Armstrong to Science and Education*, Ph.D thesis, Durham University.
2. Bastable, Marshall J. (2004) *Arms and the State: Sir William Armstrong and the Remaking of British Naval Power 1854–1914*, Aldershot: Ashgate Publishing.
3. Warren, Kenneth (1989) *Armstrongs of Elswick: Growth in Engineering and Armaments to the Merger with Vickers*, London: Macmillan.
4. Quoted in MacLeod, Christine (2007) *Heroes of Invention: Technology, Liberalism and British Identity 1750–1914*, Cambridge: Cambridge University Press.
5. MacLeod, *op. cit.*
6. Beeton, Samuel Orchart (1869) *Beeton's Dictionary of Universal Information*, London: Ward Lock.
7. *Hansard*, 4 March 1859.
8. *Report of the Select Committee on Ordnance*, Parliamentary Papers, 1863.
9. Bastable, *op. cit.*
10. *ibid.*
11. *ibid.*

12. *ibid.*

13. Buckle, G. E. (1926) (ed.) *The Letters of Queen Victoria, 1862–69, Vol. 1*, London: John Murray.

14. *Dictionary of National Biography*, entry on Joseph Whitworth, online edition.

15. Hamer, F. E. (1931) (ed.) *The Personal Papers of Lord Rendel*, London: Ernest Benn.

16. Hamer (ed.), *op. cit.*

17. *ibid.*

18. Bastable, *op. cit.*

19. *The Times*, 15 March 1864.

20. Bastable, *op. cit.*

Chapter 9 (pp.135–150)

1. Foss, Edward (1864) *The Judges of England: With Sketches of Their Lives, and Miscellaneous Notices Connected with the Courts at Westminster, from the Time of the Conquest*, Vol. IX, 1820–64, London: John Murray.

2. *Dictionary of National Biography*, entry on Benjamin Jowett, online edition.

3. Browne, Janet (2007) *Darwin's Origin of Species*, London: Atlantic Books.

4. Rolt, L. T. C. (1957) *Isambard Kingdom Brunel: A Biography*, London: Longmans Green.

5. Noble, M. D. (1925) *A Long Life*, Newcastle upon Tyne: Andrew Reid & Co.

6. Scott, J. D. (1962) *Vickers: A History*, London: Weidenfeld & Nicolson.

7. Noble, *op. cit.*

8. Scott, *op. cit.*

9. Hamer, F. E. (1931) (ed.) *The Personal Papers of Lord Rendel*, London: Ernest Benn.

10. Bastable, Marshall J. (2004) *Arms and the State: Sir William Armstrong and the Remaking of British Naval Power 1854–1914*, Aldershot: Ashgate Publishing.

11. Hamer (ed.), *op. cit.*

12. Bastable, *op. cit.*

13. Cited in Manchester, William (1968) *The Arms of Krupp 1587–1968*, Boston, USA: Little Brown & Co.
14. Manchester, William (1968) *The Arms of Krupp 1587–1968*, Boston, USA: Little Brown & Co.
15. *ibid*.
16. Dougan, David (1971) *The Great Gun-Maker: The Story of Lord Armstrong*, Newcastle upon Tyne: Frank Graham.

Chapter 11 (pp.166–78)

1. Dixon, David Dippie (1903) *Upper Coquetdale, Northumberland: Its History, Traditions, Folklore and Scenery*. Newcastle upon Tyne: Robert Redpath.
2. From a BBC radio programme marking the opening of Cragside by the National Trust on 5 June 1979.
3. Blake, Jeremy (1977) *Cragside*, architectural dissertation, University of Newcastle upon Tyne.
4. The first known use of this phrase occurred in an article in *World* magazine, 1879.
5. From the unpublished diary of Rose Horsley (wife of J. C. Horsley), 30 May 1868.
6. Saint, Andrew (1976) *Richard Norman Shaw*, London and New Haven, USA: Yale University Press.
7. *ibid*.
8. From a BBC radio programme marking the opening of Cragside by the National Trust on 5 June 1979.
9. Saint, *op. cit*.
10. Dixon, Hugh (2007) *Cragside* guidebook, National Trust; and information from Andrew Sawyer.
11. Dixon, *op. cit*.
12. *ibid*.
13. From a BBC radio programme marking the opening of Cragside by the National Trust on 5 June 1979.
14. *ibid*.
15. Davison, Thomas Raffles from an article in *British Architect*, May 1881.
16. Noble, M. D. (1925) *A Long Life*, Newcastle upon Tyne: Andrew Reid & Co.

Chapter 12 (pp.179–97)

1. Warren, Kenneth (1989) *Armstrongs of Elswick: Growth in Engineering and Armaments to the Merger with Vickers*, London: Macmillan.

2. McGuire, D. F. (1988) *Charles Mitchell 1820–95, Victorian Shipbuilder*, Newcastle upon Tyne City Libraries and Arts.

3. *ibid.*

4. *ibid.*

5. Keys, Dick and Smith, Ken (1997) *From Walker to the World: Charles Mitchell's Low Walker Shipyard*, Newcastle upon Tyne City Libraries and Information Service.

6. McKenzie, Peter (1983) *W. G. Armstrong: The Life and Times of Sir William George Armstrong, Baron Armstrong of Cragside*, Northumberland: Longhirst Press.

7. Bastable, Marshall J. (2004) *Arms and the State: Sir William Armstrong and the Remaking of British Naval Power 1854–1914*, Aldershot: Ashgate Publishing.

8. Smith, Ken (2005) *Emperor of Industry: Lord Armstrong of Cragside*, Newcastle upon Tyne: Tyne Bridge Publishing.

9. Bruce, J. Collingwood (1887) *The Bridges and the Floods of Newcastle upon Tyne*, Newcastle upon Tyne: R. Robinson & Co.

10. *ibid.*

11. Bastable, *op. cit.*

12. Hamer, F. E. (1931) (ed.) *The Personal Papers of Lord Rendel*, London: Ernest Benn.

13. *ibid.*

14. Bastable, *op. cit.*

15. *ibid.*

16. Hamer (ed.), *op. cit.*

17. Bastable, *op. cit.*

18. McKenzie, *op. cit.*

19. Bastable, *op. cit.*

20. McKenzie, *op. cit.*

21. Bastable, *op. cit.*

22. Hamer (ed.), *op. cit.*

23. Keys and Smith, *op. cit.*

24. *Dictionary of National Biography*, entry on George Rendel, online edition.

25. Hamer (ed.), *op. cit.*

26. Warren, *op. cit.*

27. *ibid.*

28. Keys, Dick and Smith, Ken (1996) *Down Elswick Slipways: Armstrong's Ships and People, 1884–1918*, Newcastle City Libraries.

29. Bastable, *op. cit.*
30. *ibid.*
31. Hamer, *op. cit.*
32. Bastable, *op. cit.*
33. Keys and Smith, *From Walker to the World.*
34. *ibid.*

Chapter 13 (pp.198–213)

1. Short, Alice (1989) *The Contribution of William Lord Armstrong to Science and Education*, PhD thesis, Durham University.
2. Cochrane, Alfred (1909) *The Early History of Elswick*, Newcastle upon Tyne: Mawson Swan and Morgan.
3. Papers of the Elswick Works' Literary and Mechanics' Institute, Tyne & Wear Archives.
4. Dougan, David (1971) *The Great Gun-Maker: The Story of Lord Armstrong*, Newcastle upon Tyne: Frank Graham.
5. Allen, L. W. 'Factors in the Selection and Recruitment of Personnel for an Engineering Company', North-east Apprentice Training Centre, Newcastle upon Tyne, 1969.
6. Short, *op. cit.*
7. *Mining Journal*, 11 September 1852.
8. North of England Institute of Mining Engineers (NEIME) Transactions, Vol. 1, 1852–53.
9. NEIME Transactions, Vol. IV, 1855–56.
10. *Report of the South Shields Committee Appointed to Investigate the Causes of Accidents in Coalmines*, 1843.
11. *Dictionary of National Biography*, entry on Charles Lake, online edition.
12. *Newcastle Daily Chronicle*, 13 March 1871.
13. Short, *op. cit.*
14. Fowler, J. T. (1904) *Durham University: Earlier Foundations and Present Colleges*, Durham: F. E. Robinson.

Chapter 14 (pp.214–30)

1. Dougan, David (1971) *The Great Gun-Maker: The Story of Lord Armstrong*, Newcastle upon Tyne: Frank Graham.
2. Allen, E., Clarke, J. F., McCord, N., and Rowe, D. J. (1971) *The North-east Engineers' Strikes of 1871: The Nine Hours' League*, Newcastle upon Tyne: Frank Graham.
3. Burnett, John (1872) *Nine Hours' Movement: A History of*

the Engineers' Strike in Newcastle and Gateshead, London, Newcastle and Manchester.

4. Allen, Clarke, McCord, and Rowe, *op. cit.*
5. *ibid.*
6. Burnett, *op. cit.*
7. *ibid.*
8. Allen, Clarke, McCord, and Rowe, *op. cit.*
9. Burnett, *op. cit.*
10. Allen, Clarke, McCord, and Rowe, *op. cit.*
11. Cochrane, Alfred from an article in *Northern Counties Magazine*, November 1900.
12. Allen, Clarke, McCord, and Rowe, *op. cit.*

Chapter 15 (pp.231–47)

1. Hamer, F. E. (1931) (ed.) *The Personal Papers of Lord Rendel*, London: Ernest Benn.
2. Armstrong, W. G. (1873) *A Visit to Egypt in 1872*, Newcastle upon Tyne: Literary and Philosophical Society.
3. Hamer (ed.), *op. cit.*
4. Noble, M. D. (1925) *A Long Life*, Newcastle upon Tyne: Andrew Reid & Co.

Chapter 16 (pp.248–64)

1. 'The Utilization of Natural Forces', as reported in *The Times*, 3 September 1881.
2. Dixon, Hugh (2007) *Cragside* guidebook, National Trust; and information from Andrew Sawyer.
3. Swan, Mary E. and Swan, Kenneth, R. (1929) *Sir Joseph Wilson Swan, Inventor and Scientist*, Newcastle upon Tyne: Oriel Press.
4. From an article in the *Newcastle Evening Chronicle*, 4 September 1831.
5. Jones, Evan Rowland *Heroes of Industry*, Sampson Low, London, 1886.
6. Noble, M. D. *A Long Life*, Andrew Reid & Co., Newcastle upon Tyne, 1925.
7. McGuire, D. F. *Charles Mitchell 1820–95, Victorian Shipbuilder*, Newcastle upon Tyne City Libraries and Arts, 1988.
8. *ibid.*
9. *ibid.*

Chapter 17 (pp.265–81)

1. Smith, Ken (2005) *Emperor of Industry: Lord Armstrong of Cragside*, Newcastle upon Tyne: Tyne Bridge Publishing.
2. Conte-Helm, Marie (1994) 'Armstrong's, Vickers and Japan' in: Nish, Ian (ed.) *Britain & Japan, Biographical Portraits*, Richmond, Surrey: Japan Library.
3. *Newcastle Courant*, 19 March 1885.
4. Conte-Helm, Marie (1989) *Japan and the North East of England: from 1862 to the present day*, London, and Atlantic Highlands, New Jersey: The Athlone Press.
5. Bastable, Marshall J. (2004) *Arms and the State: Sir William Armstrong and the Remaking of British Naval Power 1854–1914*, Aldershot: Ashgate Publishing.
6. Ruxton, Ian C. (1998) (ed.) *The Diaries and Letters of Sir Ernest Mason Satow (1843–1929)*, Lampeter: Edwin Mellen Press.
7. Bastable, *op. cit.*
8. Correspondence published in *The Times*, 15 March 1864.
9. Satow, Ernest (1921) *A Diplomat in Japan*, London: Seeley Service & Co.
10. Bastable, *op. cit.*
11. Conte-Helm, 'Armstrong's, Vickers and Japan'.
12. Bastable, *op. cit.*
13. Weightman, Gavin (2007) *The Industrial Revolutionaries*, London: Atlantic Books.
14. Conte-Helm, *Japan and the North East of England*.
15. Kanitake, Kume (1998) *The Iwakura Embassy, 1871–73*, Richmond, Surrey: Japan Library.
16. Conte-Helm, *Japan and the North East of England*.
17. *ibid*.
18. *ibid*.
19. *ibid*.
20. *ibid*.
21. Keys, Dick and Smith, Ken (1996) *Down Elswick Slipways: Armstrong's Ships and People, 1884–1918*, Newcastle upon Tyne: Newcastle City Libraries.
22. *Newcastle Daily Chronicle*, 28 June 1899.
23. Keys and Smith, *op. cit.*
24. *ibid*.
25. Conte-Helm, *Japan and the North East of England*.
26. *ibid*.
27. *ibid*.

28. Dolman, Frederick 'Notable Men and Their Work', published in *Ludgate Monthly*, October 1893.
29. Masuji, Yamanouchi (1914) *Kaikoroku (Memories of the Past)*, Japan; quoted in Conte-Helm, 'Armstrong's, Vickers and Japan'.
30. Conte-Helm, 'Armstrong's, Vickers and Japan'.
31. Conte-Helm, *Japan and the North East of England*.
32. *Newcastle Daily Chronicle*, 21 July 1911

Chapter 18 (pp.282–98)

1. Saint, Andrew (1976) *Richard Norman Shaw*, London and New Haven, USA: Yale University Press.
2. Blake, Jeremy (1977) *Cragside*, architectural dissertation, University of Newcastle upon Tyne.
3. From a BBC radio documentary marking the opening of Cragside by the National Trust on 5 June 1979.
4. Girouard, Mark (1971) *The Victorian Country House*, Oxford: Clarendon Press.
5. Letter published in *Engineer* magazine, 17 January 1881.
6. Girouard, *op. cit.*
7. Saint, Andrew 'Art and Science in the Service of Romance', lecture on Cragside at Newcastle University, 22 April 2010.
8. Pevsner, Nikolaus (2005) *Pioneers of Modern Design*, London: Yale University Press.
9. Blake, *op. cit.*
10. Dolman, Frederick 'Notable Men and Their Work: Lord Armstrong and Newcastle upon Tyne', *Ludgate Monthly*, October 1893.

Chapter 19 (pp.299–313)

1. From a personal memoir of his great-uncle by William Watson-Armstrong, published in *Cassier's* magazine, 1896.
2. Bamburgh Castle guidebook, printed in the 1950s by H. C. Coates & Son, Alnwick.
3. *Newcastle Weekly Courant*, 28 April 1894.
4. Bates, Cadwallader John (1894) *Bamburgh Castle: Its history and architecture*, reprinted privately for Lord Armstrong.
5. Ash, David (1961) *Bamburgh Castle, Northumberland*, architectural thesis, King's College, University of Durham.
6. Gibson, William (1860) *A Memoir on Northumberland*, London and Newcastle.
7. *Newcastle Weekly Courant*, 28 April 1894.
8. Brochure for the Bamburgh Bazaar, held in aid of the Soldiers'

& Sailors' Families' Association at Bamburgh Castle, August 1900.

9. Ash, *op. cit.*

10. Emery, Anthony (1996) *Greater Medieval Houses of England and Wales, 1300–1500: Northern England*, Cambridge: Cambridge University Press.

11. Bamburgh Bazaar brochure.

12. Ash, *op. cit.*

13. Bamburgh Castle guidebook, 1950s.

14. Ash, *op. cit.*

15. *Alnwick and County Gazette*, 11 June 1927; *Newcastle Daily Journal*, 9 June 1927.

16. Watson, Robert Spence (1897) *The History of the Literary and Philosophical Society of Newcastle-upon-Tyne, 1793–1896*, London and Newcastle: Walter Scott.

17. Cochrane, Alfred (1909) *The Early History of Elswick*, Newcastle upon Tyne: Mawson Swan and Morgan.

Chapter 20 (pp.314–26)

1. Worsnop, John 'The Late Lord Armstrong, His Association with Rothbury', *Newcastle Daily Journal*, 28 December 1900.

2. Warren, Kenneth (1989) *Armstrongs of Elswick: Growth in Engineering and Armaments to the Merger with Vickers*, London: Macmillan.

3. Dolman, Frederick 'Notable Men and Their Work: Lord Armstrong and Newcastle upon Tyne', *Ludgate Monthly*, October 1893.

4. Warren, *op. cit.*

5. *ibid.*

6. Hamer, F. E. (1931) (ed.) *The Personal Papers of Lord Rendel*, London: Ernest Benn.

7. *The Throne*, 4 August 1906.

8. *Newcastle Daily Journal*, 1 January 1901.

Chapter 21 (pp.327–41)

1. Quoted in Warren, Kenneth (1989) *Armstrongs of Elswick: Growth in Engineering and Armaments to the Merger with Vickers*, London: Macmillan.

2. Warren, *op. cit.*

3. Lane, Michael R. (1989) *The Rendel Connection: A Dynasty of Engineers*, London: Quiller Press.

4. Hamer, F. E. (1931) (ed.), *The Personal Papers of Lord Rendel*,

London: Ernest Benn.

5. Lane, *op. cit.*
6. Hamer (ed.), *op. cit.*
7. Lane, *op. cit.*
8. Hamer (ed.), *op. cit.*
9. Noble, M. D. (1925) *A Long Life*, Newcastle: Andrew Reid & Co.
10. Hamer (ed.), *op. cit.*
11. Quoted in Warren, *op. cit.*
12. Trebilcock, Clive (1977) *The Vickers Brothers*, London: Europa.
13. *The Times*, 12 May 1909.
14. Elswick Works album, Vickers Archives, Cambridge University Library.
15. Cochrane, Alfred (1909) *The Early History of Elswick*, Newcastle upon Tyne: Mawson Swan and Morgan.
16. Evans, Harold (1978) *Vickers: Against the Odds 1956–77*, London: Hodder & Stoughton.
17. Correspondence about William Watson-Armstrong quoted in Bastable, Marshall J. (2004) *Arms and the State: Sir William Armstrong and the Remaking of British Naval Power 1854–1914*, Aldershot: Ashgate Publishing.
18. *The Times*, 3 April 1908.
19. Smith, Bill (2005) *Armstrong Siddeley Motors*, Poundbury, Dorset: Veloce Publishing.
20. Christie, Manson & Woods, annotated catalogue of 'Important Modern Pictures and Water Colour Drawings removed from Cragside, Rothbury', 24 June 1910.
21. From a BBC radio programme marking the opening of Cragside by the National Trust on 5 June 1979.
22. Engelbrecht, H. C. and Hanighen, F. C. (1934) *Merchants of Death: A Study of the International Armament Industry*, New York: Dodd Mead & Co.

The Armstrong and Watson-Armstrong Families

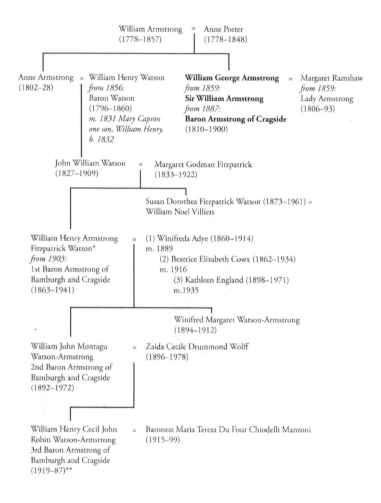

William Armstrong = Anne Potter
(1778–1857) (1778–1848)

Anne Armstrong = William Henry Watson
(1802–28) *from 1856:*
Baron Watson
(1796–1860)
m. 1831 Mary Capron
one son, William Henry,
b. 1832

William George Armstrong = Margaret Ramshaw
from 1859: *from 1859:*
Sir William Armstrong Lady Armstrong
from 1887: (1806–93)
Baron Armstrong of Cragside
(1810–1900)

John William Watson = Margaret Godman Fitzpatrick
(1827–1909) (1833–1922)

Susan Dorothea Fitzpatrick Watson (1873–1961) =
William Noel Villiers

William Henry Armstrong = (1) Winifreda Adye (1860–1914)
Fitzpatrick Watson* m. 1889
from 1903: (2) Beatrice Elizabeth Cowx (1862–1934)
1st Baron Armstrong of m. 1916
Bamburgh and Cragside (3) Kathleen England (1898–1971)
(1863–1941) m.1935

Winifred Margaret Watson-Armstrong
(1894–1912)

William John Montagu = Zaida Cecile Drummond Wolff
Watson-Armstrong (1896–1978)
2nd Baron Armstrong of
Bamburgh and Cragside
(1892–1972)

William Henry Cecil John = Baroness Maria Teresa Du Four Chiodelli Manzoni
Robin Watson-Armstrong (1915–99)
3rd Baron Armstrong of
Bamburgh and Cragside
(1919–87)**

*In 1889 his name was changed by royal licence from Watson to Watson-Armstrong.
** After the death of the 3rd Baron Armstrong of Bamburgh and Cragside, his adopted children, Francis
and Isabella Watson-Armstrong, acceded to the family estates.

Index